SCOTT BICENTENARY ESSAYS

SCOTT BICENTENARY ESSAYS

*Selected Papers read at the
Sir Walter Scott Bicentenary Conference*

Edited by
ALAN BELL

BARNES & NOBLE
BOOKS
10 East 53d St., New York 10022
(a division of Harper & Row Publishers, Inc.)

Published in the U.S.A. 1973 by:
HARPER & ROW PUBLISHERS, INC.
BARNES & NOBLE IMPORT DIVISION

ISBN 06-490354-0

Printed by R. & R. Clark Ltd. Edinburgh

Contents

Preface   ix

Scott
WILLIAM BEATTIE, *Edinburgh*   1

Scott and the Corners of Time
EDGAR JOHNSON, *City University of New York*   18

Scott and Scotland
DAVID DAICHES, *University of Sussex*   38

Scott and the Novel in Scotland
FRANCIS R. HART, *University of Massachusetts*   61

The *Journal*
W. E. K. ANDERSON, *Abingdon School*   80

Scott as Story-Teller: An Essay in Psychobiography
N. T. PHILLIPSON, *University of Edinburgh*   87

Scott's Shortcomings as an Artist
DAVID CRAIG, *University of Lancaster*   100

Scott among the Partisans: A Significant Bias in his
Life of Napoleon Buonaparte
ROBERT C. GORDON, *San José State College, California*   115

The Problem of Coherence in *The Antiquary*
ROBIN MAYHEAD, *University of Stirling*   134

Scott Manuscripts in Edinburgh Libraries
ALAN BELL, *National Library of Scotland*   147

The Manuscripts and Proof Sheets of *Redgauntlet*
G. A. M. WOOD, *University of Stirling*   160

Deceptions in the Works of Scott; or, Lying Title-pages
WILLIAM RUFF, *University of Florida*   176

Scott and the Picturesque: Afforestation and History
MARCIA ALLENTUCK, *City University of New York*   188

Scott and Turner
ADELE M. HOLCOMB, *New York*   199

v

Scott and Delacroix, with some Assistance from Hugo
and Bonington
  MARTIN KEMP, *University of Glasgow*   213

Scott as Pageant-Master—The Royal Visit of 1822
  BASIL C. SKINNER, *University of Edinburgh*   228

Scott's Foreign Contacts
  E. H. HARVEY WOOD, *London*   238

Waverley Ueber Alles—Sir Walter Scott's German
Reputation
  PAUL M. OCHOJSKI, *Seton Hall University, New Jersey*   260

The Impact of Sir Walter Scott in Hungary
  ANNA KATONA, *University of Debrecen*   271

Scott and Italy
  R. D. S. JACK, *University of Edinburgh*   283

Scott and Old Norse Literature
  JOHN M. SIMPSON, *University of Edinburgh*   300

Periodicals in the Age of Scott
  DONALD A. LOW, *University of St. Andrews*   314

Susan Ferrier
  WENDY CRAIK, *University of Aberdeen*   322

John Galt and the Analysis of Social History
  JOHN MACQUEEN, *University of Edinburgh*   332

List of papers read at the Conference   343

List of Plates

1 Eugène Delacroix. *Lucy Ashton's Bridal Night* (*Bride of Lammermoor*, ch. xxiii), pencil; Paris, Claude Roger-Marx Coll.

2 Eugène Delacroix. *Amy Robsart, Costume Design for Victor Hugo's 'Amy Robsart'*, watercolour; Paris, Maison de Victor Hugo

3 Eugène Delacroix. *Queen Elizabeth, Costume Design for Victor Hugo's 'Amy Robsart'*, watercolour; Paris, Louvre (RF 10010). Cliché des Musées Nationaux

4 Richard Bonington. *The 'Buckhurst' Armour*, pencil; London, British Museum (1857-2-28-158)

5 Eugène Delacroix. *The 'Buckhurst' Armour and other Studies*, pencil; London, Library of the Wallace Collection (WCM 43.B)

6 Richard Bonington. *Amy Robsart and the Earl of Leicester* (?), oil; Oxford, Ashmolean Museum

7 Eugène Delacroix. *Lord Shrewsbury, Costume Design for Victor Hugo's 'Amy Robsart'*, watercolour; Paris, Maison de Victor Hugo

8 Eugène Delacroix. *William de la Marck, Called the Wild Boar of the Ardennes* (or the *Murder of the Bishop of Liège*) (*Quentin Durward*, ch. xxii), oil: Paris, Louvre (RF 196113). Cliché des Musées Nationaux

9 Richard Bonington. *Vaulting of Westminster Hall*, pencil; Edinburgh, National Gallery of Scotland (3598)

10 Eugène Delacroix. *Cromwell at Windsor* (*Woodstock*, ch. viii), oil; U.S.A., private collection

11 Eugène Delacroix. *Front-de-Boeuf and the Sorceress Ulrica* (*Ivanhoe*, ch. xxx), lithograph; Paris, Bibliothèque Nationale

12 Eugène Delacroix. *Ravenswood and Lucy at the Mermaidens' Fountain* (*Bride of Lammermoor*, ch. xix), brown and black inks heightened with white; Detroit, Institute of Arts (31.339)

13 Eugène Delacroix. *Self-portrait as Ravenswood* (?), oil;

vii

Paris, Louvre (RF 195338, Société des Amis d'Eugène Delacroix). Cliché des Musées Nationaux

14 Eugène Delacroix. *Abduction of Rebecca by Bois-Guilbert* (*Ivanhoe*, ch. xxxi), oil; Paris, Louvre (RF 1392). Cliché des Musées Nationaux

Preface

ETWEEN 15 and 21 August 1971, scholars of many national-
ities and several disciplines met under the auspices of the
Institute for Advanced Studies in the Humanities of the University of Edinburgh to celebrate the bicentenary of the birth
of Sir Walter Scott by a major conference. An ample programme of lectures and seminars, excursions, receptions, exhibitions and concerts was arranged, and there was a memorable
dinner. At the concluding session the participants urged the
organizers to prepare a volume of the papers delivered. A small
committee was set up (under Professor John MacQueen, who had
presided throughout), contributions were invited, and a publisher
found. The response was so overwhelming that it proved impossible to print more than a selection, and an independent
reader chose 24 essays for publication. In July 1972 I was invited
to prepare them for the press. My task has been the mechanical
one of organizing the disparate texts into a convenient form, and
I have been much helped by the secretarial assistance of Miss
Jane Fingland and the typographical advice of Mr Max Begg.

This selection opens with four of the five major lectures
delivered to the full conference; the fifth, Mr Thomas Crawford's
'Scott as a Poet', is printed in *Etudes Anglaises* XXIV (1971),
478-91. The remainder of the volume consists of papers delivered
at various seminars, which at the conference were grouped as:
Scott the Poet and Novelist; Scott's Place in Intellectual History;
Scott—Biography and Bibliography; Scott and the Arts; and
Scott and his Scottish Contemporaries. A list of the papers delivered but not printed is given at the end.

These *Scott Bicentenary Essays* and the affectionate memories
of a busy week are not the only memories of the occasion. The
work of the conference continues in one important way. The
Biography and Bibliography section heard Dr David Hewitt's
working paper 'What should we do about Scott's Letters?'
(*Scottish Literary News* ii (1971), 3-10). It was agreed that a
systematic survey of the entire body of published and unpublished

material was urgently necessary. A supplementary or completely revised edition of Scott's letters cannot even be considered until detailed information is available on the whole documentation of the subject. The National Library of Scotland, with the help of a small working party, has undertaken a survey, with the aim of establishing full indexes and photographic collections which will be of use to scholars even if no great editorial project emerges from them. Information about the location of Scott letters will be gratefully received by the Department of Manuscripts, and those contributing will in a real sense be carrying on the work begun at the Bicentenary Conference of August 1971.

December 1972   A. S. B.

Scott

WILLIAM BEATTIE

J UST under two hundred years ago, when the Author of Waverley was a boy, Colonel Mannering came to Edinburgh with
Dominie Sampson. If our conference should ever be in danger
of being too solemn, let us remember Dominie Sampson and
Dandie Dinmont, the first in that long gallery of comic characters
who have endeared themselves so much to us. The period was that
in which the New Town, since much extended to the North, had
just been commenced; so most of the events of that week when
Mannering came to see the lawyer Pleydell took place quite near
where we are now met.

I cannot forbear from quoting the description of Pleydell's
library:

> It was a well-proportioned room, hung with a portrait or two of Scottish
> characters of eminence, by Jamieson, the Caledonian Vandyke, and sur-
> rounded with books, the best editions of the best authors. 'These', said
> Pleydell, 'are my tools of trade. A lawyer without history or literature is a
> mechanic, a mere working mason; if he possesses some knowledge of these,
> he may call himself an architect.'

This is like the Advocates' Library, the parent of our National
Library, of which Scott was to become a Curător (not Curător) or,
as we would say today, a Trustee, and which was never, even in its
beginning in the seventeenth century, merely a law library but a
good general one. Pleydell's library must remind us also of Scott's
own library at Abbotsford. The catalogue of the Abbotsford
Library, issued by the Bannatyne Club in 1838, repays constant
study. The compiler, J. G. Cochrane, did an admirable and original
piece of work, giving, where needed, references to Scott's use of
an author.

But in quoting the passage about Pleydell's library, I had in
mind another matter. I quoted from the author's manuscript and
the first edition. In his revisions for the 'Magnum' edition towards the end of his life, to the phrase 'the best editions of the

best authors' Scott added 'in particular, an admirable collection of classics'; and the clause 'he may call himself an architect' was to grow into 'he may venture to call himself an architect'. You see what an admirable improvement is achieved in the rhythm by the change from 'may call himself' to 'may venture to call himself'. Many readers still know too little about revisions in Scott; so they tend to accept him at his own value as a careless and hasty writer. Admittedly he did not often if at all search for the *mot propre*. You remember the melody of that passage of Stevenson about the Edinburgh climate:

But Edinburgh pays cruelly for her high seat in one of the vilest climates under heaven. She is liable to be beaten upon by all the winds that blow, to be drenched with rain, to be buried in cold sea fogs out of the east, and powdered with the snow as it comes flying southward from the Highland hills. The weather is raw and boisterous in winter, shifty and ungenial in summer, and a downright meteorological purgatory in the spring. The delicate die early, and I, as a survivor, among bleak winds and plumping rain, have been sometimes tempted to envy them their fate.

Perfect, every sound and every word in its right place. Scott is not like that, but he *has* harmed his reputation by writing himself down as a stylist. When we think of the merely mannered writers of English prose, we must admire and envy Scott's manly, flowing style. Of course, he had his mannerisms, and Lady Louisa Stuart could not understand how anyone should be so blind and deaf as to fail to guess the authorship of the Novels. But along with his little tricks of phrase, Scott had in his bones an understanding of the difference between a style and a manner, an understanding of the need to get on with the job. On the whole, his was the prose of a professional man. This is well seen in an earlier chapter of *Guy Mannering*, where the sheriff quietly sets down the evidence about the disappearance of Harry Bertram. This chapter, which is by the way one of the sources of the detective story of more recent days, is a good foretaste of a device that Scott will use from time to time to give himself and his readers a breathing-space—the deliberate introduction of flatness, flatness in the treatment of character and story alike. After it we take up the chase with new strength.

On the Sunday, Mannering was offered a variety of hospitality and entertainment, beginning with the choice of being accompanied to the Presbyterian kirk or the Episcopal meeting-house or being left alone. 'I am delighted', he replied to Pleydell, 'I am delighted to put myself under your pilotage. I should wish much to hear some of your Scottish preachers whose talents have done such honour to your country—your Blair, your Robertson . . .'. They went 'to the Greyfriars church, to hear our historian of Scotland, of the Continent, and of America [William Robertson, the Principal of this University]. They were disappointed—he did not preach that morning.' But the next day there came the notes of introduction.

On looking at the notes of introduction which Pleydell had thrust into his hand, Mannering was gratified with seeing that they were addressed to some of the first literary characters of Scotland. 'To David Hume, Esq.' 'To John Home, Esq.' 'To Dr Ferguson.' 'To Dr Black.' 'To Lord Kaimes.' 'To Mr Hutton.' 'To John Clerk, Esq. of Eldin.' 'To Adam Smith, Esq.' 'To Dr Robertson'.

Not a bad galaxy! And some time between the Monday and the next meeting with Pleydell on the Thursday, when the venison and claret were disposed of near Bristo Port, the Principal of the University had an opportunity of meeting Guy Mannering. Not so that notoriously shy figure, the Professor of Rhetoric and Belles Lettres, Dr. Hugh Blair, even though Mannering had expressed a desire to hear him preach. But his absence has been atoned for by at least three of his successors in what is still called the Chair of Rhetoric and English Literature.

Saintsbury not only revised the text of Scott's edition of Dryden. His short book on Scott is one of the good volumes in the uneven 'Famous Scots' series. I suppose it must be hopelessly out of date and hopelessly prejudiced; but there are other books to complement it. In some tracts of English literature, textual studies are still in their infancy; so if Saintsbury, rehandling Scott's Dryden, should be the blind leading the blind, he is likely to remain for a long time yet in a goodly company. As well as the Dryden and the little book, Saintsbury must have done a great deal for Scott studies, first and last. There comes to mind his illuminating treatment of one of the best early critics of Scott as a poet—John Keble.

As the editor of Scott's letters, Grierson was inclined to be like Scott editing Dryden or like Scott editing Scott. In the 1930s some of us thought that the recension of somebody else's letters, whoever that somebody might be, was a job unworthy of so eminent a professor as Grierson. We could not foretell the bright future of this kind of scholarship. But there *was* a certain justice in our doubt of the advisability of harnessing to a prosaic task the great critic of metaphysical poetry, whose edition of Donne, but for the outbreak of war in 1914, would possibly have had a deeper effect on the course of poetry than it seems to have had.

There was at least one altogether happy outcome of Grierson's work on the letters, and that was his life of Scott, supplementary to and corrective of Lockhart. This is an essential work, which should never have been allowed to go out of print. Grierson had come to it fresh from the study of the letters. Also, earlier in life, he had been, like Scott, fond of country sports; in boyhood he had been sent on a visit to Cheltenham, as Scott had been sent to Bath; so that long before his Oxford days he had learned to escape from what could so easily have become narrow, professional surroundings. The effect on his work was a freedom from pedantry and a closeness to his subject, which we find again in John Buchan's life of Scott, with its understanding of authors and publishers.

Along with his own impatient nature, Grierson had to contend, as editor of the letters, with an interfering printer, much as Scott had had to do; and a work that should have filled many years had to be concluded, without an index, in five. In spite of all this, Grierson again and again, silently or almost silently, corrects dates that have puzzled others. He also told, as it were, his own Tales of a Grandfather; his talks on Scott for the young are, for young and old, one of the best short books since Saintsbury's.

William Renwick was spare of build, with a dry sense of humour; and his volume in the Oxford History of English Literature may strike some readers as dry and spare. But that little book is worth a great deal. It seems to me to have the qualities that a work on the age of Scott should have—shrewd sense, the accurate and apparently easy learning of a scholar, a gentlemanly acquaintance with society and politics, and a leisured grace of presentation. And in a review stretching to no more than a page, Renwick, who lived in Dalkeith Road where some of you are staying, could conjure up the Edinburgh of Scott, as he saw it on his daily bus-ride to the University. It was not irrelevant that he had edited Spenser. Scott, a master of metrical form, brought to the Spenserian stanza something that James Thomson, for example, had not been able to give.

O wake once more! how rude soe'er the hand
    That ventures o'er thy magic maze to stray;
O wake once more! though scarce my skill command
    Some feeble echoing of thine earlier lay:
Though harsh and faint, and soon to die away,
    And all unworthy of thy nobler strain,
Yet if one heart throb higher at its sway,
    The wizard note has not been touch'd in vain.
Then silent be no more! Enchantress, wake again!

In the intellectual background of Mannering's visit to Edinburgh, several elements are touched upon—the philosophy of common sense, the idea of sympathy (in the philosophical but also in the everyday meaning), the classics, the law, the sciences, the new scope of history, and the acceptance of faith. These were parts of Scott's upbringing. But in his nature there was another element.

Scott was a poet; and the question to be asked about the *Minstrelsy* is not whether he was a less good editor of ballads than Child or his Danish master, but whether Walter Scott was not a better poet than Francis James Child. Of course, old Mrs. Hogg, the mother of the Ettrick Shepherd, was right: the ballads had been made for singing and not for reading.[1] But if we want to enjoy them as poetry, there is no better work than the *Minstrelsy* or than one of the many selections derived from it. Again and again the *Minstrelsy* has something rarely to be found in Percy or Robert Jamieson or any other editor. It is magic, that 'glamourie' cast over Lady Cassilis by the gipsies:

As soon as they saw her weel far'd face,
    They coost their glamourie owre her.

Scott achieved his magic with fewer changes, fewer liberties than Child and T. F. Henderson would have us believe. To see that, we have only to look at the manuscript materials for the *Minstrelsy* in the National Library of Scotland. People are often so solemn about the ballads. If we want to know how a ballad came to be written and then to be rubbed and worn like an old coin, we cannot do better than read Scott's preface to *Auld Robin Gray* by Lady Anne Lindsay, one of those Scottish ladies of the eighteenth and

---

[1] 'There war never ane o' my sangs prentit till ye prentit them yoursel', an' ye hae spoilt them awthegither. They were made for singing an' no for reading; but ye hae broken the charm now, an' they'll never be sung mair.' James Hogg, *The Domestic Manners . . . of Sir Walter Scott* (1834), 61.

nineteenth centuries who gave us lovely words for lovely tunes.
Lady Anne had written to Scott:

There was an ancient Scotch melody, of which I was passionately fond;
— —[1] who lived before your day, used to sing it to us at Balcarras.
She did not object to its having improper words, though I did. I longed to
sing old Sophy's air to different words . . . While attempting to effect this
in my closet, I called to my little sister . . . who was the only person near me,
'I have been writing a ballad, my dear; I am oppressing my heroine with many
misfortunes. I have already sent her Jamie to sea—and broken her father's
arm—and made her mother fall sick—and given her Auld Robin Gray for her
lover; but I wish to load her with a fifth sorrow within the four lines, poor
thing! Help me to one'.—'Steal the cow, sister Anne', said the little Elizabeth. The cow was immediately *lifted* by me, and the song completed.

The Lay of the Last Minstrel is a metrical store-house. There is
not only the 'Christabel' metre. There is the lay within the lay, the
dirge of lovely Rosabelle. There is the stanza that we find in
Christopher Smart's *Song to David* in the eighteenth century and
in Ralph Hodgson's *Song of Honour* in the twentieth:

> Costly his garb—his Flemish ruff
> Fell o'er his doublet, shaped of buff,
>   With satin slash'd and lined;
> Tawny his boot, and gold his spur,
> His cloak was all of Poland fur,
>   His hose with silver twined.

This is a fair specimen of the stanza in *The Lay*. At that time Scott
was not at home with it. Few poets have been. (Johnson was not,
though he tried it once or twice from the age of seventeen onwards.)

For the enjoyment of *The Lay* we have one advantage denied to
its first readers. We see how some themes were developed in
Scott's later work. There is the passage about Arcturus and Orion
and the Bear. The River Spirit asks:

> Tell me, thou, who view'st the stars,
> When shall cease these feudal jars?

and so on—a hint of something that was to happen in the novel
whose sub-title is *The Astrologer*.

There is a better example in a better poem, *Marmion*. It is the
description of Lord Marmion and his men at Gifford:

> And oft Lord Marmion deign'd to aid,
> And mingle in the mirth they made;

[1] Sophy Johnstone. See *Lives of the Lindsays* (1849), ii. 392.

For though, with men of high degree,
The proudest of the proud was he,
Yet, train'd in camps, he knew the art
To win the soldier's hardy heart.
They love a captain to obey,
Boisterous as March, yet fresh as May;
With open hand, and brow as free,
Lover of wine and minstrelsy; . . .

It might be a sketch for the portrait of Lord Crawford in *Quentin Durward* fifteen years later:

[He] sat as it were on thorns at the royal board, until an opportunity occurred of making his escape to the revelry of his own countrymen. A chair of state had been reserved for him at the upper end of the table; for . . . although their leader and commander, . . . their Captain sat with them at the same table without impropriety, and might mingle when he chose in their festivity, without derogation from his dignity as commander.

At present, however, Lord Crawford declined occupying the seat prepared for him, and bidding them 'hold themselves merry', stood looking on the revel with a countenance which seemed greatly to enjoy it.

'Let him alone,' whispered Cunningham to Lindesay, as the latter offered the wine to their noble Captain, 'let him alone—hurry no man's cattle—let him take it of his own accord.'

In fact, the old Lord, who at first smiled, shook his head, and placed the untasted wine-cup before him, began presently, as it were in absence of mind, to sip a little of the contents, and in doing so, fortunately recollected that it would be ill-luck did he not drink a draught to the health of the gallant lad who had joined them this day.

When I said *Marmion* was a better poem than *The Lay*, I had in mind among other things Scott's growing mastery of the octosyllabic couplet, one of the simplest and hardest of metres. Try it and see for yourself. Unless you are very skilful, it will sit down in the middle of the road and refuse to budge, or else it will run away with you. It was this fatal facility that Scott was afraid of, when he began.

In English poetry the octosyllabic couplet had been put to two excellent uses. It was used by Dryden and Swift in their epistles, and it was not for nothing that Scott had edited Dryden. In the introduction to the first canto of *Marmion* there is an admiring echo of the master:

And Dryden, in immortal strain,
Had raised the Table Round again,
But that a ribald King and Court
Bade him toil on, to make them sport;

> Demanded for their niggard pay,⎫
> Fit for their souls, a looser lay,   ⎬
> Licentious satire, song, and play;⎭
> The world defrauded of the high design,
> Profaned the God-given strength, and marr'd the lofty line.

The six Epistles from the Ettrick Forest, each introducing a canto
of *Marmion* and each addressed to a friend, follow the good
eighteenth-century custom of writing familiar, often amusing,
letters in verse:

> For omens, we in Livy cross,
> At every turn, *locutus Bos.*
> As grave and duly speaks that ox,
> As if he told the price of stocks;
> Or held, in Rome republican,
> The place of Common-councilman.

At the same time the Epistles follow the course of the seasons,
beginning in November and going a little more than once round,
until the Christmas of the next year—not unlike Thomson's
Seasons in idea but quite different in effect, far fuller of movement
and people.

But the Epistles also continue the other good use of the octosyllabic couplet, and that is for sketches of natural scenes. We find
it so used in Marvell's 'Nunappleton House', and we find it quite
late in the nineteenth century, in an entrancing evocation of Hyde
Park:

> Bright was the morn and south the air;
> The soft-couch'd cattle were as fair
> As those that pastured by the sea,
> That old-world morn, in Sicily,
> When on the beach the Cyclops lay, ⎫
> And Galatea from the bay   ⎬
> Mock'd her poor lovelorn giant's lay.⎭

Very fine, I think, down to the triple rhyme which Dryden himself,
and Scott, had managed so well. The cattle must have gone long
ago from Hyde Park, but we still see them there through Arnold's
eyes. Yet the scene is set not with London names but with names
from the poetry of the ancient world. Because of the plentiful use
of names familiar to a Borderer like myself, I sometimes find it
difficult to judge Scott's poetry as poetry. When he writes

> No longer Autumn's glowing red
> Upon our Forest hills is shed;

> No more, beneath the evening beam,
> Fair Tweed reflects their purple gleam;
> Away hath pass'd the heather-bell
> That bloom'd so rich on Needpath Fell;
> Sallow his brow, and russet bare
> Are now the sister-heights of Yair . . . .

I suspect that the pleasure conveyed by such lines is the pleasure of association rather than the pleasure of poetry.

But in *Marmion*, names are also used from another part of the world. The passage falls in the Third Canto, and it introduces the song 'Where shall the lover rest' sung by Fitz-Eustace at Gifford. That wild, sad air reminds the poet of songs he had heard rising from busy harvest-fields in Scotland:

> Oft have I listen'd, and stood still,
> As it came soften'd up the hill,
> And deem'd it the lament of men
> Who languish'd for their native glen;
> And thought how sad would be such sound
> On Susquehana's swampy ground,
> Kentucky's wood-encumber'd brake,
> Or wild Ontario's boundless lake,
> Where heart-sick exiles, in the strain,
> Recall'd fair Scotland's hills again!

For any but an American poet like Philip Freneau (whose poems are at Abbotsford in the 1809 Philadelphia edition), perhaps even for an American poet like Philip Freneau, it was almost as fine a feat to wring poetry from such names at that time as it had been for an earlier English poet to catch the magic of names like Vallombrosa and Fiesole.

You may care to be reminded that Susquehana was to haunt a later[2] Scottish poet:

> Of where or how, I nothing know,
>   And why I do not care.
>   Enough if even so,
> My travelling eyes, my travelling mind can go
> By flood and field and hill, by wood and meadow fair,
> Beside the Susquehanna and along the Delaware.

These lines were written by Stevenson on the emigrant train on which he crossed the States in 1879, 'between Pittsburgh and Chicago, just now bowling through Ohio'; and in her edition of

---

[2] As it had already appealed to Thomas Campbell in *Gertrude of Wyoming*, which Scott had reviewed in the *Quarterly* in May 1809.

Stevenson's poems Dr. Janet Adam Smith draws attention to the corresponding passage in *Across the Plains*:

Our American sunrise had ushered in a noble summer's day . . . I stood on the [driver's] platform by the hour . . . And when I had asked the name of a river from the brakesman, and heard that it was called the Susquehanna, the beauty of the name seemed to be part and parcel of the beauty of the land. As when Adam with divine fitness named the creatures, so this word Susquehanna was at once accepted by the fancy. That was the name, as no other could be, for that shining river and desirable valley.

But beautiful as the passage from Stevenson is, beautiful as is the one I quoted from Arnold, they lack something that is present in Scott. This is the movement and sound of people. In *Marmion*, before we come to Susquehana, we have the busy harvest band and its wild chorus swelling the song; and when the sound of Susque-. hana has died away, we still have with us the heart-sick exiles This feeling for people is often to be found in Scott; and we find it not only in the Scottish portrait-painters Ramsay and Raeburn but in painters like David Allan and Walter Geikie and David Wilkie, some of whose work is to be seen in the Scott Exhibition in Parliament House.

Even with the lyrics in the Waverley Novels, as with Shakes-speare, it is best to know what comes before and after the song. Take Lucy Ashton's song in *The Bride of Lammermoor*:

. . . Sir William Ashton heard the sound of his daughter's lute. . . . The statesman, though little accustomed to give way to emotions . . . natural and simple . . ., was still a man and a father. He stopped, therefore, and listened, while the silver tones of Lucy Ashton's voice mingled with the accompaniment in an ancient air, to which some one had adapted the following words:

> 'Look not thou on beauty's charming,
> Sit thou still when Kings are arming,
> Taste not when the wine-cup glistens,
> Speak not when the people listens,
> Stop thine ear against the singer,
> From the red gold keep thy finger,
> Vacant heart, and hand, and eye.
> Easy live and quiet die.'

The sounds ceased, and the Keeper entered his daughter's apartment. The words she had chosen seemed particularly adapted to her character.

The words are much more than a poem of resignation. So far as the secret of poetry can ever be discovered, their secret lies somewhere in the tension between the strong metre and the languishing sense. The strong beat is characteristic of our poet in

whose work, whether in prose or verse, there is so much action and
so little languor.

I would ask you to consider one more poem, an early one,
written in 1797 on an excursion from Gillsland, in Cumberland,
the lines 'To a Lady with Flowers from a Roman Wall':

> Take these flowers which, purple waving,
>   On the ruin'd rampart grew,
> Where, the sons of freedom braving,
>   Rome's imperial standards flew.
>
> Warriors from the breach of danger
>   Pluck no longer laurels there;
> They but yield the passing stranger
>   Wild-flower wreathes for Beauty's hair.

I would ask you to set beside that the lines from *The Betrothed*
twenty-eight years later:

> Soldier, wake—the day is peeping,
> Honour ne'er was won in sleeping,
> Never when the sunbeam still
> Lay unreflected on the hill: . . .

It is uncanny, this continuity in poetry. We have seen it from
Dryden, through Scott, to Arnold. And now the rampart, Rome,
the breach of danger, laurels, and all four of the later lines, culminating in that inversion of the *l* sound to open and close the line
'Lay unreflected on the hill', rather like the inversion of *l* and *k* in:

> And like a skylit water stood
> The bluebells in the azured wood.

But I am less concerned with unconscious echoes in a learned poet,
like Housman, than with a tendency in English poets from time to
time, after a period of faded sophistication, to renew their art,
more or less consciously, at what they see as the source, whether
that be the ballads, or the alliterative Middle English poets, or
poets like Scott and Campbell, or more recently Blake and
Coleridge.

So far I do not detect any similar tendency among novelists in
these islands. When I use that limiting phrase 'in these islands', I
have in mind what I see is suggested by the fine Norwegian critic,
Professor Francis Bull, in the admirable pages on Scott in his short
history of literature; and that is that an important novel like

Sigrid Undset's *Kristin Lavrinsdatter* owes a great deal to Scott. It seems to me natural that after a period when Ibsen and Strindberg[3] and so many of the other Scandinavian writers and artists were radicals, not just in the political and social sense, but in the sense that they turned art and literature upside down and looked at the roots—it seems to me natural that such a period should have been followed by one with a more tender feeling for the past.

Two radical writers have made useful contributions to the appreciation of Scott by irritating us into liking him more than ever. George Borrow, however vituperative, concluded that after all there were no novels to match Scott's, and this is true praise when one thinks of that wonderful woman Isopel Berners standing in the wood, taking farewell of the Romany Rye. She is the creature of a novelist who understood the gipsies as one of themselves. Mark Twain, that great writer, is if anything more bitter, and I sometimes think that, in order to be consistent, he should have refused to be honoured by a medieval university! What Borrow and Mark Twain held against Scott was his medievalism, which they looked on as reactionary, and which our ancestors generally took more seriously than we do, perhaps too seriously.

There were gaps (shall I say?) in Scott's idea of the dark and the middle ages. Even by eighteenth-century standards he was not much of a medievalist, in the sense in which historians and literary scholars now use the word. Looking back, we have only to think of the influence of the great Benedictine scholar Mabillon on the Maule family, or of the list of early authorities that David Hume wanted to know about in his letter of 1757 and that were, some of them, selected for editing in the Rolls Series in the next century. While Scott read Ariosto and Tasso, he had little use for Dante either as a person or a poet; he disliked what he called excessive alliteration in Anglo-Saxon and Early English poetry; and even in the province of medieval Scots literature, while he read Dunbar to Crabbe and no doubt enjoyed the busyness of Dunbar, he does not seem to have greatly appreciated the quieter (admittedly less well known) Henryson or the poets who had inspired him. In the Moralitas to Henryson's *Orpheus*, and even more in his Annunciation poem, there is a taut, almost Latin, Boethian quality, some-

---

[3] This passage should be qualified by words of Strindberg quoted by Sigfús Blöndal in 'Scott in Swedish Literature' in *The Sir Walter Scott Quarterly* for January 1928: 'To get myself into the proper mood and into the presence of the past I did the same thing, as I usually do, when I am writing historical plays, I read Walter Scott.' I am grateful for this reference to Mr. John M. Simpson.

thing of which is to be found again, perhaps surprisingly, in a version of Boethius about the year 1765:

Tho' when Orpheus made his Moan	But what Laws can Lovers awe?
For his lovely Consort gone,	Love alone to Love is Law:
Tho' the Hind approach'd to hear	Just emerging into Light,
Where the Lyoness stood near,	Orpheus turn'd his eager Sight,
And attentive to the sound	Fondly view'd his following Bride,
Hares forgot the following hound . . .	Viewing lost and losing died.

(What part in the collaboration in that poem was played by Dr. Johnson and what by Mrs. Thrale could, I fancy, be distinguished off-hand only by an editor of Johnson.) My argument from these random instances is that, Gibbon apart, we need to know far more than we know at present about the eighteenth-century acquaintance with late Latin and with medieval literature and thought, before we can judge Scott's Gothick medievalism and what have been called its reactionary influences. While Newman loved and admired Scott (praying for him, and then in later years at Abbotsford wearing his spectacles with great delight), it seems to me that Newman's thought and his final decision were based too firmly on intellectual and, as he saw them, logical grounds for him to have been influenced in that way by his reading of the Waverley Novels.

In his work Scott was not a reactionary but an innovator. He was a novelist in the eighteenth-century tradition; and in the novels laid in earlier centuries the best characters are those who are treated as though they have lived near his own time. But into the English novel he infused two elements that had seldom been there before and have seldom been absent since.

First, he introduced poetry. This was observed by a young poet writing to his brothers as early as January 1818 (when, by the way, they had guessed the secret of the authorship, although in another letter from the same hand nearly a year later there is a distinction between 'Scott' and 'the scotch novels'):

You ask me what degrees there are between Scotts Novels and those of Smollet. They appear to me to be quite distinct in every particular—more especially in their aim—Scott endeavours to throw so interesting and romantic a colouring into common and low Characters as to give them a touch of the Sublime—Smollet on the contrary pulls down and levels what with other Men would continue Romance. The Grand parts of Scott are within the reach of more Minds than the finest humours in Humphrey Clincker—I forget whether that fine thing of the Sargeant is Fielding's or Smollet's [it is in *Tom Jones*, ix. 6] but it gives me more pleasure than the whole Novel of the Antiquary—you must remember what I mean. Some one says to the Sargeant—'That's a non sequiter,' 'if you come to that' replies the Sargeant 'you're another'.

This is excellent criticism, as far as it goes; and Keats might well have continued to level it, to include even Jeanie Deans. But after all, in six months, he was to do very well out of the predecessor of *The Antiquary* with his lines:

> Old Meg she was a Gipsey
> And liv'd upon the Moors;

and in his letter is there not also a 'defence of poesy', an intimation that the novelist is beginning to encroach on what had been poets' territory? Such an instinct was right; for since Wordsworth and Keats there have been few if any great poets, only excellent ones, in the English-speaking world, and on the other hand there have been plenty of great novelists. And from Dickens onwards, with a few notable exceptions like Trollope and Bennett, they have had in them in various kinds a streak of poetry. This, I would suggest, may be a legacy from Scott.

But Scott brought to the novel something beyond what Keats called an interesting and romantic colouring. He had known too much of real life to stop there. The story, the plot, was the thing; but he was more than a good story-teller. He had understanding of character and motive—what would now be called psychology, even psychiatry, for (like Swift and Johnson and Boswell) he knew about that side of life, the 'black dog' and worse than that, and he used his knowledge in, for example, *The Bride of Lammermoor*. But the reader of the Waverley Novels has also a constant sense of an understanding of character and motive in everyday business and bustle and danger. One has only to stay for a little among the Mucklebackits of more recent times to know the truth of the great sentence in *The Antiquary*, 'It's no fish ye're buyin'—it's men's lives'.

In the Advertisement to *The Antiquary*, the Author of 'Waverley' and 'Guy Mannering' took a grateful and respectful leave of the public, 'as one who is not likely again to solicit their favour'. The third novel, he wrote, completed a series of fictitious narratives, intended to illustrate and to describe minutely the manners of Scotland at three different periods, from the age of his father to the last ten years of the eighteenth century. Of the country people of Scotland, among whom he sought his principal personages, he wrote, 'The antique force and simplicity of their language often tinctured with the oriental eloquence of Scripture . . . give pathos to their grief, and dignity to their resentment.' The farewell to the public was premature, but in it, I think, we have the recipe for the best parts of all the novels, down to that splendid one, *Castle Dangerous*. By strength of imagination, by force and simplicity of language, Scott makes the past actual.

But he is not an easy author for anyone to study, and he is unlikely to become easier. The range of his mind and imagination will occupy the learned for many centenaries to come.

We should go on reading Scott and enjoying him by his own light. We should read not only the great, familiar works but his obscure ones, even (I would say, above all) the notes contributed towards the end of his life to Croker's edition of Boswell—the notes on the Finnon haddock, or discomfort in the Highlands, or Young Col running down the greyhound, or Johnson's proposal that Macdonald should call out his clan. 'Sir, I would have a magazine of arms.'—*Sir Alexander*. 'They would rust.'—*Johnson*. 'Let there be men to keep them clean. Your ancestors did not use to let their arms rust.' Scott's note runs:

Dr. Johnson seems to have forgotten that a Highlander going armed at this period incurred the penalty of serving as a common soldier for the first, and of transportation beyond sea for a second offence. And as for 'calling out his clan', twelve Highlanders and a bagpipe made a rebellion.

These and other notes by Scott can easily be dug out of the index to the great Hill-Powell edition of Boswell and may be read with profit and entertainment alongside *Rob Roy* and the Highland tales. I think there is just time to insert here Scott's account of Lord Auchinleck's view of his son's association with Johnson:

'There's nae hope for Jamie, mon,' he said to a friend. 'Jamie is gaen clean gyte.—What do you think, mon? He's done wi' Paoli—he's off wi' the land-louping scoundrel of a Corsican; and whose tail do you think he has pinned himself to now, mon?' Here the old judge summoned up a sneer of most sovereign contempt. 'A *dominie*, mon—an auld dominie: he keeped a schŭle, and cau'd it an acaademy.'

We must sympathize with that Boswellian scholar who had to modify his first impression of this passage, which had been 'Like all Scott's Boswelliana, it should be read as historical fiction, not as a record of fact'. Scott's father, Walter Scott, Writer to the Signet, had been in practice at the time, and it may well have been from him that Scott had the seed of the anecdote.

We should enjoy Scott in the light of his near contemporaries like Dorothy and William Wordsworth, Jane Austen (of whom he wrote so well), Susan Ferrier, Galt and Hogg and Lockhart, but also in the light of many predecessors. I must not exaggerate the value of Scott's reading of Livy at the High School of Edinburgh: it is one thing to quote *locutus Bos* and another to consider the causes of the grandeur and decadence of Rome. Yet the ancients, and Montesquieu, and the other French writers made known here by Hume are all part of the world of Scott. Much of his reading was done so early in life as hardly to be conscious study at all. It could be recalled at will. Or it was there all the time.

'What do the dates matter if the story is true?' That was written by Scott in his *Journal*, when Ballantyne was plaguing him about errors in *Napoleon*. 'What do the dates matter if the story is true?' It may be so; but in nearing at last the end of an introductory talk I would record gratefully that fifty years ago I entered this University. At the beginning of the term some of us came in 'the little train', the railway-train that is no more. We passed the Eildon Hills, cleft in three by

> the wondrous Michael Scott,
> A Wizard, of such dreaded fame,
> That when, in Salamanca's cave,
> Him listed his magic wand to wave,
> The bells would ring in Notre Dame!

We passed Melrose Abbey.

> If thou would'st view fair Melrose aright,
> Go visit it by the pale moonlight.

Drawn by an engine called I forget what, perhaps 'Rob Roy' or 'Redgauntlet', our train steamed into the *Waverley* Station. We had come to 'Mine own romantic town'.

The phrase 'the little train' invites a comparison between two novelists, the one born two hundred years ago and the other a century later. It may be far-fetched. Yet Scott and Proust, however different as men and authors, share an interest in class, society, psychology and places and, above all, in time. Their novels came out over almost the same feverish span of their lifetimes. At the end, despite early death, we are left in each case with the impression of work finished, an *œuvre* held together by two continuing characters, the Narrator and Time himself. A Scottish grammarian had once to explain the difference between 'has been' and 'had been' and he used the phrase 'tyme perfitely and mare than perfitely bygane'. In Scott and Proust time goes on and on and is never 'bygane', never lost, but in the end is time regained. There could not have been a better title than the Waverley Novels. But, if there had had to be another one, what could be more natural than that the Clerk of Session, sitting day after day in Court, 'thinking of anything but his business', should have anticipated Proust's title in C. K. Scott Moncrieff's brilliant rendering, 'Remembrance of Things Past'?

> When to the sessions of sweet silent thought
> I summon up remembrance of things past.

There is one aspect of the Court of Session that you will not see this time. During the law terms, every morning from Tuesday to Friday, there is a procession of lawyers up the Mound. In the afternoon the procession goes down again. It was during the walk down the Mound that Scott's tears fell as he told his Whig friends that their reforms would so alter Scotland that it would never be the same again. The scene has been depicted by an Englishman, our well-remembered historian Richard Pares,[4] in these words:

If you take your stand on the hill which leads from the New Town of Edinburgh to the Old about 10 o'clock in the morning, you will see gentlemen ascending it in the black clothes and the prosperous-looking hats which lawyers wear: these are the judges and the Faculty of Advocates who are going up the hill to administer the law of Scotland. They and their predecessors have played an important part as bearers and defenders of nationality. It is not for nothing that the great Sir Walter Scott was something in the law line.

[4] 'A Quarter of a Millennium of Anglo-Scottish Union', in *The Historian's Business and Other Essays* (Oxford, 1961), 89.

Scott and the Corners of Time

EDGAR JOHNSON

SCOTT led a dual life, one as a legal functionary, man of affairs, public-spirited citizen, and prominent figure much in the world's eyes, the other as poet, imaginative writer, and reflective thinker exploring in the solitude of his spirit the meaning of human experience. But he was no divided man, no split personality; fundamentally the public figure and the private, the man of action and the man of vision, were one, bringing a single though widely comprehensive gaze to bear on both the outer world around him and the inner world of thought and feeling. For these reasons, though I hope to show their unity, I am dividing this paper into two parts, moving toward an analysis of the nature of his achievement and imaginative vision, but beginning with some aspects of his life as an active participant in his nineteenth-century world.

On 15 December 1808 Scott enthusiastically greeted the Declaration of Claremont affirming Britain's support to all peoples who resisted the imperialistic aggressions of Napoleon. 'Tell Mr. Canning,' he wrote impetuously, 'that the old women of Scotland will defend the country with their distaffs, rather than that troops enough be not sent to make good so noble a pledge.' It was one of those corners in time of which Tinidril speaks in *Perelandra* when he says, 'Among times there is a time that turns a corner and everything this side of it is new.' With that pledge, and the carrying out of that pledge, Britain's history and the history of Europe turned a corner.

Scott welcomed the decision; he recognised the crucial significance of the international struggle—more clearly indeed, Tory though he was, than Jeffrey and Cockburn and many of Scott's other friends among the radical Whigs. Unlike them, he refused to believe that Napoleon was invincible, and he saw that the Emperor's word on the most solemn treaty was a scrap of paper. Almost seven years were to pass before Napoleon was finally brought down, but at this turning point in history Scott knew that the supreme challenge for all Europe was resistance or submission to the despotism of one man. He firmly declared for defiance at a time when half of those who believed themselves the voices of enlightenment were crying out for surrender.

His position was emblematic of his course throughout his entire career. During the Napoleonic Wars he enraged the radical Whigs by insisting that not the Tories but Napoleon himself made accommodation impossible; in 1826 he enraged a Tory government headed by his own friends—though without thereby conciliating the Whigs—with his slashing Malachi Malagrowther papers, which defeated singlehanded the administration's banking legislation for Scotland; in 1829, despite his antagonism to the Church of Rome, he joined the Whigs in petitioning Parliament to pass the bill for Catholic emancipation. He was no runner with crowds, either reformist or reactionary, but neither, as he told Edward Cheney in the last year of his life, was he an enemy to constitutional change. 'If the machine does not work well,' he said, 'it must be mended.'

So understood, Scott is a figure quite different from the blind and obstinate traditionalist of the myths about him, building a sham Border castle crammed with Wardour Street antiques, and retreating into the past because he disliked and feared the present. I am not denying, of course, that Scott had in him a broad streak of Jonathan Oldbuck, delighting, as he himself put it, in

> a fouth o' auld nicknackets,
> Rusty airn caps and jinglin' jackets,

but such hobby-horsical indulgences were only a strand in his nature, growing out of the deeper and more meaningful core of his rich response to the literary and historical significance of old legends and old ballads. None of these facts, however, implies any distasteful recoil from the stresses of current experience. If every banker or industrialist who collects Renaissance paintings, medieval sculpture, rare editions, or African masks is a refugee from the present there are mighty hosts of fugitives from reality crowding the world.

All these strictures voiced by Scott's adverse critics seem to me representative of a strange tendency to judge Scott by more censorious standards than they apply to themselves or to other men. If he got large sums for his books he was greedy; if he spent lavishly he was improvident; if he rejoiced in making Abbotsford a large and handsome dwelling he was vainglorious; if he lost his fortune in the general crash of 1826 he was somehow more financially incompetent than Constable or the thousands of others who were ruined in the same catastrophe.

The attitude is perhaps tempting for literary critics who have seldom lost a fortune because they have seldom made a fortune. But it is not obvious why the facts about Scott make him less competent or less at home in the world than his detractors. Samuel Johnson—an exception to such biases—may have been over-generous in declaring that men were seldom more harmlessly employed than in making money, but Scott's monetary dealings do not constitute major defects in his make-up. He was not grasping; his publisher Cadell testified that Scott might successfully have demanded larger sums than he did for his books, and he was always open-handed in helping others. But neither was Scott incompetent as a business man; he built up the printing firm of James Ballantyne and Company into an enterprise that survived the wreck in which Constable foundered. And as for Abbotsford, I must confess that few ambitions seem to me more innocent than the desire to build a beautiful house and leave it to one's children.

The truth about Scott is that he adjusted himself realistically to all the challenges of his age. Instead of fearing the corners of time he welcomed them. Though he deplored the bitter social and economic consequences of the ways in which industrialists were exploiting the new technology, he had no sentimental desire to retain or return to handicraft industry. He installed steam presses in his own printing plant. When he visited Glasgow in 1817 he was delighted by the new process of 'singeing' muslin by passing it over bars of red-hot iron to remove the knots and irregularities. 'The man that imagined that', he exclaimed, 'was *the Shakespeare of the Websters.*' He enormously admired the creative scientific imagination of Sir Humphry Davy.

He was among the earliest of home-owners to put gas lighting in their own homes. Both in Castle Street and at Abbotsford he rejoiced in the brilliant illumination of his library and drawing room. (Virginia Woolf's essay 'Gas at Abbotsford' recognizes the symbolic significance of that innovation.) So enthusiastic for gas, indeed, was Scott, that he became president of a new company engaged in making gas from oil. On occasion his ardour for the new even carried him to oddity; he honeycombed the walls of

Abbotsford with winding tubes in which the compression of air was supposed to ring the bells in the various rooms—an invention that never worked satisfactorily.[1]

Unlike many English landowners, Scott did not oppose what Thomas Creevey called 'the new loco-motive monster navigated by a tail of smoke and sulphur'; he invested in the Melrose branch of the Berwick to Kelso Railroad which was to bring the road into the very valley of the river Tweed where he had his own dwelling. His vigorous applause for Constable's scheme of making cheap books available to the masses by the hundreds of thousands was no doubt coloured by his own professional interests as a writer, but it helps to underline his general receptivity to new ideas.

Against all these facts the outcry is that in Scott's political and social philosophy he was a Tory. He was; but his Toryism was neither reactionary nor subservient. As we have seen, it did not prevent him from successfully opposing a Tory government of his own friends and patrons, and at a time when such opposition might well have endangered his son Charles's appointment to the diplomatic service; and he did not hesitate to join forces with the Whigs when he thought their course was wise. Far from being founded on a blind attachment to the past and an uncritical fear of change, Scott's Toryism represented a balanced realization of the degree to which the individual and society are shaped by the historical past and the forces that have created social institutions.

His profound awareness of the delicate intermeshing of feeling and tradition that gave society its durability made him distrust sweeping panaceas even for clearly recognizable abuses. He felt suspicious of radical reforms that might subvert the habits of order and endanger society's equilibrium. Great as were the evils that had precipitated the French Revolution—and Scott painted them without extenuation in the first two volumes of his *Life of Napoleon Buonaparte*—the noble enthusiasts who fired its opening shots had been overwhelmed in the mob of fanatics and demagogues who drove on to the Reign of Terror and the bloodbaths of the guillotine. Scott saw that unchecked enthusiasm led naturally to fanaticism, and fanaticism, no matter how noble its cause, 'robbed men of their balance, destroyed their judgment, perverted their sense of truth, and finally ended by destroying their sanity,

---

[1] In making this last statement I have been misled by Lockhart; Mrs. Patricia Maxwell-Scott has demonstrated to me that the bells are still in use and work perfectly well.

charity, human compassion'. Scott's massive sanity perceived these dangers and preserved him from extremism.

For Britain, consequently, with its long-established government, he believed in the monarchical and gradated social organization which it had developed. But in *Anne of Geierstein* he paid tribute to the virtues engendered and fostered by the political organization of the republican Swiss. Even in Britain, as I shall presently note, he did not oppose change, and in his survey of her past he strongly condemned the tyrannous aggressions of Charles I, defended the Great Rebellion, and lauded the Revolution of 1688. The American Revolution too he regarded as justified by the attempt of George III and Parliament to assert absolute dominion over the Colonies. But with James Madison—himself hardly a reactionary —Scott realized the importance of not sweeping away the entire past in unlimited change. 'When the examples which fortify opinion', Madison wrote, 'are *ancient* as well as *numerous*', they have 'a double effect'; frequent appeals for constitutional revision 'deprive government of that veneration which time bestows on everything, and without which perhaps the wisest and freest government would not possess the requisite stability'.

Counter to the view I have been presenting has been urged Scott's almost agonized protest against the legal reforms pressed by a victorious Whig administration in 1807. Lockhart paints a moving picture of Scott's distress. Walking down the Mound with him after a meeting of the Faculty of Advocates, Francis Jeffrey, who took the proposals more calmly, teased him playfully about the violence of his emotions. 'No, no,' Scott exclaimed, '—'tis no laughing matter; little by little, whatever your feelings may be, you will destroy and undermine, until nothing of what makes Scotland Scotland shall remain.' He turned away to conceal his agitation, leaning his head against the wall of the Mound, but Jeffrey saw tears falling down his cheeks.

In actuality, though, the episode makes for my case. What the Whigs were demanding amounted to the almost total destruction of the Scottish system of the administration of justice and the substitution of a machinery closely resembling the legal institutions of England. It was not modification but uprooting. In Scott's own 'Essay on Judicial Reform' he accepts measured change, but at the same time quotes Montesquieu's *l'Esprit des lois* from the significant chapter 'Qu'il ne faut pas tout corriger'. Later, as Secretary to the Commission on the Administration of Justice in

Scotland, Scott accepted, among other reforms, the extension of jury trial to areas that had previously been matters of judicial decision.

When in 1817 Scott's friend Morritt was working in Parliament for reforms in the Poor Laws, instead of lagging behind, Scott argued for drastic action. Thousands of peasant farmers had been forced to sell their smallholdings and sink into the ranks of hired labour. One-fifth of the rural population was on parochial relief and the national contribution to the poor rates since 1750 had multiplied almost twelvefold. In the hideously proliferating industrial towns, unemployed factory workers overflowed filthy cellars and airless courts, while their children toiled fifteen hours a day at labour that crippled their limbs, rotted their lungs, and stunted their minds.

Though the state of the agricultural classes was bad enough, Scott agreed, the crying evils both in England and in Scotland were those of the industrial districts. Why should financial adventurers be allowed to bring hordes of people into crowded slums, assume no responsibility for the conditions they had created, and then fling labourers into destitution by discharging them as soon as there was a stoppage of trade? Scott therefore insisted that employers should be taxed in proportion to the number of men they normally employed and that the public funds thus created be applied to relieving the poor.

'If it should be alleged that this would injure the manufacturers I would boldly reply "And why not injure or rather limit speculations the excessive stretch of which has been productive of so much damage to the principles of the country and to the population which it has in so many respects degraded and demoralized?" '
Still later, 'God's justice is requiting, and will yet further requite,' he exclaimed, 'those who have blown up the country into a state of unsubstantial opulence at the expense of the health and morals of the lower classes.'

During the miseries of 1819 when the entire country was suffering from a depression, Scott too was under heavy financial pressures. But instead of dismissing any of his workers at Abbotsford, he created additional jobs to give employment to those out of work. He devised, in fact, a sort of one-man public-works programme of road-making, tree-planting, and other enterprises, including the erection of a sawmill, the last of which, Dr. James Corson has told me, is still in operation. Scott urged similar projects upon the Duke of Buccleuch and other neighbouring land-owners.

As he grew older, he did not grow more conservative. Unlike many another ageing man, he did not gloomily feel that the decades were one long decline from the great days of his youth; if anything he had been more worried about radicalism and rebellion as a young man during the 1790s, and even in his forties, than he was in his sixth decade. The country was despaired of by good citizens every twenty years, he said, but always righted herself 'without much assistance from the crew and sometimes when their strength was employed in a direction that would have swampt her'. During the agitation that led to the Reform Bill of 1832 not Scott but his son-in-law Lockhart feared the outbreak of what he called a 'servile war', while Scott urged him not to let the *Quarterly Review* become an instrument of the reactionaries.

Scott did oppose the Reform Bill, though not, as the Jedburgh labourers who shouted 'Burke Sir Walter' imagined, because it would aid them. He opposed it because it would give enhanced power to precisely those industrialists whom he thought largely responsible for the sufferings of the working class. Though he well knew from his own political experiences in Roxburghshire and Selkirkshire how venal and selfish were many of the existent electorate, he did not believe that a crew of greedy men, often with scanty educational qualifications, would be less corrupt, and they had shown themselves even harder of heart.

Consequently Scott indignantly rejected as a remorseless deception the propaganda that led workers to believe the Bill would ameliorate their woes. And though in the long perspective of time the Bill may ultimately have helped them by showing that political institutions were not immutable, students of economic and political history know how little it aided the labouring classes in the 1830s and 1840s.

In the political sense Scott was no democrat, but he had a strong feeling for the dignity of all human beings. Though he believed in respect for rank, it never occurred to him that lofty position made the Prince Regent a better man than Tom Purdie. For him the Earl of Buchan was always 'a trumpery body' who had been 'wrong in the head all his life', and the egregious Sir John Sinclair was the 'Cavaliero Jackasso'. Though Scott was generously charitable, he sharply condemned the Mrs. Pardiggle kind of domineering charity that might undermine pride and destroy what he called

'the precious feeling of independence'. All his efforts were directed
to helping people to help themselves. In the work programme that
he instituted at Abbotsford, he paid no paupers' wage but the full
rate, and at the same time insisted on a full day's performance
for a full day's pay. Any other course would sap the roots of
character.

Nevertheless, Scott shared none of Rousseau's idealization of
'the natural man'. Even in imagination he would never have
followed Chateaubriand to the forests of North America and
fantasized the red Indian into a noble savage. The Indians were
no better—and no worse—than other peoples; no doubt their
culture had its values, but it was no pastoral idyll. Shelley's vision
of a world in which power has fallen before the resistless persuasion of love Scott would have dismissed as a rainbow-hued
Utopian dream. But, as Prior Aymer of Jourvaulx in *Ivanhoe*
reveals, Scott was equally far from the notion Carlyle was to
elaborate in *Past and Present* that in the middle ages Abbot
Samson typified the relation of the clergy to the populace; and I
suspect he would have been as derisive as Dickens was about the
idea that people should humbly submit to the feudal benevolence of
Sir Joseph Bowley. Scott's creed was that men should be fitted or
fit themselves for responsibility before taking it.

For that reason, like John Stuart Mill, Scott thought that a
broadened base of education should go along with any extension
of the franchise. During the last year of his life he penned an
article urging upon the Tory government a revival of the income
tax and the use of its revenue for free education of the children of
the poor and a great programme of public works. His publisher
Robert Cadell was terrified by the radical sound of Scott's proposals and trembled lest they injure the sales of his novels. It was
to be another forty years before the Government made any pro-
visions for public education, and many years more before any
government tried anything resembling Scott's remedies for dealing
with periods of financial distress and unemployment. But the
generous vision and bold scope of Scott's plan show that he was a
Tory of a very different case from what Franklin Delano Roosevelt
called the economic Bourbons of the twentieth century.

Scott was, in fact, a Tory progressive, almost a Tory radical.
His sympathies were broad and humane, his thought rationally
flexible. He was not afraid of new ideas, but he did not believe
that a thing was true merely because it was novel or strange.

Neither did he exalt as true all beliefs that were old. But he did think that ideas that had survived the repeated examination of learned and thoughtful men were more likely in general to be true than if they had never been subjected to testing at all. Himself a rationalist, Scott thus had at the same time a profound respect for tradition. In a way, its power over men's minds and hearts represented a salutary prejudice, an antidote against giving uncritical belief to crackpots.

As even this brief survey of his public career shows, the historical crises of his age engaged Scott's vigorous concern, but did not throw him into a panic. He was acutely aware of what, in the phrase I have borrowed from C. S. Lewis, I have called the corners of time; he was not afraid to turn them. When he thought his contemporaries were turning the wrong corner, he did not even fear to take an unpopular stand and call out that they had taken the wrong turn.

I turn now to the world of Scott's art, the realm of his creative imagination. In less than thirty years he produced seven long narrative poems and twenty-six full-length novels, all of them set in a past that ranges from the eleventh century to the earlier decades of the nineteenth. These, too, facile critics have slurringly dismissed, in part because of their number and the rapidity with which they were written, in part because of their occasional carelessnesses of structure and style, but most of all because of the very fact that they were set in the historical past. Their concern with the past has been interpreted as the supreme proof that Scott did not feel at home in the present, the warning sign of that dreadful infirmity disparagingly labelled 'escapism'.

I do not intend here to deal elaborately with what I hope is the exploded notion that Scott was a 'romantic'. I did consider it in my life of Scott, because there I felt it an obligation to examine the more important of the errors about him, but here, and before this audience, I trust, to do so would be belabouring a dead issue. Romanticism is a state of feeling, not a body of subject matter. Intrinsically there is nothing more romantic about portcullises than about plumbing, about wimples than about atomic warheads. Those who cannot see the difference between the past in Scott and the past in Dumas cannot tell a hawk from a handsaw, and I intend to waste no time on them. Certainly Scott, like almost all of us, had a romantic strain, but the fundamental nature of his mind and feeling was realistic, rationalistic, and stoic. What Francis Russell Hart calls the 'arid debate over whether Scott was Romantic or anti-Romantic' may well be transcended in the realization that for Scott the existence and power of romantic feeling was incorporated in his realistic vision of the totality of human experience.

Within that vision the past was not a refuge from the present, but the matrix in which the present had been formed. Its struggles were in fact the paradigms of the problems that still confront us; its fascination for Scott was not that it was remote but that it was relevant. History is the great public world in which we are all embroiled, and if we refuse to draw light from its past victories and defeats we condemn ourselves to repeat its disasters.

This, as I have pointed out elsewhere, is the dominant theme that runs through the entire body of Scott's work—in the phrase Wordsworth used of himself in *The Excursion* the 'haunt, and the main region 'of his thought. That theme is the clash of loyalties battling on the stage of time, of men struggling in the torrent of history. More profoundly still, it is the collisions of history itself, the contention between different degrees of civilization and different stages of society, between a predatory tribalism and the establishment of an ordered society, between the endeavour to hold back—sometimes even to turn back—the clock of history and the forward movement of its hand, between the desire to hold on to ways of life rooted in the past and the forces making for progress, between the powers of stability and change.

The exploration was lifelong. The great struggle extends through all Scott's work—Highlander and Lowlander, pastoral Scotland and commercial England, Catholicism and Protestantism, Established Church and Covenanter, freedom of conscience and orthodoxy, law and rebellion, tyranny and constitutional government, feudalism and nationalism, barbarism and culture, Europe and Byzantium, Christianity and Islam. These fell encounters of mighty opposites dominate Scott's greatest work and provide his most exciting theme.

The corners of history—as men turn them, or half turn them, or fail to turn them—both through the contentious early nineteenth century in which Scott himself lived, with its tremendous political, social, and economic problems, and throughout the past from which it had descended—all these multiple corners of time were the cruces of Scott's theme. And past and present are not discrete, but interconnected. Scott's history, as Morse Peckham has pointed out, is an analogue for his vision of the present, which was a product of that history.

And for Scott history is not all war, kings, and politics, though it embraces them. It is the impact on everyday people of their present, their environment, and their times. What his great eighteenth-century forerunners in fiction had seen as the relation between the feelings and the material circumstances of men and women, Scott sees as moulded not exclusively by their individual pasts but as moulded also by all the communal past. Scott's penetrating insight, as Georg Lukács observes, is that 'the great transformations of history' are 'transformations of popular life'. He thus becomes, Lukács concludes, 'the great poet of history because he has a deeper, and more genuine and differentiated sense of historical necessity than any writer before him'.

Scott well knew that the past was not merely the present in plate armour or periwig, but he also knew that in essence it shared, as he remarked in the opening chapter of *Waverley*, 'those passions common to men in all stages of society'. Thus he simultaneously emphasizes both the deep-rooted elements in men and women and the thousands of ways in which they are shaped by the society of which they are a part, by the beliefs and attitudes of their milieu, in short, by the culture of their time. This was his revolutionary insight as an imaginative writer.

In a paper of this length I cannot illustrate Scott's achievement from more than a brief selection of the poems and novels. Even in the earliest of the narrative poems, *The Lay of the Last Minstrel*, he demonstrated his mastery over the manners of an earlier age; his fifteenth-century Scots and their Northumberland foes are portrayed with commanding truth. But he did not in that poem attain to any significant confrontation of cultural forces; the clash between the Scots and the English was only one of innumerable Border hostilities, and, as he himself noted, both parties were in fact more akin to each other than they were to their own compatriots farther south or farther north. Nor in *Marmion*, though it deals with the crucial defeat of Scottish arms at Flodden, does Scott portray or dramatize the differences between the England of Henry VIII and the Scotland of James IV.

In *The Lady of the Lake*, however, the great theme emerges unmistakably. Roderick Dhu and James V are two lions locked in mortal combat, and they are also the past and the future. Roderick voices the resentment of a proud and valiant people despoiled of their heritage by what they regard as alien invaders. Unquestionably Roderick has tradition on his side; his clansmen for generations have lived in the predatory ways in which they persist and have always regarded the lowland Scots whom they call Saxons as aggressors to be resisted and raided.

But if Scott understands and portrays their feelings with deep sympathy, he knows and renders even more strongly the fact that the new reign of law and order represented by James V is a step forward in the organization of society and must and should triumph. Though there was, of course, no historical Roderick Dhu, he epitomizes countless clan chiefs in the long struggle, and the poem is a fictional archetype of the actual movement of history. James's victory is the victory of civilization over barbarism.

Scott's first three novels explore other crucial moments of time. *Waverley* shows the last confused and broken endeavour of the clan chiefs to dominate Scotland. Their defeat at Culloden ends the old feudal society for ever. In *Guy Mannering* Godfrey Bertram's banishment of the gipsies and his prosecution of the smugglers represent a premature and ill-considered attempt to subdue old folk-ways to an order for which Western Scotland in the mid-eighteenth century is not yet ready. The period of *The Antiquary* is almost a generation later still, but in it the present is even more dominated by the past. Almost all its major characters are trying to live in a past that is already dead; and the novel is constructed around the recovery, the redemption, the true understanding and use of the past. In *Waverley* the Jacobite leaders seek to turn backward to a corner that had been passed by the Revolution of 1688; in *Guy Mannering* Godfrey Bertram tries to turn a corner that had not yet been reached; in *The Antiquary* Sir Arthur Wardour and the Earl of Glenallan must cease ignoring the corners that have already been turned and adapt themselves to the present. Time was thus to loom gigantic through all Scott's future work.

With these three novels, even more clearly than in his narrative poems, Scott has grasped his essential theme. Hemmed in and impelled in opposing directions by the clash of vast impersonal forces, how is the individual to survive and achieve a meaningful and fruitful life? Among those forces, which are those of a dead hand, which nurture and enrich, which are a confused mingling of the two? The Waverley Novels in their long sequence are a tremendous effort to grapple with these immemorial struggles of the human spirit.

Old Mortality is both a study of fanaticism and a study of revolution. The intolerance of the government, determined to enforce religious conformity, is balanced by that of the Covenanters, no less bent on compelling all Scotland to their mode of worship. If the Covenanters are demanding religious freedom for themselves they are as tyrannous as the government in denying it to others.

Claverhouse and Burley, the two great symbolic antagonists of the book, are mirror-images of each other, alike in their fanaticism, their unscrupulousness, and their brutal contempt for human life and moral sympathy. Burley believes deception, treachery, and murder are justified by his religious aims. Claverhouse, more self-analytic, knows he is a fanatic, but draws a distinction between what he calls 'the fanaticism of honour and that of dark and sullen superstition', and between the blood of gentlemen 'and the red puddle that stagnates in the veins of . . . crack-brained demagogues and sullen boors'.

'God gives every spark of life,' Henry Morton replies, '—that of the peasant as well as of the prince.' It is the reply of the book, Scott's reply, but he shows it almost drowned out in the rage of civil strife. Morton's plea for moderation and reason seems merely prudential and time-serving to the passionate contenders, and subjects him to the distrust and antagonism of both sides. In the end, the bigotry of the government crushes the rebellion of the bigoted Covenanters; reason will have no hope until after the Revolution of 1688.

The Covenanters nevertheless had been an early swell of that great flood that in 1688 was to sweep a dynasty from the throne. Their forces had been too scanty and poorly armed, and they had commanded too little general sympathy, to give them any chance of success. Their revolt, nevertheless, exhibits the typical characteristics of all revolutionary movements, and Scott gives a brilliant human cross-section of the kinds of people inevitably and necessarily involved. Within their ranks there are bound to be men like Burley, driven by the lust for power but concealing their motivation even from themselves, ruthless but insidiously persuasive; madmen like Habbakuk Mucklewrath and enthusiasts like Macbriar; less magnetic moderates like Pound-text; timorous followers like the Laird of Langcale; and, finally, many like Cuddie

Headrigg, drawn in by the force of accident or circumstance. Morton yields to these realities when he accepts the fact that though he does not desire to be their associate they *are* the rebellion. Nor is their revolt an utter failure. Though they have not turned this corner of time, the next corner will be a different one in consequence of their struggle.

Another kind of revolution dominates *Rob Roy*, the change from the older world of the feudal landowner to the new world of commerce. William Osbaldistone in London and Bailie Nicol Jarvie in Glasgow stand for that new world; Sir Hildebrand in Northumberland and Rob Roy in the Highlands for the old. Osbaldistone Hall shows the rural world of the country squire sunk in a vegetative and fat-witted decay; Rob Roy has heroic stature but in his Highland glens almost all that Frank Osbaldistone can find is dirt, ignorance, violence, and squalor. Bailie Jarvie, the progressive Glasgow businessman, is the real protagonist of the book, with his strain of sentiment for the brave past but his courageous and forward-looking dedication to the prosperity and welfare of Scotland.

So far, then, is Scott from idealizing the old England and the old Scotland and violently opposing the new. His loyalties were not rooted in an uncritical devotion to the past; in *Rob Roy* he shows the ancient and traditional ways of life to have been straitened and savage and now dead or dying; it is the new ways that he celebrates. Scott sees the daring entrepreneur William Osbaldistone and the sober businessman Nicol Jarvie as creative forces, and their lives as no less adventurous and exciting—and a good deal more fruitful—than the life of the knight errant.

When at the close of the book Frank Osbaldistone enters into the partnership with his father that he had formerly refused, and at the same time inherits Osbaldistone Hall, the ending is symbolic, drawing into a unity the hitherto separate worlds of finance and the landed gentry. It is not unlike the course followed by Scott himself, the scion of an old Border family who entered the world of law and business, became the partner in a printing house, and built up for himself a country estate in Roxburghshire. It was another significant corner in time that England was to turn in the course of the nineteenth century.

The Heart of Mid-Lothian probes into deeper corners of the human heart itself. If Ephraim Macbriar had shown the extremes to which faith may be driven by fanaticism and persecution, Jeanie

Deans reveals the heights to which it can rise with love. Her character has been formed by the conscience of her stern Cameronian father; she is the child of his unbending rectitude. Beset on all sides and wrung within by the need to save the sister whom she loves, Jeanie nevertheless cannot force herself to tell the lie she believes forbidden by God. Her ordeal makes the book profoundly searching in its exploration of the problems of justice and compassion as they weigh on the human heart conditioned by all the forces that have shaped it.

Jeanie can solve her problem, in fact, neither by compromise nor by surrender, but only by transcendence, by an appeal from law to mercy. The revelation 'came, as she described it, on her mind, like a sun-blick in a stormy sea'. Her spiritual illumination is a personal epiphany, but it is one of universal significance. The harsh Cameronian conscience turns a deep inward corner and is thereby transformed. Bathed in David Deans's tears and irradiated by Jeanie's love, it can never afterward be the same.

The later novels I must survey more briefly, and I cannot discuss them all. We may note, however, the even-handed portrayal of both the Whigs and the Tories in *The Bride of Lammermoor*, where there is small moral choice between the political corruption of Sir William Ashton and the Privy Council and the slippery tactics of the Tory Marquis of A——, or between the duplicity and fraud by which Caleb Balderstone tries to support the traditional 'rights' of the house of Ravenswood and the tricky legal evasions of the villagers of Wolf's Hope. In *Ivanhoe* Scott is hardly less impartial in rendering the realities of the feudal system, the ferocious and greedy Normans, the sluggish Athelstane, the fanatical Cedric, and the brutal anti-Semitism of both the Normans and the Saxons. Rebecca's loyalty to her father and his devotion to her are in sharp contrast to the behaviour of the Christians, of whom Cedric has disinherited his son, Prince John is conniving at the murder of his brother, and Front-de-Bœuf has slain his father. *The Monastery* and *The Abbot* render with a like impartiality the fierce struggle of the sixteenth-century Reformation preacher Henry Wardour with the Catholic Father Eustace, and of Mary Queen of Scots with her violent and contentious nobles.

Still another decisive corner of time is dramatized in *Quentin Durward*, the breakdown of feudalism and the emergence of the French national state. The colourful and magnificent Charles of

Burgundy and the wily and unscrupulous Louis IX are equally violators of feudal tradition. But there is no doubt of the issues; only if the King can establish a stable government can he prevent the country from being dismembered and falling into a chaos of warring petty states. Between the cynical political realism of the King and the fiery self-aggrandizement of the Duke there is thus shown to be only one choice.

Redgauntlet, even more than *Waverley*, deals with an endeavour to turn back to a corner of time already passed. The passionate devotion of Herries of Birrenswork to the Stuart cause has become an anachronism in the 1760s. It is far more hopeless than the revolt of the Covenanters at Drumclog, it faces backward to the past, and its devotees are a mere remnant. Only one or two fire-brands share Redgauntlet's visions of triumph; all the few dozen other conspirators are either half-hearted or terrified at the perils into which he is striving to plunge them. Reality shatters the romantic dream. Time cannot be made to turn back. 'Then, gentlemen,' Redgauntlet exclaims, clasping his hands in anguish, 'the cause is lost forever!'

Woodstock centres upon one crucial turning in English history, the Great Rebellion, and ends with another, the Restoration. The moderate Presbyterian, Markham Everard, and the fugitive King, Charles II, are its two balanced protagonists. Everard has some-what reluctantly given his support to Cromwell. 'It is true,' the narrative points out, 'that in thus submitting to a successful soldier those who did so forgot the principles upon which they had drawn the sword against the late King. But in revolutions stern and high principles are often obliged to give way to the current of existing circumstances . . .' Cromwell, on the other hand, insists, 'Not wealth nor power brought me from my obscurity. The oppressed consciences, the injured liberties of England, were the banner that I followed.'

Though Cromwell hovers over the whole book, it is primarily Everard and Charles who embody its historical forces—the Rebellion arousing itself to challenge absolutism, and the Restoration that was to follow, only to find itself obliged to sanction much of the work of the Commonwealth. These two, the King and the sober Everard, subsume a fusion of contending group and personal loyalties. They are not only themselves, individuals, they are history itself, made concrete and symbolic in them.

An entire constellation of opposing codes is integrated in *The*

Fair Maid of Perth—not only the codes of Highlander and Low-lander, but of the burghers of Perth and the court world of rulers and nobles, and ultimately of the warlike contention for power and an unworldly pacifism. The psychological analysis of cowardice and courage melts into the larger philosophic study of how far non-violence may survive in a world of violence, Henry Gow's courtship of the unbendingly pacifistic Maid is almost the court-ship of Mars and Venus, of war and peace. Henry's belligerence must learn justice and restraint, but the rather priggishly self-righteous Catharine must also learn that in a world of chaotic brutality like that of fourteenth-century Scotland virtue needs a strong arm in its defence. In the end, Henry repeats his delight in contention and Catharine at last sees that valour must be the weapon of the distressed. Both have turned corners that are significant for themselves but that are still crucial for the savage world that surrounds us today.

The scene of *Anne of Geierstein* enlarges to one of international conflict and the theme to an analysis of imperialism. Charles the Bold reappears, bent on swelling his Duchy into a kingdom stretching from the German Ocean to the Mediterranean. His ambitions involve overrunning the sturdy republican Swiss and absorbing helpless Provence. He stands for the same forces of aggressive nationalism as his rivals, the scheming Louis XI, the warlike Edward IV, and the coldly calculating Richmond, who is to become Henry VII of England. In the game of power politics they are all playing, international morality is a helpless victim.

Among the actors in the story, however, only a few recognize the issues. Young Arthur Philipson and his father the Earl of Oxford are still living in the now moribund world of chivalry, and appeal to ideals of knighthood that had hardly ever been honoured in practice. Burgundy looks on those ideals as a dream of his romantic youth. Only Arnold Biederman, the elected magistrate of Unterwalden, and the leaders of some of the other cantons, believe in a government of law with no oppressive designs upon the rest of Europe. But when Charles demands submission they see their course clear. 'Then farewell peace and welcome war.' Biederman exclaims. 'We will meet you on our frontiers with our naked swords . . .' At Nancy, Burgundy's army is utterly destroyed and he lies a mangled corpse on the battlefield. The true theme of this vastly ambitious novel is the nationalist aggression embodied in the Duke of Burgundy, and its verdict is absolute condemnation.

Count Robert of Paris is the last of the major novels. Its theme is again international conflict, but the clash is not the war of nations but of cultural values—on the one side the cultivated, subtle, and decadent Greeks of the Byzantine Empire, on the other the half-barbarous but forceful Western Crusaders. Can the hostility of their attitudes and interests be resolved in any kind of mutual understanding? Ultimately that understanding is achieved in all three of the central characters. Count Robert is taught to moderate his barbarous contempt for strange manners and peoples; the Saxon Hereward purges himself of his bitterness against the Normans who had conquered his own homeland; and the cynicism of the Emperor Alexius is brought to recognize and value faith and integrity.

In part, *Count Robert of Paris*, like *Ivanhoe*, is a critique of chivalry, but it is much more than that. It is an involved and elaborate analysis of the issues raised by the strife of worldliness and idealism, of irrational excess and sordid calculation. East and West have been brought face to face with each other, and each has been forced to respect the virtues of the other and to reassess itself. In their confrontation another corner of time has been turned.

Scott's total achievement—and for the first time in either fiction *or* history—was to dramatize the basic processes of history. He was the first, G. M. Trevelyan notes, to show that 'thoughts and morals vary according to the period, the province, the class, the man'. It was a revolution, and since Scott's time all history has learned from him. It learned to listen to what the *people* were saying: to realize, as G. M. Young observes, that what men *thought* was happening was as important as what was really happening, and their feelings as significant as fact. It learned that history embraces the common man as well as kings and statesmen —in Gibbon and in Hume the common man had appeared rarely if at all. From Scott historians learned to look for the patterns of meaning within the flow of events. Even Toynbee's principle of challenge and response is implicit in Scott.

Scott's own approach to history strongly resembles that of the French *philosophes*, and he was philosophical in the same way that they were: his real concern, like theirs, was with life in society, the study of social man. But, unlike them, he was no doctrinaire; he was more subtle and flexible, far more aware of the power of the irrational. Though himself a rationalist and an empiricist, he understood how profoundly the stability of society depends upon folk-ways of feeling, habit, tradition. Here he had learned from Burke, but brought to Burke's insights an added richness and inclusiveness of observation.

Though Scott's history is philosophic, it is not tendentiously propagandist. 'The candour of Sir Walter's historic pen', wrote William Hazlitt, 'levels our bristling prejudices . . .' Coleridge pays eloquent tribute to Scott's philosophic insight. 'The essential happiness and wisdom', he says, of Scott's work, 'consists in this, that the contest between loyalists and their opponents'—between all Scott's contending groups—'can never be *obsolete*, for it is the contest between the two great moving principles of social humanity; religious adherence to the past and the ancient, the desire and admiration of permanence, on the one hand; and the passion for increase of knowledge, for truth, as the offering of reason—in short, the mighty instincts of *progression* and *free agency*, on the other. In all subjects of deep and lasting interest, you will detect a struggle between the opposites, two polar forces, both of which are alike necessary to the existence of the other.'

Scott understands and dramatizes this eternal Apollonian-Dionysian struggle with an imaginative sympathy that enables him to comprehend how all the contestants took the stand they did, and thereby to represent the very logic of historical development. He anticipates the sociological-economic historians in showing that people are the products of their ways of earning a living and their relationship to the institutions of which they are both the fathers and the children. His insights, too, are analogous to Darwin's generalization that biological forms are the consequences of a mutually inter-related pressure of general laws, making all living things the offspring of their environments and their past.

The aspects of that past that Scott chooses for representation are those great watershed moments in history, those corners of time, that are pregnant for men's lives. He does not sentimentalize his rendering of them; he shows the past as, like the present, full of ferocity, ignorance, prejudice, and suffering, but shot through, too, again like the present—his present and our present—by gleams of heroism and nobility. His work, therefore, in its meaning for the present, is not only still relevant—it is superbly luminous. 'To be steeped in his books', wrote one of my own teachers, John Erskine, 'is to be on familiar terms with the noble men and women who dwell in them, to share their courage, their zest in life, their self-reliance, their intellectual sincerity, until their outlook becomes our own—this would be a good protection against most of the romances which today it is our frailty rather than our fate to read . . .'

Scott's great theme was always the struggle between the dying and the emerging, between spiritual stultification and spiritual fruition, between the life-denying and the life-fulfilling. That great theme he explored and developed with unexampled fertility. The courage with which he confronted the problems of his own time was clarified by his realization that the present is the child of the past. No novelist in his century saw life more sanely or portrayed it more lucidly. That is his heritage to us. Under his gaze the corners of time are not quaint and obscure crannies; they are light-filled openings into meaning and enlargements of understanding and the spirit.

Scott and Scotland

DAVID DAICHES

IT was almost predictable that the historical novel should have been invented in eighteenth-century Scotland. 'I believe this is the historical age and this the historical nation', observed David Hume of his time and people in 1770. He was right. The Scots in the eighteenth century were engaged in a prolonged contemplation of their own history to a unique degree, and history itself was responsible for this. The Union of 1707, resulting from the Scottish Parliament's having voted itself out of existence in order that Scotland might form an 'incorporating union' with England, ended the separate political existence of the Scottish nation, and thoughtful Scots spent much of the succeeding century considering the meaning of this event and devising different ways of coping with its consequences. This activity stimulated general ideas about the historical process. The movement from consideration of the recent history of Scotland—which included putting the case for and against Mary Queen of Scots, arguing the pros and cons of the Union of 1707, and reacting often in unexpected ways to the Jacobite Rebellion of 1745—to consideration of larger historical issues is seen again and again in the work of the Scottish literati of the eighteenth century. The first professor of history at Edinburgh University began in 1719 as Professor of Universal History and then had his title expanded to Professor of Universal History and Scottish History—a reversal of the more usual development. William Robertson, the most wide-ranging historian of his time, began with a *History of Scotland* in 1759 (in which David Hume among others found a too great tenderness towards Queen Mary) before moving on to other countries and continents. In the same year that saw the publication of Robertson's *History of Scotland*, William Tytler published his defence of Queen Mary, *The Inquiry into the Evidence against Mary Queen of Scots*; his son, Alexander Fraser Tytler, became Professor of Universal History at Edinburgh University in 1780 and young

Walter Scott attended his lectures in the academic year 1789–90. The movement from Scottish particularism to more general historical interests reflected in the relation between Tytler *père et fils* is seen also in the development of Scott's own historical concerns. Scott was led into history by his deep emotional involvement with the recent past of his own country, and what this involvement taught him he then applied to other times and other countries.

Scott lived in an age of improvement. The Union had opened up the English colonies to Scottish merchants and so helped to compensate them for the cruel and humiliating failure of the Darien Scheme. It was the Union, as Bailie Nicol Jarvie points out in *Rob Roy*, that enabled Glasgow to grow into a flourishing mercantile city importing sugar from the West Indies and tobacco from the southern American colonies. The Union also encouraged Scottish landowners to turn to England for models of how to improve their land. Alexander Tytler's *Memoirs of the Life and Writings of Lord Kames* (published in 1807, after he had become Lord Woodhouselee) traces the history of what he calls 'the improvement of agriculture' from about 1720.

> The continual intercourse of [the great Scottish cattle-dealers] with England, made them acquainted with various modes of husbandry, which they successfully introduced at home on the land-estates which their wealth enabled them to purchase. The example was imitated by a few spirited and opulent landholders in different parts of the country. . . . These noblemen and gentlemen formed, in 1733, the plan of a *Society for the Encouragement of Agriculture*, which, in a short time, comprehended three hundred of the principal landholders of Scotland; and this institution, subsisting in vigour for above twenty years, diffused the spirit of improvement over a considerable part of the kingdom.

If the Union was seen by the Scottish literati of the eighteenth century as assisting agricultural improvement in Scotland, that other Scottish traumatic experience of the century, the Fortyfive, was also seen by many of them as resulting in the opening up of the Highlands to improvement. Again, I quote Tytler's *Memoirs of Lord Kames*:

> The Rebellion of 1745 brought a great recompence for the temporary evils that attended it, in the many valuable improvements to which it gave rise in Scotland. Among these, the opening of the country by highways, the first step to all advancement in agriculture, and the primary engine of civilization; the suppression of the heritable jurisdictions; the abolition of the personal services of the peasantry, which kept them in the most abject dependance, and

repressed all ingenuous exertions to improve their condition, were great and permanent benefits. Nor is it to be denied, that, in a few instances, even the forfeiture of many of the great estates, and their temporary annexation to the Crown, while it tended more effectually than any other means that could be employed to break the feudal bondage, was the immediate introduction to a better system of husbandry, and the cause of many material improvements in the state of the country.

This view of the ultimately beneficent results of the Union and of the defeat of the '45 rebellion is reflected in Scott's novels. 'Whisht, sir!—whisht!' exclaimed Bailie Nicol Jarvie to Andrew Fairservice when the latter was complaining about the Union,

it's ill-scraped tongues like yours that make mischief between neighbour-hoods and nations. There's naething sae gude on this side o' time but it might have been better, and that may be said o' the Union. Nane were keener against it than the Glasgow folk, wi' their rabblings and their risings, and their mobs, as they ca' them now-a-days. But it's an ill wind blaws nae-body gude—Let ilka ane roose the ford as they find it.—I say, Let Glasgow flourish! whilk is judiciously and elegantly putten round the town's arms, by way of by-word. Now, since St. Mungo catched herrings in the Clyde, what was ever like to gar us flourish like the sugar and tobacco-trade? Will onybody tell me that, and grumble at a treaty that opened us a road west-awa' yonder?

The whole rhetorical rhythm of the novel at this point makes it clear that the Bailie is here speaking for Scott, just as it is clear that Darsie Latimer is speaking for his creator in *Redgauntlet* when he defends, as Tytler defended, the Heritable Jurisdictions Act, a direct result of the defeat of the '45 rebellion. Darsie is talking to his sister about their uncle Redgauntlet's attempt to rouse the people in favour of a new Jacobite rebellion: 'Whatever these people may pretend,' he says, 'to avoid your uncle's impor-tunities, they cannot, at this time of day, think of subjecting their necks again to the feudal yoke, which was effectually broken by the Act of 1748, abolishing vassalage and hereditary jurisdictions.'

Scott was a man of the Scottish Enlightenment, who believed in progress, rationality, moderation, reconciliation. The prime use of history was to help us to improve ourselves. 'Our ancestors lodged in caves and wigwams,' he wrote to his younger son Charles in November 1821, 'where we construct palaces for the rich and comfortable dwellings for the poor. And why is this but because our eye is enabled to look back upon the past to improve on our ancestors improvements and to avoid their errors. This can only be done by studying history and comparing it with passing events.'

Is this Scott or Macaulay? It might almost come from Macaulay's famous manifesto of progress in his review of Southey's *Colloquies*.

It is Scott, of course, but—and this is the important point—it is one side of Scott only. This is the Scott who stage-managed George IV's visit to Scotland in 1822 and succeeded in presenting him, on one occasion even wearing the kilt, amid every kind of tartan pageantry, as legitimate leader of the Highland clans. 'I am sure such a man is fitter for us than one who would long to head armies, or be perpetually intermeddling with *la grande politique*', he wrote of the King in his *Journal* in October 1826. This is the Scott who installed gas to illuminate Abbotsford, who became first chairman of the Oil Gas Company, who welcomed 'steam carriages' going 'at the rate of 30 miles per hour', who interested himself in the development of a railway for transporting coal and lime. This is a rather different Scott from the man who exerted himself to achieve the recovery of the old Scottish Regalia in 1818 or the man involved in an incident of 1806 described by Lockhart:

At a debate of the Faculty of Advocates on some of these propositions [for the reform of Scottish legal procedure], he made a speech much longer than any he had ever before delivered in that assembly; and several who heard it have assured me, that it had a flow and energy of eloquence for which those who knew him best had been quite unprepared. When the meeting broke up, he walked across the Mound, on his way to Castle Street, between Mr Jeffrey and another of his reforming friends, who complimented him on the rhetorical powers he had been displaying, and would willingly have treated the subject-matter of the discussion playfully. But his feelings had been moved far beyond their apprehension: he exclaimed: 'No, no—'tis no laughing matter; little by little, whatever your wishes may be, you will destroy and undermine, until nothing of what makes Scotland Scotland shall remain.' And so saying, he turned round to conceal his agitation—but not until Mr Jeffrey saw tears gushing down his cheek—resting his head until he recovered himself on the wall of the Mound.

This is the Scott who twenty years later confided to his *Journal* that 'they are gradually destroying what remains of nationality' and complained bitterly of the 'lowering and grinding down all those peculiarities which distinguished us as Scotsmen'. This Scott is very much a high Tory. His famous remark to Croker in March 1826 that 'if you *unscotch* us, you will find us damned mischievous Englishmen' has often been quoted out of context. Just as in the *Journal* entry I have quoted he went on to complain that the destruction of traditional distinguishing features of Scottish national life would 'throw the country into a state in which it will be universally turned to democracy, and instead of canny Saunders, they will have a very dangerous North British neighbourhood', so the mood of Scottish nationalist conservatism in which he wrote the *Letters of Malachi Malagrowther* arose from his fear of the development of bourgeois democratic views. He tells Croker that the Scottish popular 'desire for speculation in politics' can only be 'restrained by some proud feelings about their own country', and adds: 'The late Lord Melville knew them well and managed them accordingly'. Now most modern Scottish Nationalists regard Lord Melville as a Quisling, a man who ruled Scotland for his English masters. What we have here is a case of Scott drawing on Scottish national feeling as a means of preventing the development in Scotland of liberal democratic measures. We may perhaps be uncomfortably reminded of the way in which German fascism used the nationalism of small nations (in Croatia and the Ukraine, for example) as a cover for exploitation.

The analogy is, however, unfair to Scott, for the paradox goes far deeper than anything that can be explained by reference to modern concepts of nationalist political manœuvring. Though Scott believed in progress and welcomed it, and though he accepted eagerly any technological aids to the easing of the conditions of life that he could find—whether it was gas or railways or pneumatic bells—he was deeply troubled at the break-up of organic structures in society which the industrial revolution brought with it. In a letter to Lord Montague in January 1820 he analyses the break-up of traditional community loyalties:

Formerly obliged to seek the sides of rapid streams for driving their machinery, manufacturers established themselves in sequestred spots and lodged their working people in villages around them. Hence arose a mutual dependence on each other between the employer & employd for in bad times the Master had to provide for these peoples sustenance else he could not have their service in good & the little establishment naturally lookd up to him as their head. But this has ceased since manufacturers have been transferd to great towns where a Master calls together 100 workmen this week and pays them off the next with far less interest in their future fate than in that of as many worn-out shuttles.

This puts Scott in the tradition of the Victorian 'prophets', the attackers of *laissez-faire* capitalism from Carlyle to William Morris. This attack can lead the attacker to the political Left or the political Right: an objection to bourgeois democracy is later a

feature equally of Socialism and Fascism. Marx would have understood what Scott was complaining about, for he made the same
point himself in the Communist Manifesto: 'The Bourgeoisie,
wherever it has got the upper hand, has put an end to all feudal,
patriarchal, idyllic relations. It has pitilessly torn asunder the
motley feudal ties that bound man to his "natural superiors", and
left no other nexus between man and man than naked self-interest,
than callous "cash payment"'.

But Scott's complex of feelings about Scotland cannot be
explained by simply counterpointing his attitude as a 'progressive'
who welcomes the Union and its prospects for the peaceful commercial development of Scotland as North Britain against his
paternal Scottish nationalist Toryism. There were other factors
involved, and these are deeply bound up with the circumstances of
Scott's life and character.

Scott's concern with progress was bound up with his view of
history as *process*, a view which he developed early in an instinctive
way and which he first heard formulated when he attended the
lectures of David Hume (nephew of the philosopher), professor
of Scots Law, between 1790 and 1792. In his autobiographical
fragment Scott has recorded the impression made on him by
Hume's lectures:

I copied over his lectures twice with my own hand, from notes taken in class,
and when I have had occasion to consult them, I can never sufficiently admire
the penetration and clearness of conception which were necessary to the
arrangement of the fabric of law, formed originally under the strictest influence of feudal principles, and innovated, altered, and broken in upon by the
change of times, or habits, and of manners, until it resembles some ancient
castle, partly entire, partly ruinous, partly dilapidated, patched and altered
during the succession of ages by a thousand additions and combinations, yet
still exhibiting, with the marks of its antiquity, symptoms of the skill and
wisdom of its founders, and capable of being analysed and made the subject
of a methodical plan by an architect who can understand the various styles of
the different ages in which it was subjected to alteration. Such an architect
has Mr Hume been to the law of Scotland, neither wandering into fanciful
and abstruse disquisitions, which are the more proper subject of the antiquary,
nor satisfied with presenting to his pupils a dry and undigested detail of the
laws in their present state, but combining the past state of our legal enact-
ments with the present, and tracing clearly and judiciously the changes which
took place, and the causes which led to them.

'The changes which took place, and the causes which led to
them.' Here is a clear enough statement of one aspect of Scott's
view of history. But this view of the development of Scots law as

bound up with changes in social habits and institutions—a view very much in conformity with the sociological interests of the Scottish historians and political economists of the latter half of the eighteenth century—was not in this case presented to a mind untouched by historical interests. The young Scott, when he attended Edinburgh University, had since earliest childhood been developing a passionate interest in history of a kind very different from that shown by the Edinburgh literati, and it was the interaction of these two kinds of interests which eventually produced the historical novelist.

Scott tended to underestimate the contribution of the literati and the Scottish Enlightenment to his view of history, though he did recognize that it interacted fruitfully on his other kind of historical interest. Talking of his state of mind at the time when he entered Edinburgh University, he says in the autobiographical fragment:

My memory . . . seldom failed to preserve most tenaciously a favourite passage of poetry, a playhouse ditty, or, above all, a Border-raid ballad; but names, dates, and the other technicalities of history, escaped me in a most melancholy degree. The philosophy of history, a much more important subject, was also a sealed book at this period of my life; but I gradually assembled much of what was striking and picturesque in historical narrative; and when, in riper years, I attended more to the deduction of general principle, I was furnished with a powerful host of examples in illustration of them. I was, in short, like an ignorant gamester, who kept up a good hand until he knew how to play it.

Ideas of change and development such as those that had been developed by Adam Ferguson in his *Essay on the History of Civil Society* (1767)—especially in Parts IV and V—and those which Scott learned from the lectures of Professor Hume, worked on the mind and imagination of a youngster who as a child, living on his grandfather's farm at Sandy-Knowe, had become fascinated by Border traditions and had listened eagerly to innumerable anecdotes of tragic slayings, of feats of heroic endurance, of grim slaughter, of escape and rescues and struggles. Not only did the little Walter Scott hear such stories told round the fireside and encounter them in ballads sung by farmers and farm servants and in tales about particular places that he could see with his own eyes, imagining the acting out of those old heroic deeds on the very scene before him and thus associating the stability and continuity of place with the perpetual movement of time—not only did he hear all this, but he also listened with equal eagerness to stories of recent history told by Jacobite survivors of the '45. He later recalled hearing news of the progress of the American War from his uncle at his weekly visits to the farm and at the same time listening to 'songs and tales of the Jacobites'. 'This latter political propensity', he tells us in the autobiographical fragment, 'was deeply confirmed by the stories told in my hearing of the cruelties exercised in the executions at Carlisle, and in the Highlands, in the battle of Culloden. One or two of our own distant relations had fallen on that occasion, and I remember detesting the name of Cumberland ["Butcher" Cumberland, the victor at Culloden] with more than infant hatred. Mr. Curle, farmer at Yetbyre, husband of one of my aunts, had been present at their execution; and it was probably from him that I first heard these tragic tales which made so great an impression on me.' Dr. Arthur Melville Clark made a very important point when he observed of Scott that 'it was by the spoken and often casual reminiscences of his elders, even more than by books, that he recreated the past of the three or four generations before his own—not in respect of the history-book facts, but in respect of the unrecorded details of day-to-day existence and the ways in which real persons really behaved and spoke and felt.' The combination of interest in quotidian details of daily life in the past with interest in violent or desperate or tragic or comic incidents that had occurred against the background of that daily rhythm gave Scott his first view of Scottish history: it is a view very appropriate to a future novelist. Again, one is tempted to quote from the autobiographical fragment:

My grandmother, in whose youth the old Border depredations were matter of recent tradition, used to tell me many a tale of Watt of Harden, Wight Willie of Aikwood, Jamie Telfer of the fair Dodhead, and other heroes— merrymen all of the persuasion and calling of Robin Hood and Little John. A more recent hero, but not of less note, was the celebrated Diel of Little-dean, whom she well remembered, as he had married her mother's sister. Of this extraordinary person I learned many a story, grave and gay, comic and warlike.

So it was not only, and indeed not principally, 'old unhappy far-off things and battles long ago' that fascinated the young Scott when he lived on his grandfather's farm at Sandy-Knowe: it was also, and very significantly, the recent past as transmitted by survivors. The sub-title of Scott's first novel was ' 'Tis Sixty Years Since', and his first three novels are about the recent Scottish past.

We must not, however, underestimate the effect of Scott's wide reading in romantic and heroic narratives when he was a youngster. It was pretty much the reading attributed to his hero in chapter 3 of *Waverley*, and it certainly affected his view of Scottish history. It gave him, for example, an emotional predisposition in favour of the Stuart cause, so that the young Scott considered himself both royalist and Jacobite. The mature Scott, the Scott of the Scottish Enlightenment, retained much of this youthful emotion, while his reason pronounced a very different verdict. He was quite aware of this ambivalence in his attitude. Writing to Robert Surtees in December 1806, in reply to a letter in which Surtees had urged him to take up 'the interesting periods of 15 and 45', he mentions his early Jacobite associations (including 'one old man, called Stuart of Invernahyle, who had been out both in 1715 and 1745, and whose tales were the absolute delight of my childhood') and affirms that he 'became a valiant Jacobite at the age of ten years old' before continuing: 'and, even since reason & understanding came to my assistance, I have never quite got rid of the impression which the gallantry of Prince Charles made on my imagination. Certainly'—he adds—'I will not renounce the idea of doing something to preserve these stories, and the memory of times and manners, which, though existing as it were yesterday, have so strangely vanished from our eyes'. The following year, in a letter to Southey, he defends Claverhouse and talks of 'the perfidy, cruelty, and stupidity' of 'the beastly covenanters'. (Twenty-one years later, in a letter to John Richardson, he called them 'a set of cruel and bloody bigots'.) But we must put side by side with these remarks other observations which are equally important, such as this, made in a letter to Miss Clephane in July 1813: 'I am very glad I did not live in 1745 for though as a lawyer I could not have pleaded Charles's right and as a countryman I could not have prayed for him yet as a soldier I would I am sure against the conviction of my better reason have fought for him even to the bottom of the gallows'. Writing to Lockhart of Robert Burns's Jacobitism he remarked, quite rightly: 'I imagine . . . his Jacobitism belongd like my own to the fancy rather than the feelings', while of Mary Queen of Scots he admitted that his head contradicted his heart: 'my opinion in point of fact is contrary both to the popular feeling and to my own'. This ambivalence of attitude is given another dimension in the novels: his presentation of Jacobitism in *Waverley* and in *Redgauntlet* is enriched by his concern for the viability or non-viability of older heroic codes of behaviour while set beside the rational progressive attitude of the Scottish Enlightenment and by the interaction of social, historical and psychological factors which that concern made visible. Scott could not have become a historical novelist without this double vision; it is this that prevents him from having any historical villains or historical heroes in his novels: I mean by this that none of his villains or heroes are bad or good because of the side on which they find themselves. A man of good-will may find himself on either side of a historical conflict: he can be trapped by his own generous impulses to accept at their face value the swagger and panache of a heroic code which has in fact outlived its social usefulness—and this is in some degree what happened to Waverley— or he can be motivated by a desire for compromise and bridge-building to join one side in order to try to moderate its extremism and help bring about a peaceful accommodation with the other side. We see this latter figure in many of Scott's novels—in *Old Mortality* and *Woodstock* among others—and he represents something very deep in Scott's own character. High Tory though he was, he was by temperament a mediator, and he disapproved violently of the party-political rancour which Lockhart and his friends introduced into their writings. The conclusion of his revealing preface to *The Minstrelsy of the Scottish Border* seems to lament the assimilation of Scottish manners to those of England, yet he gently and courteously refers to England as Scotland's 'sister and ally'.

The well-known passage is of interest for other reasons: 'By such efforts, feeble as they are, I may contribute somewhat to the history of my native country; the peculiar features of whose manners and character are daily melting and dissolving into those of her sister and ally. And, trivial as may appear such an offering, to the manes of a kingdom, once proud and independent, I hang it upon her altar with a mixture of feelings, which I shall not attempt to describe.' The 'mixture of feelings' represents something quite fundamental in Scott: he simultaneously looked back with excitement on Scotland's violent heroic past and welcomed the peaceful progress which he saw as guaranteed by the merging of Scotland with England in a common British culture. He wanted to preserve Scotland's individuality and resented every innovation which tended to whittle it away, yet he knew that change was a necessary and desirable part of the historical process and he had no illusions about the cruelty and often the simple nastiness of life under the old heroic codes. He was in his fashion a Scottish

nationalist, but his Scottish nationalism was modified and complicated in so many ways that it represented a unique version of this
political stance.

Scott's first long narrative poem, *The Lay of the Last Minstrel*,
and his last novel, the short and broken-backed *Castle Dangerous*
written when he was a dying man, are both about conflicts
between English and Scottish forces. In neither case is it a question
of 'goodies' against 'baddies'. The English knights are if anything
more chivalrous and considerate than the Scottish. *Castle Dangerous*
is set in the early fourteenth century, in that period of bitterest
conflict between England and Scotland, when Robert the Bruce
was a fugitive from the forces of Edward II and Scottish castles
were being held with increasing difficulty by English garrisons
against the patriotic onslaughts of the Scots. Here if anywhere
Scott, who prided himself on nothing so much as his Scottishness,
could have been expected to throw his sympathies clearly on the
side of the struggling supporters of Scottish independence. But
what we find is a fully sympathetic picture of the English soldier
in Scotland—his problems, difficulties, frustrations, confusions—
which reminds us of Kipling's picture in *Puck of Pook's Hill* of the
Roman soldier on garrison duty on the Wall. The patriotic Scots,
roughened and toughened by their years of guerrilla warfare
against the English, are never idealized, but presented with what
I can only call a gruff sympathy. Even in *The Lord of the Isles*, the
narrative poem in which he introduces Bruce himself and describes
the Battle of Bannockburn, the note of historical and psychological
curiosity is far stronger than the note of simple patriotism. At the
same time we must remember the famous patriotic opening of
Canto VI of *The Lay*:

> Breathes there the man, with soul so dead,
> Who never to himself hath said,
>   This is my own, my native land!

And we remember the autobiographical introduction to the third
canto of *Marmion* in which he described his childish visions of
patriotic Scottish achievement:

> And ever, by the winter hearth,
> Old tales I heard of woe or mirth, . . .
> Of patriot battles, won of old
> By Wallace wight and Bruce the bold;
> Of later fields of feud and fight,
> When, pouring from their Highland height,

> The Scottish clans, in headlong sway,
> Had swept the scarlet ranks away.
> While stretch'd at length upon the floor,
> Again I fought each combat o'er,
> Pebbles and shells, in order laid,
> The mimic ranks of war display'd;
> And onward still the Scottish lion bore,
> And still the scatter'd Southron fled before.

Scott the novelist tempered the simple patriotic feeling of Scott the discursive autobiographer and continually presented both conflicts within Scotland and conflicts between Scotland and England as bound up with a fascinating historical process rather than as conflicts between loyalists and rebels or between patriots and invaders. And when he introduces Scottish characters in novels set elsewhere—in England in *The Fortunes of Nigel* or on the continent in *Quentin Durward*—it is more often than not with a wry recognition of the awkwardness of the Scottish character. Yet there is a warmth about this recognition, a sense that he is dealing with his own people, that helps to give depth and conviction to the portrait.

It is a commonplace of Scottish cultural history that Scottish response to the Union of 1707 worked in two equal and opposite directions. One response was to cultivate Scottish feeling in song and ballad, to look to the Scottish folk tradition—which had survived, in however attenuated a fashion, the decline of the Scottish Court tradition largely attributable to the loss of Scotland's Court in 1603. Thus we find the deliberate cultivation of the Scottish vernacular, no longer, since the decline of Scots as a literary language, a full blooded literary medium in its own right but more and more a series of vernacular spoken dialects. This is on the whole a view of Scottish literature as deliberately 'low', for it is in poems of rustic life or city debauchery that the vernacular was now most effectively used. Side by side with this new vernacular poetry, largely of low life or imitative of older ballad and folk-song, there were attempts to make available the older 'art' literature of Scotland, produced when Scotland was an independent country and non-Gaelic Scotland had a distinctive literature written in its own literary language. But the folk tradition was the stronger. Though this movement began with James Watson's *Choice Collection of Comic and Serious Scots Poems both Ancient and Modern* (1706–11), which assembled examples of everything then available in the Scots literary tradition, both courtly and popular, its real influential monuments were Allan Ramsay's *Tea-Table Miscellany* of 1724 and David Herd's enlarged, two-volume edition of his *Ancient and Modern Scots Songs* (1776), both of which emphasize the folk tradition, the latter handling it exclusively. Interest in 'Scotch airs', Scottish songs and Scottish ballads grew apace throughout the century, and received additional impetus from the interest in early and primitive poetry that was developing both in England and in Scotland and of which the example most mentioned in text-books of literary history is Percy's *Reliques* (which was only one of very many such collections). Seen in this context, Scott's first important work, his *Minstrelsy of the Scottish Border*, is a contribution to the already well-established tradition of collecting, editing and reviving Scottish folk literature.

The other response to the Union of 1707 also tried to compensate for a lost political independence by cultural means, but through Enlightenment rather than nostalgia. The aim here was not to produce antiquarian collections of old songs or transcriptions of oral ballads or imitations of older Scottish popular modes, but to write in elegant English works of philosophy, history and literary criticism that were addressed to Europe as a whole. The men of the Scottish Enlightenment were no less patriotic Scotsmen than the folklorists and collectors of old songs and ballads in Scots. But their aim was to assert their country's claim to greatness by operating in the van of European progress in order to show that Scotland, small and poor though she might be and chequered though her history might have been, could nevertheless represent Britain before the world at least as well as, and perhaps better than, any English writer. And this aim was realised not only in philosophy, history and literary criticism—in the works of David Hume, William Robertson, Hugh Blair, Lord Kames, among many others—but also in architecture, portrait-painting, medicine, political economy, geology, chemistry and even road-building. (One need mention only Robert Adam, Sir Henry Raeburn, the dynasty of the Doctors Monroe, Adam Smith, James Hutton, Joseph Black and John Loudon McAdam.)

In his attitude to the history of his own country Scott combined both the responses to the Union of 1707—the nostalgic, antiquarian and folkloristic and also the enlightened and progressive. In doing so he avoided the excesses of either side. He understood precisely the nature of Burns's achievement in producing an Indian

Summer of Scots poetry by combining a reinvigorated vernacular folk tradition with elements of a sophisticated art tradition, and he knew that this was the end, and not the beginning, of a road. He knew that Scots no longer existed as a full-blooded literary language, and that, like the literati, he must write in English, but he triumphantly found a new way of using the vernacular in the dialogue of his Scottish novels while at the same time avoiding the masochistic desire of the literati, whose *spoken* language was for the most part the Scots vernacular, to castigate their own spoken speech as corrupt and uncouth. 'Is it not strange', wrote David Hume to Gilbert Elliot of Minto in July 1757, 'that, at a time when we have lost our Princes, our Parliaments, our independent Government, even the Presence of our chief Nobility, are unhappy, in our Accent & Pronunciation, speak a very corrupt Dialect of the Tongue which we make use of; is it not strange, I say, that, in these Circumstances, we shou'd really be the People most distinguish'd for Literature in Europe?' Scott knew better than that. Though he shared Hume's pride in Scottish achievement, he would never have castigated the Scots tongue as 'a very corrupt dialect': he understood enough of the history of language to know that 'corruption' in such a context is a wholly misleading term and that in fact Scots preserved many Germanic words that had become lost in standard English as well as preserving other words in their earlier Anglian form. And Scott's pride in Scottish achievement did not lead him, as it had led David Hume, to hail as the greatest of poets either Thomas Blacklock, the 'Scottish Pindar', John Home, the 'Scottish Shakespeare', or William Wilkie (author of the ineffable *Epigoniad*), the 'Scottish Homer'. Nor did Scott's national pride lead him, as it led so many of the literati, to champion Macpherson's *Ossian* against all comers. Introduced at an early age to *Ossian*, he soon found himself—in his own words—'disgusted' with 'the tawdry repetitions of the Ossianic phraseology'. Perhaps most important of all, Scott's almost feudal paternalistic attitude to society, however reactionary it might seem to modern eyes, saved him from the false gentility to which so many of the literati succumbed.

In spite of the tartan pageantry which Scott arranged for George IV's visit to Scotland, he was far from believing that the Highland tradition was the one truly Scottish tradition. Many times in his letters he points out to correspondents that they must not think of all Scots as wearing the tartan. Writing to the painter

Haydon in January 1821 he made the point quite clear: 'In general there is a great error in dressing ancient Scottish men like our Highlanders, who wore a dress, as they spoke a language, as foreign to the Lowland Scottish as to the English'. In 1806 he explained to Lady Abercorn his difficulty in writing a Highland verse romance: 'My great difficulty is that being born and bred not only a lowlander but a borderer I do not in the least understand the Gaelic language and therefore am much at a loss to find authentic materials for my undertaking'. He regarded the Highlands as having been in a sense left behind by history until after the '45, and this gave them their special kind of interest and fascination.

My early recollections of the Highland scenery and customs [he wrote in 1829 in the General Preface to the Waverley Novels], made so favourable an impression in the poem called the *Lady of the Lake*, that I was induced to think of attempting something of the same kind in prose. I had been a good deal in the Highlands at a time when they were much less accessible, and much less visited, than they have been of late years, and was acquainted with many of the old warriors of 1745, who were, like most veterans, easily induced to fight their battles over again, for the benefit of a willing listener like myself. It naturally occurred to me that the ancient traditions and high spirit of a people who, living in a civilized age and country, retained so strong a tincture of manners belonging to an early period of society, must afford a subject favourable for romance, if it should not prove a curious tale marred in the telling.

Fifteen months later, writing a retrospective introduction to a new edition of *The Lay of the Last Minstrel*, Scott made a similar point about life in the Borders in the mid-sixteenth century, referring to 'the obscure feuds of barbarous clans, of whose very names civilized history was ignorant'. Though Scott was anxious to make clear the difference between Highland and Border customs, he thought of both as belonging to an older, heroic way of life that had been left behind by civilization. An important difference between them was that civilization caught up with the Borders before it caught up with the Highlands. The fascination for Scott of the Highlands, and in particular of Highland involvement in the Jacobite rebellion of 1745, was that this represented an older kind of heroic culture surviving right into the eighteenth century. The meaning and the fate of that kind of survival are examined in three of Scott's novels, *Waverley*, *Rob Roy*, and *Redgauntlet*. The concern in each of these novels is with the effect of historical process on older surviving social forms, codes of behaviour and personal

ideals rather than with Scottish patriotic feeling as such. Redgauntlet's identification of his anachronistic and hopeless Jacobitism with the movements for Scottish independence led in earlier
centuries by William Wallace and Robert the Bruce is presented
as socially and psychologically interesting, but historically absurd.
And indeed the identification by so many eighteenth-century
Jacobites of the exiled house of Stuart with the national welfare of
Scotland, though quite precisely explicable in terms of the history
of Scottish national feeling, is one of the great absurdities of
history. The truth is that ever since James VI of Scotland inherited
the throne of England to become also James I of England the
Stuart kings neglected their poorer northern kingdom in favour of
their richer southern one. For the most part, Scotland was either
neglected or simply used by the later Stuarts. It is true that the
succeeding dynasty did no better, and sometimes did very much
worse (one is sometimes tempted to wonder how Scottish national
feeling might have developed in relation to the exiled Stuarts if
there had been no Massacre of Glencoe and no Darien Scheme);
and it is true also that the Catholic Highlands had their own
reasons for turning to the Stuarts and that Protestant Scottish
Nationalism, of the kind that earlier had been professed by
Fletcher of Saltoun when he led the battle against the Union at the
beginning of the century, had gradually been led to support the
House of Hanover just because the exiled Stuarts were Catholics—
though even here there were the kind of people whom Burns called
'sentimental Jacobites', people who would not in the least have
welcomed a Stuart restoration but who felt a glow of Scottish
feeling when they contemplated the Jacobite cause. The Jacobite
cause, in fact, after it had been well and truly lost at Culloden,
could be safely indulged in as a sentimental nationalist exercise,
and the indulgence was common. Scott understood all this very
well: from one point of view, *Redgauntlet* is a probing of that very
indulgence, and the splendid scene in the novel when the belated
little band of Jacobite rebels are dismissed with something like
contempt by the Hanoverian General Campbell, who laughs good-
humouredly at their pretensions and punctures their rhetoric with
quiet realism and humane reasonableness, is one of those great
moments in Scott when historical and psychological insight come
memorably together.

If Scott saw the movement towards enlightened progress in
Scotland as both inevitable and desirable, this does not mean that

he was unaware of its cost. The division between Scott's head and
heart, as he saw it, or the super-imposition of the ideals of the
Scottish Enlightenment on a temperament inclined to a passionate
love of the violent heroic past, as we might see it, produced insights which could operate on either side of the division. *Waverley*
wavers—the man a swell as the novel—and the reader is led into
an exploration of the moral and psychological aspects of Highland
society in such a way as to keep *him* wavering too. The character-
spectrum of the novel, as so often in Scott, is an important part of
its meaning. Between Colonel Talbot, the enlightened Englishman and Donald Bean Lean, the Highland freebooter, there is a
whole gallery of characters each of whom occupies a revealing
position between these two extremes. Fergus Mac-Ivor, high-
minded Highland gentleman though in some ways he is, is nearer
to Donald Bean Lean than this dedicated idealistic sister Flora. The
pedantry of Baron Bradwardine, who confuses the forms in which
things have traditionally been done with the substance of the things
themselves, mediates between heroism and eccentricity, between
history and antiquarianism, in a way which is very central to
Scott's vision, for so often in Scott pedantry is shown as a personal
way of modulating the past into the present. It is from one point
of view sad that the heroic way of life has to give way to learned
theses and even learned disputes about it by antiquaries—this
happens often in Scott—but the sadness is also partly comic and it
is aerated by a kind of wry fatalism which represents for Scott a
curious razor-edge of feeling. The nearer Scott comes to the
present in his Scottish novels the easier he finds it to walk that
razor-edge. He can walk it in *The Heart of Mid-Lothian*, for all the
disturbing brilliance with which he describes at the opening of the
book the Porteous Riots, which he understood very well were at
bottom a protest against the Union, and he can walk it easily in
The Antiquary. He comes down more openly on the side of the
Enlightenment in *Rob Roy*, where the titular hero is seen at the
end to be a histrionic freebooter who has no place in the modern
world. But when he goes even a little further back in time, notably
in *The Bride of Lammermoor*, the deep underlying suspicion of
change which finds expression intermittently in his letters and is
revealed in many anecdotes about him, leads him to present the
forces of progress with tragic pessimism. Indeed, Robert Gordon
has called this novel 'a novel of Tory pessimism', and up to a point
this is just, though Scott is not saying that progress always comes

through the machinations of opportunities and parvenus (yet this is precisely what happens in several of the novels—in *Guy Mannering*, for example, although the parvenu there loses out in the end).

All of Scott's greatest novels are concerned with the relation between tradition and progress, and in his novels dealing with Scotland this subject has for him a compelling fascination, so that he cannot leave it alone. In two novels published in 1822—*The Pirate* and *The Fortunes of Nigel*—he deals with it in very different ways. In the former he explores the impact on the traditional, long-isolated late seventeenth-century Shetland society of forces from the outside world, and in the latter, centring the story on the fortunes of a young Scotsman in the London of King James VI and I, he shows progress and corruption as closely related without any suggestion that the solution was to go back to the good old days. In *The Fair Maid of Perth*, published as late as 1828, he sets the heroic Highlander and the bourgeois Lowlander very clearly against each other in a brilliantly clear-eyed way, and though the novel is set in the late fourteenth century it is curiously 'modern' in feeling, in the sense that it opposes what might be called the enlightened claims of middle-class progress to traditional patterns of loyalty and violence.

Scott had no illusions about the internecine violence that filled the pages of Scottish history. We see it in *Old Mortality*, as well as in *The Monastery*, *The Abbot* and *The Fair Maid of Perth*, not to mention the Jacobite novels. Yet he saw *something* admirable in those older codes which produced that violence, and his novels keep searching for the mediator, the bridge-builder, the man who can find a way of carrying the past into the present or discover middle ground between two factions. It is significant that Scott left the Presbyterian Church of Scotland to which his father had belonged to join the Scottish Episcopal Church, as a kind of *via media* between Catholicism, which he considered riddled with superstition, and Presbyterianism, which he considered narrow and untraditional. The reasons for this, as Lockhart tells us, were historical rather than religious. He wanted to belong to a Church which had continuity with the past yet which had reformed the errors of the past. Counsellor Pleydell, one of Scott's many mediating characters, tells the Colonel in *Guy Mannering*: 'I am a member of the suffering and Episcopal Church of Scotland—the shadow of a shade now, and fortunately so—but I love to pray where my fathers prayed before me, without thinking worse of the Presbyterian forms, because they do not affect me with the same associations'. And Provost Crosbie in *Redgauntlet* similarly reflects the ambiguities of Scott's own attitude in his combination of loyalist Hanoverian principles with understanding of and sympathy for the Jacobites. Mediation for Scott is not only the function of civilized man: it is also the function of history and one of the main justifications of historical study. We must not let Scott's Toryism, and the particularly strident Toryism of his last years, obscure our realization of this. It is all in the novels.

In the end the 'mixture of feelings' with which Scott contemplated the recent history of his own country and which provided him with a model for the understanding of other periods and other countries yielded no certain insight into the prospects for Scotland. *St. Ronan's Well*, the novel in which he tried to write of the social life of the Scotland of his own day, fails because of the uncertainty of its insights. It is a curious mixture of comedy of manners and Gothic melodrama, in which Scott made an uncharacteristic concession to the growing Mrs. Grundyism of the time by falsifying a central situation. His fictional imagination was genuinely historical; he could see the past in its relation to the present; but he could not imagine the present in its relation to the future. I have already referred to Scott's curious attitude with regard to the *Malachi Malagrowther* letters. In his letters to Sir Robert Dundas and J. W. Croker written in connexion with the Malagrowther business he talks strongly about what he calls his 'Scottish feelings —prejudices, if you will; but which were born, and will die with me', and draws on them to prophesy doom. 'I have only the prospect of being a sort of Highland Cassandra', he tells Croker. Yet what strange Scottish feelings they are! He is appalled by the repeal of the first Lord Melville's acts against sedition; he shudders at the thought that 'the whole burgher class of Scotland are gradually preparing for radical reform'; he tells Croker that 'Scotland, completely liberalized, as she is in a fair way of being, will be the most dangerous neighbour to England that she has had since 1639'. He is arguing that the only way to preserve the Union is to keep enough of Scotland's separate customs and institutions to ward off the contagion of English 'liberalization'. But again we must remember that what Scott was afraid of was the disruption of traditionally evolved social patterns and the emergence to power of a *laissez-faire* bourgeoisie with no sense of history or community or social responsibility. He saw change as necessary not to destroy the past but to enable the past to modulate into the present in a way that made progress possible. Change was part of history, not a repudiation of it. This insight was more valuable to Scott as the historical novelist of Scotland than to Scott the Scottish politician.

Yet Scott would never have used the traditional conservative argument about 'human nature being what it is'. For he differed from the historians of the Enlightenment in his realization that—within limits of course—human nature could and did change. Gibbon and Hume in their histories had taken for granted, as so much neo-classic literary criticism took for granted, the basic uniformity of human nature in all times and places. But Scott had the novelist's understanding of radical differences between certain kinds of human beings combined with the historian's awareness of the social and historical factors involved in these differences. Though he never asked himself the chicken-and-egg question whether these differences were the causes of or were themselves caused by these social and historical factors—he was clearly aware that causation worked in both directions—he knew that the differences existed and that they posed moral and psychological as well as political problems. Bailie Nicol Jarvie and Rob Roy were cousins, yet the differences between them—morally, psychologically, socially—were profound: each emerged from a different stratum of Scotland's history, one stratum running successfully into the future and the other thwarted and blocked. The character-spectrum that I referred to in *Waverley* and that is characteristic of all Scott's best novels relates differences in character to ways in which the historical process operates, and neither the brilliant philosophical mind of Hume nor the panoramic historical imagination of Gibbon achieved this kind of insight.

What Scott knew best of all was the history of his own country from the sixteenth century to his own day. He knew the literature, the polemical pamphlets, the correspondence, the traditions, the folklore. He understood the nature of the divisions within the country, the options that were open to it, the forces at work which operated in favour of one option rather than another. In writing of sixteenth-century Scotland he understood the religious reformers' reasons for wanting reform while understanding equally the traditionalists' desire to maintain the old religion, and he was also clear-eyed about reforming fanaticism and traditionalist obscurantism. While he had no love for the Covenanters of the seventeenth century he could portray them with understanding and sympathy—and, more surprisingly, with humour—while losing none of his admiration for their arch-enemy, Claverhouse. He supported the Union of 1707 while showing a full and sympathetic awareness of the attitudes of those who opposed it and I have sufficiently discussed his view of the Jacobite rebellions. All this, as I have said, is in the novels. What we do not find anywhere in the novels is anything resembling the Wellsian kind of vision of the future. Scott did have a view of the future, a future made more agreeable by the enlightened use of technology. But it was not a *vision* of the future; there was no imaginative leap. He discussed the future, as it were, with his back to it—as indeed most of us do, seeing the past unrolling as we travel into the future with our back inevitably to the engine. I think that it could be argued that this was to Scott's advantage as a novelist.

Scottish Nationalists today tend to judge a Scotsman's attitude to Scotland by his attitude towards the Union. It is interesting that about the same time as Scott was writing his letters to Dundas and Croker he was also composing his *Tales of a Grandfather* for his grandson. This child's history of Scotland opens with an unequivocal statement of his view of the relation between England and Scotland:

England is the southern, and Scotland is the northern part of the celebrated island called Great Britain. England is greatly larger than Scotland, and the land is much richer, and produces more crops. There are also a great many more men in England, and both the gentlemen and the country people are more wealthy, and have better food and clothing than in Scotland. The towns, also, are much more numerous and more populous. . . .

Now, as these two nations live in the different ends of the same island, and are separated by large and stormy seas from all other parts of the world, it seems natural that they should have been friendly to each other, and that they should have lived as one people under the same government. Accordingly about two hundred years ago, the King of Scotland becoming King of England, . . . the two nations have ever since then been joined in one great kingdom, which is called Great Britain.

But, before this happy union of England and Scotland, there were many long, cruel, and bloody wars between the two nations; and, far from helping or assisting each other, as became good neighbours and friends, they did each other all the harm and injury that they possibly could, by invading each other's territories, killing their subjects, burning their towns, and taking their wives and children prisoners. This lasted for many hundred years; and I am about to tell you the reason why the land was so divided.

This opening chapter concludes thus:

> The English are very fond of their fine country; they call it 'Old England', and 'Merry England', and think it the finest land that the sun shines upon. And the Scots are also very proud of their own country, with its great lakes and mountains; and, in the old language of the country, they call it 'The land of the lakes and mountains; and of the brave men'; and often also, 'The Land of Cakes', because the people live a good deal upon cakes made of oatmeal, instead of wheaten bread. But both England and Scotland are now part of the same kingdom, and there is no use in asking which is the best country, or has the bravest men.

It is grossly unfair to reduce the attitude to his country of a great historical novelist to a simplified statement written for a child. But it is interesting to see where Scott thought he stood on this question in the last part of his life. I say 'thought he stood', because of course where he really stood, what his novelist's imagination really told him, can be found only in the novels. The maxim 'Never trust the artist; trust the tale' applies at least as much to Scott as to D. H. Lawrence. It is to Scott's novels about Scotland that we must go if we really want to know his response to the history of his own country—especially to *Waverley*, *Old Mortality*, *Rob Roy*, *The Heart of Mid-Lothian*, *Redgauntlet*, and *The Fair Maid of Perth*. I would add *The Two Drovers*, that remarkable story in the first series of *Chronicles of the Canongate*.

A final word about Scott and change. Though in his last years he presents the picture of a man fiercely battling to preserve things as they are, in terror of the future, it must never be forgotten that Scott's first impulse to write a novel came from his profound sense of the changes that had occurred in Scotland in the recent past. Let me remind you, in conclusion, of Scott's Postscript to *Waverley*:

> There is no European nation, which, within the course of half a century, or little more, has undergone so complete a change as this kingdom of Scotland. The effects of the insurrection of 1745,—the destruction of the patriarchal power of the Highland chiefs,—the abolition of the heritable jurisdiction of the Lowland nobility and barons,—the total eradication of the Jacobite party, which, averse to intermingle with the English, or adopt their customs, long continued to pride themselves upon maintaining ancient Scottish manners and customs,—commenced this innovation. The gradual influx of wealth, and extension of commerce, have since united to render the present people of Scotland a class of beings as different from their grandfathers, as the existing English are from those of Queen Elizabeth's time. . . . But the change, though steadily and rapidly progressive, has, nevertheless, been gradual. . . . Such of the present generation as can recollect the last twenty or twenty-five years of the eighteenth century, will be fully sensible

of the truth of this statement; especially if their acquaintance and connections lay among those, who, in my younger time, were facetiously called 'folks of the old leaven', which still cherished a lingering, though hopeless attachment, to the house of Stewart. This race has now almost entirely vanished from the land, and with it, doubtless, much absurd political prejudice; but also, many living examples of singular and disinterested attachment to the principles of loyalty which they received from their fathers, and of old Scottish faith, hospitality, worth, and honour.

To Scott, history was about change, Scotland was the most changed country in Europe, so novels about recent Scottish history would be the most searching kind of historical novels. And so they proved to be.

Scott and the Novel in Scotland

FRANCIS R. HART

THE first Edinburgh International Festival took place 149 years ago, the last fortnight in August 1822, when Sir Walter marked his 51st birthday by welcoming a Stuart-tartaned Hanoverian monarch, his Fat Friend, First Gentleman of Europe. Scott found himself, he says, a sort of adviser-general in the matter of ceremonial and so forth, and went tirelessly about amid the throngs, the bustle, the flaming rivalries of chief and faction, as Edgar Johnson says, 'soothing, conciliating, directing, controlling'—the consummate stage-manager. What a disquieting centrepiece in the spectacular allegory of Scott's life! Lockhart finds it 'a sort of grand "terryfication" of the Holyrood chapters in *Waverley*'. Johnson likens it to 'Leicester's entertainment of Elizabeth in Kenilworth'. More apprehensive viewers will recall more precarious spectacles: the feuding of Jacobite followers in *Waverley* and *Redgauntlet*, the *wappenschaw* that opens *Old Mortality*, the peace-making that climaxes *Quentin Durward*, Lady Peveril's ominous banquet, the anxious staging of Argyle when ingenuous Jeanie confronts a jealous queen. Here is Scott's dominant theme: the precariousness of human conciliation, assimilation, continuity; the need for a blend of romance, humanity, and opportunism—consummate stage management in such endeavours. And if we are troubled by the theatrical, we might recall the otherwise ironic Lockhart's comment on the King's Visit: 'All captiousness of criticism sunk into nothing before the grandeur of this vision'.

Vision of what? Of an anachronistic, pseudo-Celtic Scotland ruled by a sentimental Stuart Hanoverian? Of a precarious, somewhat fictive, nonetheless operative Union? N. T. Phillipson and Janet Adam Smith see Scott's as the task of perfecting the Union—and his lifetime came at the precise moment. But how ironic and prophetic that less than four years later the visionary of the King's Visit should find himself forced to play Malachi Malagrowther.

Planning a spectacle, observes Phillipson, is easier than doing something constructive about one's growing uneasiness with the assumptions of Unionist ideology. Phillipson's summary of Mala-growther's 'passive ideology' is the most devastating assessment I know of Scott's ideological significance for Scottish culture, because it *rings* true, and if it *is* true, then conferences such as this become as ludicrous as the King's Visit.

As Phillipson observes in his paper on 'Nationalism and Ideology' contributed to the 1969 Edinburgh University *Government and Nationalism* seminar, what was needed was:

a passive ideology; one that would combine a stoical acceptance of the passing of an old Scottish way of life with a legitimate means of protesting against it without in any way harming the essential economic and political structure of the union. Scott provided such a formula. . . . He encouraged [Scots] to believe simultaneously in the contradictory truths of fact and fancy. . . . He taught Scotsmen to see themselves as men whose reason is on the side of the Union and whose emotions are not, and in whose confusion lies their national character. Finally, Scott showed Scotsmen how to express their nationalism, by focusing their confused national emotions upon inessentials. . . . By validating the making of a fuss about nothing, Scott gave to middle class Scotsmen and to Scottish nationalism an ideology—an ideology of noisy inaction.

My own reading of Malachi, against the background of the account of the Union in the *Letters from a Grandfather*, is more modest.

But I don't think we are ready to *assess* Scott as Scottish ideologue until we have a fuller understanding of his curious and evolving position as Scottish mythmaker. And the best way to begin is to place him in the several contexts of the novel's development in Scotland. The contexts I shall mention, in a succession of outrageous generalizations, are five: the roughly identifiable Blackwoodian group; the later Scottish romancers; the novelists of the Highlands culminating in Neil Gunn; the theological warfare of Kailyard and anti-Kailyard; and the twentieth-century mythmakers, from Lewis Grassic Gibbon through Eric Linklater to Robin Jenkins and Alan Sharp. What can we begin to learn as we reflect on Scott the novelist in these several contexts of the novel in Scotland?

In his essay on 'Tradition and the Individual Talent', T. S. Eliot suggests that 'what happens when a new work of art is created is something that happens simultaneously to all the works of art which preceded it. The existing monuments form an ideal order among themselves, which is modified by the introduction of the new.' Recently, the structuralists have given philosophical dignity to this idea: 'To be transitively understood,' writes Geoffrey Hartman, 'to be understood in such a way that it can play its role in society [my italics], the work must be placed among other works, and finally among that ideal order.' That order, that living tradition, is a continuous process of cultural mythmaking. Myths, Levi-Strauss proposes, are 'logical techniques to resolve the basic antinomies in thought or social existence. . . . The function of myth is to allow man to keep on functioning' [Hartman]. In some such faith let me propose some generalizations toward the definition of Scott's relation to the novel in Scotland.

Ian Watt associates the 'rise' of the novel in England with an early eighteenth-century socio-economic individualism, with Locke and the secularizing of spiritual autobiography, with the decorums of a newly affluent bourgeoisie and the providential optimisms of a new religious liberalism. The rise of the novel in Scotland almost a century later belongs to extraordinarily different formative circumstances, and it is surprising how tangentially most of them touched Scott. I derive them from recent social historians: Craig, Davie, Ferguson, Kellas, Mitchison, Phillipson, Sanders, and Smout.

The late Enlightenment in Scotland was a time of pioneering social thought, tracing man's societal evolution not from a contract but from primitive societal impulses—and for some, this is a reassertion of the societal emphasis in Calvin, and a refutation, as Smout shows, of the applicability of Max Weber's thesis to a Scotland long dominated by a kirk-session ethic and a communal tradition of guild and burgh. It was a time of burgh reform exceeding in importance the 1832 Reform of a remote British Parliament in a country which had been bourgeois for centuries. It was a period marked by the importation from Germany and Spain of the first cultural nationalisms roused in resistance to the French Imperialist. It was the time of first real apprehensiveness, especially among the legal aristocracy, concerning the survival of definitive national institutions: Kirk, education, law. It was a time of widespread religious revival, stirring populist sentiment for parochial self-determination and climaxed by what Mrs. Mitchison calls that 'act of tremendous courage' and Ferguson cites as Scotland's 'most momentous single event of the nineteenth century', the Great Disruption of 1843. The religious-patriotic reaction carried with it an awakened fascination with the seventeenth century as an age of national heroes and martyrs and generated a Romantic mythography which modern historians would exorcize, one with which Scott felt little sympathy—to his credit perhaps as a lover of truth, but to his detriment as a fictional interpreter of Scotland's moral life. It was a time of incredibly rapid socio-economic change. 'Scotland packed into about thirty years', notes Mrs. Mitchison, '. . . the economic growth that in England had spread itself over three centuries.' Until Neilson's 'hot blast' of 1828, it was predominantly agrarian: it was in the *countryside* the shock could be felt; it was in the *glens* that the central moral metaphor of the Clearances was generated in the name of 'improvement', 'progress', 'loyalty to the Chief'. Finally, in literature it was an age of memoir, of the romantic cult of visionary subjectivity, of the gothic cult of demonic irrationalism. This was the age when the novel took its 'rise' in Scotland, and the life of an Edinburgh advocate, a child of eighteenth-century moderation, a Stoic episcopalian, a rational antiquarian, a founder of an Edinburgh Academy with an Oxonian Welsh headmaster— the life of Walter Scott seems remote from a number of its formative cataclysms.

But what were the results of these formative circumstances in fiction? To come, for example, back to the present and the 1971 Festival, we find that the 'terryfication' of *Rob Roy* has given way to the dramatizing of what we read is 'the greatest novel of Scotland, a lonely, single work', rediscovered in the 1920s with international éclat by Gide, who marvelled that it was unknown to 'surrealists who are so particularly drawn by the demonic in every shape'. Our own contemporary cultists of the Gothic and Fantastic find the demonism of Hogg's *Justified Sinner* 'curiously refreshing'. If we recognize that the book is variously typical of early *Blackwood's*, we glimpse a cultural continuity in Scottish fiction that by-passes Scott.

The 'swithering of modes' which disturbs David Craig in the book is recognizably Blackwoodian, out of such sensationally diverse inspirations as Hoffmann, Godwin's psychosadistic thrillers, the horror Gothic of *Melmoth the Wanderer*, and a sustained Richardsonian subjectivism, all whimsically mingled with a serio-comic Scottish diabolism and a Presbyterian sense of the awful power and corruptibility of theological doctrine. It was Lockhart who first drew the essential distinction between such a mixed bag of a mode and the essentially dramatic, humorous mode of Scott.

Scott can see the antinomian madness as picturesque terror and humour—little more. For Scott, demonic possession is a disease of the will, not a doctrinal infatuation. Scott's Gothicism comes from a more 'enlightened' human world, a world essentially uniform, where, whatever the differences of customs and manners, men share a common humanity. The Blackwoodian voice of the counter-enlightenment is heard in Hogg's *Sinner*, raising the awful Gothic question: do we know of what sublimity of evil, what frenzy of self-destruction, man is possessed? What is the 'truth' of this wild tale? What is fact or fiction in a world where the moral mystery of man dazzles the senses? Scott's world is rationally explicable; history and tradition, romance and reality, are distinct phases in a progress from barbarism to enlightenment. Blackwoodian mystification—here in *The Sinner*, later transformed into the transcendental irony of Carlyle's *Sartor*—challenges all that. The truth of the local, demonic past in Hogg is compelling but mysterious; in Scott, paradoxically, the truth of the past is more remote and more clear.

Scott's Waverley programme was to record fading local manners in the service of timeless humanity. The 'truth' of a passing Scotland, as the author of *Waverley* sees it, may be of a salutary interest to an enlightened international world. But consider a Blackwoodian appeal to a profoundly different idea of cultural truth. At the end of *Adam Blair*, Lockhart says, 'I have told a TRUE STORY. I hope the days are yet far distant when it *shall be doubted in Scotland* [my italics] that such things might have been.' Waverley's discovery of Scotland is addressed as cultural enlightenment to a foreign world. The Blackwoodian speaks from and to Scotland. What is at stake is Scotland's belief in its moral and religious self; what is addressed is a contemporary Scotland that has lost itself. The difference dictates a basic difference of narrative stance, for the diagnosis of a self-alienated culture must be carried on from within. Such is the stance of the Blackwoodian.

Scott's normal narrator is the philosophic historian with antiquarian enthusiasms and a genius for dialogue; he is at home in intercultural enlightenment. The narrator of John Galt is a limited, implicated subjectivity. Scott felt uneasy *without* the convention of judicial omniscience, Galt *with* it. Turning from the minister of *Annals of the Parish* and the apologist of *The Provost* to the gossipy chronicler of *The Last of the Lairds*, Galt regretted having to change from autobiography to narrative and thus (in his words) to lose 'that appearance of truth of nature which is, in my opinion, the great charm of such works'. Balwhidder and Pawky are triumphs of dramatic irony, cultural representatives in themselves, sensitive impressionistic media for rendering traditional community in flux. Galt's technical expertise is seen in both. Skilful, too, is the communal variation on Smollett's epistolary convention in *The Ayrshire Legatees*. And Scottish fiction has little to match *Ringan Gilhaize*, a book, says Ian Jack, with 'a technical expertise or sophistication . . . seldom to be found in Scott', a corrective to *Old Mortality* in the voice of the Covenanting hero's grandson, whose providential reincarnation he believes he is. This is 'literary ventriloquism' with a historical dimension, a narrative method expressive of the mystery of hereditary identity.

It is not mere technique. Galt's expertise would *not* have fitted Scott's purposes. Galt's theme is of the Blackwoodian counter-enlightenment: the folly, the sterility, of metropolitan anti-provincialism. It is obvious and central in *The Ayrshire Legatees* and *Andrew Wylie*. But if we recall Galt's most admired novel, *The Entail*, we recognize another deep thematic division between the Blackwoodian and Scott. Like most nineteenth-century novelists, both use and explore the problem of inheritance. Yet for Scott, inheritance is a problem of social morality; for the disinherited, the natural virtues of historical piety and courageous prudence may be efficacious. For Galt, Susan Ferrier, and Lockhart, and even their Victorian heirs, Margaret Oliphant and George MacDonald, the problem of cultural inheritance is seen in religious perspective: disinheritance is the fruit of idolatry; true inheritance is gained only through painful conversion. In their pervasive concern with cultural idolatry, the Blackwoodians manifest a sensitivity to neo-calvinist religious revival which scarcely touched Scott.

But we must turn to a second continuity of the Scottish novel, one which *seems* closer to Scott, yet raises some comparable questions of discrimination: the later romancers, Stevenson, Munro, and Buchan.

Frank Kermode finds the novel the central literary form of 'our phase of civility', but since the late Enlightenment those wishing to challenge in fiction 'our phase of civility' have challenged novelistic norms with incursions of romance. Richard Chase suggests that romance from the beginning seemed to American novelists the best means for fictionalizing 'the narrow profundity of New

England Puritanism, the skeptical, rationalistic spirit of the Enlightenment, and the imaginative freedom of Transcendentalism'.
The terms make it easy to recognize the closeness of Scottish and
American cultures at the time Chase is recalling, and thus to
glimpse in what he says a rationale for the persistence of romance
in Scotland as well. But forms do not cross oceans without significant change.

Northrop Frye defines romance under three distinct heads: as
mode, mythos, and genre. As mode, romance relates the marvellous actions of a hero superior in power to other mortals. As
mythos, romance traces the perilous quest through struggle to
ritual death and triumphant re-instatement. As genre, romance
represents personality not as a social mask, but as a quasi-
archetype in a borderland of allegorical intensity. The three may
but need not co-exist. There are useful discriminations here.
There is, for instance, a romance pattern shared by Scott and
Stevenson: the bystander or *ingénu*, representative of the reader's
normal world, is kidnapped into significant peril in a strange world
—in Scott a world of quixotic activism, in Stevenson a world of
exhilarating sensation. But in *genre* the two are different. John
Buchan's heroes are themselves urbane escapists fleeing the ennui
of the normal, hence Buchan differs in *mode* from the others, whatever the kinships. In Neil Munro, the normal has faded with the
marvellous into bitter melancholy, and thus the romance *mythos*
has vanished. For all four, the return from 'romance' transforms
reality; yet the differences of method and meaning are significant.

Stevenson saw Scott as progenitor of an 'extended curiosity
and an enfranchised imagination'—a fuller realist; while Stevenson, late Victorian anti-realist, found in romance what Robert
Kiely calls an escape hatch from a closed moralistic universe.
Paradoxically, the escape is to a world of vivid sensation, yet the
vividness, in Stevenson's own word, is 'emasculate'. Scott offers
no such sensory vividness, yet his 'romance' world is inferentially
more real. Stevenson delights in violence, yet it is 'emasculate',
game-like, while Scott's heroes are immunized against violence
because, even in its potentiality, Scott finds violence awful. For
Stevenson the immanence of the precivilized is exhilarating, while
for Scott the precariousness of civilization is frightening.

Buchan, with his 'very thin crust of civilization', is in between.
As man and author he seems much closer to Scott; yet he began
as a Stevensonian of topographical romance, and his own favourite

Witchwood is, like *The Master of Ballantrae*, a romance of neo-calvinist terror Scott could not have written. Yet it is in his English Association lecture on Scott (1923) that Buchan offers his own idea of romance: 'The kernel of romance is contrast, beauty and valour flowering in unlikely places. . . . The true romantic is not the Byronic hero; he is the British soldier whose idea of a *beau geste* is to dribble a football into the enemy's trenches . . .' Curiously, Buchan came back to Scott by way of the first master of international thrillers, E. Phillips Oppenheim, who had transformed Scott's wide historic world into sinister, explosive modern Europe. The Buchan hero (Hannay, Leithen, MacCunn) is charged extra-legally with saving it. And the discovery of Nicol Jarvie's descendant Dickson MacCunn in *Huntingtower* is an echo with significant variations of Waverley's: 'it sounds ridiculous, I know, in Britain in the twentieth century, but I learned in the war that civilization anywhere is a very thin crust'. The strategy for survival in Buchan, however, is Stevensonian: eminent barristers, bankers, M.Ps. unite as the poacher John MacNab, play in exhilarating earnest at a game, meet the wilderness as a lover on its own terms, and find in atavistic adventure the vitality and shrewdness to guard civilization beneath the crust.

Buchan's heroes are implicitly complex, but his narrative economies are such that we scarcely care—and this, too, is Stevensonian. Stevenson's basic distinction is between romance, circumstance, incident, and drama, conduct, character. Adventure in Scott invariably leads to the discovery of character and the imperatives of conduct. Yet the distinction is complicated by the fact that Stevenson's most admired romance is closer to Scott: *The Master of Ballantrae*, says Professor Daiches, is 'more complex and less adolescent in its moral implications' and 'more essentially dramatic' in its mode.

But the apparent closeness only identifies a deeper ideological difference. *The Master* recalls *The Bride of Lammermoor* and *Redgauntlet* only to reveal a truer kinship with the Blackwoodians and their theme of cultural idolatry. Stevenson may have been haunted by the idea of damnation and he did say the Master had all *he* knew of the devil. But the Master is no epic Heathcliff or Ahab, as some suggest; and to think so is to commit the idolatry that destroys the House of Durrisdeer, infatuates poor Allison, de-Mades hapless Henry, and *almost* deludes the idolatrous servitor grackellar. 'Hell may have noble flames.' But the Master wants some dirty money, that's all; he's 'a footpad that kills an old granny'; 'to think that this great force for evil should be swayed by the same sentiment that sets a lassie mincing to her glass'. The Master has the last word: he and Mackellar have a 'common strain'; they 'both live for an idea'—both are idolatrous, false, and in between poor Henry tries to live for his love, is degraded into the same idolatry, and is destroyed. Stevenson has attacked the tragic idolatry of devil-worship as a form of cultural suicide. Scott might have done so had he come later, had he been endowed with Stevenson's imaginative insight into the power of the disease, had he been inclined to be diagnostician of Scotland's cultural ills.

Add one more complication to this sketch of romance, one more variant of *The Bride of Lammermoor*, *Doom Castle*, by the novelist one critic scorns as Stevenson of the Celtic Twilight and another sniffs at as the Scott tradition going bad. Neil Munro is neither. But the critical confusion is interesting. In *Doom Castle*, romance finds in 'a country of marvels and dreads' only the tawdry and mean. The Ravenswood here is an ageing baronet playing at masquerade. The would-be Alan Breck is actually a decadent Fergus MacIvor, trapped by a small-town Argyllshire Emma Bovary. *John Splendid* is less bitter but equally melancholy; romance muses in the midst of adventure on the sad unreality of life. The vividness of long retrospects stresses the unreality. It is all DAFT; romance is child's play and Dance of Death, grotesque *fin de siècle* elegy. If this is tradition gone bad, the badness must be moral, for the art is superb. Indeed, Munro's finest book, *The New Road*, is the finest historical romance in Scotland since Scott. Jacobitism is now mean racketeering and pathetic delusion. The 'great adventure' is to learn that you have been robbed, that your father was not killed in Glenshiel or drowned in Loch Duig, but murdered by an impostor and buried in the dovecot at home. And what does the New Road promise? Only that in a thousand years it too will be the Old Road. The veneer of civility periodically stripped off, the savagery will last—the savagery and the long sad memory.

Kurt Wittig complains that Munro should have treated the fate of the modern Gael. For a Gael of the *fin de siècle*, there *was* no modern fate. This, too, the central problem of the Highland novel, had its beginnings in Scott and casts a curious light backward. And here is our third context.

Some ancient civilizations were revealed to the new cultural historicism of the later Enlightenment only in their decadence and hence were seen through an aesthetic of picturesque ruin. Scott knew parts of Gaelic Scotland at first hand but *in extremis*, a moribund feudality, last gleamings of barbaric splendour, remnants of nameless clans. The short stories show that it could have been otherwise, yet the novels have almost no Gaelic counterparts to Mucklebackit, Dinmont, and Deans. The novel of domestic economy Scott could have set in the Highlands he set instead in the Norse Shetlands. The vignette of Sergeant More M'Alpin's return shows that Scott knew what was happening to the Highlands and would say so. But Scott was not a tragic pastoralist; the comic ideology of his fiction placed the Highlands in the role of fitfully gleaming Old Way, in conflict with pragmatic, civilized New Way, and this dialectic left no place for present or future Highlands.

A Highland novel was possible only when the comprehensive domestic tragedy of the Clearances had displaced the tragic absurdity of Culloden. The Clearances came strongly to public attention in the 1840s, the time of the Disruption, and these two events captured the Scottish moral imagination for generations—indeed, their joint impact is enough to explain the pastoral-parochial locale of Scottish fiction for almost a century.

Three impressive novels of our century suggest alternatives in fictionalizing the Clearances. Their most striking reflection as a group on Scott is that while all three recreate a bitter *history*, all three move *away* from history to other modes. Iain Crichton Smith insists that *Consider the Lilies* (1968) is simply 'a fictional study of one person, an old woman who is being evicted'. The novel's final meaning, through Donald Macleod's perspective, is that the achievement of communal legend, 'story', is truer and more lasting than the blighting record of history. Fionn MacColla's *And the Cock Crew* (1945) moves to a different pole. The historic has limited reality in a psychic war between the paralysing prophetic fatalism of Zachary the minister and the activist theodicy of the poet Fearchar. In Neil Gunn's *Butcher's Broom* (1934) historic reality is basic, but history as a way of knowing is part of the problem. What man in his callous rationalism calls history, says Gunn, is actually a legendary continuity of 'innumerable women whose suffering and endurance were like little black knots holding the web of history together'. History is the enemy, the partial or disintegrated vision. Life is affirmed beyond history through atavistic epiphany and the ceremony of myth.

For numerous moderns, salvation from the historicism of Scott's century must come through renewed mythic consciousness. The modern novel was borne with the displacement of history by myth. Yet Scottish fiction, from its inception in social history, had been dominantly historic. So, the emergence of the Highland novel shows two conflicting imperatives: one, the post-Waverley drive toward an honest particularity of cultural realism; the other, the anti-realistic mythic impulse of early modernism. Both are seen in two near contemporaries carelessly lumped together as pseudo-Celticists, William Black and Sharp's Fiona Macleod. Black's anti-romantic steps toward a constructive realism should not be lost in his Ruskinian sunsets—especially in *Macleod of Dare*, one of the most interesting Scottish novels between Galt and Brown. And Fiona's Yeatsian commitment to the remythologizing of the world imagination should not be buried under derisive cliches about twilit pseudo-Celticism.

The Black sunset and the Fiona twilight are, as ideological symbols, radically different. Black suggests real possibilities of saving a viable traditional culture by land reform, Crofters' Councils, and progressive resident landlords (see *Donald Ross of Heimra*). He is aware of the precariousness of such efforts at renewal, and in this he is Scott's ideological heir. Sharp's Fiona derives from a Victorian Celticism propagated by Matthew Arnold. Her theme is that the essential Celtic must be abstracted from doomed local cultures to enter the mainstream of civilization. Toward this anti-nationalist end, Fiona mythologizes the sublimities of the archetypal Celt to provide talismans for the reanimation of the cosmopolitan imagination. And in this, *Fiona* is Scott's ideological heir. The ideological rift between these two progenitors of the Highland novel helps to identify a division in Scott himself. There are three ambitious twentieth-century attempts in fiction to heal the rift: Compton Mackenzie's six-volume, 3000-page *The Four Winds of Love* (1937–45), which conceives an international psychologized Celticism as preserver of small nations, and Jane Duncan's Proustian cycle of Easter Ross, the Reachfar Story. But perhaps the reason for Neil Gunn's unique importance is his own effort (in twenty novels, 1926–54) at a synthesis of cultural realism and a renewed Celtic mythopoeia.

To think of Scott and Gunn together is endlessly suggestive. In Scott, the 'givens' of Enlightenment fable—the historic, the psychological, the natural—exclude the mythic. Scott's interest in the local is generic, moral. When the local is displaced in Gunn, it is onto the 'other landscape' of myth. In Scott, the archaic and irrational are revisited prudently in a desire for enlightened liberation. In Gunn, 'man must forever renew himself in the primeval intensity'; 'must for ever move, like a liberator, through his own unconscious'. For both, history is the necessary antagonist: 'The Scots are pretty good at history', says Gunn, 'which, perhaps, is why most of them mistrust it. For it is full of facts, most of them ugly.' But the historic quest need not lead to dark barbarisms and fitful gleams; the source of the river, for Gunn, the bottom of the well at the world's end, is light, and the way to it is the way of humour. Both envision the conquest of history by virtues associated with high comedy, but their ideas of the comic are as different as Cervantes and Aristophanes. The comic dialectic in Scott opposes two views of history, fatalistic-tragic and providential-comic, with the latter normally winning. The dialectic in Gunn opposes two views of time, historic and mythic. The Scott hero triumphs by winning through the ironies of history to the timelessly natural. The Gunn hero wins when he becomes legendary, has his story, moves on a level of being truer than mere history. Scott is a moral realist exploring problems of loyalty, commitment, valid neutrality; Gunn is a humorous metaphysician exploring problems of reality, enlightenment, valid escapism. Scott avoided repetition by setting new historical locales to his dialectic of fidelity and change. Gunn necessarily repeated himself, because all stories are one, or two, 'the story of Cain and the story of Christ'. Among countless illuminating differences, there is a momentous negative kinship. Both seem remote from that major warfare of the Scottish imagination, the battle of Kailyard and anti-Kailyard, the fourth of our five contexts. Like most spiritual wars, it seems largely a battle of shadows, but it is nonetheless crucial and symptomatic.

It is difficult for an alien to interpret. The Kailyard, of course, is chiefly Victorian pastoral, sometimes elegaic (Maclaren), sometimes ironic (Barrie), sometimes neo-pagan (Crockett). The anti-Kailyard is more mysterious. The battle between them is theological. Anti-Kailyarders are enraged by sentimental images of man's goodness because they find man grotesquely fallen. They find more salutary force in the evil grandeur of a Calvinist megalomania than in glimpses of kindliness behind the dour facades of Thrums or Drumtochty. When Brown claimed his *House* was 'more complimentary to Scotland'. I take it he meant it is truer doctrine to have a powerful vision of evil than a wishful vision of innocence. The anti-Kailyard *furor* is theological, and suitably, the Kailyard was sown in an alien theological liberalism. Recent historians say little of Erskine of Linlathen. Ian Maclaren calls him 'our Scottish Maurice' and George MacDonald's son calls him 'that loving support to all who dared preach universal redemption'. The ferment he caused led to the heresy trials of numerous young anti-Calvinist ministers. The heritage of the Kailyard is the line of Erskine–MacDonald–Maclaren.

Barrie's Little Minister has his auld licht nurture exploded, falls in love with an aristocratic gypsy of Chartist sympathies, and is torn by the need to be loyal to his orthodox parishioners in spite of his new liberalism. The 'I' of Maclaren's *Beside the Bonnie Briar Bush* becomes the boisterous Free Kirk minister of *Kate Carnegie*, whose anti-Calvinist scorn is modelled on his creator's liberalism, who must undergo a painful heresy trial, and who emerges chastened—not from his liberalism, but from his cultural arrogance toward old orthodoxies. And what of poor Crockett, whose *Lilac Sunbonnet* even old-fashioned critics damn as senti-mental, and anti-Kailyarders find nauseating? Crockett has dared to envision an Eden of innocent love. Edenic allusion is pervasive; there is no Serpent; orthodoxy is devastated with humour; youth is ripe, unabashed, ready for midnight trysts. The kiss of surrender in a sinless garden is a late Victorian neo-paganism, mildly antici-pating the mythic Galloway yearned after in *A Green Tree in Gedde*. This is distressing to the reader who finds any vision of a sinless world theologically revolting.

The unspeakable T. W. H. Crosland, whose book could seem salutary only to the Scot who delights to hear of his damnation and confuses honesty with flagellation, says Thrums and Drum-tochty are 'little bits of Heaven dropped on to the map of Scot-land'. But Barrie calls Thrums a town without pity. Seen from an old woman's *Window in Thrums*, it is a place of hard, lonely domesticity. For Sentimental Tommy, it is a fancied 'home of heroes and the arts' which turns out to be the place where his mother is buried in a cold-dark hole, and his playmate Grizel lives with *her* mother, a poor drunken maniac who trysts with respect-able local gentlemen in the wooded den where Tommy plays at Jacobite fantasies. Drumtochty is less ambiguously idyllic. But it is a place of incessant critical severity and death; its centre is not kailyard but kirkyard, locus of endless gossip and omnipresent mortality. Even the story of young love, *Kate Carnegie*, is told by one who has seen it all fade into ruin and exile.

Barbie, continues Crosland, 'is not of heavenly origin in the least'. Indeed not: it is Hell. But why this late Victorian fury of neo-orthodoxy? 'Calvinism', what Ferguson calls 'that bogeyman of the *avant garde* from David Hume's day to our own', is receiving increasingly careful historical attention these days as a cultural energy. Smout follows Buckle's view that Calvinism 'seems to be released as a psychological force for secular change just at the moment when it is losing its power as a religion'. Edwin Muir's Sandy, in *Three Brothers*, says, 'Calvinism makes all other creeds look like bairns' play'. In *Grey Granite*, Ewan the Marxist says he always liked the 'funny chaps the Covenanters . . . the advance guard of the common folk of those days, their God and their Covenant just formulae they hid the social rebellion in'. Mrs. Mitchison sums up the positive impact: 'Calvinism was a fighting faith. . . . As with Marxism, men would act freely and strongly in its cause because they felt that it was inevitable that they should.' V. S. Pritchett suggests the negative side: 'Extreme puritanism gives purpose, drama and intensity to private life. . . . Puritanism burns up the air and leaves a vacuum for its descendants.' In such terms, we may begin to understand the contradictory ferocity of anti-Kailyardism, so vital an impulse of Scottish culture, so remote from Scott's moderatism.

The three most promising of early modern Scottish fictions have a common theme: a weak humanitarianism cannot cope with the Manichaean warfare carried on behind man's facade of civility. Stevenson's Archie Weir has to learn in circumstances of primitive violence a true sympathy for his father's toughness. The would-be destroyers of the soulless evil of Gillespie (in Hay's ornate novel) learn it through disaster and blood bath. There is scarcely anyone left to learn it in Brown's *House*, but the theological lesson is there. Barbie's terrible lack is charity; the deacon is an 'artist in spite'; the baker is 'the only kind heart in Barbie'. The book is a contest in malignity; Gourlay's devilish destruction of his son is the triumph, wherein the book's theological vision is fulfilled: 'the hell on which man is built' is brought 'to the surface'. Man is not tragic, but fallen a blotch, on nature: 'amid the suave enveloping greatness of the world, the human pismires stung each other, and were cruel, and full of hate and malice and a petty rage'.

Maurice Lindsay is right: 'Kailyardism must satisfy some continuing Scottish need'. But anti-Kailyardism does too: they are poles of the same field. What Chase found true of American romanticism applies to this phase of the Scottish moral imagination: it is theological, but not tragic and Christian; rather, Manichaean and melodramatic, deeply polarized.

Is Scott as remote as he seems from these infernal precincts? In his normally comic providential world, evil often seems humorous and self-destroying. His serious vision is not of the degradation of human nature but of the precariousness of community, the deviousness of continuity. Kailyard and anti-Kailyard find history irrelevant, but for Scott, a conservative moral utilitarian in the line of Johnson and Burke, history with all its vicious ironies is inescapable. Moral realism working in history must be pragmatic. The nobility of Fergus is less dependable than the opportunism of Dalgetty; the amoral cynicism of King Louis may be more necessary than the adventures in conciliation of King Richard. The restorers Touchwood and Mannering are imperfectly wise; the pious burghers—Jarvie, Joshua, Glover, Magnus Troil—are limited by circumstances. Yet the permanence of a natural humanity is assured, and grounded in this assurance, the progressive will is, within limits, efficacious. Scott's is a sober vision, free of melodrama. But sobriety alone cannot reanimate a culture.

The war of Kailyard and anti-Kailyard isn't over. We turn to our fifth and final context and find that the poor minister of *Sunset Song* knew how it was to be caught between a bonnie brier bush and a house with green shutters, and for Moseby and Gibbon of Alan Sharp's trilogy the poles are still a 'West Coast Scottish . . . preoccupation with guilt and sex and sin and its image of man as a monster' and a haunting vision of 'the garden genesis, old green Eden, wherever and whatever it had been'. But a way beyond the battle was glimpsed when, at the end of *Cloud Howe*, her minister husband dead, Chris Colquhoun could stand up at the Kaimes and bless all 'the pitiful gossiping clowns' of Segget.

The novel in Scotland began with Scott and the Blackwoodians. Some have seen it beginning again with *A Scots Quair*. Scott took off from the Scottish Enlightenment's concern with societal evolution; Leslie Mitchell began from a fascination with archaeology and archaic man. Young grey granite Ewan turns from a flinty archaeology to a flinty Marxism. Some Marxists accept Scott as an ancestor. What they must think of Gibbon's vision of a Golden

Age is suggested in Hugh MacDiarmid's words: Gibbon had 'a conception of history that seemed to me a pipe-dream'. The fate of Chris Guthrie takes her from a hard but vital pastoralism to a burgh corrupted by history and ideology, and finally to the amorphous, inhuman city. Total vision is still possible on the essential battleground of the burgh, but, as William Montgomerie observed, Duncairn is a city without history, without development, depth, or background. At least for Chris. Young Ewan, Marxist descendant of the Scott protagonist, learns from the city that 'It is a hell of a thing to be history!' But *Gibbon's* Scotland is still *Chris*, and from her lonely feminist vision, history is a male fanaticism, a fall into cloudy creeds; woman is pre-civilized, able to believe in nothing but the land and her naked self. Would not our moralistic youth call this a cop-out? The strengths and limits of the *Quair* are pastoral. The great voice of *Sunset Song* flows incessantly like the memory of the land, modulating into the fallen world of gossip for *Cloud Howe*, fading into little more than a style in *Grey Granite*. Scott and Gibbon in their opposite ways are great impersonators; both have voices that live in local tradition; but neither can be heard in a world of industrial urbanism. The essential problems of the modern Scottish novel were left unsolved by *Grey Granite*. George Blake, lacking Gibbon's grand moral and linguistic intensity, faced them more squarely in *Shipbuilders*, as he had earlier in *Mince Collop Close* and elsewhere.

And then, in the forties and fifties of our century, the world changed, and with it the essential problems; and marvellously, Scottish novels of the past decade—novels such as *The Prime of Miss Jean Brodie*, Linklater's *A Man Over Forty*, Sharp's *A Green Tree in Gedde*, Jenkins's *A Very Scotch Affair* (in Glasgow) and *The Holy Tree* (in Malaysia)—are still vitally related to traditions of Scottish fiction and yet uniquely meaningful for a changed world. Ferguson suggests a reason: in a post-imperialist world, the far-flung adaptability and small-nation mentality preserved in Scottish tradition have unique advantages.

Consider Sharp's vision of urban rootlessness, of a flight from and to Glaswegian Scotland. The polarities of anti-Kailyard are still evident, but the difference is that this feverish provincial burgh dreaming of transcendence is now the world. The quest for cosmopolitan identity, Juanesque imperialism, now sends one home again: provinciality is no longer the Scottish problem, for mankind has been culturally humbled to discover its inevitable provinciality. The neo-orthodox vision of man's dividedness, his guilts and yearnings, has entered the existentialist mainstream, and the Scottish novelist finds himself with a timely paradigm and a dreadfully useful Calvinist heritage. The world, especially the third world outside of two or three monolithic bureaucracies, is becoming Scotland, and the question of cultural survival is now mankind's, for a planet is a tight little island forced into a small nation mentality, with cultural tolerance and compassion a planetary imperative, imperative, too, an abiding awareness of the precariousness of our community and the need for situational prudence and existential courage. We have come back to Scott's theme, with a difference, and the return is surprisingly evident in two very different recent masters of the novel in Scotland, Eric Linklater and Robin Jenkins.

They are both novelists of survival, and a fiction of survival focuses on the anti-hero, the rogue, the chastened quixote, the picaro, the resilient soldier of fortune, and on the perilous folly of romantic attitudes in a diminished world. Yet both, like other Scottish fantasists, are haunted by visions of innocence: the maimed heroes of Linklater survive by the resiliency of the child, and Jenkins, like poor Miss Carmichael in *Love is a Fervent Fire*, has the faculty of 'being able to see in any man or woman the child betrayed and corrupted'. Betrayal is an inevitable moral revelation in the fallen worlds of both. Both are artists in grotesque, and the grotesque vision of the persistence of the divine in a ludicrously fallen world is akin to the innocent eye. The grotesque serves both well as urban novelists: Linklater in showing the ludicrous vitality that breaks through the gentility even of Edinburgh, Jenkins in showing the vestigial and necessarily lovable humanity that persists even in the horror of a Glasgow slum.

Linklater's book on the Union (*The Lion and the Unicorn*) and his *Fortnightly Review* article on 'The Novel in Scotland' came out the same year (1935) and sit strangely together: one a vision of the humane utility of small nations against modern bureaucratic imperialism; the other a pessimistic vision of the limited options of the Scottish novelist. But it is characteristic of Linklater to juxtapose a strenuously adventurous dream and a hard-headed sense of limitation. Running through his twenty-three novels of romance at war with itself are a mock-epic of inheritance, a comic-picaresque search for identity, a brilliantly grotesque vision of the persistence of 'ripeness' in a murderous world, an anti-egalitarian,

often fantastic-alcoholic 'enjoyment of the polychromatic but mono-
gene world' that eventuates in a Priapian vision of the brother-
hood of man. 'Critics, I am told,' wrote Linklater (in 1968),
'prefer an author who . . . will mark his territory and stay within
it. . . . I rarely write the same thing twice.' Yet the same vision of
comic fertility and existential courage runs through the Juanesque
vision of romance America, the tragical farce of Edward Ballintore
(*A Man Over Forty*), the ritual maiming of the bureaucrat in
Laxdale Hall. It is summed up splendidly in the finale of *Position
at Noon*: 'Belief came back as I rehearsed the troubled tale of my
ancestry, because—though patched like a cottage quilt with farce,
futility, and gross ineptitude—it was a tale so stiff and stubborn
with intent to live, to propagate and persist'. It is summed up, too,
in the final polychromatic community of the fertile and Voltairean
Private Angelo: an international pastoral on the theme of Ripeness
is All.

In the grotesque world of Jenkins, cultural pluralism is less
easily domesticated, and ripeness is *not* all—not even the *dono di
coraggio* is enough. Two cultural problems alternate in Jenkins's
fifteen novels: how to humanize, to dignify, and not to betray in
one's flabby humanitarianism the life of the innocent among the
brutalities of modern life; and, related, how under the same conditions to humanize and preserve the life of the native pawn in post-
colonial or neo-colonial small nations. Every effort at humane
conciliation leads to a terrible revelation of betrayal; one's love is
an enemy that knows one profoundly; the revelation may turn the
supposedly innocent into a changeling in one's grotesque eye, or
cause one to reject one's maimed humanity and prefer trees to
people, or bring one to a cultural and moral humility—'that
maturest of virtues', Jenkins calls it—and even to a glimpse of
'some kind of grace'. The lovely villain is the unforgettable sight
of Eden; the imperative is to live humbly in a clear sense of one's
awful distance from it. But under such conditions community and
survival are possible. And the final vision of the splendid book
Dust on the Paw, the vision of Wahab and Paula running down
sunlit roads, and of the Moffats' long postponed inter-racial
children, is, I think, not ironic, and is akin to the polychromatic
finale of *Private Angelo*.

Indeed, it is this shared vision of diminished survival in a plural-
istic community that calls us back to Scott and to his vision of the
King's Visit. For here is the Scott—of comic conciliation and

existential courage and cultural humility and ironic romance—that remains alive and usable for us. Naturally, it is not quite the same Scott that enchanted the bizarre world of Regency Britain. It is not even the same Scott that George Eliot worshipped or the one that saved Ruskin from a Carlylean fixation on the 'faultfulness and gloom of the present'. But great authors, like literary traditions and even national ideologies, must and can change to stay alive. And some such admonition and reassurance is what we lesser mortals can learn from them.

The *Journal*[1]

W. E. K. ANDERSON

OVER the past five years I have been reading and rereading the *Journal* in the very intensive and very slow way that is an inevitable part of transcribing, editing and annotating. Many of you have experienced this method of reading a great author and are aware of the curious perspectives which it gives. It fixes the attention on minutiae, but these can be interesting in themselves and also hint at truths of a larger kind. I propose to divide this paper into two halves, therefore. In the first, I should like to talk about some of the minutiae, some of the technically interesting points that have arisen in the course of re-editing the *Journal*. After that I shall look briefly at Scott the man as he reveals himself in that remarkable work.

The first sentence of the *Journal* runs as follows. 'I have all my life regretted that I did not keep a regular.' That seems to me an entirely characteristic beginning. It reminds us that the *Journal* is a totally uncorrected work. It is also the first example of the kind of omission that occurs regularly throughout. Sometimes, as in this case, a whole word is omitted; sometimes it is part of the word only. Usually these slips occur at the end of a line or at the end of a page. Writing about a statue of George IV by the self-taught sculptor Greenshields, Scott says it 'attain a wonderful [*turn of page*] expressing ease and majesty at the same time', omitting 'likeness' as he turns the page. 'Irritabi' for 'irritability' and 'imagina' for 'imagination' come at the end of their lines. It is tempting to read too much into what after all are relatively infrequent omissions of this kind, but when one also comes across slips like 'I will leave on what they leave me', the evidence of a mind moving faster than the hand looks inescapable. The testimony of Robert Hogg, when he acted as amanuensis for Scott, was that while dictating one sentence Scott sometimes slipped in a word

[1] References throughout are to my edition of *The Journal of Sir Walter Scott* (Oxford, Clarendon Press, 1972).

which showed that he was already composing the next, 'perhaps four or five lines farther on'. In the *Journal*, though, the distance seems to be four or five words rather than four or five lines.

His mis-spellings have a certain interest, too. I am not thinking of the words for which he had his own particular spelling—'segar', 'shufle', 'knowlege', 'plege' for 'pledge', 'aflicted', 'untill', 'wellcome' and the like—but rather of the revealing occasional mistakes. One of his novels, he reports, is 'setting *sale* with a favourable breeze'; a portrait is not worth much because 'the face has been *reprinted*'. These are slips which would delight the literary psychoanalyst. But there is greater interest, to my mind, in a tendency (and significantly it grows as the *Journal* goes on) to omit the final letter of certain words. We have 'bein' for 'being', 'good-lookin', 'look' for 'lookd' (Scott's normal but not invariable practice was to shorten 'ed' to 'd' in the past participle), and later 'crep' for 'crept', 'lef' for 'left', 'wen' for 'went', and 'an' for 'and'. Miss Claire Lamont, who is editing *Waverley*, tells me that she has not come across this kind of omission there. It seems to be characteristic of Scott's later work only, and it is most marked after the strokes which we know to have affected his speech. Does this suggest that Scott was one of those people who listen to themselves as they write, for whom the written word is a transcript of the words they hear themselves dictating inside their heads?

If so, another class of curious slips and mis-spellings is easily explained. Their number is not large, and I must not exaggerate their importance. But we have, for instance, 'a fear task' where 'a fair task' is intended; 'over' instead of 'offer'; 'perils' for 'pearls'; 'date' for 'debt', and 'debt' for 'date'. Scott spoke with a Scots accent and was proud to do so. 'Scotch,' he wrote to Constable on one occasion 'was a language which we have heard spoken by the learnd and the wise & witty & the accomplishd and which had not a trace of vulgarity in it but on the contrary sounded rather graceful and genteel . . . But all that is gone and the remembrance will be drowned with us the elders of this existing generation.' Sir Frederic Madden, who met him in London in 1831 just before he set off to Malta and Italy, noted with surprise his 'slow and thick manner of speaking—and broad Scotch accent'. The mis-spellings I have noted above, and others like them, preserve, I believe, the characteristic vowel sounds of his native speech (where 'fear' is almost indistinguishable from 'fair' and 'debt' from 'date'), and in one place at least ('perils' for 'pearls') the authentic Scottish 'r'.

The absence of any great number of deletions in the *Journal* is very marked, although it can scarcely be cause for surprise that an author as experienced and prolific as Scott should write quickly and confidently in a private notebook. Only a few are of interest. In his description of a visit to the King in 1828 there are three deletions in two sentences: 'I was ~~most likely~~ received most kindly as usual. It is impossible to conceive a ~~kinder~~ more friendly manner than his Majesty ~~possesses towards~~ used towards me.' Clearly the passage was written with unusual care, a fact which may give some satisfaction to those (of whom I am not one) who believe that Scott was a snob.

There is an interesting deletion in the Entry for 26 March 1831, when Scott was ill, and worried about Reform in general and about his own son's part in quelling the radicals in particular. The Entry for 26 March finishes with a rather bitter reference to 'the half bred mass who would fain see the field exclusivel[y] filld by such raff as they themselves'. Scott originally added 'Most likely it will come to a civil war one day', but scored it out again.

Of more significance is the Entry for 10 April 1827, which begins with three sentences scored out. The following day's Entry begins with very similar words, and this time they are left to stand. This gives us the clue—confirmed by the evidence of other Entries as well—that Scott often made up his *Journal* in arrears. In this case he realized half-way through his Entry for the 10th that the events he was describing had happened on the 11th, scored out, and began again. In other cases the mistake was not so speedily put right. As a result, his dates are not always reliable, and it is as well to check them wherever possible from other sources. In the new edition of the *Journal*, Entries have been assigned to their correct days wherever these can be ascertained with reasonable certainty, although a note of the date given by Scott is always added.

Several kinds of error are possible in dating a private diary and most of them occur in the *Journal*. When making up past Entries it is easy, for instance, to forget to re-date in the middle. There are a number of examples of composite Entries like this. Less frequent is the opposite error, the Entry to which Scott adds a paragraph later in the day, absent-mindedly giving it the next day's date at the same time. A third type of mistake is caused by turning the page. It was Scott's habit to repeat the date in the margin at the top of a new page. Sometimes he turns the page and writes down the next date in the sequence although he is still in the middle of an Entry. On one occasion, when the previous Entry began almost at the bottom of a page, Scott failed to see the numeral when he turned back to find out the date of the last Entry (his finger may well have covered it), and as a result we have two succeeding Entries assigned to the same date.

Such mistakes breed a whole series of misdatings in the Entries that follow. When Scott eventually realizes that he has gone wrong he is likely to go back until he finds a dateless paragraph and slip in the extra date required there. That is a rough and ready method, but on the whole Scott did not care much about dates and treated them in the same cavalier fashion as he used towards proper names and petty financial bills.

Let us pass now to Scott himself. To read even a few pages of the *Journal* is to discover his generosity (which displays itself not only in money matters but in a generosity of judgement), his common-sense, and his courage. A closer look confirms first impressions and deepens them. Despite frequent references to his lack of method, Scott was in some respects very much more a creature of habit than he liked to admit. Even allowing for the financial circumstances that made every moment at the writing-desk important, we can only marvel at the staggering amount that he wrote, and the regularity with which he settled to his task. Once he completed half a volume in six days; in one fortnight shortly after his financial crash he wrote a whole volume, adding 'I think for a bett I could have done it in ten days'; he set himself an average of three leaves a day, and he frequently exceeded it; he once wrote eight leaves in a day and on another occasion ten (seventy being enough to fill 'a volume of the usual novel size'). With a few exceptions, generally forced on him by the need to see company, he wrote something every day, term-time and vacation, week-day and Sunday.

It is clear from the *Journal* Entries that of everything he wrote in those final years the *Life of Napoleon* was the hardest. When he writes that it 'engrosses me morning noon and night' he means exactly that. He had always written in the morning (that is, before breakfast). As *Napoleon* swelled to seven volumes, then eight and finally nine, he was also working at it from breakfast until one o'clock and again, after a perfunctory dinner, throughout the evening. Even his time of exercise in the afternoon was not sacrosanct, and there seem to have been many days when he worked until dinner-time, or varied his labours with only a short walk. The *Journal* confirms that Anne was not exaggerating when she wrote to Sophia on 26 January 1827 that 'he is working very hard, ten minutes at dinner is all I see of him'. We can have some sympathy with her view of the book: 'I shall be glad when Buonaparte is done what a horrid long dose of History we will have to *read*'.

Scott's zeal for work is all the more impressive when we notice how often he was not well. The major diseases, the attacks of gall-stones and the strokes, are obvious. They did stop him writing for a time, although never for long enough. What is less easily noticed and perhaps more significant is the history of minor ailments chronicled by the *Journal*. More than a hundred and fifty different pages out of seven hundred and forty-five (and considerably more Entries) have at least one reference to bile, headache, depression, sleeplessness, lameness, or rheumatism, and each of those pages may record several days of pain or disability. What is more it is depression that is mentioned most often of all. We are brought starkly up against the realities of Scott's heroic fight to pay off his debts. He was not buoyed up by the sense that he was doing the right thing; he was often profoundly dejected and miserable. His struggle is all the more remarkable and all the more heroic.

It is equally remarkable that no one, not even his daughter Anne, knew how depressed he was. It had always been his practice to cultivate cheerfulness in the family circle, whatever his real feelings might be, and even in those dark days he succeeded for the most part in doing so.

In one respect the *Journal* may disappoint the reader. It is informative in places about the life of the times—about the pursuits of the country gentleman and the Edinburgh lawyer, about visits and topics of conversation, about etiquette and the details of everyday living. It is candid about Scott himself. It is neither informative nor candid about other people.

There are notable exceptions to the general rule. Constable's death calls forth that magnificent portrait of the 'Prince of Booksellers' who knew 'the rarer volumes of his library'—it is unmistakably 'rarer' in the original by the way, not 'rare' as previous editions have printed it—'not only by the eye but by the touch when blind-folded', the 'violent temperd man with those that he dared use freedom with' who was 'easily overawed by people of consequence'. It is magnificent, but it is a set-piece. There are the references to Lord Buchan and to the 'Gran Giag Asso', Sir John Sinclair, which are not without malice: 'I hear it reported that Lord Buchan is very ill. If that be true it affords grounds for hopes that Sir John Sinclair is not immortal. Both great bores. . . .' There is a fine account of 'the brute of a laird', old Scott of Raeburn. But by and large the pointed remark is left unwritten. 'The fact is', as Scott says in the Entry for 11 November 1826, 'I have refraind as much as humane frailty will permit from all satirical composition', and as far as the *Journal* is concerned that is certainly true. He is not incapable of a barbed letter. There is one to Walter cautioning him against Mrs. Thomas Scott, and another to Ballantyne at the time of Walter's wedding, half in jest half in earnest, describing the bride's mother, Mrs. Jobson, as 'a perfect allegory on the banks of the Nile . . . and all for nonsense of the first water'. But there is nothing like this in the *Journal*. Anne in her letters has plenty to say about visits to Abbotsford by Mrs. Jobson; Scott merely records her arrival and departure. Lockhart describes to Sophia a Hogmanay party in gleeful detail: 'Mary [Ferguson] invisible for headache—Margaret much as of yore only she has lost *all her teeth* & went out in convulsions here on Hogmanae at hearing yr papa expatiate, as is his custom, on the minutiae of Duff James's murder.' Scott has no account of the evening.

What is more there is no pen-picture of such important people as John Gibson junior, who was his Trustee and man of business. Many of his letters have survived as well as the *Reminiscences* which he wrote late in life, and he emerges as the kind of meticulous cautious Scottish lawyer who might not have been out of place as an adviser to Puir Peter Peebles or as part of the congregation in the Greyfriars when Mannering visits it with Pleydell. His inability to think on a large enough scale is well illustrated, for instance, by a letter about the proposed engravings for the Magnum Opus edition of the *Waverley Novels*. He wonders 'whether something might not be saved on this head, & whether Mr. Cadell does not over-rate the necessity for splendid illustrations'. He would have them '*respectable* only, & not so *splendid* as Mr. Cadell contemplates'. Scott must have been amused by him, but of that too nothing is said in the *Journal*.

Scott may have intended the *Journal* for publication. Certainly he knew after his bankruptcy that anything he wrote would have to be sold for what it would fetch after his death. This may to some extent explain the reticence of the *Journal* about other people. It does not entirely explain it though, for his *Journal* could have been edited by Lockhart (as indeed in part it was for the *Life*) just as other journals were. It is explained, I think, by Scott's genuine conviction that it was better not to speak ill of one's neighbours, that it was right to refrain 'from all satirical composition'. The *Journal* reveals, as no other work of Scott's does, the man himself. Even in what it does not give us, it reminds us that he was as generous-spirited a writer as ever lived.

Scott as Story-Teller;
An Essay in Psychobiography[1]

N. T. PHILLIPSON

CULTURAL historians have paid surprisingly little attention to the fascinating problem of Scott's relations with Scottish society. Nevertheless, there does exist a revived tradition, which derives from Lockhart, which explains Scott's remarkable hold over the imagination of his contemporaries in the following terms. Scott, it is held, gave Scotsmen a sense of national identity; he reminded them that however much they felt that their society and its culture was threatened by modernization and by English values, at least it possessed an ancient and distinctive past which was safe from the destructive forces of progress. However, history showed that the desire for material improvement and a closer union with England which characterized the present generation was actually as old as Scottish history, and that the perplexities of the present, so far from being an aberration and a betrayal of the past, were in fact a consummation of everything that patriotically-minded Scots had ever stood for. Scott thought that his fellow countrymen would be able to sustain their flagging sense of identity under these paradoxical circumstances by accepting the benefits of material progress, destructive though they might appear to be, with stoical dignity, safe in the belief that they were helping to act out their country's destiny. At the same time, they should be encouraged to think of their country's independent past as unique and in no way dishonourable. They should dwell on its historic achievements and its traditional ways of life with senti-ment and affection, and find in their memory a source of consola-tion for the apparent vicissitudes of the present rather than an

[1] I am very grateful to Dr. Margaret Donaldson and Mr. Steven Englund for their criticism of this paper.

excuse to impede the forces of material progress in the name of a narrow and defensive nationalism.[2]

This paper is offered in the belief that this explanation of contemporary ideological role, although generalized and raising as many questions as it answers, is nevertheless on the right lines. My purpose is to ask what it was that made Scott so peculiarly suitable to fill an ideological role of this sort. Clearly he had a sense that the artist was well suited to provide such a society as his with a sense of identity. Clearly he had a keen and complex sense of the past as a source of authority to be drawn upon and to be rejected. Clearly he could understand that the consolation the past could offer to a disorientated society was not simply pleasing but in some sense necessary. But instincts such as there are are the product of experience rather than the intellect, and it is well worth asking what role literature played in Scott's life. This is not simply to ask what Scott's explicit intentions were in writing particular works. It is to ask what role the business of creating works of literature played in structuring his identity, and whether there is any recognizable sense in which the pursuit of literature can be seen as the activity which defined and gave coherence to a complex personality.

Psychobiographical questions of this sort are often distrusted because they are said to be speculative, and it is true that it is much more difficult to make biographical material yield psychological fruits than some enthusiasts are prepared to admit. However, I do believe that autobiographical material is particularly amenable to psychological analysis, and in this paper I propose to offer you a partial and preliminary analysis of Scott's first formal exercise in autobiography, the Ashestiel Memoir of 1808. Autobiography is normally and rightly valued for the information it gives about the author's past. However it is even more valuable for the interpretation the author provides of his own past, for that interpretation will tell us something—perhaps a great deal—about the author's sense of identity. Let me explain.

It is normally believed that psychological analysis seeks to explain the formation of personality and behaviour in terms of those inner impulses (usually sexual) whose structure is determined in infancy, which propel the individual through life. Historians have rightly felt that such a view of human behaviour is too generalized to be of much use in explaining the particular actions of a man long since dead. However, ego-psychology provides a much more promising model. It teaches us to pay particular attention to the structure of the ego, that mechanism which Erik Erikson defines as 'the organisational principle by which the individual maintains himself as a coherent personality with a sameness and continuity both in his self-experience and in his actuality for others'.[3] The ego, then, not only defines the individual's conception of what he is and what he must do to maintain his sense of identity. It also necessarily defines the expectations and fears the individual has of ordinary social life, and the means by which those expectations and fears can be legitimately realized or avoided. It is the mechanism that knits together the inner man, his impulses, hopes and fears, with the external, social world. For our purposes, it is important to notice that it is an essential function of the ego to provide the individual with a sense that his past is a source of strength which will sustain and reinforce his sense of identity rather than cripple it. To quote Erikson once again,

To the ego the past is not an inexorable process, experienced only as a preparation for an impending doom; rather, the past is part of a present mystery which employs a convenient mixture of forgetting, falsifying and idealizing to fit the past to the present, but usually to an extent which is neither unknowingly delusional nor knowingly dishonest. The ego can resign itself to past losses and forfeitings and learn not to demand the impossible of the future.[4]

Thus autobiography can be seen as the most formal manifestation of an activity that is normally less consciously and less formally undertaken, and less systematically executed. Its value for the historian is the information it gives him about the author's ego-structure and about his sense of identity. But an author will only derive ego-strength from autobiography provided he has a real capacity to recognize at some level the real inner needs that he must attempt to satisfy in his ordinary life. It is the major premiss of this essay that Scott's autobiographical exercises were undertaken with great seriousness (perhaps with as much seriousness as

[3] Erik H. Erikson, *Identity: Youth and Crisis* (London, 1968), 73.
[4] Erik H. Erikson, *Young Man Luther: A Study in Psychoanalysis and History* (New York, 1962), 217.

those of Boswell);[5] that they are the work of a man deeply concerned with problems of identity; that they show us that Scott had
a remarkable and perhaps frightening capacity to recognize the
precise needs that he required his literary life to satisfy.

Throughout his life, Scott was deeply preoccupied with autobiography. His autobiographical writing is concentrated in two
periods. The first was a period of success and personal happiness
which culminated in the composition of the Ashestiel Memoir in
April 1808. The second was the period of sickness, financial ruin
and sense of personal failure at the end of his life in which he wrote
the *Journal* and autobiographical introductions to the Magnum
Opus edition of the Waverley Novels and the Poetical Works.
The Ashestiel Memoir was composed after one of those periods of
personal crisis in which the individual's sense of identity is tested
by an unexpected and disturbing experience which threatens to
dislocate his sense that there is a continuity between past and
present, and forces on him the task of re-establishing that sense of
continuity by reflecting on his past and its relation to his
present.

The background to the crisis was this. In 1792 Scott had
entered the Faculty of Advocates, the career of his father's choice,
and for the next ten years had allowed his literary life to be contained by the requirements of his professional career. The death
of his father in 1799, the success of the *Minstrelsy of the Scottish
Border* in 1803, and merely modest success at the Bar, encouraged
him to seek to satisfy his expectations of life through literature
rather than in law, and in 1806 his honourable withdrawal from an
active career in that profession was marked by his appointment as
Clerk of Session. Scott's feeling that it would be possible to enjoy
a sense of achievement by the pursuit of literature was confirmed
by the favourable opinions his aristocratic and literary friends gave
to drafts of various sections of *Marmion* in the autumn of 1807. His
sense that he had turned his back on his past is shown in the introductory autobiographical epistles to the six cantos of *Marmion*
which so irritatingly hold up the action of the poem. What he
clearly did not expect was that the poem would be a quite spectacular critical and social success. This became clear immediately

[5] B. H. Bronson, *Johnson Agonistes and other Essays* (Cambridge, 1946), 53–99,
especially pp. 64–5.

following its publication on 23 February 1808. Later in life Scott recollected that the experience 'gave him such a heeze he had for a moment almost lost his footing', a reaction confirmed by the shrewd, observant Mrs. Grant of Laggan.[6] Clearly Scott found this success disturbing; it was exactly the sort of experience to force the attention of an introspective man on his sense of himself as a writer, on his relationships with the world around him, and on his past. In March 1808, he left for the relative peace and quiet of Ashestiel and composed his first autobiographical essay in which, as we shall see, he explains the precise role that he believes literature played in his life.

In his essay Scott reviews his past from his earliest recollections to his entry to the Faculty of Advocates in 1792. There is no time to discuss the manuscript certainly composed at two sittings in April 1808.[7] Apart from an interesting reconstruction of the narrative at the point where it seems that he broke off at the end of the first sitting, the structure of the essay was never changed although the text was embellished with sundry details in 1809 and 1826 (a fact not always recognized in the text produced by Lockhart in chapter I of the *Life*). More important, the narrative provided Scott with an explanation of his early years from which he never subsequently departed. The theme of the essay—and indeed of most of Scott's autobiographical writing—is his relationship with those around him, and it is particularly interesting to notice that nearly all of the relationships he describes are associated with difficulty and strain. Indeed it is impossible to read the essay without recalling the most famous remark Scott ever made about himself, 'From childhood's earliest hour my heart rebelled against the influence of external circumstances in myself and others'.[8] The two external circumstances of which the 37-year-old Scott was most acutely aware were his lameness and his father; of the two, the former is given more prominence than the latter.

Scott's lameness was the result of an attack of infantile paralysis in 1773 at the age of 18 months. His parents decided that his health would benefit by living in the country and he was sent to the country to live with his paternal grandfather at Sandyknowe. Lameness, later reinforced by bouts of severe illness, obliged Scott to spend much of his early life in the country away from his natural

[6] Lockhart, *Life*, ii. 149–50.
[7] The manuscript of the Ashestiel Memoir was acquired by the National Library of Scotland in 1970. Its temporary reference number is MS. Acc. 4991.
[8] *Journal*, 22 June 1826 (misquoted by Lockhart, i. 65).

family. In his essay Scott attaches great importance to the role of sickness in shaping his life. Every episode in his early life is made to hinge on this fact, and having told us that he 'bade farewell both to disease and medicine' in 1785,[9] his narrative at once switches to an account of compensatory activities such as long walks, violent exercise and conscientious conviviality. At the same time the theme of the narrative switches from failure and disappointment to success and achievement in work and social relationships. Indeed, having done with sickness, Scott seems to have done with his essay. Of the 60 pages the essay occupies in the first edition of Lockhart, no less than 49 deal with the years of sickness. We cannot doubt the importance Scott attached to lameness in shaping his life. In the preamble to *My Aunt Margaret's Mirror*, written in 1828, he recalls a foolish and irritable maid 'upbraiding me with my infirmity, as she lifted me coarsely and carelessly over the flinty steps [of a stile], which my brothers traversed with shout and bound. I remember the suppressed bitterness of the moment, and, conscious of my inferiority, the feeling of envy with which I regarded the easy movements and elastic steps of my more happily formed brethren.'[10] George Allan (an invaluable source for Scott's early years) records a similar though more complex experience, to which Scott never referred in print or in correspondence, although it clearly remained with him throughout his life. When he was about ten, a local flirt, driven to spite by Scott's rudeness and his refusal to allow her to disturb his reading, left the room, calling after her 'hob-goblin Wattie'. 'The epithet sunk deep,' Allan recalls, 'for not many years before his death he asked her, if he were still hob-goblin Wattie.'[11] And, with the problem of the status of literature for Scott's identity still before us, it is interesting to learn from the same source that 'his favourite attitude while studying . . . was lying upon his back on the carpet, with all his books around him, his lame leg resting upon his left thigh as on a reading-desk. This habit he retained at least as late as the year 1796' (i.e. until that time at which he started to publish on his own account).[12]

Scott's father occupies an equally prominent place in his narra-

[9] This quotation and the unacknowledged quotations which follow are taken from the Ashestiel Memoir. I have used material only from the original unembellished text of 1808.

[10] *My Aunt Margaret's Mirror*, Magnum ed., xli. 298.

[11] G. Allan, *Life of Sir Walter Scott, Bart.* (Edinburgh, 1832–4), 26.

[12] Allan, *Life*, 25. Scott's first published work, various translations of Bürger's verse, appeared in 1796.

tive as a force shaping his early years. That of course is scarcely surprising. What is remarkable, however, is the impression Scott gives us of his father. His close friend, William Clerk, recalled that Walter 'stood in great awe of his father and never joked before him nor displayed his wanton vivacity'.[13] This sense of awe and of remoteness is likewise to be found in Scott's own narrative. Mr. Scott is presented as an external force, inscrutably directing his son's future. Never once are we given a sense of intimacy between father and son, a sense that theirs was a close and affectionate relationship that could be taken for granted. In a short paper it is, unfortunately, impossible to develop this important point in the detail it deserves; however the character of the relationship becomes clear if it is contrasted with Scott's treatment of his grandparents' family at Sandyknowe. He tells us very little about them as individuals, it is true. But if there are no character sketches, the manner in which they are introduced to us speaks volumes. All of them, his grandmother, his 'kind and affectionate' aunt Jenny (who, Allan was told, 'did all but bear him'),[14] and his uncle Robert are written of easily and unselfconsciously, with intimacy and affection. They belong to the action of the story, meshed in, as it were, to Scott's own life. They are taken for granted in a way that Mr. Scott is not. However, it is interesting that Scott does not show resentment at what appears to be the impersonal and inexorable exertion of parental authority; indeed he frequently uses adverbs of approval to describe actions which resulted in his being forced to do things he found unpleasant. Equally revealing is the character sketch he gives of his father. Here he picks out characteristics in his father's personality which are equally striking in himself. He presents his father (like himself) as a fairly successful lawyer who was, nonetheless, fundamentally miscast in his profession. His heart lay, Scott guesses, more in letters than in law (Scottish church history, to be precise). Did he, he wonders, perhaps read his beloved historians in secret in his study when he should have been busy at his law-papers? It is a fascinating speculation for what it tells us about the son rather than the father. Scott is forced to speculate about things many sons would have known. More important, he wonders whether his

---

[13] 'Memoranda taken down from Mr. Wm Clerk's Oral Communication', compiled by Robert Cadell for Lockhart in December 1834, now National Library of Scotland, MS. Acc. 5425. I am grateful to Mr. A. S. Bell for telling me of this recent acquisition.
[14] Allan, *Life*, 9. The more we can discover about aunt Jenny, the more we shall learn about Scott. At present Allan is our best source.

father was guilty of the sort of secret reading in office hours to which he is to plead guilty later in the essay. Scott is projecting patterns of behaviour he recognizes in himself onto his father, a classic device for achieving a substitute intimacy with a remote figure with whom a deeper intimacy is sought. As we shall see, it is a faculty Scott was to recognize too often as the means he used to achieve intimacy with those individuals and groups on whose approval he depended for ego-strength.

Scott's portrait of a remote and impersonal father is buttressed by equally problematical portraits of other members of his family. His mother and his mother's family are given very little space (though there is a great deal about his father and his father's family). Indeed Scott seems to have felt a little guilty about this because he added a couple of additional and rather perfunctory sentences to the original draft in 1809. She comes over as rather a negative figure, although he says she was kind to him at a difficult period of his life—his return from Sandyknowe to Edinburgh. She tried to tell her son stories as aunt Jenny had done, but he says they were stories taken from polite literature and he did not really like them. And the sense we have of a lack of any real intimacy between mother and son is confirmed by a letter he wrote to her on that most testing and revealing of occasions, the death of her husband. Although there is no space to quote it here, it is remarkable for its awkwardness, its self-consciousness and its formality which is all the more striking when we recall the charm, compassion and spontaneity which he could show when writing to those with whom he felt at ease.[15] Scott's account of his brothers and sisters suggests a similar lack of intimacy, this time coupled with a sense of threat. Collectively he speaks of them only once, in the context of his return to his natural family in 1775, an experience which he tells us caused him agony. Individually, they appear equally unattractive. Robert, in spite of being a poet and a singer, was a bully. Anne is associated with sickness, which led her to live in 'an ideal world which she framed to herself by the force of imagination', with eccentricity and, finally, with death. Daniel (who had died in disgrace in 1806, disowned by Scott) is associated 'with the same determined indolence that marked us all' which finally overcame him, and with self-destruction. Scott's discussion of his brother and sister is made all the more striking on account

---

[15] Scott's letter to his mother, dated 19 April 1799, is cited in Lockhart's *Life*, i. 299–300; see also *Letters*, i. 90–2.

of his seeing in them weakness conspicuously present in himself which he associates with self-destruction. He has presented his father and family as externalized and even forbidding, and it is striking that the narrative not only ends with the story of health and success in personal relationships and in his career, but also with his entry to the Faculty of Advocates and to the profession that meant so much to his father. Scott seems to have assumed that by 1792 he had surmounted the two most formidable external obstacles that had governed his early life.[16]

What does Scott say about the relationship between these two obstacles? In purely literary terms, lameness is presented as the more prominent. However, psychologically, the desire for the affection of a remote father seems likely to have been the more formidable. Thus one is lead to wonder whether is any sense in which Scott sought to blame lack of intimacy in his relations with his father on the lameness which had caused his physical removal from him. It may be that Scott was retrospectively trying to 'save his father' by blaming a failure in their relationship upon the physical weakness for which neither of them was responsible. In this respect it is interesting to observe that Scott was to see literature—or story-telling as we shall now call it—as a form of activity which provided the means of surmounting these obstacles simultaneously.

Scott writes of his attraction to stories and story-telling in connexion with the two unsatisfactory family environments in which he spent his childhood—the kindly world of Sandyknowe which was flawed by the absence of his father, and the formidable, rather menacing world provided by his natural family. We have already seen how affectionately he regarded his grandfather's family and his beloved aunt Jenny. Yet the mature man refused to allow himself to use the crucial word 'family' to describe it. In the manuscript, having written the word 'family' to qualify Sandyknowe when he first uses the word, he scores it out and substitutes the neutral word 'farm-house'. Moreover, the picture of Sandyknowe is subtly and unconsciously distorted, to show us how isolated Scott felt even in an environment which held pleasant associations for him. The men are presented as interlopers from the outside world. The other grandchildren who lived there and with whom we know Scott played are not mentioned.[17] Sandyknowe appears

---

[16] It is arguable that Scott recognized that he acquired identity in 1792.
[17] Allan, *Life*, 10.

as a kindly though remote world dominated by women. (The same
sort of picture is drawn of aunt Jenny's home at Kelso, where she
was to live after the death of her father and where Scott was to
spend much time in later childhood.)[18] At the same time Scott
presents himself as a boy with a highly idealized sense of family
relationships. When visiting Bath with aunt Jenny (a fascinating
episode, which deserves detailed discussion)[19] he recalls his first
visit to the theatre to see *As You Like It*. He was clearly greatly
excited by what he saw ('The witchery of the whole scene is alive
in my mind at this moment') and he describes his sense of shock
at seeing the forest scene of the first act (which he could associate
with Sandyknowe) violated by the quarrel between Orlando and
his brother. 'A'n't they brothers?' he remembers shouting. In
telling this story, he seems to recognize that he had a powerful
capacity to idealize family relationships and so to expect more of
them than, perhaps, they could provide.

It was in this setting that Scott remembered himself as a lame
boy seeking to satisfy basic inner needs by story-telling. He
remembers being told stories about Borderers and Jacobites by
the various women of the Sandyknowe family—above all by aunt
Jenny. But he couples these stories with his father's family—an
association that makes all the more sense if we recall that aunt
Jenny, in the classic manner of maiden aunts of insecure social
status, was a family genealogist and something of a snob.[20] At this
point we begin to wonder whether Scott saw himself as a child
who was beginning to make out of these story-book heroes some
sort of substitute for the paternal family from which his lameness
had alienated him. These suspicions are sharpened by his recollection, in this very context, of a powerful emotional hatred of
Butcher Cumberland ('I remember I detested the name of Cumberland with more than infant hatred.') In slaughtering the Jacobites,
Cumberland seemed to Scott to have been slaughtering his father.
Thus far Scott has offered us, at a pre-conscious level, an explana-

[18] 'Scott appears to have formed no intimacy with any of his schoolmates at Kelso.
He was among them, not of them.' This, coupled with his aunt's snobbery, encouraged
him to spend his days 'almost exclusively restricted to the circle of his aunts and
cousins; and weak in body, and accustomed to their society, he does not seem to have
entertained a desire for any other' (Allan, *Life*, 14–15).

[19] There are three different versions of the visit to Bath. Two are to be found in the
Manuscript—the final version being an interesting reconstruction of material contained in an earlier draft. The third was written in 1826 and is part of a review of
Boaden's *Life of Kemble* (*Misc. Prose Works*, xx. 145–6, cited by Lockhart, *Life*, i.
84–6.)

[20] Allan, *Life*, 14–15.

tion of the initial attraction story-telling had for him. Sandyknowe was a pleasant though remote world, fatally flawed by the absence of his father. For that his lameness was responsible. No doubt part of the attraction of story-telling was that it offered a world of escape. But its real importance, Scott suggests, was that it offered a means of redeeming the fatal flaw in an otherwise secure and happy environment.

In his account of his early schooldays he portrays himself putting to use the discovery he believes he had made at Sandy-knowe. His account of his return to his natural family in 1775 is the story of a powerful and unpleasant experience. He speaks of 'The agony of mind which I internally experienced' in trying to assimi-late himself to the life of his natural family. His narrative leads us to suspect that this was the point at which he recognized that his extraordinarily idealized expectations of the sort of security family life could provide would be frustrated. It is interesting to see that at this point he recognizes for the first time in the narrative his very powerful desire for achievement. This took the form not simply of doing well but of doing better than everyone else around him and earning high approval and even admiration from those in authority. Again it is interesting to notice that Scott attributes this urge to lameness, although in Freudian terms it is legitimate to explain a powerful desire for achievement with the desire to win the approval of a remote authoritative figure such as a father. In writing of his early days at the High School when he was a member of Luke Fraser's class, we find Scott preoccupied with the frustra-tion caused by his failure to satisfy his overpowering need for achievement in the classroom and in the playground in an orthodox way. He found Fraser's Latin teaching pedantic, pointless, and temperamentally alien to him and he blames this on the lameness which disrupted his education. And although we know he did well enough in class by conventional standards,[21] this level of achieve-ment did not satisfy him. Indeed, we know from another source that being unable to excel in orthodox ways, he attempted to dis-place a rival by an extraordinary piece of cheating so successful that he retained a profound sense of guilt until the end of his life when he confessed the episode to a friend.[22] His powerful desire for achievement was also frustrated in the playground. Lameness prevented him from joining in the ordinary hurly-burly around

[21] E. Johnson, *Sir Walter Scott* (London, 1970), i. 34–5.
[22] Lockhart, *Life*, i. 94.

him.[23] So, unable to excel by running with the herd, he resorted to improvisation and sought, so to speak, to assimilate the herd to himself.

In the winter playhours, when hard exercise was impossible, my tales used to assemble an admiring audience around Luckie Brown's fireside, and happy was he that could sit next to the inexhaustible narrator. I was also, though often negligent of my own task, always ready to assist my friends, and hence I had a little party of staunch partisans and adherents, stout of hand and heart, though somewhat dull of head, the very tools for raising a hero to eminence.

What he has done, he tells us, is to take the social world of the playground—or at least a section of it—when it could not function in its normal way, and re-constitute it around himself, holding it together by means of his story-telling. It is interesting to notice how Scott describes the means by which he holds his little circle together. He addresses them *de haut en bas*; they are 'somewhat dull of head, the very tools for raising a hero to eminence'. They are lost in admiration, trying to get as close to the story-teller as possible. The boys form a group whose identity depends solely upon the activities of its lame author.

Both in this episode and in the account of Sandyknowe, Scott has made story-telling serve him in the same way. At Sandyknowe an otherwise pleasant and secure environment was flawed not by lameness but by the absence of his father. A strong emotional attachment to the songs and stories about his absent father's ancestors was, he senses, the means by which he sought to make good this flaw. At school this sense of alienation was intensified by the physical presence of his father and by a formidable family. An overpowering need for achievement led him to have expectations of school life which could not possibly be satisfied, intensifying a sense of alienation and redoubling his reliance upon story-telling as the only means by which the curse of alienation could be overthrown. And so story-telling came to have for Scott the function not of diverting his friends but of dominating them absolutely, rendering them completely dependent upon him. In other words Scott sought to overthrow his curse not so much by

[23] *Ibid.* i. 99–102. Cf. the comments of William Clerk recorded in Cadell's 'Memoranda' (see note 13 above): 'At this time he was not remarkable for any particular qualification—he was known as being a great teller of stories to his companions when at the High School. He used to tell of their sitting him on a fragment of wall for this purpose. His conversation when Mr. Clerk first knew him was remarkably lively and clever—full of border stories and traditions. His memory appeared to his companions to be very extraordinary as he was constantly repeating Ballads and poems which he had not read more than once. He was anxious to be known for his prowess.'

making stories as by telling them. No doubt his audience was composed of the ordinary members of the busy world. But it was not the busy world itself. It was a world which had been stopped in its tracks, so to speak, diverted from its ordinary business, reconstituted around the person of the story-teller who sought to overthrow his curse not by assimilating himself to the busy world but by assimilating that world to him, binding it to him with an endless flow of stories. But Scott knew that he could not keep intact indefinitely the social world he had thus created. His account of story-telling in the school playground, like his account of the visit of the Minstrel to the Duchess's court in *The Lay of the Last Minstrel*, shows how clearly he realized that once the story had finished the group would disband and return to its ordinary business. The world would continue as before; it might applaud the minstrel and offer him approval and admiration, but it would never assimilate him.

This paper began with the rather problematical received tradition which explains Scott's hold over his contemporaries, and like that tradition the foregoing discussion has raised more questions than it answers. Within its own frame of reference, it calls for discussion of Scott's later childhood and adolescence, of his continuing efforts to win his father's approval, and of the tension between the disciplined demands of a formal education and the apparently chaotic process of self-education with which he associates story-telling. It also calls for a discussion of the relation between the essay of 1808 and the early para-autobiographical excursions built into *The Lay of the Last Minstrel, Marmion,* and above all the first seven chapters of *Waverley*. For it seems likely that Scott's recognition of the part played by story-telling in fashioning his identity came gradually between 1802 and 1808, only reaching full consciousness in the Ashestiel Memoir. This question centralizes a technical assumption which has been made in this paper. I have suggested that Scott recognized that he possessed deeply-seated and disturbing needs which he could never hope to satisfy but which would drive him to compulsive writing. I have assumed that in so doing he was recognizing real needs and was, to a remarkable extent, recognizing these needs for what they really were. But we have seen that Scott repressed difficult experiences (for example, his cheating in the classroom) or distorted others (for example, his impression of the female-dominated world of Sandyknowe). However, historically, that does not matter if we recall that the essay tells us more about the identity of the 37-year-old author than about the child—indeed it may be felt that biographers have been reckless in the literal use they have made of sources that are more problematical than they have realized. Nevertheless, a clinician would say that Scott's own story, told at a preconscious level, set against what we *do* know of Scott's childhood, provides a perfectly plausible explanation of the problems such a child might experience, of the sort of needs that he would seek to satisfy and of the sort of expectations that story-telling might be called upon to fulfil. However, if that is so, one is forced to remark that the mature Scott was not only deeply pre-occupied with problems of identity but was also led by the habit of introspection to recognize disturbing self-truths which a happier man would have repressed; self-knowledge is not necessarily a source of ego-strength. For all that, it is hoped that while this analysis may not have shown anything of the hold Scott had over his contemporaries, at least it has shown something of the complex man who held them at a time when that society, like the Great Unknown himself, could sense that it lived in a world which was happy but fundamentally flawed.

Scott's Shortcomings as an Artist

DAVID CRAIG

IT seemed to me that this paper should be cast not in the usual form of critical or scholarly *argument*. Having been present at thousands of hours of such discussion, I have seen very, very few cases of convincing or persuading actually taking place. Instead of such a train of argument, therefore, this paper will be a sequence of passages, in each case one by Scott and a comparable one by some other writer, and these passages will be left to speak for themselves, with as little commentary as possible. This way has the further advantage that literature itself is much more interesting than criticism; but my final reason is more important: I want to show, as concretely as possible, how literary-critical standards work.

The pressing need to do this came home to me particularly ten years ago when reviews were published of my book on Scottish literature.[1] Several times I was taken to task—for example, by John MacQueen in *Scottish Studies*, by Sydney Goodsir Smith in *Lines Review*[2]—for comparing various Scottish works adversely with other, usually English items. Professor MacQueen thought it pointless and illegitimate for me to compare a satire by Fergusson or Burns with one by Pope because they were not contemporary. This still seems to me the most dumbfounding mistake in critical logic. Of course my comparisons did not imply that the social environments or artistic aims of the poets were identical. That is never the case. And of course I did not imply that somehow Burns or Fergusson ought to have been writing the same poem as Pope. But the overlap between the things compared seemed quite enough to make them comparable, for example the passages on young bloods on the Grand Tour—in Book IV of *The Dunciad* the youth who

---

[1] *Scottish Literature and the Scottish People*, 1680–1830 (London, 1961).
[2] *Scottish Studies* vii, (1963), 124–6; *Lines Review* 19 (1963), 49–50.

> All Classic learning lost on Classic ground,
> And last turn'd *Air*, the Echo of a Sound!

and in Burns's 'Twa Dogs' the youth who
> takes the rout,
> To thrum *guitarres* an' fecht wi' *nowt*;
> Or down *Italian Vista* startles,
> Wh-re-hunting amang groves o' myrtles . . .

In essence my critical commentary is that 'Yes, Burns is trenchant,
he is graphic enough, but . . . but—isn't the young blood a *mere*
butt to the poet? doesn't Pope manage to be as severe while also
bringing vividly before our mind's senses the whole presence, the
speech, the air and turn-out, the entire life-style of the well-to-do
young twit? and if this were agreed, would not the judgement be
that the Pope achieved more than the Burns, that *The Dunciad*
was *better*?'

This is, obviously, a piece of comparative evaluation, and it is
often implied in academic circles that such work is rather invidious,
that the classic canon is sacrosanct: for example, a good many
papers at this conference will, I am afraid, spend a great deal too
much ingenuity on novels and poems that are in my view too
mediocre to merit that attention. Actually, comparative evaluation
is one of the most natural, and necessary, of our responses when
we are reading or choosing what to read. We take a book from
the library shelf, dip in, think 'No, that's not for me', and finally
pick something else. That is an act of comparative evaluation. We
say to someone discussing the latest Penguin books: 'Have you
read Victor Serge's *Case of Comrade Tulayev*? You must, it's very
fine, it's like *Darkness at Noon* only it brings in the whole of th *.*
surrounding Russian and European life . . .' Or again we decide,
'No, I won't go on any deeper into *The Lord of the Rings*—it's
only a story—I'd much better spend my time on *War and Peace*,
I've been wanting to read it again for years . . .'

Most of us do professionally go in for comparative evaluation
(even if it is only in the rather negative form of *not refusing* a
commission to write yet another book on 'the Brontës'); and we
do this on the tacit principle that it is good that people should
spend their imaginative energies on the more rewarding work, on
the books and poems and plays that go on yielding meaning in-
exhaustibly. Of course we have to sample many grades of work,
if we are ever to develop standards at all. But we had better keep
our minds perfectly clear as to which grade is which or we will be

misleading and distracting our hearers, whether we are choosing the books for a British Council library in Kandy or making up a syllabus or suggesting to a friend or to one of our children what they might do well to read.

The passages that follow come from what are widely judged to be Scott's better novels: first, *The Heart of Mid-Lothian*, and to start with a sequence from the core of the novel—Jeanie Deans's momentous crux of conscience: should she or should she not save her sister's life by pretending that Effie had told her she was pregnant? Her father is talking it over with her:

'Jeanie, I perceive that our vile affections—so I call them in respect of doing the will of our Father—cling too heavily to me in this hour of trying sorrow, to permit me to keep sight of my ain duty, or to airt you to yours. I will speak nae mair anent this over-trying matter. Jeanie, if ye can, wi' God and gude conscience, speak in favour of this puir unhappy—— (here his voice faltered). She is your sister in the flesh: worthless and cast-away as she is, she is the daughter of a saint in heaven, that was a mother to ye, Jeanie, in place of your ain—but if ye arena free in conscience to speak for her in the court of judicature, follow your conscience, Jeanie, and let God's will be done.' After this adjuration he left the apartment, and his daughter remained in a state of great distress and perplexity.

It would have been no small addition to the sorrows of David Deans, even in this extremity of suffering, had he known that his daughter was applying the casuistical arguments which he had been using, not in the sense of a permission to follow her own opinion on a dubious and disputed point of controversy, but rather as an encouragement to transgress one of those divine commandments which Christians of all sects and denominations unite in holding most sacred.

'Can this be?' said Jeanie, as the door closed on her father—'can these be his words that I have heard, or has the Enemy taken his voice and features to give weight unto the counsel which causeth to perish? A sister's life, and a father pointing out how to save it! O God deliver me! This is a fearfu' temptation.'

Roaming from thought to thought, she at one time imagined her father understood the ninth commandment literally, as prohibiting false witness *against* our neighbour, without extending the denunciation against falsehood uttered *in favour* of the criminal. But her clear and unsophisticated power of discriminating between good and evil instantly rejected an interpretation so limited and so unworthy of the Author of the law. She remained in a state of the most agitating terror and uncertainty—afraid to communicate her thoughts freely to her father, lest she should draw forth an opinion with which she could not comply,—wrung with distress on her sister's account, rendered the more acute by reflecting that the means of saving her were in her power, but were such as her conscience prohibited her from using,—tossed, in short, like a vessel in an open roadstead during a storm, and, like that vessel, resting on one only sure cable and anchor—faith in Providence, and a resolution to discharge her duty. . . .

It was not the least of Jeanie's distresses that, although she hoped and believed her sister to be innocent, she had not the means of receiving that assurance from her own mouth.   (Ch.19.)

That strikes me as adequate, plain, *expository* prose. Here is a comparable bit from George Eliot's *Daniel Deronda*, from the section called 'Maidens Choosing'. Gwendolen Harleth can only save herself from a life of cramped, threadbare dullness by marrying a man she has an aversion from and whose cast-off mistress has pleaded passionately with Gwendolen not to accept:

'Mr Grandcourt presents his compliments to Miss Harleth, and begs to know whether he may be permitted to call at Offendene to-morrow after two, and to see her alone. Mr Grandcourt has just returned from Leubronn, where he had hoped to find Miss Harleth.'

Mrs Davilow read, and then looked at her daughter inquiringly, leaving the note in her hand. Gwendolen let it fall on the floor, and turned away.

'It must be answered, darling,' said Mrs Davilow, timidly. 'The man waits.'

Gwendolen sank on the settee, clasped her hands, and looked straight before her, not at her mother. She had the expression of one who had been startled by a sound and was listening to know what would come of it. The sudden change of the situation was bewildering. A few minutes before she was looking along an inescapable path of repulsive monotony, with hopeless inward rebellion against the imperious lot which left her no choice: and lo, now, a moment of choice was come. Yet—was it triumph she felt most or terror? Impossible for Gwendolen not to feel some triumph in a tribute to her power at a time when she was first tasting the bitterness of insignificance: again she seemed to be getting a sort of empire over her own life. But how to use it? Here came the terror. Quick, quick, like pictures in a book beaten open with a sense of hurry, came back vividly, yet in fragments, all that she had gone through in relation to Grandcourt—the allurements, the vacillations, the resolve to accede, the final repulsion; the incisive face of that dark-eyed lady with the lovely boy; her own pledge (was it a pledge not to marry him?)—the new disbelief in the worth of men and things for which that scene of disclosure had become a symbol. That unalterable experience made a vision at which in the first agitated moment, before tempering reflections could suggest themselves, her native terror shrank.

Where was the good of choice coming again? What did she wish? Anything different? No! and yet in the dark seed-growths of consciousness a new wish was forming itself—'I wish I had never known it!' Something, anything she wished for that would have saved her from the dread to let Grandcourt come.

It was no long while—yet it seemed long to Mrs Davilow, before she thought it well to say, gently—

'It will be necessary for you to write, dear. Or shall I write an answer for you—which you will dictate?'

'No, mamma,' said Gwendolen, drawing a deep breath. 'But please lay me out the pen and paper.'

That was gaining time. Was she to decline Grandcourt's visit—close the shutters—not even look out on what would happen?—though with the assurance that she should remain just where she was? The young activity within her made a warm current through her terror and stirred towards something that would be an event—towards an opportunity in which she could look and speak with the former effectiveness. The interest of the morrow was no longer at a dead-lock.

(Bk. III, ch. 26)

The authorial analysis here is quite as ethically-minded as Scott's. But it is also wholly intertwined with the psychological, and evoked in terms so physical that 'ethical', 'psychological', 'physical' cease to be distinct and become what they really are—inseparable aspects of the one whole organism, the person. By contrast, Scott seems to be offering a kind of synopsis of experience, coherent, lucid, but done from the outside.

It could be argued that Gwendolen is a more mixed and complex nature than Jeanie. But even a so-called 'simple' person has many stirrings and pulses of feeling, and makes gestures. Scott barely evokes these. It could be argued that the novel in 1818 was not yet subtle enough to render nuance—an argument which would concede such of my case. But already, a few years before *The Heart of Mid-Lothian*, Jane Austen had shown in her finest and last-published novel, *Persuasion*, that she too could create a prose sensitive enough, in touch enough with the speaking voice, to *enact* a person's inner life. Anne Elliot is deeply disconcerted by the reappearance of Captain Wentworth at Bath:

It was fixed, accordingly, that Mrs. Clay should be of the party in the carriage; and they had just reached this point, when Anne, as she sat near the window, descried, most decidedly and distinctly, Captain Wentworth walking down the street.

Her start was perceptible only to herself; but she instantly felt that she was the greatest simpleton in the world, the most unaccountable and absurd! For a few minutes she saw nothing before her: it was all confusion. She was lost, and when she had scolded back her senses, she found the others still waiting for the carriage, and Mr. Elliot (always obliging) just setting off for Union Street on a commission of Mrs. Clay's.

She now felt a great inclination to go to the outer door; she wanted to see if it rained. Why was she to suspect herself of another motive? Captain Wentworth must be out of sight. She left her seat, she would go; one half of her should not be always so much wiser than the other half, or always suspecting the other of being worse than it was. She would see if it rained. She was sent back, however, in a moment, by the entrance of Captain Wentworth himself, among a party of gentlemen and ladies, evidently his acquaintances, and whom he must have joined a little below Milsom Street. He was more obviously struck and confused by the sight of her than she had ever observed before; he looked quite red. For the first time since their renewed acquaintance, she felt that she was betraying the least sensibility of the two. She had the advantage of him in the preparation of the last few moments. All the overpowering, blinding, bewildering, first effects of strong surprise were over with her. Still, however, she had enough to feel! It was agitation, pain, pleasure; a something between delight and misery.

(Ch. 19)

There the very nerve of the character's emotions—what Lawrence called the 'flow and recoil', the 'delicate, forever trembling and changing *balance*' of our feelings[3]—is enacted in the prose; and that is why so simple-seeming a sentence as 'She would see if it rained' demands to be *read aloud* to catch its perfectly mixed tone, part determinedly unruffled, part expostulatory.

Before leaving *The Heart of Mid-Lothian* here is an example from it of what Scott is supposed to be a master of, the rendering of adventurous actions. The Edinburgh townsfolk are storming the prison to try and get hold of Porteous, the captain of the City Guard, and lynch him:

The passive resistance of the Tolbooth-gate promised to do more to baffle the purpose of the mob than the active interference of the magistrates. The heavy sledge-hammers continued to din against it without intermission, and with a noise which, echoed from the lofty buildings around the spot, seemed enough to have alarmed the garrison in the Castle. It was circulated among the rioters that the troops would march down to disperse them, unless they could execute their purpose without loss of time; or that, even without quitting the fortress, the garrison might obtain the same end by throwing a bomb or two upon the street.

Urged by such motives for apprehension, they eagerly relieved each other at the labour of assailing the Tolbooth door; yet such was its strength that it still defied their efforts. At length a voice was heard to pronounce the words, 'Try it with fire.' The rioters, with an unanimous shout, called for combustibles, and as all their wishes seemed to be instantly supplied, they were soon in possession of two or three empty tar-barrels. A huge red glaring bonfire speedily arose close to the door of the prison, sending up a tall column of smoke and flame against its antique turrets and strongly-grated windows, and illuminating the ferocious and wild gestures of the rioters who surrounded the place, as well as the pale and anxious groups of those who, from windows in the vicinage, watched the progress of this alarming scene. The mob fed the fire with whatever they could find fit for the purpose. The flames roared and crackled among the heaps of nourishment piled on the fire, and a terrible shout soon announced that the door had kindled, and was in the act of being destroyed. The fire was suffered to decay, but, long ere it was quite extinguished, the most forward of the rioters rushed, in their impatience, one after another, over its yet smouldering remains. Thick showers of

<hr>

[3] *Lady Chatterley's Lover* (Stockholm, 1946), 128; *Phoenix* (London, 1936), 'Morality and the Novel', 528.

sparkles rose high in the air, as man after man bounded over the glowing embers, and disturbed them in their passage. It was now obvious to Butler and all others who were present that the rioters would be instantly in possession of their victim, and have it in their power to work their pleasure upon him, whatever that might be.

(Ch. 6)

This is all action, in the obvious sense of that word. Yet I cannot see with my mind's eye or hear with my mind's ear the actual jolt or din of anyone doing anything. The 'mob' are also doing everything with incredible unanimity, literally 'as one man'. Here is a sequence from Conrad's *Nostromo*, presenting the wild surge of a rebel army into the capital city of Costaguana:

During the night the expectant populace had taken possession of all the belfries in the town in order to welcome Pedrito Montero, who was making his entry after having slept the night in Rincon. And first came straggling in through the land gate the armed mob of all colours, complexions, types, and states of raggedness, calling themselves the Sulaco National Guard, and commanded by Senor Gamacho. Through the middle of the street streamed, like a torrent of rubbish, a mass of straw hats, ponchos, gun-barrels, with an enormous green and yellow flag flapping in their midst, in a cloud of dust, to the furious beating of drums. The spectators recoiled against the walls of the houses shouting their *Vivas!* Behind the rabble could be seen the lances of the cavalry, the 'army' of Pedro Montero. He advanced between Señores Fuentes and Gamacho at the head of his llaneros, who had accomplished the feat of crossing the Paramos of the Higuerota in a snow-storm. They rode four abreast, mounted on confiscated Campo horses, clad in the heterogeneous stock of roadside stores they had looted hurriedly in their rapid rise through the northern part of the province; for Pedro Montero had been in a great hurry to occupy Sulaco. The handkerchiefs knotted loosely around their bare throats were glaringly new, and all the right sleeves of their cotton shirts had been cut off close to the shoulder for greater freedom in throwing the lazo. Emaciated greybeards rode by the side of lean dark youths, marked by all the hardships of campaigning, with strips of raw beef twined round the crowns of their hats, and huge iron spurs fastened to their naked heels. Those that in the passes of the mountain had lost their lances had provided themselves with the goads used by the Campo cattlemen; slender shafts of palm fully ten feet long, with a lot of loose rings jingling under the ironshod point. They were armed with knives and revolvers. A haggard fearlessness characterized the expression of all these sun-blacked countenances; they glared down haughtily with their scorched eyes at the crowd, or, blinking upwards insolently, pointed out to each other some particular head amongst the women at the windows. When they had ridden into the Plaza and caught sight of the equestrian statue of the King dazzlingly white in the sunshine, towering enormous and motionless above the surges of the crowd, with its eternal gesture of saluting, a murmur of surprise ran through their ranks. 'What is that saint in the big hat?' they asked each other.

(Part III, ch. 5)

This can be seen and heard; one's kinetic sense is caught up in the movement of it; and Conrad also remembers that different people, even in an excited crowd, do different things. The scene is totally envisaged. Indeed it is cinematic, which may be why nobody has filmed this most cinematic of novels, or rather it may be why one of the best dozen films to come out of America, Elia Kazan's *Viva Zapata!* with Marlon Brando in the name part, was heavily plagiarized from *Nostromo* by its script-writer, John Steinbeck.

I thought we should have a battle, since Scott was so fond of them and so fond of weapons: to quote his most recent (and I hope his last) biographer, Edgar Johnson: 'Redmond [hero of *The Lord of the Isles*] is the young Walter Scott who galloped his black charger along the surge on Portobello sands, cracked the skulls of the Irish brawlers in the Edinburgh Theatre, and hacked with his sword at the Tranent rioters.'[4] Here is a piece from what seems to me Scott's second-best novel, also from his prime and also set in Scotland—the battle of Drumclog from *Old Mortality*:

> The soldiers behind him, as they beheld the increasing number of enemies who poured over the morass, became unsteady; and, at every successive movement, Major Allan and Lord Evandale found it more and more difficult to bring them to halt and form line regularly, while, on the other hand, their motions in the act of retreating became, by degrees, much more rapid than was consistent with good order. As the retiring soldiers approached nearer to the top of the ridge, from which in so luckless an hour had descended, the panic began to increase. Every one became impatient to place the brow of the hill between him and the continued fire of the pursuers; nor could any individual think it reasonable that he should be the last in the retreat, and thus sacrifice his own safety for that of others. In this mood several troopers set spurs to their horses and fled outright, and the others became so unsteady in their movements and formations, that their officers every moment feared they would follow the same example.
>
> Amid this scene of blood and confusion, the trampling of the horses, the groans of the wounded, the continued fire of the enemy, which fell in a succession of unintermitted musketry, while loud shouts accompanied each bullet which the fall of a trooper showed to have been successfully aimed—amid all the terrors and disorders of such a scene, and when it was dubious how soon they might be totally deserted by their dispirited soldiery, Evandale could not forbear remarking the composure of his commanding officer. Not at Lady Margaret's breakfast-table that morning did his eye appear more lively, or his demeanour more composed. He had closed up to Evandale for the purpose of giving some orders and picking out a few men to reinforce his rear-guard.
>
> 'If this bout lasts five minutes longer,' he said in a whisper, 'our rogues will leave you, my lord, old Allan, and myself the honour of fighting this

4 Edgar Johnson, *Sir Walter Scott: The Great Unknown* (London, 1970), i. 470.

battle with our own hands. I must do something to disperse the musketeers who annoy them so hard, or we shall be all shamed. Don't attempt to succour me if you see me go down, but keep at the head of your men; get off as you can, in God's name, and tell the king and the council I died in my duty!'

So saying, and commanding about twenty stout men to follow him, he gave, with this small body, a charge so desperate and unexpected that he drove the foremost of the pursuers back to some distance. In the confusion of the assault he singled out Burley, and, desirous to strike terror into his followers, he dealt him so severe a blow on the head as cut through his steel head-piece and threw him from his horse, stunned for the moment, though unwounded. A wonderful thing, it was afterwards thought, that one so powerful as Balfour should have sunk under the blow of a man to appearance so slightly made as Claverhouse; and the vulgar, of course, set down to supernatural aid the effect of that energy which a determined spirit can give to a feebler arm. Claverhouse had in this last charge, however, involved himself too deeply among the insurgents, and was fairly surrounded.

(Ch. 16)

This could be worse, but again, as in the riot scene, the Latinate syntax prevents the prose from staying close to the incessant movement in the scene; the diction is again stilted ('English is not kept up', as Keats said of *Paradise Lost*); and no sooner has he managed to hit us a little—'stunned for the moment, though un-wounded'—than he moves away back again, into the stance of a historian or impassive recorder. Scott's treatment of history is a thing for which he is noted and which has been found useful by professionals in that field. For my own part I would much rather have my history, Drumclog and Bothwell Bridge and Prestonpans, done as history and not cluttered with elaborately-dressed puppets.

The comparison asking to be made is with *War and Peace*, which is consummate in its presentment of all actions from the most intimate to the most public. Indeed the two are not separable. Napoleon nauseated at the failure of his mass-attacks at Borodinó, Kutuzov stubbornly waiting for the winter and the harryings of the peasant guerillas and the sheer size of Russia to rout the *Grande Armée*: these sequences are rich in characterization and are therefore all the more able to expose the nature of warfare, whether one's interest in it is military or patriotic or historical or whatever. But I will put beside the Scott something which is more ordinary though I admire it greatly—Sholokhov's *Quiet Don*. Its hero, Grigory Melekhov, is charging in a cavalry troop for the first time:

Grigory, who was in the front ranks, had hardly brought his lance to the ready when his horse, carried away by a lashing flood of other horses, broke into a gallop and went off at full speed. Ahead of him the figure of the commanding officer bobbed up and down against the grey background of the field. A black wedge of ploughed land sped irresistibly towards him. The First Squadron raised a surging quivering shout, the Fourth Squadron took it up. The ground streaked past close under the horses' straining bellies. Through the roaring whistle in his ears Grigory caught the sound of distant firing. The first bullet whined high above them, furrowing the glassy vault of the sky. Grigory pressed the hot shaft of his lance against his side until it hurt him and his palm sweated. The whistle of flying bullets made him duck his head down to the wet neck of his horse, and the pungent scent of the animal's sweat penetrated his nostrils. As though through the misty glass of binoculars he saw the brown ridges of trenches, and men in grey running back to the town. A machine-gun hurled a fan of whistling bullets tirelessly at the Cossacks; in front of them and under the horses' feet the bullets tore up wooly spurts of dust.

The part of Grigory that before the attack had sent the blood coursing faster through his veins now turned to stone within him; he felt nothing except the ringing in his hears and a pain in the toes of his left foot. His thoughts, emasculated by fear, congealed in a heavy mass in his head.

Cornet Lyakhovsky was the first to drop from his horse. Prokhor rode over him. Grigory glanced back, and a fragment of what he saw was impressed on his memory as though cut with a diamond on glass. As Prokhor's horse leaped over the fallen cornet, it bared its teeth and stumbled. Prokhor was catapulted out of the saddle and, falling headlong, was crushed under the hoofs of the horse behind him. Grigory heard no cry, but from Prokhor's face, with its distorted mouth and its calf-like eyes bulging out of their sockets, he realized that he must be screaming inhumanly. Others fell, both horses and Cossacks. Through the film of tears caused by the wind in his eyes Grigory stared ahead at the grey, seething mass of Austrians fleeing from the trenches.

The squadron, which had torn away from the village in an orderly stream, now scattered and broke into fragments. Those in front, Grigory among them, had nearly reached the trenches, others were lagging behind.

A tall, white-eyebrowed Austrian, his cap drawn over his eyes, fired almost point-blank at Grigory. The heat of the bullet scorched his cheek. He struck with his lance, at the same time pulling on the reins with all his strength. The blow was so powerful that it plunged for half a shaft length into the Austrian's body. Grigory was not quick enough to withdraw the lance. He felt a quivering convulsion in his hand, and saw the Austrian, bent right back so that only the point of his unshaven chin was visible, clutching the shaft and clawing at it with his nails. Grigory dropped the lance and felt with numbed fingers for his sabre-hilt.[5]

This isn't extraordinary: there are better battle scenes in Isaac Babel and in Sholokhov himself. But the physical attack of its imagery is surely what such a scene needs. After reading it one

[5] Part III, ch. 4, trans. Stephen Garry, rev. Robert Daglish (4 vols., Moscow, n.d.), i. 438–40.

can never again forget that 'foul and fierce' truth of history that Taine found lacking in Scott.[6]

Old Mortality also yields a very different kind of prose—Scott's attempt at the Bible-punching style of the field preachers who were active in the south-west in the time of the Covenanters. He had read many of their sermons, but you wouldn't think it. Wherever I have sampled the actual sermons they have turned out far less bombastic and stiffly Latinate than Macbriar's sermon after Drumclog:

> 'Your garments are dyed, but not with the juice of the wine-press; your swords are filled with blood,' he exclaimed, 'but not with the blood of goats or lambs; the dust of the desert on which ye stand is made fat with gore, but not with the blood of bullocks, for the Lord hath a sacrifice in Bozrah, and a great slaughter in the land of Idumea. These were not the firstlings of the flock, the small cattle of burnt-offerings, whose bodies lie like dung on the ploughed field of the husbandman: this is not the savour of myrrh, of frankincense, or of sweet herbs that is steaming in your nostrils; but these bloody trunks are the carcasses of those who held the bow and the lance, who were cruel and would show no mercy, whose voice roared like the sea, who rode upon horses, every man in array as if to battle; they are the carcasses even of the mighty men of war that came against Jacob in the day of his deliverance . . .
>
> (Ch. 18)

And so on and on and on: no sense arises of the give-and-take with his hearers, the stock phrase given a twist to jog or kindle the crowd, or any of the other turns vital to speaking in public. Here are samples from the preaching on the moors by the most popular minister during the time of the Covenanters, James Renwick:

> The commodity is good, come away, we shall not cast out about the price: If ye have hearts to receive, I have an heart to give: Come away then, hearty good fellows, we will never stand upon it; for it is not with him as with the men of the world . . .
>
> O remember this! Ye who have any one predominant whose head ye clap . . . Remember this, ye moral civilians, who are not chargeable with gross profanity in your private walk, yet have your hands imbrued in blood, and have them defiled with public land-sins, and which procure land-judgements . . . do not think that he will sympathise with any that are not his true members; for it is as if you should tie a tree-leg to a man; let him wear it never so long he will not find life in it . . .
>
> O! how unconstant and unsure is he to lippen to! like a loose tooth, or foot out of joint, that dow thole nothing.[7]

[6] *History of English Literature* (1883 ed.), iii. 434–6.
[7] From James Renwick, *A Choice Collection of Very Valuable Lectures, Prefaces, and Sermons, preached upon the Mountains and Muirs . . .* (Glasgow, 1776), 17, 26, 197, 496.

This quick slipping from register to register—the demagogy, the stern denunciation, the relishing of his own images—this could not be other than public speaking, and above all it is in Scots. In creating Macbriar Scott, as usual deferring to lame conventions, evidently felt he had to paint the preacher as an El Greco saint— emaciated, inspired, and speaking the English of the Oxbridge divines who made the Authorized Version.

This series of comparisons will finish with a passage which has been generally admired in the highest terms, Meg Merrilies's curse on Godfrey Bertram, laird of Ellangowan, from *Guy Mannering*. I would like first to tune in, so to speak, by quoting (though only the recorded voice could make the right impression) an old woman, still alive in Aberdeenshire, who can sing such medieval stories as the ballad of the battle of Harlaw and the doom that fell on the defeated:

> An siccan a paleerachie
> The likes I never saw
> Was in among the hielandmen
> When they saw Macdonald fa.
>
> When they saw that he was dead,
> They turnt an run awa,
> They buried him at Leggat's Den
> A lang mile fae Harlaw.
>
> O some they rode an some they run
> An some they did accord,
> But Forbes an his merry men
> They slew them a the road.
>
> On Monday mornin
> The battle had begun.
> On Saturday at gloamin
> Ye'd scarce ken fa had won.
>
> An siccan a weary buryin
> The like I never saw
> Wis in the Sunday efter
> In the moors beneath Harlaw.
>
> If anybody askit ye
> For them ye took awa,
> Ye can tell them this an tell them plain,
> They're sleepin at Harlaw.[8]

[8] Record of *Lucy Stewart, Traditional Singer from Aberdeenshire*, I (New York, 1961), side 1, band 1.

Scott was a fairly early pioneer of folk-song collecting, and a skilled imitator, if one thinks of that fine lyric, 'Proud Maisie', or of the 'ballad' 'The Twa Corbies' which on stylistic and other grounds seems probably his own work. The single most ballad-like passage in his novels is Meg's curse:

'Ride your ways,' said the gipsy, 'ride your ways, Laird of Ellangowan— ride your ways, Godfrey Bertram!—This day have ye quenched seven smoking hearths—see if the fire in your ain parlour burn the blyther for that. Ye have riven the thack off seven cottar houses—look if your ain roof-tree stand the faster.—Ye may stable your stirks in the shealings at Derncleugh— see that the hare does not couch on the hearthstane at Ellangowan.—Ride your ways, Godfrey Bertram—what do ye glower after our folk for?— There's thirty hearts there, that wad hae wanted bread ere ye had wanted sunkets, and spent their lifeblood ere ye had scratched your finger. Yes— there's thirty yonder, from the auld wife of an hundred to the babe that was born last week, that ye have turned out o' the bits o' bields, to sleep with the tod and the black-cock in the muirs!—Ride your ways, Ellangowan—Our bairns are hinging at our weary backs—look that your braw cradle at hame be the fairer spread up—not that I am wishing ill to little Harry, or to the babe that's yet to be born—God forbid—and make them kind to the poor, and better folk than their father!—And now, ride e'en your ways; for these are the last words ye'll ever hear Meg Merrilies speak, and this is the last reise that I'll ever cut in the bonny woods of Ellangowan.'

So saying, she broke the sapling she held in her hand, and flung it into the road.

(Ch. 8)

This works quite powerfully—and Scott is nearer than usual to folk originals. But I am perhaps not alone in finding the 'originals' stronger than this novelistic counterpart. For one thing Meg's speech is rather too symmetrical in its sentence structures for the kind of utterance it is meant to be; but the root fault is pervasive in the novel: Meg is brought on-stage with altogether too many of the 'black and midnight hag' type of trappings—elf-locks, dark eyes flashing, even a witch's cauldron. Think how much more telling it would have been if Scott had shown Bertram's landowner heartlessness as it struck at more ordinary countryfolk—as ordi- nary, say, as the Mucklebackits in *The Antiquary*—and if one of *them* had risen (as country-folk could do) to a fiery malediction. To remind you again of the real voice for this kind of thing here is a ballad, very short and perhaps incomplete, about raid- ing and counter-raiding in the Cabrach, that grim upland region beyond upper Donside, on the boundary of Aberdeenshire and Banffshire:

As I cam in by Fiddich side
On a May mornin,
I spied Willie Mackintosh
An hour before the dawnin.

Turn again, turn again, turn again I bid ye,
If ye burn Auchendoun, Huntley he will heid ye!
Heid me or hang me, that shall never fear me;
I'll burn Auchendoun tho the life leave me,.

As I cam in by Fiddich side
On a May mornin',
Auchendoun was in a bleeze
An hour before the dawnin.

Craw on, craw on,
For a your crouse crawin
Ye brunt your crops an tint your wings
An hour before the dawnin.[9]

I am afraid that working mainly by examples will not have
changed many more minds than the usual sort of paper. It will be
said that my examples from Scott were unfairly chosen; or perhaps
the more telling argument will be used that a novelist can seem
lame in small samples but accumulate to something powerful.
But this is part of the stock-in-trade of those who resist modern
criticism, for example by saying that detailed stylistic analysis
suits only certain sorts of literature such as the short Metaphysical
poem. *Anna Karénina* seems to me palpably, and demonstrably,
much better than *Tess of the D'Urbervilles*, or *Middlemarch* much
better than *Emma*, whether the samples are small or complete.
Even when I view a Scott novel as a whole, or his works as a
whole, I cannot see that he counts for much in the literary tradition.
True, he wrote some of the first historical novels. But how many
important successors have there been? and wouldn't Stendhal have
done justice to Waterloo or Tolstoy to the retreat of the *Grande
Armée* even if they hadn't read a word of Scott? At best he seems
to me more of a catalyst than an active contributor to the tradition
of significant literature. His significance strikes me as lying in the
mass of lore that he brought together and in the extraordinary
case-study that he poses for the historian of taste, of the media;
for how could so faulty a writer have so spellbound a generation
of readers, from the most gullible to the most discriminating?

[9] Record of *English and Scottish Popular Ballads, sung by Ewan MacColl*, I (New
York, 1961), side 1, band 5.

Scott among the Partisans: A Significant Bias in his 'Life of Napoleon Buonaparte'

ROBERT C. GORDON

I N the introductory survey of the French Revolution that begins his biography of Napoleon, Sir Walter Scott describes in dramatic terms the change in the nature of warfare that the revolution had brought about:

Europe was now arrived at a time when war was no longer to be carried on according to the old usage, by the agency of standing armies of moderate numbers; when a battle lost and won, or a siege raised or successful, was thought sufficient for the active exertions of the year, and the troops on either side were drawn off into winter quarters, while diplomacy took up the contest which tactics had suspended. All this was to be laid aside; and instead of this drowsy state of hostility, nations were to contend with each other like individuals in mortal conflict, bringing not merely the hands, but every limb of the body into violent and furious struggle.[1]

Such a warfare of armed nations inevitably appeared to Scott as a test of the health of each political unit involved, whether a province, a city, or a separate state. Thus in his early letters to politically sympathetic correspondents on the Peninsular War he clearly sees that the strength of Spain as a political entity is being measured by her capacity to resist the French armies.[2]

In thus evaluating a state's powers of resistance and, therefore, its degree of political health, Scott was bound to raise certain questions. How responsible and capable were its rulers and generals? How pious was the clergy? How committed to the independence and continuance of the state were its merchants and intellectuals? How loyal and effective were the lower orders in the common struggle? Above all, how capable were the various order and estates of coordinated effort?

---

[1] *Life of Napoleon Buonaparte, with a Preliminary View of the French Revolution*, ii. 138. (In *Miscellaneous Prose Works*, vols. viii–xvi; hereafter cited in this chapter and notes as *Napoleon*, with volumes numbered i–ix).

[2] Scott, *Letters*, ii. 75–6, 139–40; 225, 474–5; iii. 115. For similar discussions of the Spanish situation see *Napoleon*, vi. 58–62, 78–98, 286–91.

The answers Scott received were often dispiriting. Describing the débâcle in the Kingdom of Naples, when the regular army quickly gave up, leaving the *lazzaroni* to hold out against the French, Scott exhibits exasperation: 'What can we say of a country, where the rabble are courageous and the soldiers cowards? what, unless that the higher classes, from whom the officers are chosen, must be the parties to be censured' (*Napoleon*, iii. 392).

Such comments reveal an interest in the composition and character of irregular forces natural to any Briton of the time. Britain's most sustained and successful military effort on the land was the Peninsular campaign, and this campaign led inevitably to discussions regarding the effectiveness as allies of the Spanish guerillas and their leaders. The Whigs of the *Edinburgh Review* regarded the partisans as genuine patriots victimized by rulers so corrupt that they betrayed their people to Napoleon as a matter of course. This is the tenor of the review's famous 'Don Cevallos' article, which refers to Napoleon's 'faithful allies, the old royal sovereigns and courtiers of Europe'. With such rulers, the populace had little chance against the disciplined French armies, especially when their ally happened to be an unreformed British government.[3] Later, a radical and an enthusiastic Bonapartist, William Hazlitt, went further and expressed near-contempt for resistant peasants and irregular insurgents. Those who consider the word 'rabble' a Tory shibboleth might ponder his comment on an anti-French insurrection in Valencia, where 'a priest named Calvo incited the rabble to massacre upwards of two hundred French residing in that city, on no other ground than their being French'.[4] That the sentence was stolen from Scott's *Napoleon* (vi. 69) does not invalidate my point.[5] Hazlitt, unlike Scott, had little patience with legitimist rebels or 'Church and King' mobs.

The Tories believed otherwise. The guerillas were indeed heroic and patriotic defenders of national institutions against foreign Caesarism, but the institutions they defended were sancti-

[3] *Edinburgh Review* xiii (1808), 215–34. The passage quoted is on p. 229. For a good discussion of the *Review*'s treatment of the Spanish question see John Clive, *Scotch Reviewers, 1802–1815* (London, 1957), 99–102. Clive, I believe, somewhat underestimates the anti-Bonapartism and Francophobia of the Don Cevallos article.

[4] *The Life of Napoleon Buonaparte* in *The Complete Works of William Hazlitt*, ed. P. P. Howe (London and Toronto, 1931), xiv. 33. See, in addition, his dismissal of the much-admired Andreas Hofer as one of the 'plebeian volunteers in the cause of Legitimacy' who 'expiated their mistake in not knowing their own side of the question, as rebels and traitors on the scaffold' (*ibid.* xiv. 353).

[5] Robert E. Robinson, *William Hazlitt's 'Life of Napoleon Buonaparte'* (Geneva and Paris, 1959), app. B, pp. 82–5.

fied by tradition and their efforts deserved support. As Southey wrote Scott: '. . . every day adds to the discipline of the Portugueze and no people in the world can make better soldiers. Their past history abundantly proves this, and the manners and habits and character of the peasantry remain unchanged. Only keep up the heart of England against such politicians as Whitbread and Brougham and Jeffrey, and we shall live to sing Te Deum for the destruction of Buonaparte.'[6]

Thus the irregulars and partisans become a force for conservatism, and what some might call a mob or a rabble achieves the status of a patriotic militia. It is this view of primitive rebels that Scott sustains with little qualification in his *Life of Napoleon Buonaparte*. However, as we shall see, his realism led him to share some of the views of the *Edinburgh Review* concerning the effectiveness of guerillas. In order to reconcile some of his apparent contradictions on this subject and to understand better not only his opinion of primitive and irregular forces, but also his view of primitivism itself, we must first observe his attitude towards the dominant classes in certain crucial European political or social areas.

First, we may be surprised to see how much of Scott's biography, not to mention other writings both formal and informal, is devoted to the vituperation of the European ruling classes. His fear that 'the Castilian nobility are more sunk than the common people' (*Letters*, ii. 75) is later echoed in *Napoleon* with an intense and comprehensive denunciation of Spain's upper and middle social orders. The nobles are decadent because of inbreeding, the clergy is bigoted and superstitious, the middle class—especially its professionals and intellectuals—respond to clerical obscurantism by flying off into scepticism. Only the peasantry remain as possible saviours of the kingdom (vi. 58–61). Despite their indolence, they are still hardy, uncorrupted by luxury, capable of strenuous resistance to injustice, fiercely patriotic, and proud to a fault. Such people, able 'to part with the advantages of civilized society upon . . . easy terms', (vi. 60), are potentially unbeatable. They, not their political or military leaders, are the true guardians of Spain.[7]

---

[6] *New Letters of Robert Southey*, ed. Kenneth Curry (New York and London, 1965), i. 551.

[7] At the time of the Spanish war Scott shared the general British anxiety about the regular military forces of Spain. See *Letters*, ii. 75–6, 139–40, 174. Although the *Napoleon* is less explicit, its emphasis on the popular origins of Spanish resistance implies no change in his opinions. See *Napoleon*, vi. 68.

As with Spain, so with other states. The example of Naples has already been cited. Prussia was lost in 1805 because most of her generals exhibited a military incompetence that amounted to infatuation, and because her fortresses were easily bribed out of the hands of their governors and commanders (v. 178–84). Malta's knights were so degenerate an assembly of voluptuaries that the memory of their heroic past merely provided Scott an opportunity to mark an ironic contrast (iii. 313–14). Pre-revolutionary France does not escape censure. Faults that Burke concedes, Scott proclaims. France's kings, from the time of Louis XIII, had progressively abated the power of the nobility and attracted them away from their feudal estates (i. 58–9). Scott thus continues a line of argument that he had begun earlier in *Paul's Letters to his Kinsfolk*: the peasantry lacked 'a *noblesse campagnarde*, who found their importance, their power and their respectability, dependent on the attachment of the peasants among whom they lived, and over whom their interest extended'.[8] Furthermore, France's third estate was enraged by a sense of opportunities for advancement unjustly denied, her clergy was like that of Spain, and her intellectuals, both alienated and pampered by excessive dependence upon patronage by a cynical and licensed nobility, were encouraged to express social and religious heresies that simultaneously amused their complacent superiors and corrupted the commons (*Napoleon*, i. 37–40, 32–5, 43–5).

Such lordly, panoramic accounts of European decadence would suggest the arrogance of the self-satisfied islander, were it not for similar remarks about Britain. In his letters, of course, Scott was more candid about such matters than in *Napoleon*. After the Canning–Castlereagh duel he wrote to Ellis that the French might conquer the British Isles largely because the British aristocracy was so corrupt that it would probably betray Britain for duty-free champagne. Elsewhere he laments the growth of factionalism after the death of Pitt, fears the Regent's efforts to break up groups that might interfere with his own power of patronage, and caricatures a royal scandal in the spirit, if not with the finesse, of a Saint-Simon (*Letters*, ii. 249, 327, 537; vi. 216). In the more discreetly pro-British *Napoleon* he is less vehement, but the attack on British disunity remains (i. 261), the policy of acquiring 'sugar islands' is criticized (*Napoleon*, iv. 204–5), and the defence—if it may be so

---

[8] *Paul's Letters* (*Misc. Prose Works*), v. 191.

called—of the Convention of Cintra is lukewarm.[9] Scott was convinced that the English rulers could be guilty of many of the follies of their Continental counterparts.

Decadent societies, in Scott's opinion, not only invite revolution, they also encourage despotism. If Napoleon could not resist the temptation to play the part of a Cromwell rather than a Washington (iv. 61), he could be at least partially excused on the grounds that the most decadent society of a decadent Europe offered him no worthwhile examples to follow: 'We are not to expect, in the course of ordinary life, moral any more than physical miracles. There have lived men of a spirit so noble, that, in serving their country, they had no other object beyond the merit of having done so; but such men belong to a less corrupted age than ours, and have been trained in the principles of disinterested patriotism, which did not belong to France, perhaps not to Europe, in the eighteenth century' (iv. 54–5).

But the Spanish irregulars, properly understood, offered hope. Despite such concessions to their unruliness as were to prove of use to Hazlitt, Scott concludes his first extended account of Spanish affairs with a narrative of the defence of Saragossa in which he ascribes to its citizens a 'spirit of indomitable courage' having, perhaps 'no equal in history, excepting the defence of Numantium by their ancestors' (vi. 97). Such heroism was possible because, as Fouché had warned, the Spaniards 'are attached to their laws; their government; their ancient customs. It would be an error to judge of the national character by that of the higher classes, which are there, as elsewhere, corrupted, and indifferent to their country' (vi. 22). The Spanish lower orders were the nation's true patriots. In thus defining them, for the most part truthfully, as legitimist insurgents, Scott symbolically captured them for the Tories. In a world turned upside down the Spanish populace embodied a saving ideal for their own nation and for Europe as well.

It was inevitable, given the British involvement on the Peninsula, that Scott should have defended the character of the Spanish irregulars. More surprising is his sympathetic picture of the Cossacks in his account of Napoleon's Russian campaign. Scott's view that Napoleon had, in effect, sown the wind and reaped the whirlwind (vii. 247) made any dogged defence of the Tsar's auxiliaries unnecessary. Nationalistic whirlwinds directed against

[9] *Letters*, ii. 151–2, contains a clear expression of agreement with Wordsworth on Cintra.

foreign invaders are notoriously impolite. Nevertheless, without denying their ferocity, their occasional desultoriness, and their dependence upon plunder (v. 229–30; vii. 147), Scott in fact tidies them up to a degree remarkable even by the standards of romantic history and biography. Scott's favourite published source for his story of the Russian campaign was Ségur, whom he goes out of his way to defend as a man of superior honour and reliability (vii. 49–50n). Nevertheless, Ségur presented Scott with a problem, simply because he consistently depicts the Cossacks as despicable and unworthy enemies. They were a horde 'plus bruyante que redoutable', 'insectes importuns' who nevertheless lack initiative, cowards who could be put to flight by a single determined Frenchman, barbarians incapable of defending their country or avenging her wrongs with honour.[10]

Scott, on the other hand, had admired the Cossacks for years. In 1812 he wrote to Southey that they reminded him of borderers and moss-troopers (*Letters*, iii. 421). In 1815, describing the scene in Paris after the allied victory at Waterloo, he praises the appearance of the Cossacks of the Russian guard, and reports that the irregular Cossacks, whom he affectionately calls 'the children of the desert', are seldom seen. At the same time he notes the Parisians' refusal to distinguish between Cossacks and the more savage Tartars as if he were reporting a local eccentricity.[11]

By the time he wrote *Napoleon* Scott's enthusiasm seems to have grown. The Cossacks are loyal vassal soldiers who combine the qualities of civilized men with the strength of disciplined primitives. At home they exhibit domestic virtues and are gentle and devoted to their families, but in war they are ferocious and, perhaps, the best light cavalry in Europe (v. 229–30). Concerning a successful action near Haberstadt in 1813, Scott writes: 'It was seen on this occasion, that these sons of the desert were something very different from miserable hordes, as they were termed in the language with which the French writers, and Napoleon himself, indulged their spleen' (vii. 304). The result of such an attitude is that Ségur's narrative suffers an almost total purge of embarrassing evidence or derogatory comment. There are no imputations of cowardice, no dwelling on atrocities, no deliberately insulting epithets. Ségur habitually refers to the Cossacks as 'ces barbares',

[10] M. Le Général Comte de Ségur, *Histoire de Napoléon et de la Grande-Armée pendant l'année* 1812, 3rd ed. (Paris and Brussels, 1825), i. 407; ii. 189; i. 362; ii. 183. (Hereafter referred to as *Histoire*.)
[11] *Paul's Letters to his Kinsfolk* (Edinburgh, 1816), 271.

but Scott avoids such language. Even good stories that would appeal to a historian as fond of anecdotes as Scott are omitted. Ségur records with considerable relish the story of the Cossacks' response to the wounding of one of their officers. He reports that they demanded that their sorcerer be flogged for failing to turn aside the French bullets that had hit him (*Histoire*, i. 363). In Scott's view, however, legitimist irregulars are religious, not superstitious, and Ségur's story is omitted. At other times Scott takes passages from Ségur and includes them after seeing to it that they have been given the proper turn. Two brief examples will illustrate his way with his honourable and reliable source. The first concerns the destruction of the Kremlin by Mortier. Here is Ségur's account:

Mortier se hâte de fuir, mais, en même temps qu'il s'éloigne rapidement, d'avides Cosaks et de sales mougiks, attirés, dit-on, par la soif du pillage, accourent, s'approchent; ils écoutent, et s'enhardissent du calme apparent qui règne dans la forteresse, ils osent y pénétrer; ils montent, et déjà leurs mains avides de pillage s'étendaient, quand tout à coup tous sont détruits, écrasés, lancés dans les airs avec ces murs qu'ils venaient dépouiller, et trente mille fusils qu'on y avait abandonnés: puis, avec tous ces débris de murailles et ces tronçons d'armes, leurs membres mutilés vont au loin retomber en une pluie effroyable.

(*Histoire*, ii. 150-51)

Here is Scott's account of the same incident:

Aware that some of the Russians who were left behind, men of the lowest rank and habits, would crowd in to plunder the palace when the French retreated, they attached long slow-matches to the gunpowder which was stored in the vaults of the palace, and lighted them when the rear of the French column marched out. The French were but at a short distance, when the explosion took place, which laid a considerable part of the Kremlin in ruins, and destroyed at the same time, in mere wantonesss, a number of wretches, whom curiosity or love of plunder had, as was anticipated, induced to crowd within the palace.

(vii. 153)

Thus Ségur's Cossacks and mujiks are transformed into an urban mob of 'wretches' in a burned and abandoned metropolis and the barbarism of the looters draws less attention than the cruelty of the French.

On another occasion Scott is perhaps more artful. It occurs after the incident at Malo–Yaroslavetz in which Napoleon and his party were overrun by a party of Cossacks. After the skirmish, in describing which even Scott has to admit that the Cossacks were too interested in booty to notice the presence of Napoleon, Ségur writes:

Cependant, plusieurs de ces barbares s'étaient montrés audacieux jusqu'a l'insolence. On les avait vus se retirer à travers l'intervalle de nos escadrons, au pas, et en rechargeant tranquillement leurs armes. Ils comptaient sur la pesanteur de nos cavaliers d'élite et sur la légèreté de leurs cheveaux, qu'ils pressent avec un fouet. Leur fuite s'était opéreé sans désordre: ils avaient fait face plusieurs fois, sans attendre, il est vrai, jusqu'à la portée du feu, de sorte qu'ils avaient à peine laissé quelques blessés et pas un prisonnier. Enfin, ils nous avaient attirés sur des ravins hérissés de broussailles, où leurs canons, qui les y attendaient nous avaient arrêtés.

(*Histoire*, ii. 131)

Scott's rendition turns Ségur's insolent and cowardly 'barbares' into exemplars of Cavalier insouciance:

In the mean time, the audacity of the Cossacks in their retreat, was equal to the wild character of their advance. They halted between the intervals of the French cavalry to load their pistols and carabines, perfectly secure that if pressed, their horses, at a touch of the whip which is attached to their bridle, would outstrip the exhausted chargers of the French Imperial Guard.

(vii. 147–8)

Finally, Scott flatters the Cossacks by depicting them, in one significant instance, as more enthusiastic and aggressive than Kutuzov (vii. 245). Thus the motif of the partisan as inspiration, or as embodiment of the national will, prominent in his account of the Spanish revolt, is restated.

That it is not restated more emphatically in Scott's story of the Russian campaign is no surprise. The society for which the Cossacks fought was fundamentally sound. Scott knew that Russia was a despotism. Even in praising Russian resistance to Napoleon he acknowledges serfdom: '. . . from the palace of the Czar to the hut of the slave, there was nothing breathed save resistance and revenge' (*Napoleon*, vii. 124–5). But despotism was natural to the Russians, and in no way impeded their capacity for unified and cohesive action. The nobles were loyal, the merchants generous, and the people were governed by a 'natural spirit of obedience and instinct of discipline . . .' (vii. 105; vii. 86–7).[12] Both people and prince preferred death to disgrace (vii. 248), and the army was successful, despite the relative ignorance of the junior officers, because the soldiers possessed the hardihood of semi-barbarians, and the 'passions, courage, love of war, and devotion to their country, which is found in the early periods of society. . . .' If the junior regimental officers were comparatively ignorant, they were

[12] Ségur offered interesting support for Scott's enthusiasm for the Russian nobility. He reports that they lived with their families rather than at court and maintained an independence that the Tsar had to respect. See *Histoire*, ii. 9.

also 'naturally brave, kind to the common soldier, and united among themselves like a family of brothers . . .' (v. 227–8). Unlike the armies of Austria and Prussia, in which the common soldier felt like an unimportant part of a great machine (v. 226), here was an army, and a people, united and to a large extent disciplined by common interests and common passions. When Scott describes the Cossacks repulsing Murat's cavalry 'under the eye of their sovereign' (vii. 385–6) we receive the impression of a great chivalric order coming to the rescue of all Europe. To be sure, the Russian peasants regarded all foreigners with an unenlightened suspicion that could have brutal consequences (vii. 130), but in describing their actions and beliefs in the service of their Tsar, Scott is revealing his strong preference for the natural bigotry of primitive men over the attitudes of men who, in Burke's well-known words, had 'subtilized' themselves 'into savages'.

Nevertheless despite Scott's admiring tribute to Holy Russia, there were other sections of Europe about which he wrote with even greater affection. They were the Tyrol and the Vendée. In extolling these areas, Scott emphasizes their isolation, their parochialism, their hardiness which fostered by harsh natural environments made them naturally skilled in war, and their rustic freedom from excessive differences in rank and wealth. Both regions, although their names sound less exotic than that of Tsarist Russia, are turned into the precise opposites of cosmopolitanism. His account of the Tyrol, after the treaty of Pressburg had subjected it to Bavaria, may be naive, but it is typical enough to deserve quotation at length:

Those wild regions, which had been one of the oldest inheritances of Austria, had been torn from her by the treaty of Pressburg, and conferred on the new kingdom of Bavaria. The inclination of the inhabitants had not been consulted in this change. The Austrians had always governed them with a singular mildness and respect for their customs; and had thus gained the affection of their Tyrolese subjects, who could not therefore understand how an allegiance resembling that of children to a parent, should have been transferred, without their consent, to a stranger sovereign, with whom they had no tie of mutual feeling. The nation was the more sensible of these natural sentiments, because the condition of the people is one of the most primitive in Europe. The extremes of rank and wealth are unknown in those pastoral districts; they have almost no distinction among their inhabitants; neither nobles nor serfs, neither office-bearers nor dependents; in one sense, neither rich nor poor. As great a degree of equality as is perhaps consistent with the existence of society, is to be found in the Tyrol. In temper they are a gay, animated people, fond of exertion and excitation, lovers of the wine-flask and the dance, extempore poets, and frequently good musicians. With these are united the more hardy qualities of the mountaineer, accustomed to the life of a shepherd and huntsman, and, amidst the Alpine precipices, often placed in danger of life, while exercising one or other of the occupations. As marksmen, the Tyrolese are accounted the finest in Europe; and the readiness with which they obeyed the repeated summons of Austria during former wars, showed that their rustic employments had in no respects diminished their ancient love of military enterprise. Their magistrates in peace, and leaders in war, were no otherwise distinguished from the rest of the nation than by their sagacity and general intelligence; and as these qualities were ordinarily found among inn-keepers, who, in a country like the Tyrol, have the most general opportunities of obtaining information, many of that class were leaders in the memorable war of 1809.

(vi. 191–2)

Two features of this eulogy are worth noting: its flirtation with egalitarianism, indicating that a persistent opponent of the radicals could also dislike extremes of wealth and poverty, and its inescapable linkage between loyalty and primitivism. The Tyrolese are, in some respects, remarkably similar to the 'children of the desert', with one tragic difference—they were beaten. After his glowing account of their social order and its rustic virtues, Scott records their defeat, repeatedly insisting that lack of Austrian support against overwhelming military force was its major cause (vi. 193; 218–20), and concludes with a definition of Andreas Hofer's place of execution as 'sacred to the thoughts of freedom, as the precincts of a temple to those of religion' (vi. 220).

Hazlitt distrusted Scott's tribute to those he regarded as ignorant victims of their own blindness to Austrian perfidy, but he need not have been suspicious of Scott's emphasis on Tyrolese near-egalitarianism.[13] In honouring Russia, for example, Scott as we have seen was often cunningly selective in his omissions. One of the most significant exclusions is that of a paragraph by Ségur strenuously denouncing the extreme inequalities of Russian society (*Histoire*, ii. 42). Moreover, Scott, earlier in the *Napoleon*, had already presented a glowing account of yet another region's heroic resistance to aggression, and once again, in addition to the theme of noble primitivism, there is a reference to the advantages of moderate differences in wealth. The region concerned was the Vendée, and this backward province of the most sophisticated country in Europe draws a remarkable tribute.

Scott begins by describing a terrain and climate that are as impassable as other European or Asiatic wastelands. Emphasizing

[13] *Works*, xiv. 353.

the length of the rainy season, he portrays a damp social paradise in which all orders are in harmony partly because the exigencies of nature render political despotism superfluous. The 'ladies of rank . . . went in carriages drawn by bullocks; the gentlemen, as well as the peasants, travelled chiefly on foot; and by assistance of the long leaping-poles, which they carried for that purpose, surmounted the ditches and other obstacles which other travellers found impassable' (ii. 141–2). The *noblesse* was indeed deferred to by the peasantry, but plain friendship was also possible, since so many sports and activities were enjoyed by both ranks in common (ii. 142–3). Although the priests were not very learned, they were natives of the region 'distinguished for the primitive duty with which they discharged their office . . .' (ii. 145). (Scott is gently suggesting that they are happily isolated from the attentions of Rome and thus free to minister to their parishioners in a pure and Apostolic manner.) In a passage reminiscent of eighteenth-century British novels, with their country estates that are, in effect, microcosms of benign Erastianism, Scott writes that the *curé* 'took frequent share in the large hunting parties, which he announced from the pulpit, and after having said mass, attended in person with the fowling-piece on his shoulder' (ii. 145).

Unlike Alphonse Beauchamp, who is a major source for Scott's account of the Vendean wars, and who assumes a more impartial posture than Scott, Scott sees the Vendée as France's *only* region of heroes.[14] Influenced by religion and natural affection, they resist the revolution when they hear with disgust the stories of its atrocities (ii. 144). Allowing for a different ecclesiastical situation, the following paragraph of Scott's account could have been taken from *Old Mortality*: 'The peasants maintained in secret their ancient pastors, and attended their ministry in woods and deserts; while the intruders, who were settled in the livings of the recusants, dared hardly appear in the churches without the protection of the national guards' (ii. 146).

But the Covenanters were tainted by divisive doctrinal frenzy; the Vendeans are worthier. In France the source of excess is Paris, and the Vendeans take to their thickets because of the 'absurd and persecuting fanatacism' of the Assembly's anti-clerical decree. Moreover, Scott specifically denies that their priests ever went to battle as warriors (ii. 145 and n.).

[14] Alphonse Beauchamp, *Histoire de la guerre de la Vendée et des Chouans*, 2nd ed. (Paris, 1807), i. 15–27.

They did, however, exhibit an emotion akin to fanaticism, the same emotion that governed the Spaniards, the Cossacks, and the Tyrolese; the legitimate enthusiasm of a region defending its way of life. Consequently, this society, whose manners were simple, virtuous, and patriarchal (ii. 143), confronted the revolutionary forces of Europe's most sophisticated nation, not only with the armed tactics of 'ancient Swiss and Scottish soldiers', but also with those of American 'red warriors, accompanied by whoops and shouts, which seemed, from the extended space through which they resounded, to multiply the number of the assailants' (ii. 151). France, in its finest region, had both its Mohicans and its Natty Bumppos.

Thus the Vendeans, despite their ultimate failure, which occurred, like that of the Tyrolese, largely because of the failure of a larger power to support them, in this case a factious and indecisive Britain (ii. 160–4), set a pattern for guerrilla resistance that was later to be followed in Spain, Russia, and the Tyrol. Although each country had to be capable of acting alone, the mere enthusiasm of such rebels, when sustained long enough to attract the sympathetic attention of countries threatened by Napoleon, was a tributary cause of his ultimate defeat. It is perhaps no coincidence that Scott, in a letter written in 1808 criticizing Jeffrey's determination to keep enthusiasm of any sort at arm's length, went on to express a desire to visit Spain (*Letters*, ii. 116–17). He was inspired by the courage of the Spanish patriots, despite their obvious need of a leader to discipline their self-defeating over-confidence and pride (*Letters*, ii. 75–6; 139–40; 474–5 and *Napoleon*, vi. 79–81). Later, in *Napoleon*, he noted that Kutuzov cited the Spaniards as an inspirational example to his own troops (vii. 138), and it was the Russian example in its turn that revived Europe.[15] Europe was saved from military dictatorship by a type of enthusiasm that included furious provincialism and a frequently quixotic heroism. She was rescued by noble savages from her *fainéants*, her intellectual poseurs, her middle classes who, like the burghers of Vienna, preferred peace to honour and who, despite their usefulness as socially stabilizing ballast, usually needed to be 'struck and struck like flints / Ere their hid fire will sparkle'.[16]

[15] *Letters*, iii. 221–2. For an illustration of the Cossacks' effect on the Prussians see *Napoleon*, vii. 279.
[16] These lines from Dryden's *The Duke of Guise* were among Scott's favourites. In his *Napoleon* Scott often exhibits a lukewarm attitude towards the burghers of all countries. See i. 306; ii. 55, 83, 110.

Scott's admiration for men and women who, like the Spanish insurgents and even the Neapolitan *lazzaroni*, embodied the national will more effectively than their leaders, was, we must remember, qualified by his concern over discipline. A mere rabble too easily dissipated its ferocity. The Cossacks required their Platoff, the Swiss and Tyrolese *montagnards* their Hofer, the Vendeans their Charette. Otherwise they risked becoming like the Calabrians, who, because they were 'tumultuous, sanguinary, and unmanageable', were of little use to their allies (v. 28). In this respect Scott, the old Pittite, joins hands with E. J. Hobsbawm, a modern student of primitive rebels well acquainted with Marxist theory, to insist that to be 'effective champions of their people, bandits had to stop being bandits. . . .'[17] We must be careful, however, not to confuse discipline with *embourgeoisement*. Discipline facilitated the effective use of primitive men in battle, making more forceful their brute force. The celebrated Charette may have drawn strength from his privateering ancestors, but fortunately he did not dissipate his energies in piracy (ii. 147).

In summarizing Scott's account of his legitimist rebels, certain inescapable facts are evident. They did not defend their traditional ways of life out of sentimental nostalgia, for to be nostalgic about the past is obviously to be separated from it. These rebels were living specimens of antiquity playing a salvationist role in the modern world. They were hunters, shepherds, herdsmen, peasants, sometimes disciplined bandits, living in patriarchal societies that had known little or no change for centuries. Inevitably they exhibited characteristics directly opposed to ideals of the Enlightenment as commonly interpreted. They distrusted or hated foreigners, remained faithful to traditional religions, and lived lives so hardy that they could with ease part with whatever advantages of civilized society they may have known.

The last characteristic is of particular importance. Both the occupations and the natural surroundings of Scott's primitives facilitated both the transition to warfare and the return from it. Scott feared and disliked conscription as well as the systematized militarism of large standing armies. Flora MacIvor, who complained that 'On the hill or the glen if a gun should appear, / It is only to war with the heath-cock or deer',[18] would have relished Scott's tributes to the martial skills of the Tyrolese and the Vendeans, just as Scott enjoyed describing the skill with which the

[17] *Primitive Rebels* (New York, 1965), 27. [18] *Waverley*, ch. 22.

Cossacks managed their horses while escorting an emissary of the Tsar through hostile country (*Napoleon*, vii. 176) or the address with which the Tyrolese ambushed their imperial enemies with the help of the boulders of their own mountains (vi. 218–19). Among the chief evils of the French revolution was that it had made the army a badge of honour for all rather than a refuge for inferior beings.[19] Eventually the French army found its proper commander—a military genius to be sure, but also a man too easily seduced into a bombastic and affected prose style (*Paul's Letters*, 62; *Napoleon*, viii. 202), the creator of a 'half-feudal, half-oriental establishment of grand feudatories' (v. 137), an emulator of false neo-Roman ideals (iii. 287–8), and an admirer of the pseudo-bardic effusions of Ossian (ix. 244–5). The empire led by such a figure was clearly a 'modern antique'; it was Scott's pleasure to record its frustration by the genuine article. Scott's poem *The Field of Waterloo* is itself open to the charge of being a particularly bad example of a modern mini-epic, but it was sincerely meant, and it is no coincidence that the same poem that celebrates the heroism of Cameron of Lochiel cannot help remembering the 'Children of the Don'. Summarizing the liberal dilemma of 1815, a modern historian writes: 'Cossacks in the streets of Paris proclaim the triumph of reaction everywhere'.[20] Scott, fond of picturesque contrast, was obviously more amused than shocked at the spectacle of the Champs Elysées turned into a 'Scythian encampment' (viii. 170). He could not refrain, in fact, from mocking the village provincialism of the City of Light. The Parisians, he reports, were terrified because they had heard that Tartars, Baskirs, and Kalmouks had 'a taste for the flesh of children . . .' (viii. 58–9). Vulgar superstitions were not confined to the Highlands.

What conclusions can be drawn from Scott's admiration for the legitimist partisans and insurgents? Certainly he was not an atavist. His accounts of the Tyrol and the Vendée indicate a preference for the discipline of proximity and example over the discipline of the knout. His emphasis on the absence of extremes of wealth in these ancient regions is clearly the result of this preference. The excessive wealth and excessive poverty of so-called

[19] For Scott's comments on French conscription, see *Napoleon*, v. 368–73; for his views on standing armies and militarism see *Paul's Letters*, 31, 37–8, 61; *Napoleon*, v. 361–7; viii. 293; ix. 326–7.

[20] Stanley Mellon, *The Political Uses of History: A Study of Historians in the French Revolution* (Stanford, 1958), 6.

'advanced' societies rendered impossible the shared life of leaders and followers that does so much to create a feeling of common interest. One sees why he regretted the development of extremes of wealth in Britain.[21] Nevertheless, the evidence of *Napoleon* cannot be ignored. Allowing for the license of the romantic biographer or historian, we are still justified in observing with surprise how Scott tampers with his evidence, distorts his sources, in effect, turns perjurer on behalf of some of the wildest forces in Europe. Their superstitions become venerable religions, their pillaging an occasion for apology or an implied admission that boys will be boys (vii. 147), their cruelties spontaneous expressions of loyalty to place, region and way of life in the face of Caesarism and organized militarism.

In view of so emphatic a bias on behalf of ancient primitivism we are now justified in asking a pointed question. What has become of the Scott who we have been hearing so much about of late—the child of the Enlightenment, the typical eighteenth-century man, the artistic comrade of Biedermeyer, the mocker of chivalry and other outmoded patterns of behaviour, the rationalist, the extremely proper Burkean, the apostle of progress?[22]

Francis R. Hart has defined Scott as 'an unphilosophical, somewhat erratic artist, vaguely in touch with Hume, Robertson, and Gibbon, but also with Montesquieu, Ferguson, the German Romantics, and Burke. . . .' He then goes on to attack the oversimplification of the eighteenth century and its Enlightenment that usually accompanies the oversimplification of Scott.[23] I agree with Hart. Like most of its great and rebellious sons, Scott took from eighteenth-century art and thought what he considered useful or prophetic and ignored or condemned the rest. Nevertheless, I would add that Scott was passionately acquainted with gazettes as well as with philosophers and social thinkers. In a letter to Southey, expressing dark thoughts about the power of the enemy, he concludes: 'I am almost driven to the pass of the Covenanters,

[21] *Journal*, 24 November 1826.
[22] I will restrict myself to a few fairly emphatic examples: Duncan Forbes, 'The Rationalism of Sir Walter Scott', *Cambridge Journal* vii (1953), 20–35; Joseph E. Duncan, 'The Anti-Romantic in *Ivanhoe*', *Nineteenth-Century Fiction* ix (1955), 293–300, reprinted in *Walter Scott, Modern Judgements*, ed. D. D. Devlin (London, 1968), 142–7; Mario Praz, *The Hero in Eclipse in Victorian Fiction*, trans. Angus Davidson (Oxford, 1956), 54–64; Alexander Welsh, *The Hero of the Waverley Novels* (New Haven and London, 1963); and, perhaps the most extreme instance, John Henry Raleigh, '*Waverley* as History, or 'Tis One Hundred and Fifty-six Years Since', *Novel* iv (1970), 14–29.
[23] *Scott's Novels: The Plotting of Historical Survival* (Charlottesville, 1966), 182.

when they told the Almighty in their prayers, he should no longer be their God; and I really believe a few Gazettes more will make me turn Turk or Infidel' (*Letters*, ii. 151–2).

Obviously, the breathless reader of gazettes participated in the writing of Napoleon's biography and as a consequence I am inclined to think that Scott cannot be considered either a 'child of the Enlightenment' or a believer in progress. The answer cannot be one-sided. As Edgar Johnson has pointed out, Scott could annoy as perceptive a reader as Lady Louisa Stuart by writing too condescendingly of the ignorant superstitions of the past.[24] Those who approach him with rigorously monistic ambitions will receive the refutation that Scott's writings will be happy to supply. The most one can do is assert a preponderance.

Scott was a follower neither of the Enlightenment nor the idea of progress, if the Enlightenment entailed the rejection of primitive ignorance, religious and patriotic fury, and parochialism, and if progress was seen as a law of history. Scholars who assert that Scott belittles the past and exalts the Age of Enlightenment usually get into deeper trouble than that encountered by those who resignedly acknowledge exceptions. They begin by assuming, quite wrongly, that Scott anatomizes every other age except that of Voltaire. The *Life of Napoleon Buonaparte*, as we have seen, suggests otherwise. The man who spoke of his own time as 'the iron age' and 'this monster-breeding age' (*Napoleon*, iii. 221; *Journal*, 25 October 1831) did not conceive of his era as having begun in 1800. The execution of Louis XVI was a disgraceful parody of the execution of Charles I, symbolizing the difference in quality between the English and French revolutions (*Napoleon*, ii. 80). Even an apparent compliment to Voltaire becomes a deprecation of his role as unknowing instigator of a revolution he would have deplored (ix. 246–7). As for the chief voices of the Enlightenment, they are the 'infidels of the Encyclopédie' contributing to the 'indecencies and impieties of French philosophy' (ii. 281; 291).

Such remarks indicate a hostility to a nation as well as to an age, but we should remember that that nation achieved imperial power during Scott's time because of the moral and intellectual weaknesses of the eighteenth century. Moreover, I have yet to mention the most significant indication of eighteenth-century corruption— the partition of Poland. This diplomatic butchery was, of course, deplored by many, but Scott is unusually vehement on the subject.

---

[24] *Sir Walter Scott, The Great Unknown* (London, 1970), ii. 1144–5.

'The partition of this fine kingdom', he writes, 'by its powerful neighbours, Russia, Austria, and Prussia, was the first open and audacious transgression of the law of nations, which disgraced the annals of civilized Europe' (v. 218; also 218–23; vii. 13–15; viii. 34–5). The international politics of the eighteenth century had 'the primal eldest curse upon't', a nation's murder. No wonder Scott once saw Napoleon as a scourge, sent by Providence, to flay Europe for her sins (*Letters*, ii. 236).

Such evidence possibly explains the difficulties encountered by Duncan Forbes when he insists that Scott believed in the 'necessary progress of society through successive stages', only to support his assertion by citing Scott's denunciations of significantly regressive actions by Napoleon in the areas of law, war, and commerce. Moreover, if Scott, as Forbes says, 'had his doubts about the benefits arising from the progress of civilization',[25] then we are entitled to inquire quite sharply just what he intends by the word 'progress' in this sentence. Does it not also contain a contradictory meaning?

The answer may be that Scott believed in periods of progress within certain specific areas. One of the arguments he used against the British ministry in the Malachi Malagrowther letters refers to the improvements Scotland had made under its own banking system.[26] Nevertheless, the Malachi papers were themselves intended to check a regressive Napoleonic policy on the part of the London government. Significantly, much of the third letter is devoted to a defence of the Highlanders. The Scott who read the gazettes had long been convinced of the usefulness, actual and potential, of men who had never heard the word 'progress'. His description of European cultural and political life in the *Napoleon* reads like a nightmare dreamed by Adam Ferguson, in which Europe was dominated by a France transformed into 'one immense army, under the absolute authority of a military commander, subject to no control nor responsibility' (*Napoleon*, ix. 326–7).[27] In such a situation progress was something that other nations simply could not afford.

Such a conclusion suggests that, for at least one writer, the Romantic glorification of primitive man had utilitarian motives.

[25] Forbes, 'Rationalism', 27–8.
[26] *Letters of Malachi Malagrowther*, in *Miscellaneous Prose Works*, xxi. 283–7; 352–4; 390–4.
[27] *Reflections Previous to the Establishment of a Militia* (London, 1756); *An Essay on the History of Civil Society*, ed. Duncan Forbes (Edinburgh, 1966), 230–2.

So, for that matter, did the Romantic emphasis on 'emotion' as opposed to 'reason'. The eighteenth century lacked passion. Fortunately for its tired *fainéants* and waspish philosophers, there were hot-blooded partisans to supply the energy needed to save the countries their leaders had, in effect, betrayed. The *Life of Napoleon Buonaparte* not only fails to endorse the passing away of primitive cultures, it actually celebrates what the Napoleonic wars had proved to be true on the most urgent grounds of national self-interest—their necessary continuance and vitality.

Moreover, there were other than pragmatic reasons for praising the primitive men of Europe. We must be sensitive to ethical imperatives that Scott considered of particular importance. One of these imperatives was that of gratitude. Ingratitude, and the humiliation resulting from it, disgusted Scott. He remarks sadly that such moments as Napoleon's abdication, when men abandon their previous benefactor, reveal human nature at its worst (*Napoleon*, viii. 220–1), he sympathizes with the veterans of the Napoleonic campaigns who, after the 1814 collapse, were put under the command of emigré officers who had never fought for France (viii. 297–8). As early as 1815 he had expressed his dis-like of the French Royalist ultras who felt that the British had not done enough for them (*Paul's Letters*, 316–20). More significantly, he later described the restored Ferdinand's exiling of Don Miguel Alava, who had joined the Spanish insurgents in 1811, as 'beastly' (*Letters*, ix. 23–4). The implication of such remarks is clear. The *Napoleon*, in its appreciation of warriors too often dismissed as barbarous, expresses Scott's gratitude for their efforts for Europe and Britain. If we insist on ascribing to Scott opinions that require the rejection of primitive man as representative of historically obsolete ways of life we are in fact accusing him of exhibiting a type of ingratitude which, as a moral being, he profoundly detested.

It is not the function of this paper to explore the relationship between the Scott who read the gazettes to the Author of Waver-ley, but a warning is in order. Most of the novels were written before *Napoleon*. Let us suppose that interpretations of the novels as implied endorsements of the cosmopolitan ideals of the Enlight-enment, *bourgeois* good behaviour, and the happy progress of man-kind towards politer style of life are correct. Then the *Napoleon* becomes a sprawling palinode, strongly implying that most of those novels are dangerous and suicidal nonsense. To be sure, the Scott of 1826 was not the Scott of 1814, but I doubt if he had changed so drastically. Perhaps it is time to arrest the frigid caution still creeping from journal to journal and confront the possibility that Scott neither endorsed nor resigned himself to the death of any primitive culture whatever. We have often stood before such figures as Meg Merrilees, spinning elegant theories of progress and the necessary extinction of backward and un-enlightened men in the manner of Dominie Sampson muttering his exorcisms.[28] In doing so we may have earned the response the Dominie got from the primitive saviour of Ellangowan.

Furthermore, we should begin re-examining our notions of death in the novels. Not all of Scott's traditionalist rebels die, and those that do are not necessarily doomed by some nebulous entity called History. Perhaps they die because in decadent ages some-one may have to do some very heavy and violent work in defence of the realm. Scott knew that he wrote for Miss Buskbody, and he recorded his frustration by that embodiment of invincible *bourgeois* complacency. But to himself he wrote: '. . . if there be any thing good about my poetry or prose either it is a hurried frankness of composition which pleases soldiers sailors and young people of bold and active disposition' (*Journal*, 16 June 1826). It is note-worthy that the passage follows an expression of pleasure that Lieutenant-Colonel Dennis Davidov, of the Tsar's Cossacks, had expressed an interest in Scott's work. If questions arise concerning Scott's appreciation of Davidov's interest, or his amiable treatment of the Cossacks in the *Napoleon*, we might consider his insistence, in *Napoleon*, that had the French actually invaded Britain, the war would have assumed a 'popular and national' character (iv. 303). Should such an invasion have occurred, Scott would certainly have considered the potential usefulness, not only of his beloved yeomanry, but also of the Scottish *montagnards*.

[28] I include myself in the indictment. See R. C. Gordon, *Under Which King? A Study of the Scottish Waverley Novels* (Edinburgh, 1969), 30 and 33.

The Problem of
Coherence in The Antiquary[1]

ROBIN MAYHEAD

I T was almost inevitable, I suppose, that this discussion should
start with a quick review of comments made on *The Antiquary*
by gentlemen who are playing a very prominent part in this
conference. For this book is in many ways the Cinderella of the
Scottish Waverley Novels. I am not thinking of readers who have
been frankly hostile towards it, or those who have patronized it
as a work containing some marvellous 'bits' in a welter of inco-
herence. No, I have in mind the reader who rates it high, who may
(like the author himself) have a special affection for it, but who
may equally have serious reservations which make it rather hard
for him to say convincingly just why he includes the book among
Scott's best. I myself, at any rate, have been such a reader, and I
want now to sketch my reactions to the following comments.

First there is Professor Robert C. Gordon in his valuable study
Under Which King?, who closes his third chapter with these
words: '*The Antiquary* is a very odd novel'. Indeed it is; and he
tabulates with exemplary clarity the book's 'instances where
"heterogeneous elements are yoked by violence together"', and
its 'discordant juxtapositions and "purposes mistook"'. I am
interested in Professor Gordon's view of the heterogeneity he so
vividly brings out. 'These anticlimaxes, dissonances, obscurities
suggest', he says, 'a sort of careless mannerism, as though Scott
were mocking the whole idea of coherence and perspective'; and
he remarks a declining coherence of design 'in the conventional
sense' through the first three Waverley Novels, observing that 'It
would seem that the closer Scott came to his own age the more
chaotic the world became for him'. He has, moreover, the useful

---

[1] Certain parts of this paper have been adapted, with some alteration, in chapter 5
of my *Walter Scott* (Cambridge, 1973), where a further discussion of points raised
here will be found. I am indebted to the Cambridge University Press for permission
to use the material from which my chapter partly derives.

suggestion that the book's oddities are connected with a basic 'discord' in the figure of Oldbuck himself: 'the authority on the past [who] does not know the past', with the consequent reflection that 'the impulse to study the past may involve the use of tools that in themselves remove the past farther from us'.

That, I am sure, is one of the things this novel is telling us, but it does not take me as far as I feel I need to go. If I have the nagging impression that *The Antiquary*, odd though it is, really does have a principle of coherence somewhere, I do not think it is being inappropriately 'Jamesian' to want something rather more worked out and explained.

Now for Professor Daiches, in that famous essay of 1951, 'Scott's Achievement as a Novelist'. For him *The Antiquary* clearly presents no real problem of coherence. Its 'prevailing atmosphere', he tells us, 'is comic'; and although the 'melodramatic Glenallan episode in this novel and the drowning of the young fisherman Steenie Mucklebackit give a sense of depth and implication to the action . . . they do not alter its essential atmosphere.'

No one is likely to play down the comedy in *The Antiquary*, but I wonder how many readers have queried pretty strongly, as I have, the contention that comedy constitutes the book's 'essential atmosphere'. Is it enough to 'fit in' the Glenallan and Mucklebackit strands of interest simply by saying that they 'give a sense of depth and implication'? May one not be right in suspecting that the book's 'atmosphere' (if one is going to use that word) is something both more complex and more compelling? And although I heartily agree with Professor Daiches that the 'plot' of *The Antiquary* hardly counts *as* plot, I find it hard to accept another of his views: that it is 'essentially a static novel'. Hard, because the oddities to which Professor Gordon rightly points engender in the book a textural 'irritation' and agitation quite incompatible, to my mind, with any notion of stasis. But I shall return to Professors Gordon and Daiches in a minute or two.

Professor Edgar Johnson, in his new biographical and critical study, offers a more persuasive reading of *The Antiquary*: more persuasive in that he makes the novel seem a more unified thing than does Professor Gordon, while he is at the same time more aware of its heterogeneity than Professor Daiches. He does not consider the book to be without flaws, but his over-all view is expressed in the contention that 'Far from being a cluttered ragbag of a story, like Oldbuck's study and its historical lore, the novel when truly understood is seen to have the clearest thematic unity'. He accepts the heterogeneity of the Glenallan business alongside so much that is comic, but insists that a coherent design is made out of it all: 'Both the melodrama of these events and the comedy of Monkbarns and Edie Ochiltree are in fact essentially fused into the significant action of the novel, which explores the way in which the present is rooted in the past and rectifies the errors of that present by putting it into a sound relationship with the past'. This, then, is the principle of 'thematic unity'.

Now, it would be both untrue and unfair for me to say that when I hear the word 'thematic' I reach for my revolver. Untrue because I would have to shoot myself; unfair because we must all be grateful to Professor Johnson, here and elsewhere in his critical chapters, for giving such sensible guidance as to what Scott's novels are well and truly *about*. I am sure, however, that he would agree that the thematic approach alone can cover a multitude of critical sins, or at any rate be at best a partial index to the kind of effect that a novel makes as a whole. To get our bearings by trying to say what a novel is most centrally about is the *start*; it can hardly be expected to do the whole job.

Professor Johnson makes it plain that he does not consider it as doing the whole job. He doesn't suppose that to proclaim *The Antiquary* unified on the principle of the present's being rooted in the past and the errors of the present being rectified by putting it into a sound relationship with the past is the ultimate critical insight which 'accounts for' the impression that book makes upon us. He is firm, or at least he tries to be, about real or suspected weaknesses in the book. He has something to say, for instance, about the apparently stilted language put into the mouths of Lovel and Miss Wardour, but although he is willing to agree that there is some reason genuinely to feel that Scott has not quite succeeded here, he reminds us that 'in imaginative literature all dialogue is a matter of convention and of adjustment to an established atmosphere'. That is well said, for it voices a truth too often forgotten, and I hope my saying this will remove possible offence from the remark of a moment ago that Professor Johnson is *trying* to be firm about the book's debit account. I was not meaning to patronize, but rather to draw attention to certain difficulties he seems to have in facing this admittedly odd novel as honestly as he can. Though he is inclined to feel that the language of Lovel and Isabel Wardour doesn't quite come off, his reminder about the conventional nature of all literary dialogue is an important qualification of that feeling. And take another item in his catalogue of the book's faults: 'For some readers the horseplay of Edie's tricks on Dousterswivel is too farcically out of tone with the more serious parts of the story and Dousterswivel so ridiculously transparent a swindler as to make Sir Arthur exaggeratedly credulous'. I underline those words *'For some readers'*. Professor Johnson is too honest a commentator to assert categorically that the Dousterswivel element definitely *is*, for *all* readers, a damaging flaw. Clearly, despite his firmness about the book's 'thematic unity', *The Antiquary* does present for him some problems of coherence, problems which the thematic approach does not completely solve. And for my part I have to say that although I find his comments very useful, Professor Johnson does not, for me, quite convey a sense of the book's 'established atmosphere', to use his own phrase.

This brings us back to Professor Daiches, and his remark about 'the prevailing atmosphere' of *The Antiquary*. Well, 'atmosphere', like 'thematic', is a word which can cover a multitude of critical sins. I wonder how many of us here who are teachers have told our pupils to be drastically economical in its use—or even not to use it at all! Still, it is probably in this case the most useful general word, even if it is too vague to do duty for very long. The most useful general word, because to speak of this novel's prevailing or established 'tone' wouldn't do. For it seems to me that the main reason why we have to agree with Professor Gordon that it is 'a very odd novel' is that it contains so wide a variety of differing tones. It is not just a case of finding the Dousterswivel business 'out of tone with the more serious parts of the story', but of finding umpteen things 'out of tone' with one another. Where, then, do we go from here?

It seems to me that each of the critics we have been looking at can give us a clue. First there is Professor Gordon's remark that the book's oddities 'suggest a sort of careless mannerism', and I underline *'mannerism'* particularly. Then there is, once more, Professor Johnson's salutary reminder about literary 'convention and adjustment', and I would here extend those words to apply to more things than dialogue, which he has specifically under discussion, especially the word *'convention'*. Thirdly comes a clue contained in Professor Daiches's claim that the book's 'prevailing atmosphere is comic'. If we query this, what do we substitute for the word *'comic'*? And what could one mean by 'the prevailing atmosphere', if we accept that term for the meantime? Finally, back to Professor Gordon and his observation that the first three Waverley Novels are in declining order of coherence of design *'in the conventional sense'*. Suppose *The Antiquary* has a coherence that is quite *unconventional* in the sense that it does not conform to familiar notions of unity in plot or consistency in tone, but highly *conventional* in its own terms—in the sense, that is to say, that it is very firmly based on conventions of a kind different from those of the more familiar kind of eighteenth or nineteenth-century novel, but still, very definitely, *conventions*.

There is little time for me to follow clues very far, but I shall try, in terms of the text, to suggest as many ways as possible of seeing where they lead us. I will start with the question of 'prevailing' or 'essential' atmosphere. Near the beginning of his excellent but all too short study *The Author of Waverley*, Mr. D. D. Devlin reminds us of 'a steady pessimism' colouring everything that Scott wrote, and the presence in his background of Dr. Johnson, especially the Johnson of *The Vanity of Human Wishes*. Now, consider this from Monkbarns in Chapter 16 of *The Antiquary*:

. . . To have lost a friend by death while your mutual regard was warm and unchilled, while the tear can drop unembittered by any painful recollection of coldness or distrust or treachery, is perhaps an escape from a more heavy dispensation. Look around you—how few do you see grow old in the affections of those with whom their early friendships were formed! Our sources of common pleasure gradually dry up as we journey on through the vale of Bacha, and we hew out to ourselves other reservoirs, from which the first companions of our pilgrimage are excluded;—jealousies, rivalries, envy, intervene to separate others from our side, until none remain but those who are connected with us rather by habit than predilection, or who, allied more in blood than in disposition, only keep the old man company in his life, that they may not be forgotten at his death—

There we find not only the spirit of *The Vanity of Human Wishes* but the cadences of *Rasselas*, and even something very like an echo of the first of the stanzas on the death of Robert Levett:

> Condemn'd to Hope's delusive mine,
> As on we toil from day to day,
> By Sudden Blasts, or Slow Decline,
> Our Social Comforts drop away.

It would, of course, be wrong to take Mr. Oldbuck's gloomy musings as an expression of Scott's 'central philosophy' or some such phrase. It is a commonplace that, if Monkbarns is in some ways very close to Scott, the author at the same time places him at a critical distance. I am not proposing, either, that we should invert Professor Daiches's statement and say that the prevailing atmosphere of *The Antiquary* is 'tragic'. I do suggest, however, that the note of Johnsonian pessimism in far more prevalent, and is far more of a unifying factor, than discussion of the book in terms of 'comedy of manners', for example, would imply. We all know that comedy of manners is one major ingredient of the book. We note and enjoy the counterpointing of the different attitudes towards the past, and their social-historical implications, represented by Monkbarns and Sir Arthur Wardour. We laugh at the anachronistic notions of honour and gentility exemplified by Hector M'Intyre's insistence on a duel, its bluster and bravado so absurdly parodied in his attempt on the seal. These things, too, are all in keeping with what our three critics agree to be a central preoccupation of the book: wrong-headed or right-minded ways of looking at the past, and their bearing upon the present. But does comedy of manners, even with those important implications, account for this novel's remarkable emotional quality? It is precisely this element in *The Antiquary* that even the best critical discussions underestimate or even ignore. The objection is not that they underplay the Glenallan or Mucklebackit episodes, but rather that they do not really bring out the very important truth that such things are the most overtly 'serious' expression of what we might call a 'prevailing emotional atmosphere' in the novel; though Professor Johnson does see them as thematically linked with the comic parts. And I suggest that this atmosphere is coloured throughout by the Johnsonian pessimism which, again, has its most overtly serious expression in the utterance of Monkbarns I quoted a minute or two back.

But let us now get away from the word 'atmosphere', and talk in terms of the specific. What is it that unites so many episodes in the novel, so many activities, interests, convictions, and ambitions, over and above the thematic links brought out by Professor Johnson? Surely it is the feeling of *futility* which surrounds them. *The Antiquary* seems to me a far more powerful *Vanity Fair* than Thackeray's. Think of the catalogue. Mr. Oldbuck's antiquarian pursuits are not invariably misguided and futile (the point would be lost if they were), but how often they are, as he acknowledges from time to time himself! Sir Arthur Wardour is surrounded by futility, in his ancestral bluster, and in his gulling by Dousterswivel. The whole Glenallan story, until its final determination, has been a saga of futile passions and futile guilts. One of the most powerful scenes in the book is the opening of Chapter 34, where Monkbarns finds Mucklebackit making the futile attempt to work on his boat, as though no tragedy had befallen his family; and there is an echo of the bereaved father in *Rasselas* when we are told that 'Oldbuck, beaten from the pride of his affected cynicism, would not willingly have had any one by upon that occasion to quote to him his favourite maxims of the Stoic philosophy'. This scene is the tragic expression of that same 'vanitas vanitatum' which has its farcical manifestation in the contemptible antics of Dousterswivel, right at the other end of the gamut. Some readers with whom I have discussed *The Antiquary* have complained that there is no particular reason why the death of Steenie should have been introduced, seeing it as a gratuitous occurrence whose inclusion seems to be merely an injection of seriousness, of 'tragic relief', to give the novel ballast, so to speak. But the drowning of Steenie is *meant* to be seen as gratuitous, as a piece of futile waste. Moreover, returning to the scene we were discussing, we can see how the episode links up with this book's concern with different ways of looking at the past. Sir Arthur's genealogy and Mr. Oldbuck's 'praetorium' represent two ways, and they look pretty silly, as do the latter's 'favourite maxims of the Stoic philosophy', alongside Mucklebackit's overwhelming recollection of a past which has meant so much to him, in the context of a grey present whose full reality he can as yet hardly grasp. 'The large drops fell fast from [Oldbuck's] own eyes, as he begged the father, who was now melted at recollecting the bravery and generous sentiments of his son, to forbear useless sorrow, and led him by the arm towards his own home, where another scene awaited our Antiquary.' That other scene, of course, is his meeting with Lord Glenallan, and the juxtaposition of the Mucklebackit and Glenallan stories is interesting and important. It is a mistake to think of them as possessing the same kind of seriousness. The whole Glenallan story is 'serious' enough for the Earl and for old Elspeth, and the outcome is momentous for Lovel; but its farrago of squalid and ultimately futile intrigue puts it in a very different category from the stark catastrophe of the Mucklebackits' loss. The Glenallan story is melodrama; the other is not. If the two stories are at the most serious end of the scale that has Dousterswivel at the other extreme, the Glenallan theme is already well on the way down. And if these stories embody the sorrow and futility of wasted lives, in their different ways, we have another sort of futility in Chapter 30, which leads into those chapters where their full impact is felt; Chapter 30, in which Monkbarns and Hector M'Intyre discuss Ossian (a parody of useless scholarship) and the latter makes his attempt on the seal (a parody of heroic bluster). All these chapters, seen individually, are very different in feeling; yet what I have proposed as the book's over-all emotional quality permits them to cohere. And I suggest that the copresence of all this apparently heterogeneous material, not, however, 'yoked by *violence* together', is the reason for the complex effect, the impression of being really 'stretched', that a careful reading of *The Antiquary* produces.

Here I want to go back to Professor Gordon's remark about 'careless mannerism'. He does not, of course, mean 'careless' in the sense of 'slipshod', but is thinking rather of the urbane ease of the writer introducing materials whose heterogeneity he is quite aware of, without overmuch concern for tidiness. Now, one needs to keep a sense of proportion when dealing with Scott. If one must beware of 'condemning the self-effacing Scott out of his own mouth', as Professor Hart warns, one must also heed Professor Gordon's caution not to go to the opposite extreme of supposing him to be too self-conscious an artist. We know that he could be 'careless' in a quite ordinary sense, and relied on James Ballantyne to clear up the mess. But if he didn't plan his novels with the minuteness of a Henry James constructing his scenario for *The Ambassadors*, he was far from 'careless' about the *effect* a book would have, as his letters and *Journal* show. And if such concern is not a concern with *art*, in the most important sense, I do not know what is.

Perhaps I am asking too much of Professor Gordon's use of 'careless', and in any case I said a while back that it was 'mannerism' I wanted to underline. I still want to, as it strikes me as pointing very happily to the way in which this book works. I am thinking of the word, as I take Professor Gordon to have been, as one uses it to refer to a type of painting, or architecture, or the French 'precieux' poets, or (with reservations, because of their variety) to the English Metaphysicals. Now, I am not about to claim that *The Antiquary* is a Metaphysical poem! At the same time I suggest that the ways in which Marvell's *Coy Mistress* or Donne's third *Satyre* 'stretch' the reader are not altogether absurdly remote from the impression produced by this novel. More to the point, though, is to think of writers Scott knew especially

well: Swift, Dryden, Ben Jonson, and, once again, the Samuel
Johnson of *The Vanity of Human Wishes*. Blandly to dub them
'mannerist' would be extravagant; on the other hand they are all
remarkable for compelling unity on very disparate materials, and
demand of the reader particular flexibility and attentive vigilance.
The Vanity of Human Wishes encompasses a great variety of tones.
A long time ago T. S. Eliot quoted two couplets from it to demonstrate that Johnson himself was not averse to heterogeneity, whatever he said about the Metaphysicals.

If I made perhaps too much of the word 'careless' it is because
Scott seems to me to have been very decidedly aware of what he
was doing in *The Antiquary*. The novel abounds in little oblique
references to its assorted ingredients. Take this, from Chapter 19,
where Sir Arthur, Mr. Oldbuck, and Dr. Blattergowl are hard at
it: 'But here the Baronet and Mr. Oldbuck having recovered their
wind, and continued their respective harangues, the three *strands*
of the conversation, to speak the language of a rope-work, were again
twined together into one undistinguishable strong of confusion'.
Less bold, but still telling in this novel's context, is Oldbuck's
lament in Chapter 22 on the loss of the poem he imagines Lovel
to have conceived, 'with notes illustrative of all that is clear, and
all that is dark, and all that is neither dark nor clear, but hovers in
dusky twilight in the region of Caledonian antiquities'. Consider,
moreover, the book's studied insistence upon the miscellaneous
and incongruous in any number of applications. There is the wild
miscellany of objects in Monkbarns's study in Chapter 3, to take
the most obvious case; but hardly less striking is the incongruous
appearance of his sister in Chapter 6:

> The elderly lady rustled in silks and satins, and bore upon her head a
> structure resembling the fashion in the ladies' memorandum-book for the
> year 1770—a superb piece of architecture—not much less than a modern
> Gothic castle, of which the curls might represent the turrets, the black pins
> the *chevaux de frize*, and the lappets the banners.
> The face, which, like that of the ancient statues of Vesta, was thus crowned
> with towers, was large and long, and peaked at nose and chin, and bore, in
> other respects, such a ludicrous resemblance to the physiognomy of Mr.
> Jonathan Oldbuck, that Lovel, had they not appeared at once, like Sebastian
> and Viola in the last scene of the 'Twelfth Night', might have supposed that
> the figure before him was his old friend masquerading in female attire.

Less ridiculous than Monkbarns in drag, but still gloriously miscellaneous, is Griselda's ghost story about Rab Tull the town clerk
and the 'marvellous communication about the grand law-plea

between us and the feuars at the Mussel-craig', with its linking
of the supernatural and the most mundanely practical. And while
we are on the subject of the Green Chamber, consider the contrast
between Lovel's dream (if 'dream' it is), with all the rather stock
'Gothic' associations it conjures up, and the words of the song
which wakes him—stock too, in their sentiments, but giving to the
voice of Time crisply urbane Augustan accents far removed from
the sensational:

> 'Why sit'st thou by that ruin'd hall,
>   Thou aged carle so stern and grey?
> Dost thou its former pride recall,
>   Or ponder how it passed away?'

> 'Know'st thou not me!' the Deep Voice cried;
>   'So long enjoyed, so oft misused—
> Alternate, in thy fickle pride,
>   Desired, neglected, and accused?'

On another level there is the meeting of incongruities when the
Wardours meet Edie Ochiltree on 'The beach under Halket-head,
rapidly diminishing in extent by the encroachments of a spring-
tide and a north-west wind, . . . a neutral field, where even a
justice of peace and a strolling mendicant might meet upon terms
of mutual forbearance.' It is something Edie is quick to underline,
indeed, as the three seem to face certain death, in answer to a
particularly sad piece of futility from Sir Arthur:

'Good man,' said Sir Arthur, 'can you think of nothing?—of no help?—I'll
make you rich—I'll give you a farm—I'll'—
    'Our riches will be soon equal,' said the beggar, looking out upon the
strife of the waters—'they are sae already; for I hae nae land, and you would
give your fair bounds and barony for a square yard of rock that would be
dry for twal hours.'

Or, to return to comedy, take Mr. Oldbuck's disquisition on the
meaning of a *'shathmont's-length'*, at the conclusion of the alarming
episode. To explain it psychologically as the expression of relief
at the conclusion of a harrowing affair may be sound enough, but
that does not take away from its incongruity. I could list many more
things of this sort, but there is no time for them, beyond reminding
you of the circumstances attending the false alarm of invasion, a
case of the beautifully incongruous, which Professor Gordon
singles out for special comment.

   Now, I am sure that some of you here want to protest that
similar points could be made about *Waverley*, or *The Bride of*

Lammermoor, or *A Legend of Montrose*, or *Redgauntlet*—and I would wholly agree, especially as regards *Redgauntlet*. I would still maintain, however, that although the miscellaneous and incongruous are repeatedly to be found throughout all Scott's best work, they are exploited in *The Antiquary* in a far more thorough-going way than elsewhere. Things assorted, sometimes absurdly, sometimes tragically—their use in this novel is so ubiquitous as to constitute a positive *convention*, a principle of organisation. To say which is not to argue that Scott thought out such a principle abstractly, but that it was the natural outcome of the vision of the 'vanity of human wishes' he is in this book projecting—a vision in which the best laid plans go wildly awry, in which fondly cherished theories turn out to be ludicrously hollow, in which random success sits cheek by jowl with equally random disaster, in which there is little to trust to or depend upon: just think of the Fairport post office, for example! Yes, the book ends 'happily', but what has gone before is enough to make us contemplate this with a certain wry amusement, or at least scepticism, though not with a sardonic chuckle. It is not surprising that *The Antiquary* should be Scott's most Ben Jonsonian work as well as his most Samuel Johnsonian, for the extremes of character and situation he here depicts lead to a use of 'Humour' characters, of representative types (and consider the naming of so many of them), which, again, we can find elsewhere in Scott, but not on such a scale. It is not for nothing that Monkbarns quotes from *The Alchemist* when he turns on Dousterswivel at the end of Chapter 23.

I have time for only one thing more, and as you might have predicted, it concerns Edie Ochiltree. I have avoided saying much about him so far, because, although I am second to none in my admiration for this particular creation of Scott, I am sure we need to get away from that notion of *The Antiquary* which sees it as charming muddle, with Edie's 'racy vernacular', or some such phrase, as the richest ingredient. Don't let us play that down, but let us this time try to think of Edie in relation to the suggestions I have been making about the book as a whole. If I find Scott's Vanity Fair more powerful than Thackeray's, it is because all therein is *not* Vanity. *The Antiquary* contains irony enough, but it is not the 'bottomless' irony which in Thackeray makes it hard to believe that *anything* is really to be valued. And if we do not contemplate the book's happy ending with a sardonic chuckle, Edie has most to do with this. For he is the antithesis of the shortcomings of others. To complain that he is too conveniently 'on hand' to help out is to expect a realistic convention alien to this novel, for Edie is almost an allegorical embodiment of dependability where so many others lack it, and Scott presses the point home. Where others are hag-ridden by fantasy, whether it be about Roman encampments, or codes of supposed 'honour', Edie is a realist. If Sir Arthur and Oldbuck can both be absurd about the past, and find it hard (especially the former) to adjust to the realities of the present, Edie is in tune with both past and present. He is the repository of any number of old tales and ballads, and he is also the inheritor of a tradition of rural usefulness which makes him almost an indispensable figure in the present of his locality. And his proud insistence on such points as not accepting too much in the way of alms is not an incongruity putting him into line with other characters, not a mere eccentricity or quirk, but a piece of realism showing a lively awareness of both past and present. For him to change would be at once to go against the tradition to which he proudly belongs, and to give himself an outwardly finer but essentially empty and meretricious present. He has no illusions about either past or present, and if he can at times be monumentally impressive, as in his protest to Lovel and M'Intyre before the duel, he is hardly an idealized figure, for all his worth. Nor, for all his apparent contentment, is he depicted as an ideally happy figure, a character out of pastoral convention; but it must immediately be said that he is no unhappy one either. He simply *lives*, facing situations astutely when they arise, and dealing with them as adequately as circumstances permit: this does not mean that he carries any invincible charm against misfortune.

If Monkbarns is to some extent a satirical self-portrait of the author in his antiquarian guise, Edie Ochiltree strikes me as being a kind of premonitory self-portrait. Obvious dissimilarities apart, he is very close to the Scott of the later years of disaster, bereavement, and sickness: by no means a 'happy' man in any ordinary sense, and yet certainly not 'unhappy' in feeling that he could face things and do the best he could with them. And I think, too, that the Mucklebackit whom Monkbarns meets trying to mend his boat in Chapter 34 is close to the Scott we meet in the *Journal* after the death of Charlotte. It isn't for nothing that Edie and Mucklebackit (and the Mucklebackits are by no means idealized) are the characters in the book least connected with sham or pretension.

A very odd novel, then. A novel with a sombre vision underlying much extravagant comedy: a vision which erupts once into
melodrama, and once into tragedy. It is neither a 'happy' nor an
'unhappy' book. I think there are quite a few reasons why Scott
had a special affection for it.

Scott Manuscripts in Edinburgh Libraries

ALAN BELL

THIS paper was prepared during my work on the Sir Walter Scott Bicentenary Exhibition and is therefore mainly concerned with the holdings of the National Library of Scotland, from which most of the exhibits are drawn. The Library's collections are very well known, particularly to members of the Biography and Bibliography seminar, but it is worth while taking a general look to remind ourselves of the context in which much of the research to be reported during the week is taking place. I hope that it will also serve as a general introduction for those who are not so familiar with Edinburgh's really remarkable range of primary source material for the study of Sir Walter Scott.

I am an archivist who is privileged to share the custody of the National Library's Scott manuscripts; I am not a Scott scholar in the ordinary sense. Archivists are mainly concerned with the conservation of documents—in the widest sense of that term—and not with their exploitation for scholarly purposes. There is one austere school of professional thought which argues that the use of the documents in his keeping is absolutely no part of the archivist's work. But in a great research library it is essential that the specialist staff should know something of the type of work which is being carried out on their collections. They should possess some instinctive sense of the questions which may be asked of their documents, even if the answers are the province of the literary scholar himself. Properly managed, such a dialogue can be of great advantage to curator and user alike. Words such as 'important' and 'useful' will occur frequently in this paper, and I make no apology for repeating them, for it is essential to have some idea of the relative values of different parts of the collections before one can assist visiting scholars with any confidence.

The archivist's professional point of view gives him a special eye for the provenance of documents. As we shall see, there are particular satisfactions in this respect to be gained from the Library's Scott holdings. One also develops a professional eye for handwriting. Palaeography does not stop at the Renaissance, and Scott's hand is worth much more detailed examination than it has yet received. Literary references can be matched by examples from Scott's handwriting. For example, there is the complaint the young Frank receives from his father in the first chapter of *Rob Roy*: 'I wish, by the way, you would write a more distinct current hand: draw a score through the tops of your *t*'s and open the loops of your *l*'s.' The relationship of Scott's characteristic *mise en page* to the practice of engrossing learned in his father's office needs further investigation; it may help us to understand his major prose manuscripts better.

I intend to deal briefly with the major manuscripts, and then to speak about lesser holdings in Edinburgh before returning to the National Library and its great collections.

There are five manuscripts of Scott's major works in Edinburgh libraries. The Pierpont Morgan Library in New York has a much larger collection of literary manuscripts, but in quality those in Edinburgh are of a very high standing indeed. The National Library has *Marmion*, *Waverley*, *The Heart of Mid-Lothian*, and *Redgauntlet*; next door, the Library of the Society of Writers to the Signet holds *The Bride of Lammermoor*. In addition, Edinburgh University Library has fragments of *Kenilworth* and *A Legend of Montrose* in its Laing Collection.

Such great literary monuments are so important that they need no comment from me. Summary information about their history and contents is available in Miss Gillian Dyson's admirable article on 'The MSS. and Proof Sheets of Scott's Waverley Novels' in the *Edinburgh Bibliographical Society Transactions* iv (1960). They have been exhibited, admired, and examined and collated with the printed texts for various purposes over the years. But they will stand much further literary and bibliographical inspection. The additions and revisions are often as interesting a study as that of the final handwritten text. From a palaeographical point of view, the ink, watermarks and physical make-up are of great interest, particularly for a bibliographically complicated manuscript like that of *Waverley*. Mr. G. A. M. Wood has made a special study of many of these points, and I must not anticipate his paper later in the week. But I would recall some advice given to students of Old

English literature by Kenneth Sisam: 'It [is] not altogether desirable that workers should be relieved of foraging amongst manuscripts. . . . Now that the flow of new materials and ideas is drying up, there is something to be said for the pre-systematic way of turning over one manuscript after another, with no set purpose except to follow up anything of interest that may arise.'[1]

The proof-sheets must be considered along with the manuscripts, though here again I must not anticipate Mr. Wood, whose article on 'The Great Reviser; or the Unknown Scott' in the July 1971 number of *Ariel* gives an elegant outline of the problems which revisions in proof pose for an editor. Unfortunately the National Library does not have proofs for the novels it owns in manuscript, but it has many others which help to concentrate the material for this particular stage of textual examination. The dialogue in the margins between Scott and Ballantyne greatly enlivens what can be very arid textual work. My favourite (on display in Parliament House) is a note in which Ballantyne objects to a phrase describing James VI in *The Fortunes of Nigel*: 'certainly the least *talented* of the Stuarts'. 'For the love of passion,' Ballantyne writes, 'I entreat you not to sanction by so high an example this detestable American fungus!' 'I think the word a good one,' Scott replied, but 'least *able*' is the phrase which found its way into the published text.

The Scottish Record Office contains a good deal of Scott material amongst the government records preserved at H.M. General Register House, and particularly amongst the large collections of deposited non-official papers. The official papers relate mainly to Scott's duties as Clerk of Session and as Sheriff of Selkirkshire. They are mostly formal legal documents with some additional official correspondence, covering an aspect of Scott's work not dealt with systematically by the Centenary editors. Much of Scott's Border correspondence touches on his shrievalty—the letters to his Sheriff-Substitute Charles Erskine of Melrose are an example—and the official papers will clearly be of use in annotating it.

The Record Office also contains some three hundred Gifts and Deposits, each with a separate inventory which varies greatly in the detail of description. There is no general index of correspondents like that in the National Library, but a thorough search for Scott material would be rewarding. One of the earliest of all deposits (GD 18) is the Clerk of Penicuik archive, with fourteen

[1] K. Sisam, *Studies in the History of Old English Literature* (Oxford, 1953), 150.

Scott letters, all but two of them in the Centenary Edition. A more recent accession (GD 224) consists of the Buccleuch papers from Dalkeith Palace. Boxes 32 and 33 contain 235 letters from Scott, mainly to the Duke of Buccleuch and Lord Montagu, 1807–31, with various transcripts and handlists. Nearly all of them were considered (if not wholly printed) by the Centenary editors, and I mention them only as an example of the richness of the Record Office's holdings. The Buccleuch papers are an obvious source of Scott material, but when the whole archive has been arranged and listed properly, I am sure that they will yield much further information about the financial and personal relationship of Sir Walter Scott and the senior branch of his family. I ought to add that the Duke of Buccleuch himself retains in his library at Bowhill those literary manuscripts—the illustrated early transcript of *The Lay of the Last Minstrel* and Scott's 'History of the Year 1814'—which are on show in the Bicentenary Exhibition.

Elsewhere in the Scottish Record Office there are numerous single letters and small groups which it would be interesting to examine; and the many inventories prepared by the Record Office's associated body, the National Register of Archives (Scotland), also contain references to Scott letters privately held throughout the country, information which it would be useful to have gathered together.

Edinburgh University Library holds a decent, but not sensational, representation of Sir Walter Scott. As I have already mentioned, there are good fragments of *A Legend of Montrose* and of *Kenilworth*. The bulk of the *Kenilworth* manuscript is in the British Museum, but the *Legend of Montrose* fragment is the largest to have survived. These literary manuscripts, like most of the University Library's Scott collection, derive from the bequest of David Laing, that long-lived and pertinaceous collector. There are 42 letters from Scott to Laing, of which the most important are printed in the Centenary Edition—those omitted are slight indeed. Many of the letters accompanied copy for press, or proof-sheets of Bannatyne Club publications, which have now been bound up separately. Scott's antiquarian work has not received much attention recently, and the student of the Scottish historical revival in the early nineteenth century—a subject surely worth another look both from the literary and the philosophical points of view—should find much to interest him in the Scott parts of the Laing papers.

David Laing also owned a collection of 74 letters addressed to Scott, which supplement the Abbotsford and Walpole collections in the National Library. I have not been able to establish their provenance to find out how they came to be separated from the main archive, but their quality is not in doubt and they include a good many letters from important literary correspondents. Laing himself collected over thirty letters—some of them very long—from Scott to various correspondents, which have formed the basis of the University Library's small collection of single letters and small groups. They were drawn on for the Centenary Edition.

The foundation on which the great Scott collections of the National Library of Scotland are built is the series of purchases made from Major-General Sir Walter Maxwell-Scott before the war. After Scott's death, the library and historical relics at Abbotsford were secured by a trust deed which placed them in the ultimate charge of the Dean of the Faculty of Advocates and his Council. The Trust covers all the books and objects described in the printed catalogue of the Abbotsford Library, but not the great accumulation of letters and papers of Scott and his son-in-law which were preserved elsewhere in the house. In the 1930s the National Library of Scotland was enabled to purchase virtually all the manuscript material at Abbotsford, with the exception of the catalogued manuscripts collected by Scott himself. The Abbotsford collection includes many letters written by Scott, either autograph or in the copies made in Lockhart's time and cited by the Centenary Edition as 'Abbotsford copies'. The correspondence is well known from the various publications based on it, but the supporting documents also contain much to interest the scholar. There are, for example, the working papers for the *Minstrelsy*, which have been examined by M. R. Dobie and others. There are Scott's collections for his edition of Swift; there are literary remains of Joseph Strutt and Anna Seward; there are some of the bulky collections for the Life of *Napoleon* which turned Scott to comic verse:

> When with poetry dealing,
> Room enough in a shieling:
> Neither cabin nor hovel
> Too small for a novel: . . .
> But my house I must swap
> With some Brobdingnag chap,
> Ere I grapple, God bless me! with Emperor Nap.

There are the family papers of Scott's ancestors, and his own genealogical collections. And there are letters and diaries of Scott's children, and of Sophia's husband Lockhart, which take the collection well into the succeeding generation.

It is impossible in a brief paper to give more than an outline of some of the main categories into which the Abbotsford collection may be divided. There are many pages of description and many entries in the index of the first volume of the *Catalogue of Manuscripts Acquired since 1925*, to which I refer you with one important reservation. I take it from an essay by M. R. James on medieval manuscripts: 'Be inquisitive. See books for yourself; do not trust that the cataloguer has told you everything. . . . In spite of the imperfections of catalogues, catalogues must be used, and they must be read and not only referred to. . . . besides, there is always the chance . . . that the describer of any MS. may have failed through some ignorance or want of attention to see that some article in it is of extreme interest and rarity.'[2]

I do not propose to spend much time discussing Scott's own letters, which Dr. David Hewitt will be doing when he answers his question, 'What should we do about the Letters?', later in the week.[3] He will provide us with some of the statistics and suggestions which make it necessary for me to do no more than refer to benefactions such as the Law collection—over 400 letters from Scott to his family and to J. B. S. Morritt—and to the many letters of Scott himself in the Abbotsford collection. Over the years we have added to these acquisitions of 1928 and 1931–2 by many purchases of groups of Scott correspondence and smaller sets of letters. Dr. Hewitt will be speaking about this additional material. Partly spurred by his own interest, I recently started work on a detailed survey of the Scott letters in the National Library, working backwards from the most recent accessions. This will obviously occupy me for many months, perhaps years.

The counterpart of the Abbotsford collection is the series of letter-books containing Scott's incoming correspondence, acquired by the novelist Sir Hugh Walpole at a sale at Sothebys in 1921, which formed a treasured part of his notable Scott collection during his lifetime. It is fitting that they should be generally known to scholars today as the 'Walpole collection'; more prosaically they

[2] M. R. James, *The Wanderings and Homes of Manuscripts* (London, 1919), 95–6.
[3] D. S. Hewitt, 'What should we do about Scott's Letters?', *Scottish Literary News* ii (1971), 3–10.

should be described as N.L.S. MSS. 3874–919, and it should not be forgotten that other incoming correspondence can be found elsewhere on the shelves of the Department of Manuscripts. The Walpole letter-books also derive from that part of the Abbotsford collection not covered by the trust deed, and it is particularly satisfying that these two portions of the Scott archive—Abbotsford and Walpole—should have been reunited so appropriately in the national collection.

Sir Hugh Walpole had a lifelong interest in Scott, and also owned some literary manuscripts which he left to his old school, whose collection of manuscripts includes other Scottish material well worth investigation: the manuscript of *The Fortunes of Nigel* in the Bicentenary Exhibition comes from King's School, Canterbury. Walpole bequeathed the letter-books to the National Library, where they were received in 1941. The volumes he owned, now expanded to 46, were drawn on by Wilfrid Partington for two useful volumes published under Walpole's patronage in the 1930s—*The Private Letter-Books of Sir Walter Scott*, and *Sir Walter's Post-Bag* (which also draws on the Abbotsford papers in the National Library). Partington's two books give a good outline of the contents of the Walpole collection, and make very pleasant browsing for the general reader.

The Walpole collection is very frequently used by research workers for all sorts of literary enquiries and is one of our most-used series of manuscripts. I have noticed that readers tend to approach the volumes by searching for the names of particular correspondents in the index, rather than by looking through the volumes themselves. This is unfortunate. Scott's incoming correspondence is surely worth more detailed study as a whole, in its great variety of writer, of style, and of approach. The letters were used by the Centenary editors for annotation, but they were not consistently exploited. They often enrich one's understanding of the printed letters. Dr. Hewitt will probably have something to say about the desirability of editing the correspondence of Sir Walter Scott, rather than merely editing his own letters. I myself think this highly desirable. Whether it is practicable is another matter. Whatever scale of publication is eventually attempted, it is clear that the Library with its great holdings of correspondence will make the most important contribution of all to a revised edition of the letters of Sir Walter Scott. There will always be plenty for the ordinary research worker in the Walpole letter-books. As Dr. Walter Oakeshott remarked of his own work on Malory: 'The moral seems to be that there are chances for the humblest gleaner even where the harvest has been reaped by experienced hands.'[4]

The National Library also has a great deal of material relating to Scott's business activities which should make possible a detailed and impartial study of Scott's financial crisis and recovery. Such a work would be invaluable, were it possible to find an author with the unusual combination of financial acumen, literary enthusiasm and historical understanding. The man who got nearest to this combination was the late James Glen, the Glasgow accountant and Scott student who acted as Grierson's adviser on the financial background of Sir Walter's letters. Glen's own collection of Scott letters, his correspondence with Grierson, and some of his own notes are in the Library. The notes are interesting—they include, for example, a discussion of the birth-year which at first accepts and then decisively rejects the 1770 possibility—and they show what might be done by a detailed financial study of Scott's career. Glen's successor wil find a great deal to interest him in the Library: the sederunt books of the Ballantyne trustees, the business books of Constable and of Cadell, with incoming and outgoing letters on financial matters.

It is Constable and Cadell who most obviously spring to mind as Scott's publishers, but one should not forget to add Blackwood to the list. Scott's uneasy relationship with the Blackwoods may well be worth careful modern study, and there is much direct and indirect correspondence to support a useful small piece of research of this kind. The Scott letters in the Blackwood collection are described in the third volume of the *Catalogue of Manuscripts*. In the Blackwood papers and elsewhere in the Library there is a vast amount of manuscript material which can only be loosely described as pertaining to 'Scott and his Circle'. There is much relating to particular associates such as Hogg and Lockhart, both of whom are represented by large groups of correspondence supported by letters and literary manuscripts in small batches. There are many manuscripts concerning Scott biographically, such as Robert Stevenson's journal of Scott's Lighthouse Tour (Scott's own journal is believed extant, but is untraced), or the charming, phonetically misspelt memoir by Scott's butler Dalgleish.

Then there are documents relating to the organizations Scott was

[4] *Essays on Malory*, ed. J. A. W. Bennett (Oxford, 1963), 6.

concerned with, such as the minute-book of the Royal Edinburgh Volunteer Light Dragoons, and various records of the Bannatyne Club which complement David Laing's own collection in the University Library. There is a great deal about Scott's own family, and about families he was closely connected with, such as the Russells of Ashestiel. For example, the Library holds a large collection of material relating to the Scotts of Raeburn, neatly assembled by Scott's friend the sixth laird (Maxpopple), who died in 1855. These have recently been used by Sir Tresham Lever in his book on Lessudden, the Scott house at St. Boswells which is now his home. The family interest continues beyond Scott's time with the papers of J. R. Hope-Scott, the Tractarian convert who married Lockhart's daughter and saved Abbotsford for the family and the family for Abbotsford. He was the friend of Gladstone and Manning, and an important lawyer in his time: quite apart from his Scott connexions, he is a man in need of modern scholarly attention.

Most of the members of this Biography and Bibliography seminar will be familiar with the Scott holdings I have tried to summarize. I must however add something about the Library's recent accessions of Scott material. The news will not be altogether fresh, as a preliminary announcement was made in my article in the *Times Literary Supplement* of 9 July 1971. I hope however to be able to say a little more about the various new acquisitions to fill out this short descriptive article.

The size and importance of the Library's Scott holdings imposes on us the duty of adding to them, and adding to them worthily. Over the years the opportunities for doing so have gradually diminished as less and less material of absolutely first-rate quality comes on to the market. For example, only two novel manuscripts remain in private hands—*The Abbot* in the possession of Messrs John Murray, and *Rob Roy*, believed to be in the ownership, somewhere, of the descendants of Sir Alfred Law. Really good letters— the sort which contain substantial new texts and novel information —are increasingly difficult to find, and we are only very occasionally able to justify large purchases at auction or from dealers' catalogues, though we seek them out and think about them a good deal.

There are a certain number of Scott letters in the Library's larger recent accessions. Dr. Donald A. Low's 'Walter Scott and Williamina Belsches' in the *Times Literary Supplement* of 23 July

1971, was drawn partly from the few Scott letters in the Fetter-cairn papers. The Minto papers—a vast hoard, still being sorted after several years in the Library—contain several very long letters from Sir Walter Scott on Border business. Another large archive—the papers of Messrs. Oliver and Boyd—contains a handful of letters dealing with Scott's occasional relationship with that publishing house. But generally speaking such groups are becoming more and more uncommon, and even single letters are becoming very expensive indeed. During the last couple of years, however, a combination of careful genealogical work, legal research and sheer good luck has enabled us to acquire some important new material which forms a worthy supplement to the great pre-war collections.

The first of these is of course the Ashestiel Manuscript, item A1 in the Bicentenary Exhibition, containing the fifty leaves of Scott's short but complete fragment of autobiography which was printed as the first chapter of Lockhart's *Life*. We bought it last year with the aid of the Friends of the National Libraries. It had not been available since the Centenary Exhibition of 1871. Its ownership was a complicated legal knot which had to be unravelled before we could purchase it. Its loss to scholarship over the years, and the dubious reputation Lockhart has been acquiring for the mis-handling of sources, made its acquisition by the Library particu-larly interesting, but examination has shown that Lockhart was astonishingly faithful. It is as fluently written as any of Scott's prose writings, with a characteristic lack of punctuation and of the detailed care which Scott was content to delegate to his printer. Lockhart carried out his editorial duty very tactfully, and the minor changes he made are unobjectionable—usually in the interests of art, but rarely against the interests of truth.

Scott wrote the autobiography in 1808 and reworked it after-wards, notably in 1826. Many of the later additions are given by Lockhart only as notes, though they were clearly intended to be part of the main text. There are many small linguistic revisions, but they sometimes reveal changes in critical opinion between that of the poet of 1808 and of the novelist in 1826. Some of the earlier revisions are interesting psychologically and Dr. Nicholas Phillip-son (at this very moment) will be communicating a subtler analysis of the text to the Conference. There is a good deal of interest in the Ashestiel fragment, even though the text has long been available in a reasonably accurate form. We have not yet heard the last of it, and it well deserves the attention it will provoke.

As I mentioned earlier, the National Library is particularly strong in correspondence relating to the publication of Scott's works. Our holdings have recently been increased very substantially by four related acquisitions—a deposit, two purchases, and a gift.

The first of these, the deposit, is a thick volume of Scott's letters to Archibald Constable, which has been placed in the Library by our long-standing benefactors, Messrs. T. & A. Constable, Ltd. These add the most important of all to the long (but still incomplete) run of the firm's early books of incoming letters. There are about 120 Scott letters written between 1800 and 1827; 82 of them are printed in the Centenary Edition. The remainder are all rather short, but they are far from insignificant, as they fill gaps in the publishing correspondence and add details to the profuse documentation of this important business relationship.

Robert Cadell's daughter, Lady Liston-Foulis, owned six volumes of Scott manuscripts—five containing Sir Walter's letters to her father, and the sixth containing the manuscript of *The Pirate*, which is now in Princeton University Library. This collection of six volumes was divided amongst her six grandchildren, who received one volume each. Four of the five volumes of letters were bought by the Library from the family in 1932, but the final volume was retained by the only Cadell great-grandchild who refused to sell. After some further detective work by ourselves and by Mr. John Cameron of Amherst College, followed by protracted legal negotiations, it is good to be able to report that we have managed to secure volume V to add to our MSS. 742-5. Only a handful of letters was published from this series in the very selective last volume of the Centenary Edition, and the 'Grierson rejects' (the typescript of letters copied but not published by the Centenary editors) contain rather unsatisfactory typed transcripts of the others. The originals are essential for any serious work. Over half of these new letters are particularly long and interesting, but they are all important in establishing the full sequence of this very important correspondence. Cadell methodically docketed his incoming letters, so that the problem of dating which so often bedevils Scott's later letters rarely arises. The letters reveal Scott's increasing illness and mental confusion graphically. The handwriting deteriorates rapidly, dates are given inconsistently, spelling and presentation are confused. The total effect is very moving.

Robert Cadell is the dominating personality of Scott's later years. His business acumen, however ruthless it may be thought, was the salvation of Scott's fortunes. Their business relationship developed into one of confidence and near-intimacy. These letters of 1831–2 deal with current business, including financial affairs, the progress of the Magnum Opus and the writing of *Count Robert of Paris*, Scott's health and the journey to Malta, and many other matters of biographical and bibliographical importance.

The acquisition of the fifth volume of letters led to our securing Robert Cadell's own papers as well. They form a large and apparently complete archive, including a journal of Cadell's conversations with Scott from January 1826 onwards. This is being prepared for publication by John Cameron, who is also working on a new edition of Lockhart; the discovery of the papers owes a lot to him. The Cadell papers also include thirty volumes of Robert's diary from 1824 to 1849, with much detailed information; and there are at least 1750 letters, together with the usual legal papers one would expect to find in such a family collection. The letters concern his family, his business, and the eventual settlement of his estate. As Cadell's family was closely concerned with his business activities, the whole correspondence is of great interest to the student of the history of the Scott copyrights and of the publication of the later editions. There is plenty of more obviously 'literary' correspondence, including over a hundred letters from Lockhart (Cadell published the *Life*, but some of the letters relating to its publication appear to be lost), and over four hundred from Basil Hall, which may be worth closer attention. But the most interesting general theme of the correspondence is of course the securing of the literary estate of Sir Walter Scott and the transformation of the ruined publishing business of Archibald Constable into a highly profitable enterprise.

The very day we were arranging to have the cheque drawn for the purchase of the Cadell papers, the Keeper of Manuscripts asked me into his room to look at some papers which Mr. Peter Kilpatrick (formerly of T. &. A. Constable) had brought in. He wished to present us with yet another of the volumes of Archibald Constable's incoming correspondence which he had recently discovered. The letters were from John and James Ballantyne. The coincidence was remarkable. It is the sort of discovery which quickens the pulse of scholarship. The letters cover a long period and make a notable addition to the ancillary publishing correspondence. There are over fifty letters from the two brothers, with some from John's widow, and various copy-letters from Constable to the Ballantynes. Only a few of the Ballantynes' letters are printed in that useful selection, *Archibald Constable and his Literary Correspondents*, and the new material will be very useful. The letters from James begin as early as 1801, when he was working at Kelso on Scott's *Sir Tristrem*, and they continue up to 1827. There is a certain professional confidence even in the early letters, which develops rapidly over the years. They contain much bibliographical detail—such as a discussion of the paper to be used for *Waverley*— which may be useful. John Ballantyne's letters, which run from 1809 to 1821, are much more frothy, but they are informative as well as amusing, and his wife's letters are also worth examination. Mr. Kilpatrick also presented us, with the consent of his old firm, with a volume of Constable's copies of outgoing letters between 1805 and 1807. Their Scott interest is limited, but they are a welcome addition to the series already in the Library. Incidentally, we would be glad to know the whereabouts of any stray volumes of Constable papers. There are, for example, two in the Brotherton Collection in Leeds University Library, and there may be others lying unknown in other libraries. We would be interested in trying to complete our set by means of microfilms and photocopies.

These new accessions are particularly valuable to the Library at a time when an increasing number of our visiting scholars are concerning themselves with Scott's text, either in his published works or in his letters. As I said in my *T.L.S.* article, and think I will still say later in the week when we have heard other papers in this seminar, a new or supplementary edition of Scott's correspondence may well be the most important result of our bicentenary celebrations. It is good to know that so much additional material has been acquired, and that two important runs of letters, to Constable and to Cadell, are now complete, secure and available for study in the national collection.

The Manuscripts and Proof Sheets
of Redgauntlet[1]

G. A. M. WOOD

D URING Scott's lifetime the author with whom he found himself most frequently compared, was Shakespeare. Though Scott always protested at this comparison, the scope and breadth of the Waverley Novels, with their multiplicity of well-drawn, memorable characters, or Scott's skill in creating vivid, individualizing dialogue, seemed, at least to his contemporary readers, to fully justify this linking of the two authors.

Indeed, what was known, or at least popularly believed, about their habits of composition, further validated the pairing of their names. For Shakespeare, there is Ben Jonson's famous observation, in *Discoveries*:

I remember the players have often mentioned it as an honour to Shakespeare that in his writing, whatsoever he penned, he never blotted out a line. My answer hath been 'Would he had blotted a thousand': which they thought a malevolent speech.[2]

It was similarly assumed that Scott wrote quickly and completely. Lockhart, with none of Ben Jonson's reservations, always insists on the speed and finality of Scott's prose composition. Of his many remarks to this effect in the *Life of Scott*, none is more assured than the following:

It is, I suppose, superfluous to add, that in no instance did Scott re-write his prose before sending it to the press. Whatever may have been the case with his poetry, the world uniformly received the *prima cura* of the novelist.[3]

Scott's less intimate friends were of the same opinion. When

[1] Some passages of this article have been published in my 'The Great Reviser; or the Unknown Scott', *Ariel* (University of Calgary) ii. 3 (1971), 27–43. Thanks are due to the Trustees of the National Library of Scotland, the Pierpont Morgan Library, New York, and Dr. James M. Osborn, Yale University, for permission to quote from manuscripts in their collections.
[2] Ben Jonson, *Timber* or *Discoveries*, ed. R. S. Walker (Syracuse, 1953), 52.
[3] Lockhart, *Life*, iv. 341.

Captain Basil Hall carried out his experiment to prove that it might be physically possible to produce, within three months, and using only a couple of hours each day before breakfast, manuscript to the length of a Waverley novel, he had to assume 'that Sir Walter composes his works just as fast as he can write. . . . He never corrects the press, or if he does so at all, it is very slightly—and in general his works come before the public just as they are written.'[4]

Closer investigations have shown that Lockhart grossly exaggerated. Although Scott wrote remarkably quickly, he omitted few opportunities to revise and improve, so that examination of the manuscripts and surviving proof sheets reveals many layers of rewriting between Scott's original draft and the first printed text. Miss Mary Lascelles's investigation of 'Wandering Willie's Tale' provides a beautifully detailed analysis of Scott's revising hand.[5] Consequently, from the viewpoint of the textual critic, it could seem that Shakespeare and Scott provide opposite complexities. The nature of Shakespeare's handwriting is the subject of much conjecture, for his few surviving signatures to documents, or the tantalizing fragment of *Sir Thomas More*, do little to help the textual critics' hypothesis about the nature of the copy-text behind the quarto and folio printed editions of a play. With Scott, on the other hand, there is a superabundance of autograph manuscript material, for, as Gillian Dyson reminds us, 'Scott is one of the first authors—certainly the first novelist—whose manuscripts and proof sheets have survived in any quantity.'[6] We could therefore expect that, for many of the Waverley Novels, this survival of author's manuscript, corrected proof sheets, first edition and authorially-corrected Magnum Opus edition would merely confirm the accurate transmission of the text. Collation of the text, by revealing the successive reworking and improvement of certain passages, would direct the literary critic to those places where the author wished to re-emphasize his point. An example of this reworking occurs towards the end of *Redgauntlet*, in the scene where Nanty Ewart and the traitorous Cristal Nixon fight to the death.

In the manuscript we read that Nanty 'collected his remaining strength—stood firm for an instant drew his hanger and cut

[4] *Ibid.* v. 413.
[5] Mary Lascelles, 'Scott and the Art of Revision', in *Imagined Worlds*, ed. M. Mack and I. R. Gregor (London, 1968), 139–56.
[6] Gillian Dyson, 'The Manuscripts and Proof Sheets of Scott's Waverley Novels', *Edinburgh Bibliographical Society Transactions* iv. 1 (1960), 13–42.

Cristal Nixon down'. In the proof sheets of 1824 (the first edition), the passage has been improved to read '——collected his remaining strength, stood firm for an instant, drew his hanger, and, with both hands, cut Cristal Nixon down.' Scott further modified the sentence in the 1832 Magnum Opus edition, so that the crucial passage reads 'collected his remaining strength, stood firm for an instant, drew his hanger, and fetching a stroke with both hands, cut Cristal Dixon down.'[7] The effect of this re-writing is to emphasize the last, desperate, valiant stroke of the dying man. In the novel Nanty Ewart is portrayed as a morally ambiguous character—though brave he is a smuggler, though kindly he has seduced Jess—and he is seen to be redeemed through his last heroic action.

A close examination of the available documents, manuscript and printed, reveals that Scott does indeed present problems for his editors, and that this nineteenth-century author presents complexities as involved as those which confront textual editors of Jacobean plays. There is a jostling multiplicity of variants, both substantive and accidental, and the editor is left with a baffling choice of potential copy-texts, for while there is evidence of the steady improvement of some readings, there is also ample evidence for the steady and simultaneous deterioration of other passages. The rest of this paper is devoted to discussion of this point, as related to the textual history of *Redgauntlet*. Most of the documents are still extant and the novel was written sufficiently late in Scott's career to represent his typical practice.

Redgauntlet was composed in the spring and early summer of 1824. The manuscript, complete but for two leaves, is now in the National Library of Scotland. The novel was written in Scott's normal way, on large quarto paper, with two leaves open side by side, the right-hand page for the main draft and the facing left-hand page, which was the verso of the previous right-hand page, for corrections and additions. Lockhart's insistence that 'in no instance did Scott re-write his prose before sending it to the press', can only be taken seriously if he implied that Scott did not have false starts or crossings out, and that his text was suitable for the compositor as it stood. However, the orderly appearance of the manuscript is delusive. Although the right-hand leaf text looks clean and complete at first sight, particularly when one does not

---

[7] N.L.S. Adv. MS. 19.2.29, f. 205; *Redgauntlet* (Edinburgh, 1824), iii. 284; *Redgauntlet*, Magnum edition (Edinburgh, 1832), xxxvi. 346.

attempt to decipher Scott's close, neat, illegible hand, much is in fact wanting. The left-hand leaf was habitually used for additions to the text, ranging from single words to substantial paragraphs. Evidence of different pens or inks suggests that these second thoughts were made either during or at the end of the same stint of composition, and they represent augmentations and improvements to the text, rather than corrections or crossings out. Only occasionally does the colour of ink, or the imperfect transitional wording of some passages, suggest that the revision took place at a later stage.[8]

Many of the finer details of the novel came in via the left-hand page. For example, in the scene where Darsie Latimer, kept captive in Cumberland, has his interview with Justice Foxley and his clerk interrupted by the crazed litigant Peter Peebles, this dialogue is one of Scott's second thoughts:

'The fellow must be drunk' said the Clerk. 'Black-fasting all but sin' replied the supplicant 'I have na had mair than a mouthful of cauld water since I passd the border and deils a ane of ye is like to say to me "Dog will ye drink." ' The Justice seemed moved with this appeal'.[9]

This passage reminds the reader of Peebles's earlier failings, but it also helps to add a further perspective to the novel's consideration of law, justice and charity.

At the end of each stint of writing, Scott's habit was to send his day's work off to the printer, either directly to Ballantyne's works if Scott was in Edinburgh, or else by mail from Abbotsford. The text was dispatched as it had been written, with the additional material still facing the main page. But neither page was ready for the press, as the marks of Scott's hasty composition were evident. With unimportant words left out, the punctuation and capitalization at best random, and paragraphing minimal, no compositor could have been expected to set up the text which arrived at Ballantyne's Printing Office. The copy-text of the first edition, however, was in a different shape, and a different hand, from when it left the author.

In order to help preserve the secret of Scott's authorship of the Waverley Novels, it was considered inadvisable that the text of the novels, in his well-known handwriting, should be visible to

---

[8] The footnote (MS., f. 1*v*.), printed *Redgauntlet* (1824), i. 7, is written in much blacker ink than either the right-hand page text of chapter i, or the previous left-hand page.

[9] Adv. MS. 19.2.29, f. 106.

visitors in Ballantyne's much frequented printing house. Consequently the manuscript of each novel up to 1826 or 1827 was
copied out, section by section as it became available, and the text
was set in type, not from the original manuscript, but from a copy
with very different characteristics.

Lockhart tells us that up to about 1820 John Ballantyne the
publisher had transcribed the Waverley MSS. for the press. With
the decline in John Ballantyne's health, George Huntly Gordon, a
Presbyterian minister, unplaced because of his deafness, took over
as copyist, 'in which capacity he displayed every quality that could
endear an amanuensis to an author'.[10] Unfortunately there is
evidence that Lockhart was incorrect in assuming that G. H.
Gordon was the only copyist at this time. Two letters, now in the
Osborn Collection, Yale University Library, from John and James
Ballantyne to Gordon, cast new darkness on the subject.

The first letter is dated from St. John Street, [Edinburgh], 30
December 1820.

Dear Sir / I am favd with yours: the accts. for Kenilworth are already settled
so that it is impossible any changes can be made in them; but, as a Small
proprietor of these Works, I have not the least objection to your getting
5 guineas additional for this work (as I understand is proposed by Messrs
Constable & Co) and being paid 35 for those in future: but I can assure you
the person, who copied Ivanhoe which is two sheets longer than Kenilworth,
was paid £18 & was satisfied. I am Dear Sir / Yours faithfully / *John
Ballantyne*

As *Ivanhoe* was published in 1819, this letter casts an interesting
sidelight on Lockhart's claim that James Ballantyne was the sole
transcriber prior to 1820. Because of Scott's illness, substantial
portions of *Ivanhoe* were dictated, and the extant autograph
manuscript covers just over a third of the novel.[11] If James
Ballantyne did indeed copy this section for the press, he was
therefore paid at a rate of approximately £50 for a whole novel,
or considerably more than the augmented sum of £34, grudgingly
conceded for his labours in future.

The second letter is dated from Edinburgh, 16 January 1823.

Dear Sir,
   I am now enabled to answer the letter which I received from you some
weeks since. I think it likely that copy for the new work [Scott was writing
Quentin Durward in the early months of 1823] will be sent in in a few days;
so that the sooner you can be here the better. At the same time, you need by
no means hurry yourself; as the lad, who copied Peveril, is quite expert at

[10] *Life*, vii. 100.   [11] Dyson, *op. cit.*, 28.

his task, and can easily supply your place till you find it convenient to begin. If you are here during the present month, you will be quite soon enough, or even though you should delay your journey longer. Consult, in fact, your own entire convenience.

I am, dear sir, / Very faithfully Yours, / James Ballantyne

It has been suggested that Lockhart's remarks are validated by a letter which G. H. Gordon wrote to *The Times* on 15 July 1868. This is not the case. Gordon's letter merely comments, some days after the public sale of some proof sheets, on the curious system of duplication, whereby Scott corrected one copy and James Ballantyne transformed Scott's corrections onto another. He then refers, for his competence to write on the matter, to the 75th chapter of Lockhart's *Life of Scott*. This is (in the numbering of the one-volume edition of Lockhart) the chapter which tells of Scott's sermon-writing on behalf of Gordon; the chapter which has been quoted earlier, as it records Scott's satisfaction that, as copyist Gordon 'displayed every quality that could endear an amanuensis to an author'.

The phrases 'the person who copied *Ivanhoe*' or 'the lad who copied *Peveril*' make it clear that several hands might be discerned between the author and the various first editions of the Waverley Novels. Close comparison of proof sheets with the manuscripts, and analysis of punctuation or modification of spelling, could show the particular traits of James Ballantyne, G. H. Gordon and the other copyists. Their habits are significant, for, as we have seen, Scott knew that his fictional manuscripts would be transcribed for the press, and that the copyists would attend to punctuation, layout and the like.

Although Lockhart assures us that George Huntly Gordon spent 'the autumn of 1824 [at Abbotsford] daily copying the MS. of *Redgauntlet*, and working at leisure hours on the Catalogue of the Library', his evidence, as always, is not wholly trustworthy. His chronology, in particular, is suspect, for the last batch of manuscript went to the printing office on 2 June and the novel was published the same month.[12]

As the copy-text for the first edition of *Redgauntlet* has not survived, we must deduce its characteristics from a comparison of the manuscript with the proof sheets. Both expected and unexpected changes were made. Scott's spelling was erratic, with forms (all taken from the opening leaves of the *Redgauntlet* MS.) such

[12] *Life*, vii. 101.

as 'freindship', 'stile', 'raddishes', 'tranquility', 'craggs', 'risque', or 'cobler'. These words were modernized, but not in a rigorous or systematic fashion, as traces of Scott's traditional spellings, such as 'murther', remain in the 1824 text. Capitalization was normalized, and the copyist paragraphed and punctuated the manuscript, often in an excessive manner. Quite a lot of the original was misread, or was simply not read at all, and the incapacity of the copyist, on an admittedly unenviable task, led to further complications over the correction of proof.

A complete set of the first stage of *Redgauntlet* proof sheets has been preserved, and it is now in the Pierpont Morgan Library, New York. The proof, as was customary at that time, was page rather than galley proof, and Ballantyne's compositors were accustomed to extensive re-setting and re-arrangement of type. Few pages as numbered in the proof of the Waverley Novels correspond to the page numbers of the novels as issued. Even the division of the text into volumes could be altered at will, for the opening pages of *The Heart of Mid-Lothian*, Vol. II survive in proof, numbered as the latter pages of Vol. I.

The proof was sent to the author in gatherings of eight leaves. Each gathering of *Redgauntlet*, as returned to Scott, bore James Ballantyne's invitation 'Please to read this', and was already heavily annotated. James Ballantyne was Scott's titular printer, though Scott himself had become a major partner in the firm from 1805. Ballantyne neglected both the mechanical and business aspects of the printing enterprise, a neglect which was to be of major consequence in the firm's financial collapse in 1826. The chief and devoted occupation of Ballantyne's hours was the correction of Scott's proof sheets.[13]

Some of Ballantyne's notes on the proof were designed to guide Scott to blatant errors. A large X was inserted in the margin where a misreading seemed obvious, or where the failure of the copyist to read the original resulted in a blank space being left in the proof. Ballantyne further tidied up the punctuation and strove to ease Scott's labour in various ways.

As the proofs remained private matter between printer and author, James Ballantyne grew into the habit of entering into correspondence with Scott on the margins. This record of query and answer makes fascinating reading, for Ballantyne did not restrain himself to questions of fact, but voiced opinions as to the

[13] *Life*, vi. 111.

Plates

*The publication of these illustrations
has been generously financed by the
Carnegie Trust for the Universities of Scotland*

1. Eugène Delacroix. *Lucy Ashton's Bridal Night* (*Bride of Lammermoor*, ch. xxiii), pencil; Paris, Claude Roger-Marx Coll.

2. Eugène Delacroix. *Amy Robsart, Costume Design for Victor Hugo's 'Amy Robsart'*, watercolour; Paris, Maison de Victor Hugo.

3. Eugène Delacroix. *Queen Elizabeth, Costume Design for Victor Hugo's 'Amy Robsart'*, watercolour; Paris, Louvre (RF 10010). Cliché des Musées Nationaux.

4. Richard Bonington. *The 'Buckhurst' Armour*, pencil; London, British Museum (1857-2-28-158).

5. Eugène Delacroix. *The 'Buckhurst' Armour and Other Studies*, pencil; London, Library of the Wallace Collection (WCM 43.B).

6. Richard Bonington. *Amy Robsart and the Earl of Leicester* (?), oil; Oxford, Ashmolean Museum.

7. Eugène Delacroix. *Lord Shrewsbury, Costume Design for Victor Hugo's*
'Amy Robsart', watercolour; Paris, Maison de Victor Hugo.

8. Eugène Delacroix. *William de la Marck, called the Wild Boar of the Ardennes* (or the *Murder of the Bishop of Liège*) (*Quentin Durward*, ch. XXII), oil; Paris, Louvre (RF 196113). Cliché des Musées Nationaux.

9. Richard Bonington. *Vaulting of Westminster Hall*, pencil; Edinburgh, National Gallery of Scotland (3598).

10. Eugène Delacroix. *Cromwell at Windsor* (*Woodstock*, ch. VIII), oil;
U.S.A., private collection.

11. Eugène Delacroix. *Front-de-Bœuf and the Sorceress Ulrica* (*Ivanhoe*, ch. xxx), lithograph; Paris, Bibliothèque Nationale.

12. Eugène Delacroix. *Ravenswood and Lucy at the Mermaidens' Fountain* (*Bride of Lammermoor*, ch. XIX), brown and black inks heightened with white; Detroit, Institute of Arts (31.339).

13. Eugène Delacroix. *Self-Portrait as Ravenswood* (?), oil; Paris, Louvre (RF 195338, Société des Amis d'Eugène Delacroix). Cliché des Musées Nationaux.

14. Eugène Delacroix. *Abduction of Rebecca by Bois-Guilbert* (*Ivanhoe*, ch. XXXI), oil; Paris, Louvre (RF 1392). Cliché des Musées Nationaux.

merit of various passages, the credibility of the characters, or the ways the novel might be written.

Much of Ballantyne's work was helpful, for Scott was notoriously careless over small details. He forgot how the names of various characters should be spelt, or even what they were, and Ballantyne's notes prompted him to make up his mind. The name of Nanty Ewart, for example, is variously spelled as Ewart and Ewald. Ballantyne notes on the proof 'I fancy the name is Ewald, as it began with that?' Scott's reply reads 'Ewart is finally adopted'.[14] Similarly, Ballantyne prompted Scott to be consistent with his terminology, as to whether characters address each other as 'thou' or 'you', and to remember what had already transpired in the story. An example of this latter occurs in the final pages of the novel, where, as footnote to 'Half way betwixt the house and the beach, they saw the bodies of Nanty Ewart and Cristal Nixon blackening in the sun.', Ballantyne remembered that, on an earlier page, the bodies were said to have been discovered by stragglers and carried to the house. His note prompted Scott to delete the earlier detail, so that the discovery could take place, out of doors, and before the more important characters of the novel's final scene.[15]

At times, Ballantyne betrays an endearing curiosity, as when Darsie Latimer's wanderings through Cumberland with his uncle, prompt him to enquire into the geography of the area. To Redgauntlet's 'Look eastward—do you see a monument standing on yonder plain, near a hamlet?' Ballantyne pleaded, 'Is there (for I do not know, and am curious,) is there such a monument?' Scott answered 'Yes, at Brough upon Sands'; and was then prompted to consider his readers' curiosity, for the next paragraph of text has been altered to begin 'The hamlet is Burgh-upon-Sands . . . .'.[16] Scott's ability to spell the same name, on the same page, in two different ways is worth remarking.

Scott's willingness to respond to Ballantyne's promptings becomes less praiseworthy when Ballantyne expressed anxiety over issues which are not usually the concern of a corrector of proof. Various sections were deleted in proof, because Ballantyne objected to them. Darsie Latimer's description of the Quaker Geddes's house was deprived of a lengthy passage, because Ballantyne thought it too reminiscent of a section from the Introduction to *Quentin Durward*.[17] Ballantyne also objected to a conversation

[14] *Redgauntlet*, page proof, ii. 315.   [15] *Ibid*. iii. 307, 320.
[16] *Ibid*. iii. 169.   [17] *Ibid*. i. 154.

between Darsie Latimer and the Quaker's wife, over the cruelty of killing domestic fowl, and this, too, was excised in proof.

James Ballantyne prided himself on being something of a man of taste, but his notes demonstrate that he was much less of a literary than a literal critic. Nanty Ewart's compelling autobiography relates how, when he returned to Edinburgh to learn of the evils he had done, and the consequences of his misconduct he '. . . ran downstairs, expecting, or fearing, to meet Jess at every turning'. The printer's prim note reminded the author 'But Jess had been transported'. Scott retorted that Ewart's expectation was in his mind, 'Yes he did not expect her in reality'. Even so, Ballantyne's obtuseness here was taken as a hint for textual revision, this time against the clarity and conciseness of the original manuscript, so that the printed version finally reads '. . . ran down stairs, in such confusion of mind, that notwithstanding what I had heard, I expected to meet Jess at every turning.'[18]

Virtually all of Ballantyne's hints were noted. Passages were expanded at his directive, motivations became clearer, and large chunks of expository narrative were added to command. But there were limits beyond which even Scott could not be pushed, and he refused to accept his printer's attempts at a moral censorship. An example of this occurs in the scene where, after Alan Fairford has unexpectedly rushed from Court, followed by his father, the comment is made '"What's the matter with the auld b—— next?" said an acute metaphysical judge, aside to his brethren.' 'b——' was too strong for Ballantyne, who pleaded 'b—— looks equivocal, though, used by you, it cannot be thought to be so. But such odious words occur in police-reports now-a-days, that I think delicacy itself requires b——h.' Scott was less concerned with delicacy than with effect; in the printed text there is no doubt what the 'acute metaphysical judge' intended, for the word is printed in full as 'bitch'.[19]

Sometimes Scott finally lost patience with his worthy printer. During the conversation between Nanty Ewart and Alan Fairford, Ewart demonstrates his learning by reading from Sallust. The few lines of Latin threw Ballantyne into a frenzy of dismay. 'I entreat particular attention to this Latin, which, being almost illegible in the MS. and printed by an ignorant compositor, can hardly fail to be incorrect.' Scott's reply was unforgiving: 'And why has not

---

[18] *Redgauntlet*, page proof, iii. 14, and *Redgauntlet* (1824), iii. 14.
[19] *Redgauntlet*, page proof, ii. 29, and (1824), ii. 30.

such an establishment a corrector who can read a few lines of
Latin——'20

As has been shown, Scott made many changes in the novel at the
suggestion of his printer. The majority of his additions, however,
were spontaneous. Proof-reading for Scott was a creative process,
as he read proof not against the manuscript but from memory, and
so allowed his mind to embellish rather than collate. Because Scott
read proof from memory, it sometimes happened that he unwit-
tingly made changes away from his original intentions, so that the
manuscript and the first edition present rival readings, each sanc-
tioned by the author. An example of this occurs at the opening of the
novel. The manuscript has Darsie Latimer writing to Alan Fairford,
wishing that his friend were with him 'in the same comfortable
Greyhound Inn'. The transcriber obviously botched this passage,
for the proof has a despairing 'in the same comfortable greyhound
        sun', the blank indicating an obvious misreading before
the conjectured 'sun'. The sense of the passage was direct enough,
'Inn' was the obvious word, but Scott had forgotten his original
name for the hostelry, and in the first and all subsequent editions,
Darsie Latimer resides 'In the same comfortable George-Inn'.21

After Scott had finished with each section of proof, it was
returned to Ballantyne, who copied out the changes to be made in
the text onto another set of proof, which then went to the compositor. A second stage of proof, the 'revise', was then annotated
by Ballantyne and further corrected by Scott. The few revise
sheets which have survived, such as those of *The Talisman*, show
that Ballantyne was prone to fundamental doubts about characters
and incidents at this late hour.22 No revise sheets are extant for
Redgauntlet,23 but collation of the first edition with the extant
corrected proof sheets makes it clear that Scott went over his text
for a second time. A number of changes, such as tidying up the
first chapter spelling, in manuscript and proof, of 'Fairburn' to
'Fairford' in the first edition, could have been made by Ballantyne,
and in the absence of the visual evidence of the revise sheets, no
one can tell how many alterations Ballantyne finally made to
'improve' Scott's text. The more important substantive variants.
however, have the ring of Scott's style, as when the phrase 'The

---

20 *Redgauntlet*, page proof, ii. 323.   21 *Ibid*. i. 4.
22 *Tales of the Crusaders*, page proof, iv, gatherings M, N, and Q.
23 Dyson, *op. cit.* 34, records a second set of proof sheets, 'corrected by Ballantyne
alone', which has not been traced subsequent to 1945. These sheets are probably
Ballantyne's set of the first proofs rather than the revise.

strange and improbable idea' becomes 'The faint, yet not improbable belief'.[24] There are several hundred of these substantive improvements. *Redgauntlet* was issued, in three volumes, in June 1824.

The novel was included in two collections of *Tales and Romances of The Author of Waverley*, [*St. Ronan's Well* to *Woodstock*] issued in 1827, in seven volumes octavo, or nine volumes duodecimo. These two editions reprint the 1824 text, but a very considerable amount of rearrangement took place. Names of places and personages were regularized, and attention was devoted to polishing the text, particularly in the many places where Scott had repeated words or phrases in the same sentence. A fuller discussion of the 1827 changes will appear in a forthcoming issue of *The Bibliotheck*. Although, by normal standards, the number of substantive changes made in 1827 is considerable, it seems small when compared to the major revision which the text of *Redgauntlet* was to undergo for the edition of 1832.

The Collected Edition of the Waverley Novels, referred to by Scott as his '*Magnum Opus*', was projected in early 1828 as 'an uniform reprint of the Novels, each to be introduced by an account of the hints on which it had been founded, and illustrated throughout by historical and antiquarian annotations'.[25] There are numerous references in Scott's *Journal* to his working on the notes, or reading the proof of the *Magnum Opus*, and the first volume was published in June 1829. Scott was at work on *Redgauntlet* during February 1831 and the novel was published as Volumes 35 and 36 of the *Magnum Opus* Collected Edition in April and May 1832.

At first sight the additional material seems to be conspicuous and separate. Scott contributed a relatively brief historical introduction to the novel and wrote a number of footnotes, sometimes of an autobiographical nature, together with informative material of an antiquarian kind, printed at the end of certain chapters. Consequently, the 1832 text of *Redgauntlet* served as the copy text for all reprints up to 1871, when it was superseded by the Centenary Edition, published by A. & C. Black of Edinburgh and later by A. & C. Black's Dryburgh Edition of 1892–4. The 1871 edition was based on Scott's interleaved octavo copy which he used in the preparation of the *Magnum Opus*, and from it the publishers obtained, for all the novels, 'several annotations of

---

[24] *Redgauntlet*, page proof, i. 12, and (1824), i. 13.
[25] *Life*, vii. 97.

considerable interest, never before published'.[26] The Centenary Edition restores to *Redgauntlet* one or two lines of text which were inadvertently omitted in 1832 and corrects some obvious errors, such as the misnumbering of a chapter, which the *Magnum Opus* had repeated from the 1824 first edition and the 1827 octavo edition.

The *Magnum Opus* edition offers more than a mere annotated reprint. In some respects its text of the Waverley Novels is the fullest and most complete; in other respects it offers an inaccurate and distorted reprint, reflecting a high degree of editorial interference and the inability, some years previously, of the copyist for the first edition of 1824 to make complete sense of the original manuscript.

Scott's 'Advertisement' to the first volume of his *Magnum Opus*, dated January 1829, promised that attention had been given to the text. The passage is worth reprinting in full.

But without altering, in the slightest degree, either the story or the mode of telling it, the Author has taken this opportunity to correct errors of the press and slips of the pen. That such should exist cannot be wondered at, when it is considered that the Publishers found it their interest to hurry through the press a succession of the early editions of the various Novels, and that the Author had not the usual opportunity of revision.[27] It is hoped that the present edition will be found free from errors of that accidental kind.

The Author has also ventured to make some emendations of a different character, which, without being such apparent deviations from the original stories as to distort the reader's old associations, will, he thinks, add something to the spirit of the dialogue, narrative, or description. These consist in occasional pruning where the language is redundant, compression where the style is loose, infusion of vigour where it is languid, the exchange of less forcible for more appropriate epithets—slight alterations in short, like the last touches of an Artist, which contribute to heighten and finish the picture, though an inexperienced eye can hardly detect in what they consist.[28]

It is possible to conjecture how Scott might have approached his task of revision. His eye would skip across the page, looking for some fact or reference to annotate, till it would light on an infelicitous word or phrase. A slight change might lead to a greater one, so that the whole passage would emerge substantially different and augmented. Many pages of the novel underwent

---

[26] Advertisement to the Centenary Edition (Edinburgh, 1871), page i. The 'interleaved copy' was offered for sale from the United States in 1939 and its whereabouts has since been the subject of much conjecture.

[27] The use of 'revision' is curious. Scott perhaps implies only 'final correction', perhaps he is deliberately perpetuating the myth that he never rewrote his works.

[28] *Waverley* (Magnum ed., 1829), i. pp. ii–iii.

substantial alteration between the 1824 and 1832 editions. The commonest reason for tidying up was to avoid the repetition of words, either in the same sentence, or in the same passage of text. A good example occurs when after Alan Fairford's precipitate departure, Mr. Counsellor Tough resumes his legal obfuscations, 'and succeeded in restoring the veil of obscurity and unintelligibility which had for *many years obscured the case* of Peebles against Plainstanes'. In the 1832 text, the underlined passage becomes 'many years darkened the case'.[29] This revision presents a vastly superior reading, for, with the word 'darkened', Scott not only avoids repetition, but also suggests that the lawsuit and its conduct is, despite all the wry humour, a moral abomination.

Other changes were made to strengthen the impact of a phrase, while some represent major revisions. For example, in the scene where Saunders Fairford receives a letter from Provost Crosbie about the suspected danger to Darsie Latimer, the first edition account is as follows:

Mr Fairford . . . would certainly have set out himself, or licensed his son to go in pursuit of his friend. But the case of Poor Peter Peebles, against Plainstanes was, he saw, adjourned, perhaps *sine die*, should the document reach the hands of his son.[30]

After the first sentence quoted, the 1832 edition has this addition. 'But, alas! he was both a father and an agent. In the one capacity, he looked on his son as dearer to him than all the world besides; in the other, the lawsuit which he conducted was to him like an infant to its nurse, and the case of Poor Peter Peebles. . . .' Scott's revision here is skilfully carried out. He has added the passage to the beginning of an already existing sentence, and the addition makes Saunders Fairford into a more sympathetic person, one who, like many other characters in the novel, has to contend with a clash of loyalties.

It is sometimes possible to trace Scott's revising hand through three phases of the text. Passages which were altered in the proof sheets of the first edition were themselves further changed for the *Magnum Opus*. Such an instance occurs in the scene where Darsie Latimer is disguised as a woman, in order to travel without detection. His accoutrements include a mask, of the kind which might enable a lady 'to play off a little coquetry'. The manuscript con-

---

[29] *Redgauntlet* (1824), ii. 48, and (1832), xxxv. 276.
[30] *Ibid.* (1824), ii. 35, and (1832), xxxv. 266.

tinues 'From this however I expect I shall be precluded'. In the first edition the sentence is made clearer: 'From the use of the mask, however, I suspect I shall be precluded', while the *Magnum Opus* rephrases the sentence to begin 'From the gayer mode of employing the mask, however I . . .'[31]

As with the first edition, it is clear that many of the details of the text in the *Magnum Opus* were not exclusively Scott's concern. The two editions have different conventions of accidentals; commas become semi-colons and vice versa, there is an even heavier punctuation of narrative or description, and passages of reported dialogue, which often remained unpointed in the first edition, so preserving some of the characteristics of the manuscript, are uniformly fully punctuated in the *Magnum Opus*. This edition completed the task of normalizing the spelling of characters' names, so that the variants of Chrystal and Cristal Nixon, or Father Crackenthorpe or Crackenthorp are reduced to a standard. Similarly, there is tidying up of sections where the first edition reproduces the errors of the manuscript, as when, in the final scene, the phrase 'Darsie, his sister, and Redgauntlet' is corrected to 'Darsie, his sister and Fairford'.[32] There are occasions when the two editions normalize the inconsistent spelling of the manuscript in different ways. Scott happily used both 'Stuart' and 'Stewart', the first is utilized throughout in 1824, the latter in 1832.

One kind of change seems to be inexplicable. Scott had no qualms about using the word 'Scotch'. It appears throughout the *Redgauntlet* manuscript and is so printed in the first edition. In the *Magnum Opus*, however, the word is invariably modified, to 'Scottish', even when Nanty Ewart is made to decry 'that nasty Scottish stuff that . . . Turnpenny has brought into fashion', or the spirit now universally known as Scotch whisky![33]

Equally strange is the variation between the two editions in the use of Scotticisms. There seems to be no coherent pattern. A lot of the Scotticisms in the manuscript are anglicized in the first edition and a number of the Scotticisms of the first edition have been anglicized in the *Magnum Opus*. Yet many Scotticisms have been restored to the *Magnum Opus*, and new ones added, some in the course of substantive revision, but some, seemingly, by chance or caprice. In the original printing of 'Wandering Willie's Tale',

---

[31] *Ibid.* (1824), ii. 207, and (1832), xxxvi. 56.
[32] *Ibid.* (1824), iii. 311, and (1832), xxxvi. 365.
[33] *Ibid.* (1824), iii. 33, and (1832), xxxvi. 166.

we are told that Laurie Lapraik 'liked an orra sound and a tune on the pipes'. In the *Magnum Opus*, this becomes 'liked an orra sough of this warld and a tune on the pipes'.[34] The addition reminds us of the difference between Lapraik's religious pretences and his worldly pleasures, and the spelling of the phrase, 'orra sough' [occasional sound] has been altered into keeping with the broad vernacular of Willie's narration. However, in the same story, the later edition changes 'deevil' to 'devil' or 'wad' to 'would', at the same time as it is substituting 'semple' for 'simple' or 'saunts' for 'saints'. It seems more likely that many of these latter changes represent editorial or compositorial caprice, rather than the painstaking emendations of the author. No theory of consistency in revision can explain a further example from 'Wandering Willie's Tale', when 'his friends, for the credit of his gude name', in 1824, is altered to the 'his freends, for the credit of his good name' of the *Magnum Opus*.[35]

A few of the changes in the *Magnum Opus* are not easy to justify, for they seem to reflect a more prudish public opinion. 'Damned' as an expletive becomes 'd——d', and when Darsie Latimer, in his first letter, tells of how he was 'mocked for my English accent—salted with snow as a Southern', the phrase has none of the schoolboy ruggedness of the original, to be found in both manuscript and first edition: '—mocked for my English accent—salted with snow as an English pig—'[36]

Indeed, some of the changes remind us that the first printed edition of *Redgauntlet* made inadequate sense of Scott's manuscript, and the 1832 revisions sometimes take us still further away from the author's original intentions. In the passage, as printed in proof and in the first edition, dealing with Saunders Fairford's legal assistance to his son over the case of Peter Peebles, we read 'Neither did he leave him alone to his own unassisted energies'. This sentence is obviously tautologous, and was amended in the *Magnum Opus* to read 'Neither did he leave him to his own unassisted energies'.[37] It is only when we refer back to the manuscript that we discover the original to be 'Neither did he he leave Alan to his own unassisted energies'. Either the repeated 'he', or confusion over 'Alan' led the transcriber into error, though not into nonsense. Subsequently the mistaken reading has been revised,

---

[34] *Redgauntlet*, (1824), i. 230, and (1832), xxxv. 171.
[35] *Ibid.* (1824), i. 261, and (1832), xxxv. 194.
[36] *Ibid.* (1824), i. 6.
[37] *Ibid.* (1824), ii. 12, and (1832), xxxv. 249.

by the author himself, in a direction away from his own original intentions.

This discussion of *Redgauntlet* shows that the textual history of the novel is not simple. Scott, far from abandoning his text after a first draft, made up for the initial haste of composition by extensive revision during the printing of the first edition, and was eager to further amend the text after the interval of several years. Consequently, any editor of *Redgauntlet* has no shortage of variants, both accidental and substantive. The *Magnum Opus* of 1832 represents the most complete text available within Scott's lifetime, but it is a reprint, itself based on an inaccurate version; so that some of the changes representing Scott's last intentions were made merely to cover up the inaccuracies of a first edition which never fully printed Scott's original text.

Deceptions in the Works of Scott;
or, Lying Title-pages

WILLIAM RUFF

AFTER reading too many books about Thomas J. Wise, the forger of nineteenth-century pamphlets, I begin to wonder whether there are similar deceptions among the publications of Walter Scott. However, collectors of Scott's rare editions need not worry about buying faked pamphlets. There is no trace, so far, of a Thomas J. Wise muddling this field. And yet there are a curious number of deceptions which appeared in the wake of Scott's success. Let me look at some bibliographical ghosts, American and French piracies of his works, 'spurious' title-pages, lying dates and the like.

My paper is about forgers, pirates, counterfeiters, and fakers, and concerns anyone who used crooked means to benefit by Scott's reputation. Since I have found my best material in questionable title-pages, I shall be interested in any title-page relating to Scott which is ambiguous, or a direct lie, or conceals something of its publishing history, or is a forgery. I am most interested in knowing what harm these lying title-pages did to Scott's reputation and his fortune.

Conventional title-pages are designed to give information about the name of the author, the title of his work, the name of the publisher kind enough to print him, and the date and place of publication. Scott's title-pages, however, are not always conventional. For one thing, he did not particularly like to see his name on a title-page. For example, when he allowed some of his sermons to be published for the benefit of a one-time secretary, George Huntly Gordon, Scott wrote: 'I have given Gordon leave to make a Kirk and a Mill of his sermons [i.e. do what he pleases with them] so he does not blazon my name in front of them'.[1]

If a work of fiction published before 1832 appears with the

[1] Scott, *Letters*, x. 357.

name of Walter Scott on the title-page, the book is probably a piracy. Scott's rules about putting his name on a title-page are these: his name was to appear on works of poetry, except for *The Bridal of Triermain*, 1813, and *Harold the Dauntless*, 1817. These two appeared anonymously, because Scott was testing his popularity with the public. (Were his verses sufficiently good to sell without the advantage of his name?) His name was not to appear on the title-pages of books to which he had made only a slight contribution; it was not to appear on the title-pages of annuals, or gift books, or anthologies like *English Minstrelsy*, 1810, which he edited himself. It was not to appear on works of fiction, except as 'By the Author of "Waverley"', nor on prose works like *Tales of a Grandfather*. It usually did not appear on title-pages of musical selections, though there are two exceptions: his name was on the title-page of *Albyn's Anthology*, 1816–1818, and on Thomson's *Select Melodies*, first issue, 1822, but it disappeared from the second issue, apparently at Scott's request.

As one knows, Scott rarely loses his temper when writing letters, and when he does become angry it is often because someone else has put Scott's name on his own work in order to make money. One example is enough: Scott wrote about Edward Burt's *Letters from a Gentleman in the North of Scotland*, new edition, 1818, ' . . these gentlemen [Gale and Fenner, the publishers] clapt my name upon the title page of a book of which I never read a page or wrote a line. . . . I consider myself as very unhandsomely treated, and insist upon the title being cancelled. It is a trick equally unworthy of gentlemen or honest tradesmen. . . .'[2] The original title-page, one is glad to know, was cancelled.

One may blame Thomas J. Wise, who created so many lying title-pages, for being dishonest, but no one can say that his forgeries were easily done. Imagine the work which went into eached forged title-page, the difficulty of finding the right piece to print, the care with which he had to hire printers and look after the distribution of copies, so that not too many appeared on the market at once; and how he worked to give the proper provenance to his fakes. How much simpler it would have been to create a book out of his imagination, that is, to create a ghost of a book. In 1968 Mr. John Carter wrote an entertaining note on 'Ghosts'

[2] *Ibid.* v. 274–5.

in which he defined a ghost (bibliographically speaking) as 'a non-existent book or edition or issue erroneously included in some book of reference which by repetition has achieved a misleading semblance of reality'.[3] At the end of his article he offered a complimentary copy of his *ABC for Book-Collectors* for 'the best of the first six examples contributed by readers of a full-blooded ghost *book*'.

I wish I had seen his article when it first came out, because I could have sent him a list of five ghost books, all by Scott, all supposedly printed by Ballantyne at Kelso in 1799, and all nonexistent. These ghosts are to be found in '*The Bibliography of Sir Walter Scott, Bart.*, by Albert Caplan, Bibliographical Society of America: The Head of Scott Press, 1530 Locust Street, Philadelphia, Pa., U. S. A.' This book lists the works of Scott in chronological order, and in its first eight items describes five books which never existed (so far as I know): *The Eve of Saint John*, Kelso 1799 (though there *is* a Kelso edition dated 1800); *Ballad of Glenfinlas*, Kelso 1799; *The House of Aspen*, Kelso 1799; *The Grey Brother*, Kelso 1799; and *The Fire King*, also Kelso 1799, said to be 'Limited to 12 copies, in pamphlet form'. I recommend this bibliography to all collectors of Scott not as a work of science, but of imagination.

I think I know how Mr. Caplan made up his non-existent titles. He probably read a letter from Monk Lewis to Scott, dated 6 January 1799, which begins: 'Your last Ballad reached me just as I was stepping into my chaise to go to Brocket Hall (Lord Melbourne's) so I took it with me, and exhibited both that, and *Glenfinlas* with great success.'[4] Mr. Caplan evidently thought these two ballads were in printed form, and failed to remember that Scott was in the habit of circulating his verse in the form of manuscripts. This may explain the errors in Mr. Caplan's first few items, but it does not excuse his mistakes in spelling (*Ettriche* for *Ettricke*, or *Hoggs* for *Hogg*, or his reference to 'Sir Ballantyne'). The book is amateurish; one would think it the work of a boy interested in book-collecting, if it were not for its sumptuous printing, thick paper, wide margins, with each of its 150 copies numbered and signed. But I discovered the cause of Mr. Caplan's mistakes when I found out that he was only nineteen when he published this. He

---

[3] *The Book Collector* xvii (1966), 492–3.
[4] N.L.S., MS. 3874, f. 34; printed in *The Autobiography of Sir Walter Scott* (Philadelphia, 1831), 183.

had no intention to deceive, or to make money (though each copy cost fifteen dollars). He only wanted to share in the wonderful game of book-collecting and bibliography, and to become, like Scott, the author of a book.

Mr. Caplan's work appears in Dr. James C. Corson's fine *Bibliography of Scott*, 1943, as Item No. 3, but seems to have disappeared from Dr. Corson's bibliography published in the latest edition of the *Cambridge Bibliography of English Literature*, 1969. It is a pity for such a fantastic work as that of Mr. Caplan's to become a ghost itself.

I think Mr. Caplan may have found his reference to Monk Lewis in a deception with the title, '*Autobiography of Sir Walter Scott, Bart.* Philadelphia: Carey & Lea, Chestnut Street, 1831'. I call this book a deception because Scott did not authorize such a collection of his autobiographical writings; he received no money for it; it is just an attempt by Philadelphia pirates to make something valuable out of scraps of Scott's writing. The books pirated in Philadelphia such as the *Autobiography* are not ghosts in the sense used by Mr. Carter, yet there is something spectral about them. Scott was not responsible for them yet every word (except for their title-pages) was written by Scott. All the pirates did was to assemble fragments written by Scott, and wrap around them a new title-page. The result was a saleable book. In so doing they might seem to be anticipating Wise whose favourite trick was to take a single piece from a magazine and reprint it with a date previous to its first appearance in book form.

In addition to piracies like the *Autobiography* the Philadelphia pirates also reprinted most of Scott's poetry and fiction with little or no pay for the author. These pirated editions furnish fine material for a study of Scott's text. The essential article on this subject is David A. Randall's which he published in *The New Colophon*.[5] When he found out that Carey and Lea of Philadelphia bought proofs of the Waverley Novels from workmen in Edinburgh, he compared the texts of first editions as printed in Edinburgh with first editions as printed in Philadelphia. In so doing he discovered the first state of many leaves later cancelled. But— he began his investigations with the novels printed in 1822, not those first printed in 1814. What of the novels printed before

[5] 'Waverley in America', *Colophon*, new series, i (1935), 39–55.

1822? Many were sold in early proof sheets to American book-sellers, or literary agents, and must have interesting leaves-to-be-cancelled.

The Philadelphia firm of Carey and Co., later H. C. Carey and I. Lea, had a stock answer when an English author complained of piracy: 'But see how quickly we reprint your books, and at what low cost'. And they did reprint a book quickly, sometimes over a weekend. When they reprinted *The Fortunes of Nigel* they beat the market by using nine printing houses.[6] There was no question with them of morality or of just payment to an author, only of speed in printing. Charles Dickens heard similar answers when he complained, on trips to America, about the piracies of his books. The answer from publishers which made him furious, just as it had irritated other English authors, was that, 'In the absence of an international copyright, it has always been held that the house which purchased the advance-sheets from an English author had the equitable right to the exclusive use of his works in the United States'.[7] These advance sheets need not have come directly from an author; they might have come from a go-between, and the price might have been ridiculously low (only twenty-five pounds in some cases). It was also the custom in Philadelphia and other American cities to print from plates, and to reprint from them until the print was unreadable. This practice meant that authors were paid, not by the number of editions, but by the total number of possible impressions. So even if Scott or Dickens were paid a small sum for the American rights to a novel, there was only one payment though the books might be reprinted till their stereotype plates fell to pieces.

For full details of piracies after 1820 see David Kasner's excellent study of *Messrs. Carey & Lea of Philadelphia*, and for later publishing practices 'The Dickens Controversy' included as an advertisement in R. Shelton Mackenzie's *Life of Charles Dickens*, Philadelphia, 1870. Mr. Kasner insists that Carey & Lea were not pirates, because they paid an agent in London to send them early copies of the Waverley Novels, and also paid a book-seller in Philadelphia named Thomas Wardle for advance sheets. (He had procured them from Hurst, Robinson and Co., Constable's London agents.)[8] The crooked argument is that since Carey & Lea

[6] David Kasner, *Messrs. Carey & Lea of Philadelphia* (Philadelphia, 1957), 100.
[7] Letter from T. B. Peterson & Bros., Philadelphia, 25 May 1867, in R. Shelton Mackenzie, *Life of Charles Dickens* (Philadelphia, 1870), Supplement, 'The Dickens Controversy', 4.　　　[8] Kasner, p. 95.

had paid someone, if not the author, for advance sheets, then these publishers when they grew rich at the expense of Dickens and Scott were only exercising what they called the 'usages of the trade'.

These unmoral practices of American publishers infected American authors as well. Even James Fenimore Cooper, in Paris in 1826, while trying to help Scott get money for his American publications, proposed a mode of publishing in America by entering Scott's books as the property of a citizen. Scott writes in his *Journal*, 'I will think of this. Every little helps . . .'[9] Scott must have been desperate for money to have considered this trick even for a second, or perhaps he was just irritated with pirates in general, and particularly with the 'old pirate Galignani' whom he had visited five days before the conversation with Cooper.[10] On 6 November Galignani did offer Scott £105 for the 'transmission of Napoleon to be reprinted at Paris in English'.[11] But this payment was an exception to Galignani's usual rule.

If one saw this title in a bookshop, it should be easy to know that it was not authorized by Scott: '*Lives of the Novelists*, by Sir Walter Scott, 2 volumes. Paris, published by A. and W. Galignani, at the English, French, Italian, German, and Spanish Library, 18 Rue Vivienne, 1825.' The first hint that this title was not authorized is its place of publication, Paris (English books could not be copyrighted in France). Secondly, the firm of Galignani, though respected in Paris today, with its fine shop in the Rue de Rivoli, was known in Scott's time for its habit of publishing British titles without pay for British authors. Thirdly, the work is something synthetic, for it is made up of prefaces to *Ballantyne's Novelists Library*, 10 volumes, 1821–1824, and manufactured according to its preface just to save its customers cash. Lastly, one could recognize this title-page as a cheat, because it bears the name of 'Sir Walter Scott'. As I have said, he did not use his name freely on works of prose.

When Scott referred to Galignani as 'that old pirate' he meant that Galignani (or the Galignani brothers as they were better known) had paid him nothing for his poems, and would not pay him anything for *The Life of Napoleon* unless he complained in

---

[9] *Journal*, 3 November 1826.   [10] *Ibid*. 30 October 1826.
[11] *Ibid*. 6 November 1826.

person. To all complaints the Galignani brothers gave an answer (used in their advertisements) much like that of the Philadelphia pirates: 'New Publications at One Third of the London Prices.' It is not an answer to console an author, but a familiar one in the world of bookselling.

If one looks over the books in English published by Galignani, and those published by Carey and Lea in Philadelphia, one will notice curious similarities. For instance, the edition of *The Poetical Works of Coleridge, Shelley and Keats*, as printed in Paris in 1829, and that printed in Philadelphia in 1831, are almost identical. The reason is simple: the American pirates copied the French pirates. One link between the Philadelphia and Paris pirates is Washington Irving. He was, of course, a most respectable man of letters, but one with an itch to be a business man. In 1825 he had the job of negotiating with the Galignanis on behalf of John Murray of London, and while in Paris, had at least two dinners at the Galignanis', where Matthew Carey, the pirate from Philadelphia, and Irving's American publisher, was a fellow-guest.[12] Though the negotiations between Murray and Galignani fell through, the friendship between French and American pirates lasted. No wonder, for Galignani and Carey had much in common, particularly an interest in quick ways of making money by pirating the works of respectable firms.

Where book-collectors in the time of Thomas J. Wise wanted excessively rare pamphlets, those in America and France during Scott's lifetime wanted books hot from the press, and cheaply printed. Therefore Galignani and Carey catered to this taste, and did a fine job. If Carey could not find a new long poem by Scott to reprint he would take a poem from *The Edinburgh Annual Register*, 1813, and create a whole new book which he called *The Dance of Death, and Other Poems*, 1816. Is not this what Thomas J. Wise did for the work of his own countrymen?

If you want to see fraudulent title-pages in the publications of Scott look at *A Bibliography of the Waverley Novels* by Greville Worthington, London, 1931. He has three illustrations of what he calls 'spurious title-pages', meaning counterfeit title-pages made solely to fool book-collectors. These are the title-pages of

[12] Washington Irving, *Journals*, ed. William P. Trent and George S. Hellman (Boston, 1919), ii. 144.

Tales of My Landlord, first series, 1816, *The Abbot*, 1820, and *Kenilworth*, 1821. In each case, according to Worthington, the 'genuine' title-page lists more publishers than the 'spurious'. Worthington's bibliography is good, though I wish he would tell us where he found these 'spurious' title-pages. I also wish he had been more interested in the history of publishing, because a knowledge of Ballantyne's publications might help to explain these fraudulent leaves.

One 'spurious' leaf is that of *The Abbot* where the 'genuine' title-page, in Worthington's illustration, has: 'Printed for Longman, Hurst, Rees, Orme, and Brown, London; And for Archibald Constable and Company, And John Ballantyne, Edinburgh. 1820.' And the 'spurious' has: 'Printed for Archibald Constable and Co. Edinburgh; And Hurst, Robinson, and Co. London. 1820.' A simple explanation for the difference in the list of publishers is that Constable and Co. switched its London agency from Longman to Hurst, Robinson in late 1820, and in so doing reprinted some of their title-pages to accord with the change in agents. So this 'spurious' title-page is probably the second issue of a first edition title-page, and therefore as truly from the workshop of Constable and Ballantyne as the first.

I also suggest that the 'spurious' title-page for *Kenilworth*, 1821, which omits the name of John Ballantyne, is a second issue of a genuine first edition title-page made after the death of John Ballantyne in June 1821. Hence, it is not spurious.

The third 'spurious' title-page illustrated in Worthington's bibliography is that of *Tales of My Landlord*, first series, 1816. Worthington says of it, 'I have examined a copy with "Constable" title-pages, and one of them is watermarked 1825, while the sheets are not first edition sheets'.[13] If its title-page is dated 1816, and its watermark is 1825, then Worthington is right to use the term 'spurious'. No forger who wants to fake a first edition of a Waverley Novel would reprint the whole work; instead he would forge new title-pages with the correct date of a first edition and attach them to the sheets of a contemporary edition later than the first. Yale University has a copy of *Waverley*, sixth edition, with forged title-pages done on cheap paper with crude type-setting. Its title-pages I would certainly call 'spurious'.

I would like to know at what point in the history of book-collecting it seemed important to have a first edition in its first state, and to know when collectors had to learn a great deal about the length of double lines and 'correct' imprints. I have read with some care most of the Constable and Cadell correspondence in the National Library of Scotland, yet I do not remember that these publishers concerned themselves about correct title-pages. True, Robert Cadell was much interested in 'lifting volumes to sale price', by adding illustrations, or a new preface by the author, but he was not trying to fake a first edition. When, say, Scott's *Poetical Works*, first printed in ten volumes in 1821, was not selling in 1830, Cadell added pictures, an eleventh volume with new material, and furnished new title-pages with the new date—1830. He was always willing to change the date of a book to suggest that a volume printed in 1825 was really printed five years later. But I cannot recall that he ever fiddled with a title-page to suggest that a book issued in 1830 was first printed in 1825. Scott himself talked about setting 'to work like a cunning tailor to give the old coats new capes cuffs & collars . . .',[14] but he says nothing of selling his old coat as an antique. In Scott's day, as I have said, collectors wanted books in quarto size, copies on 'thick' paper, handsomely illustrated editions, 'private' copies, limited editions and the like. So the Ballantynes and Scott gave collectors what they wanted. If collectors had demanded rare pamphlets the Ballantynes would have issued them.

Scott has always been known among the ignorant as a bankrupt. He is supposed to be a novelist who made several fortunes, only to throw everything away on building a palace. It may seem foolish of him to have spent so much money on Abbotsford, and yet he believed he had plenty of money. Was he not the most successful author of his time? Had not *The Lady of the Lake*, published in 1810, gone into eight editions the same year (if we trust the evidence of title-pages)?; had not *Rokeby* been published in five editions in 1813?; and in 1815—when Scott knew that his popularity as a poet was dying—had not *The Lord of the Isles* gone into five editions? And when he turned to writing novels, had he not made an equal success? There was the evidence of the title-pages to prove it: *Waverley*, 1814, had four editions the year of publication; *Tales of My Landlord*, first series, 1816, had six editions by 1819; *Tales of My Landlord, Second Series*, 1818, had

[14] *Letters*, xi. 202.

three editions in the year of publication; *Tales of My Landlord;*
Third Series, 1819, also had three editions the year it was published. All these editions meant money to be spent at Abbotsford,
and proof that Scott's powers as a novelist were not declining.

But this popularity and this prosperity were not so real as Scott
supposed.

To be sure, *The Lady of the Lake* had been popular, but the
number of editions published in 1810, when the first edition came
out, is misleading. Its sixth edition represents merely a new title-
page added to the sheets of the fifth edition; the eighth edition
combines the seventh edition with a new title-page. In 1813, when
Scott was nervous about the reception of *Rokeby,* he was cheered to
know that its sales were rapid. They were more rapid on paper
than in actuality, for the third edition is no more than a reissue of
the second. If he judged the popularity of *The Lord of the Isles* by
the fact that five editions were published in one year, he was fool-
ing himself, for the third edition is a reissue of the second; the
fifth is a reissue of the fourth. In short, there were three genuine
editions of *The Lord of the Isles* in one year instead of five. Yet
Scott spent money as if five editions had really been sold.

Now Scott was no bibliographer and no printer; he knew something about printing customs, but not all the tricks of selling
books. In his letters, when he rejoices over a new edition he
imagines that all copies of former editions have been sold, that
type has been reset for the new edition (usually with corrections)
and that fresh books are being offered for sale. For example, in
1814 he was delighted with the sale of *Waverley* for it meant a new
market opening at a time when he could no longer hope to write
another poem as popular as *The Lady of the Lake.* On 6 October
1814 he thought he could raise four hundred pounds by selling a
third edition of *Waverley;* on 9 October 1814, he was still dreaming
about the four hundred pounds to come from the third edition; on
26 October 1814 the *Edinburgh Weekly Journal* advertised a third
edition of *Waverley,* and Scott accordingly should have been richer
by four hundred pounds. But this third edition is a new edition
only in part, for there are two issues of the books bearing 'Third
Edition' on their title-pages. One, I shall call A, consists of the
sheets of the second edition with a new title-page and preface. The
second issue (B) is another issue with title-page, preface, and a
text wholly printed from a new setting of type. The so-called
'Fourth Edition' of *Waverley,* issued in 1814, consists of the sheets

of the 'Third Edition' (issue B) with a new title-page. In fact, no more than three editions of *Waverley* were printed in 1814, no matter what numbers appear on their title-pages, and the three represent expert juggling of new printings, plus remainder sheets. Only their printer could keep their sequence straight—and Scott was no printer.

Waverley, then, was not as popular in 1814 as the number of its editions might indicate. And the same thing is true of other Waverley Novels. *Rob Roy*'s second and third editions, 1818, are reissues of the first edition of 1818, with a few signatures reprinted to replace those which ran short. *Tales of My Landlord*, first series, appears to have had a fifth and sixth edition in 1819, but only the fifth is a genuine resetting of type. *Tales of My Landlord, Second Series*, which Scott was sure would pay for Abbotsford, seems to have had three editions in 1818, but the second and third are reissues of the first. *Tales of My Landlord, Third Series*, which came out in three editions in the same year— 1819—represents only a trick of publishing, for the second and third editions are reissues of the first. *The Fortunes of Nigel* had one setting of type in 1822, not two (the second edition is a reissue of the first); and the same operation of dividing one impression into two editions is true of *The Monastery*, 1820; *Peveril of the Peak*, 1822, and *Redgauntlet*, 1824. Moral—don't trust what you see on a title-page.

After 1825 it was apparent, even to Scott, that he was nearing bankruptcy. Then it was no longer necessary for his publishers to invent huge sales, with many editions advertised, when in fact his books were not selling at all. If Scott spent his imaginary earnings on the bright dream of Abbotsford it was because he thought his earnings were real.

In conclusion, here are some deceptions in the work of Scott: five ghost books made by a boy in a format which looks adult; piracies made in Philadelphia and Paris which anticipate the forged pamphlets of Thomas J. Wise; three title-pages presented as spurious in a first-rate bibliography which we can reduce to one sure counterfeit page; and—most important of all—a number of title-pages made by Scott's own firm of printers which carry questionable information about the numbering of editions.

None of the frauds I have mentioned in the first part of this paper harmed Scott. His reputation can withstand the mistakes of bibliographers like Caplan; the piracies of Galignani and Carey meant only that Scott lost a little money by their trickery. Forgeries like Greville Worthington's one spurious title-page are worth only a footnote. The real harm to Scott's reputation and fortune was done by the title-pages which fooled him into thinking that he had more money than was the case. They were the work of his associates and friends.

Scott and the Picturesque: Afforestation and History

MARCIA ALLENTUCK

WHILE Sir Walter Scott never wrote a fully-developed essay on the theory of the picturesque, his review-article 'On Landscape Gardening', which appears in the *Quarterly Review* for March 1828, contained many of his views on the subject. An earlier essay, 'On Planting Waste Lands', which had appeared a year earlier in the same periodical, had anticipated a few of them. I propose in this short lecture first to adumbrate the backgrounds of Scott's interest in the cult of the picturesque, and then to discuss in greater detail one particular aspect of the theory of the picturesque as explicated by Scott in the 1828 essay. Finally, I wish to relate this aspect to the larger dimensions of Scott's concern with the beauty and utility of rural economy and its connexion with history and time.

Scott's view of nature was direct, intense, active, and perhaps even somewhat compensatory, for he always regretted not having been able to master the art of rendering it in oils or water-colours: 'I could make no progress either in painting or drawing', he asserted. 'Even the humble ambition, which I long cherished, of making sketches of those places which interested me, from a defect of eye or hand, was totally ineffectual. After long study and many efforts, I was unable to apply the elements of perspective or of shade to the scene before me, and was obliged to relinquish in despair an art which I was most anxious to practise.'[1] Throughout his life, Scott consciously savoured the effects of natural landscape, yet he did not approach it topographically, but subjectively: that is, in a transforming, characterological manner. It was landscape humanized. Early on, the tranquillizing congruencies and startling incongruencies of landscape became for Scott metonyms for history. His account, for example, of the quickening effects of his sojourn

[1] Scott, *Journal*, 1 March 1826; Lockhart, *Life*, i. 51.

at Kelso in 1783, before entering the University, shows him as having been affected as much by associative qualities as by the scene's actual components. Formal and historical values interacted both to heighten his visual appreciation and to create for him a context for newly developing habits of mind:

To this period also I can trace distinctly the awaking of that delightful feeling for the beauties of natural objects which has never since deserted me. The neighbourhood of Kelso . . . is eminently calculated to awaken these ideas. It presents objects, not only grand in themselves, but venerable from their association. The meeting of two superb rivers, the Tweed and the Teviot, both renowned in song—the ruins of an ancient Abbey—the most distant vestiges of Roxburgh Castle—the modern mansion of Fleurs, which is so situated as to combine the idea of ancient baronial grandeur with those of modern taste—are in themselves objects of the first class; yet are so mixed, united, and melted among a thousand other beauties of a less prominent description, that they harmonize into one general picture, and please rather by unison than concord.[2]

It is therefore not surprising that Scott was consistently alive to the mixed modes of the picturesque—the irregular groupings, rough surfaces, calculated intricacies, broken areas of light, shade, colour, massed dispositions, striking peculiarities, arresting contrasts, and complex values—the resonances visual, emblematic, evocative, of this late eighteenth and early nineteenth-century cult —alive to them not only in landscape design, but also in the related disciplines of literature and the fine arts. His writings belie the claim made in the following passage:

I do not by any means infer that I was dead to the feeling of picturesque scenery; on the contrary, few delighted more in its general effect. But I was unable with the eye of a painter to dissect the various parts of the scene, to comprehend how the one bore upon the other, to estimate the effect which various features of the view had in producing its leading and general effect. I have never, indeed, been capable of doing this with precision or nicety, though my latter studies have led me to amend and arrange my original ideas on the subject.[3]

Yet one need only recall numerous passages in Scott's writings to conclude that he underestimated his apprehension of the picturesque—among them, for example, his Introduction (1831) to *The Monastery* in which he claimed that 'it was not the purpose of the author to present a landscape copied from nature, but a piece of composition, in which a real scene, with which he is familiar, had afforded him some leading outlines';[4] and, even more

---

[2] *Life*, i. 39.   [3] *Ibid*. i. 51.
[4] *The Monastery* (Magnum ed. xviii), pp. viii–ix.

significantly, his Introduction (1831) to *The Fortunes of Nigel*, truly a *locus classicus*:

The most picturesque period of history is that when the ancient rough and wild manners of a barbarous age are just becoming innovated upon, and contrasted by, the illumination of increased or revived learning, and the instructions of renewed or reformed religion. The strong contrast produced by the opposition of ancient manners to those which are generally subduing them, affords the lights and shadows necessary to give effect to a fictitious narrative.[5]

Scott's underestimation of his own powers was corroborated by the reviewer of *The Lady of the Lake* in the *Quarterly Review* for 1810:

Never, we think, has the analogy between poetry and painting been more strikingly exemplified than in the writings of Mr. Scott. He sees every thing with a painter's eye. Whatever he represents has a character of individuality, and is drawn with an accuracy and minuteness of discrimination which we are not accustomed to expect from verbal description.[6]

Moreover, the adjective 'picturesque' often appeared in reviews of Scott's work, and when Pichot published in Paris in 1826 his *Vues pittoresques de l' Ecosse*, he had 'un texte explicatif extrait en grande partie des ouvrages de Sir Walter Scott'. And earlier, in 1818, Scott agreed to be one of eight shareholders in *Provincial Antiquities and Picturesque Scenery of Scotland*, with illustrations by (among others) Edward Blore, John Thomson and J. M. W. Turner. Scott agreed to supply the letterpress without remuneration, provided that he received the original paintings and drawings for his own collections. Throughout, his relations with Turner as an illustrator of his works were conditioned by Scott's determined adherence to the principles of picturesque composition and tone.

However, Scott revealed his true artistic predilections in his preoccupation with Salvator Rosa, one of the prime inspirers of the British cult of the picturesque, in writing to George Ellis in 1804 about proposed illustrations for *The Lay of the Last Minstrel* by John Flaxman, that artistic apostle of the chaste, linear, neo-Hellenic style. 'I should fear Flaxman's genius is too classic to stoop to body forth my Gothic Borderers. Would there not be some risk of their resembling the antique of Homer's heroes, rather than the iron race of Salvator's engravings?'[7] Even though

---

[5] *The Fortunes of Nigel* (Magnum ed. xxvi), pp. vi–vii.
[6] *Quarterly Review* iii (1810), 512.
[7] Scott, *Letters*, i. 226–7, corrected from original now in the Pierpont Morgan Library.

Rosa was only one of the triumvirate of painters—the other two being the more subdued Claude and Poussin—whose landscapes inspired the picturesque movement in Britain, Rosa's banditti and other deracinated creatures in untamed scenes clearly ranked first with Scott, who, during his visit to the Louvre in 1815, gave pride of place to Rosa's 'Witch of Endor'. One of the finest descriptions reminiscent of Rosa's canvases occurred in *Waverley*:

The path, which was extremely steep and rugged, winded up a chasm between two tremendous rocks, following a passage which a foaming stream, that brawled far below, appeared to have won for itself in the course of ages. A few slanting beams of the sun, which was now setting, reached the water in its darksome bed, and showed it partially, chafed by a hundred rocks, and broken by a hundred falls. The descent from the path to the stream was a mere precipice, with here and there a projecting fragment of granite, or a scathed tree, which had warped its twisted roots into the fissures of the rock.

Indeed, before Waverley meets Donald Bean Lean, Scott comments:

The profession which he followed—the wilderness in which he dwelt—the wild warrior forms that surrounded him, were all calculated to inspire terror. From such accompaniments, Waverley prepared himself to meet a stern, gigantic, ferocious figure, such as Salvator himself would have chosen to be the central object of a group of banditti.[8]

While Scott was manifestly sympathetic to the aims of the cult of the picturesque and its most *outré* foreign inspirer, he was also sensitive to its excesses. Unlike Richard Payne Knight, one of the cult's most discerning and proleptic explicators, whose poem *The Landscape* and whose aesthetic treatise *An Analytic Inquiry into the Principles of Taste* Scott knew, he would not dissociate visual or pictorial elements from anthropocentric ones in contemplating a scene. Scott was less concerned with abstract categories of form than he was with man's response to the states of intensity which they induced. A duality of vision was necessary—both realistic and painterly. But the picturesque landscape was indeed Scott's local scene—to a fault, remarked Coleridge after Scott's death:

Dear Sir Walter Scott and myself were exact, but harmonious opposites in this;—that every old ruin, hill, river, or tree called up in his mind a host of historical or biographical associations,—just as a bright pan of brass, when beaten, is said to attract the swarming bees; whereas, for myself . . . I believe I should walk over the plain of Marathon without taking more interest in it than in any other plain of similar features.[9]

[8] *Waverley* (Magnum ed. i), 168–9, 177.
[9] *Specimens of the Table Talk of Samuel Taylor Coleridge* (London, 1835), ii. 225.

Yet, when Coleridge wrote of Scott's poetry he did acknowledge that 'even in these [poems] the power of presenting the most numerous figures, and figures with the most complex movement, and under rapid succession, in *true picturesque unity*, attests true and peculiar genius'.[10]

Of course, Coleridge's smack at Scott in *Table Talk* may be rooted in Coleridge's ultimate opposition to David Hartley's mechanistic associationist theories—theories which Archibald Alison and his teacher (as well as Scott's) Dugald Stewart were to refine and promulgate within a philosophical context more strongly charged than Hartley's with moral, aesthetic and intellectual values. But before Alison and Stewart concerned themselves with associationism and the picturesque (and it should be pointed out that Dugald Stewart considered the distinctions made between the beautiful and the picturesque overly subtle and paradoxical, although he did esteem the work of the arch-theorist of the picturesque, Sir Uvedale Price, 'as eminently calculated, in its practical tendency, to reform and to improve the public taste'), Robert Adam had already written of it a few decades earlier. He embodied his fascination with Vanbrugh's work, especially at Blenheim and Castle Howard, in his linking of architecture with landscape: '. . . convexity and concavity . . . have the same effect in architecture that hill and dale, foreground and distance, swelling and sinking have in landscape: . . . they serve to produce an agreeable and diversified contour, that . . . creates a variety of light and shade . . .'; '. . . the rise and fall, the advance and recess, with other diversity of form, in the different parts of a building . . . add greatly to the picturesque of the composition.'[11] Adam afforded both precept and example for the establishment of a subsequently rich Scottish context of picturesque concern.

Sir James Hall of Dunglass did no less, both in his work on Gothic architecture first published in 1798, and in his most enterprising attempt in the years 1807–13 to rebuild his house *à la* Vanbrugh in a picturesque style without abandoning utilitarian conveniences. This endeavour was primarily inspired by the writing, building and planting of Sir Uvedale Price, as well as by the treatises of Hall's own countryman, John Claudius Loudon, who boasted in his most influential *Observations on the Formation and Management of Useful and Ornamental Plantations* (Edinburgh,

[10] *Coleridge's Miscellaneous Criticism*, ed. T. M. Raysor (London, 1936), 340.
[11] Robert and James Adam, *Works in Architecture* (London, 1778), preface.

1804), that he was in Scotland 'the first who has set out as a land-scape gardener, professing to follow Mr. Price's principles'. Hall invited that polymath Alexander Nasmyth—engineer, architect, town-planner, landscape gardener, and landscape painter who assisted in the illustrations for his book—to determine an appropriately picturesque site for the house (finally the edge of a deep ravine near the ruins of a priory church), and to suggest its general disposition, before engaging the services of the architect, Richard Crichton, who was to execute much of the work. Sir James Hall's efforts demonstrated his agreement with Lord Kames's claims in his *Elements of Criticism*, in the mid-eighteenth century before the rage for picturesque improvement had become a mania for many, that in Britain, 'the books we have upon architecture and upon embellishing ground, abound in practical instruction, necessary for a mechanic: but in vain should we rummage them for rational principles to improve our taste . . . there is beauty in utility, and in discoursing of beauty that of utility must not be neglected.'[12]

It was with these concepts of utility and beauty transmuted into the picturesque that Sir Walter Scott was deeply concerned. In *Waverley*, for example, a true *Bildungsroman*, the gradual maturation of the hero is perceived by his progress from mere aesthetic responsiveness to his environment to the sensitive but practical management of it in the restoration of a lowland estate—with the considerations of patriotic duty, profitable investment and creative pleasure all implicit. And, in a more palpable sense, all that Scott achieved at Abbotsford was actuated by the two principles of the picturesque and the utilitarian, or, as he was to phrase it, the 'fantastic' and the 'convenient'. In a letter of August 1825 to Sir George Beaumont, Scott referred to himself, with emphasis on his arboricultural pursuits, as a *'pittore*, in the sense of plantations and buildings', with true picturesque idiom, 'for,' he went on, 'I have made a kind of *bravura* of a house here, a little fantastic, I own, but convenient . . . well surrounded with infant woods'.[13] In Scott's plans for Abbotsford and in his realization of them, Sir Uvedale Price's writings figured conspicuously. In the library at Abbotsford, Press S, is the last revised edition (published in Edinburgh in 1810) of Price's seminal work, *Essays on the Picturesque, as compared with the Sublime and Beautiful*, and Price corresponded

[12] Henry Home, Lord Kames, *Elements of Criticism*, 7th ed. (Edinburgh, 1788), ii. 430–1.　　　　　[13] *Letters*, ix. 216.

with Scott (Scott's letters have unfortunately not survived), who in 1813 told Lady Abercorn that he was continuing to read Price in depth.

Sir Uvedale Price's involvement with the dramatic expressiveness of trees and their compositional capabilities, his hostility to any formal arrangement of them, appealed enormously to Scott, as the noble and intricate contours and contents of the Abbotsford plantations after Scott had cultivated them testified. But before Price's first edition of the *Essay on the Picturesque* was published in 1794, Scott might have already taken seriously to heart an important section of Archibald Alison's *Essays on the Nature and Principles of Taste* (1790), in which trees as vehicles expressive of associated emotions are accorded significant attention: 'Many of the classes of trees have distinct characters. There are therefore different compositions which are beautiful in their forms; and in all of them, that composition only is beautiful which corresponds to the nature of the expression they have, or of the emotion which they excite.'[14] Yet it was Price's detailed examination of the effects of trees, in groups or singly, that exerted the greatest effect upon Scott:

It is in the arrangement and management of trees that the great act of improvement consists; earth is too cumbrous and lumpish for man to contend much with, and, when worked upon, its effects are flat and dead, like its nature. But trees, detaching themselves at once from the surface, and rising boldly into the air, have a more lively and immediate effect on the eye; they alone form a canopy over us, and a varied frame to all other objects, which they admit, exclude, and group with, almost at the will of the improver. In beauty they not only far excel every thing of inanimate nature, but their beauty is complete and perfect in itself, while that of almost every other object requires their assistance. Without them, the most varied inequality of ground is uninteresting. . . . The infinite *variety* of their forms, tints, and light and shade, must strike every body; the quality of *intricacy* they possess in as high a degree, and in a more exclusive and peculiar manner. . . . It is not enough that trees should be naturalized to the climate—they must also be naturalized to the landscape.[15]

When Scott came upon the scene at Abbotsford, he observed that the previous owner, Dr. Douglas, had planted a straight length of dark firs that looked like a hair-comb stuck in the ground. Thus, in the spirit of Price, Tom Purdie was instructed by Scott to vary the

    [14] Archibald Alison, *Essays on the Nature and Principles of Taste* (Edinburgh, 1790), 279.
    [15] *Sir Uvedale Price on the Picturesque*, ed. Sir Thomas Dick Lauder (Edinburgh, 1842), 189, 191, 193.

plantings, not only with a variety of kinds of trees, but also with trees of differing levels of maturity, to produce just those effects of accidental intricacy and eclecticism which were the cardinal tenets of the picturesque movement.

To Joanna Baillie, in 1813 Scott wrote:

I have been studying Price with all my eyes . . . So you see . . . how deeply I am bit with the madness of the picturesque. . . . I have been planting and screening and dyking against the river and planting willows and aspens and weeping birches around my new old well. . . . I have now laid the foundations for a famous background of copse with pendant trees in front and I have only to beg a few years to see how my colours will come out of the canvas.[16]

The phrase 'beg a few years' is the operative one here, for the rural embellishers among the squirearchy were much preoccupied with the length of ti m nece ssary to achieve the picturesque effects they craved in their gardens and plantations. And it is primarily with this aspect of the picturesque that Scott dealt with in the *Quarterly Review* article, 'On Landscape Gardening', although, to be sure, the first part of the essay certainly shows him to have been *au courant* with every aspect of the metamorphosis of the British garden and park from the predictably regular to the picturesque irregular, and with the vast literature upon the subject published in his time and earlier. The occasion for Scott's essay was the publication of the second edition of Sir Henry Seton Steuart's *The Planter's Guide: or, a Practical Essay on the Best Method of giving Immediate Effect to Wood, by the Removal of Large Trees and Underwood; being an Attempt to place the Art, and that of General Arboriculture, on Phytological and Fixed Principles; interspersed with Observations on General Planting, and the Improvement of Real Landscape: originally intended for the Climate of Scotland.* Well aware of the slow progress of vegetation and of the frustrations of waiting for saplings to grow into trees within the lifetime of the planter, Sir Henry developed an ingenious transplanting machine, first devised by Lancelot Brown, to move fully grown trees on his estate at Allanton in Lanarkshire. Thus he made virtually instant picturesque landscape a reality. His book was no mere description of the machine, however, but a well-reasoned and historically accurate treatise on the application of picturesque principles to the landscaping of the Scottish countryside, resonant with Scottish practicality: 'I have laid down no rule, and recommended no practice,' he maintained, 'that has not been proved in my own

---

[16] *Letters*, iii. 223.

park'; he rejoiced that his theories were leavened by 'the more correct judgement of Price, Knight, and Loudon'. Sir Henry even had a long section on Scott's transplanting successes at Abbotsford and his thinning to achieve picturesque breadth and contrast of light and shade, saying of Scott: 'He is ardently, and . . . enthusi- astically attached to the cultivation of Wood. Though possessed of the property only sixteen years, he has planted nearly five hundred acres of surface . . . few plantations are cultivated with the same skill, and none have grown with more luxuriance, than the woods of Abbotsford.'[17]

Before writing the review of Steuart's book, Sir Walter (as committee member of the Highland Society) had visited Allanton; the Society's favourable report then formed an Appendix to Steuart's book. However, another account by Scott of his visit to 'Sir Henry Steuart . . . that most fantastic person', more private and candid in nature, also exists: 'Like Malvolio he is a grave ass, a solemn prosing serious fop. He exercises wonderful power how- ever over the vegetable world and has made his trees dance about as ever did Orpheus . . .'.[18] And elsewhere: 'Sir Henry is a sad coxcomb and lifted beyond the solid earth by the effect of his book's success. But the book well deserves it'.[19] In the review itself, Scott was scrupulously laudatory of Steuart's efforts, and wrote at great length upon his techniques and achievements, or what Scott called his 'wonderful exertions'. He expressed the hope that 'earlier or later, this beautiful and rational system will be brought into general action, when it will do more to advance the picturesque beauty of the country in five years than the slow methods hitherto adopted can attain in fifty'.

Scott's concern, as a rural designer, was with trees primarily, rather than with earth and water. 'Trees', he contended in this essay, closely paraphrasing Sir Uvedale Price, 'remain the proper and most manageable material of picturesque improvement . . . as

---

[17] Sir Henry Steuart, *The Planter's Guide*, 2nd ed. (Edinburgh, 1829), pp. ix, 373. Cf. a letter from Steuart to Lady Liston, 22 September 1825 (N.L.S., MS. 5674, f. 186): '. . . I should be extremely happy to explain to you, as far as I can, the *principles of science*, which I have endeavoured to apply to an art well worthy the attention to the public . . . (I mean the Transplanting of grown trees). . . .
'Here is another thing, which I believe might strike you, were it properly explained, and that is the general purposes to which I have applied the Transplanting Art, in the *creation at once of woods and copses* intermixed with Standard or Grown Trees. You might observe some good examples of this round my Lake, which is richly wooded at present, and *wholly* done by the Transplanting Machine,—and perhaps you will be surprised to learn that 6 or 7 years ago *there was not one tree near it . . .*'
[18] *Letters*, viii. 91.   [19] *Journal*, 19 January 1829.

by their presence they not only delight the eye, with their various forms and colours, but benefit the soil by their falling leaves, and improve the climate by their shelter.'[20] But 'extensive and judicious plantation'—Scott's phrase—can be understood to have had, in Scott's universe of discourse, even greater importance than his words seemingly accord it. We recall that in the Introduction (1823) to *Quentin Durward*, in highly particularized vocabulary, he praised Sir Uvedale Price's theories of variety and intricacy for helping to 'redeem the naked tameness' of landscape.[21] And in his review of Steuart's *Planter's Guide*, Scott is, I believe, actually lauding Steuart for redeeming men—temporarily, at least—from history, or helping him at best to manipulate it. It is but the other side of the coin: at Abbotsford he dwelt in a neo-Gothic baronial structure calculated to evoke the resonances of a vanished past; in advocating and participating in active transplanting, and in advertising a machine that would accelerate its effects, Scott curved the future towards himself, and made it an inverted historical present, by leaping over the slower processes of time and history. Another great mind, always attentive to the complexities of time, history, and man's puny needs, was aroused in Scotland's western isle of Mull, only a few decades earlier, to similar ruminations upon the connexions beween afforestation and mortality: 'But there is a frightful interval between the seed and the timber. He that calculates the growth of trees, has the unwelcome remembrance of the shortness of life driven hard upon him. He knows that he is doing what will never benefit himself; and when he rejoices to see the stem rise, is disposed to repine that another shall cut it down.'[22] While Dr. Johnson could not take comfort, Scott, less possessed than Johnson of 'vile melancholy', tried by practical means, for which his preoccupation with the picturesque formed the framework, to find solace.

Yet Scott was not self-deluded: he knew what his strategies were about. In one of the most moving passages of his *Journal*, written towards the end of his life, he recorded the following:

Walked with my cousin Colonel Russell for three hours in the woods and enjoyed the sublime and delectable pleasures of being wise, and listened to, on the subject of my favourite themes of laying out ground and plantation—

---

[20] *Quarterly Review*, xxxvii (1828), reprinted in *Miscellaneous Prose Works*, xxi. 77–151; quotations from pp. 151, 109.

[21] *Quentin Durward* (Magnum ed. xxxi), p. xl.

[22] Samuel Johnson, *A Journey to the Western Isles of Scotland*, ed. Mary Lascelles (New Haven, 1971), 139.

Russell seems quite to follow such an excellent authority, and my spirits mounted while I found I was haranguing to a willing and patient pupil. To be sure, Ashestiel, by planting the high knowes and drawing woodland through the pasture, could be made one of the most beautiful forest things in the world. I have often dreamed of putting it in high order, and, judging from what I have been able to do here, I think I should have succeeded. At any rate my Blue Devils are flown at the sense of entertaining some sort of consequence—Lord, what fools we are![23]

[23] *Journal*, 12 May 1827. Professor Daiches has informed me that when his son, Alan, was assisting with the photographs for *Sir Walter Scott and his World* (London, 1971), he had to climb to the roof at Abbotsford to photograph the view of the Tweed which comforted Scott as he lay dying in the dining room. Scott would have appreciated this final irony of time: the trees he planted now obsure the prospect he so loved.

Scott and Turner[1]

ADELE M. HOLCOMB

TURNER'S engravings to the 1832–4 edition of Scott's *Poetical Works* are unique among Scott illustrations in having brought about the author's collaboration with an artist of the first rank. The circumstances of Turner's commission are, moreover, quite fully documented in correspondence, much of it unpublished, between Scott and Robert Cadell.[2] Thus it is possible in the case of this series to trace in detail the considerations that determined the choice of Turner as illustrator, the selection of subjects and Scott's attitude towards the undertaking. Such an examination indicates one of the most revealing instances of that mutual dependence of the arts that Baudelaire called 'un des diagnostics de l'état spirituel de notre siècle'.[3]

In general, Scott regarded the illustrations of his poems and novels as a concession to popular taste; the obligation was not one in which he took keen personal interest. It was apparently through the arrangements of his London publishers that Richard Westall was charged with the illustration of several of his poems between 1808 and 1815[4] (though these illustrated volumes were a minority among the many editions issued). Only a few of the novels were illustrated before the ascendancy of Cadell as prime mover behind the publication of Scott's works.[5] The first large-scale scheme of Scott illustration, that of the 'Magnum Opus', was arranged by

[1] Much of this article has appeared (with illustrations) as 'Turner and Scott' in *Journal of the Warburg and Courtauld Institutes* xxxiv (1971), 386–97; I am grateful to the editors for permission to publish this revision. I also thank the Trustees for permission to quote from manuscripts in the National Library of Scotland, where Mr. I. C. Cunningham helped my original research and Mr. A. S. Bell compared my printed texts (drawn from H. J. C. Grierson's typescripts) with the Library's newly-acquired volume of Scott-Cadell letters to produce the revised versions cited below.
[2] N.L.S. MSS. 3917–9 (Cadell to Scott); MS. Acc. 5131 (Scott to Cadell).
[3] 'La Vie et l'Œuvre d'Eugene Delacroix', *Œuvres Complètes* (Paris, 1966), 728.
[4] Engravings after designs by Westall appeared in at least eight editions of Scott's poems during this period.
[5] See Catherine Gordon, 'The Illustration of Sir Walter Scott: Nineteenth-Century Enthusiasm and Adaptation', *Journal of the Warburg and Courtauld Institutes* xxxiv (1971), 297–317.

Cadell with the encouragement of Constable, who urged in a letter to Scott of 22 December 1825 that illustrations be used in the projected edition of the Waverley novels. This 'new feature', he urged, would guarantee the prompt sale of an edition of 2,000.[6] Scott conceded what he later described as the need 'to make the new edition superior by illustrations and embellishments as a faded beauty dresses and lays on [a] prudent touch of rouge to compensate for her want of juvenile graces'.[7] Accordingly, he solicited designs from David Wilkie, Edwin Landseer, C. R. Leslie and others, who seem to have contributed their work without pecuniary reward.[8] The success of this edition, the 'Magnum Opus', exceeded Cadell's expectations and encouraged Scott to believe that the proceeds would very nearly erase his indebtedness.

Yet in 1831 when the question of illustrations for an edition of poetry was raised, Scott expressed doubt that the Waverley engravings had substantially affected the sale of the novels. Cadell knew better. In a letter to Scott of 28 March 1831, he calculated that 'without plates 5,000 less of the Waverley Novels would have sold at a difference on the whole work of £13,000 clear—or 1/- less per vol, making a much greater difference'.[9] The same letter reviews the arguments used to convince John Gibson, the agent for Scott's trustees, of the need for illustrations:

I took some trouble to open his eyes and proved most clearly that the whole plates of the Novels are paid by the sale of 2,000 books—and that all the imitators including Colburn are following the very same course. I have been more particular in alluding to this as I am fresh from the calculation of the results, and I am convinced that 5,000 less of the books would have sold without the plates—the same as to the Poetry—or, 4/- per vol. could only have been asked.

An equally compelling argument for the value of illustrations was suggested by the success of Rogers's Turner-illustrated *Italy* of 1830 which Scott praised, gracefully, for its literary content as well as for its vignettes, 'a rare specimen of the manner in which the art of poetry can awaken the Muse of painting'.[10]

[6] Quoted by H. J. C. Grierson, *Sir Walter Scott, Bart.* (London, 1938) 276 n.1., from MS. Edinburgh University Library.

[7] In a letter of 9 October 1828, *Letters*, xi. 7.

[8] Scott thanks these and other contributors at the end of his General Preface to the Magnum Opus edition (p. xxxix); moreover there is no mention in his letters of any payment for the designs.

[9] MS. 3917, f. 142. The figure of 5,000 refers to the whole edition, which by this date numbered 23 volumes. The books were also sold individually at 5s. each.

[10] *Letters*, xi. 459–60. For Roger's influence on the character of Turner's vignettes, see my 'A Neglected Classical Phase of Turner's Art: his Vignettes to Roger's *Italy*', *Journal of the Warburg and Courtauld Institutes* xxxii (1969), 405–10.

By the time Scott framed this compliment in mid-January 1831, some 4,000 copies of *Italy* had been sold in the fortnight since its appearance and the poem redeemed from the oblivion to which it had seemed destined. Scott was impressed with the efficacy of illustrations in this instance and it was Rogers's triumph that prompted the effort to secure Turner as sole illustrator of the collected poetry.

As Turner had not been among the 'most eminent living artists'[11] laid under contribution for the Magnum, his choice as illustrator would be inexplicable without the 1830 *Italy*. It would be equally inexplicable in view of the history of his acquaintance with Scott. Apparently they met for the first time in 1818 when Turner went to Scotland to make drawings for *The Provincial Antiquities of Scotland*. Various accounts of this undertaking hold that Scott was averse to giving Turner a share in the illustration as he wished to favour artists of his acquaintance such as John Thomson, but that he acceded to his publishers' insistence on the greater prestige of Turner's art.[12] Judging from anecdotes related by Thomson's biographer, Scott's personal relationship with Turner was marked by disdain for the painter's cockneyisms and general lack of refinement. Not only was Turner uncouth, in the opinion Scott formed in this encounter, he was also grasping. Indeed, Scott became an important contributor to the tradition of Turner's 'avarice'; a Scott letter of 30 April 1819 which has been published (and deplored) by Finberg, characterizes Turner as 'almost the only man of genius I ever knew who is sordid in these matters'.[13] A fair conclusion, I would suggest, is that Turner's directness in his financial dealings offended Scott's deeply held, if anomalous, conviction that concern for gain on the part of artists or writers was an ungentlemanly trait.

Nor were these grounds for personal animosity offset by an appreciation on Scott's side of Turner's merits as a painter. By all accounts, including his stated preference for works of such painters 'as produce effect on mankind at large'[14] (e.g. Wilkie and

[11] General Preface, xxxix.
[12] See William Baird, *John Thomson of Duddingston* (Edinburgh, 1895), 53–4. Thomson and Turner each contributed eleven plates to *The Provincial Antiquities of Scotland* (London, 1826).
[13] A. J. Finberg, *The Life of J. M. W. Turner, R.A.*, 2nd ed. (Oxford, 1961), 257.
[14] *Journal*, 13 February 1826; Scott's ideas may well have owed something to the views set forth in Archibald Alison's *Essays on the Nature and Principles of Taste* (1790), especially in the author's repeated appeal to opinions of the generality of

Landseer), Scott was all but completely unequipped as a judge of the visual arts. His response to painting seems to have depended solely on its associative values. The paradox of Scott's incapacity as a connoisseur and the visual bias of his imagination is suggested in the reminiscences of C. R. Leslie:

While strolling with Sir Walter about his grounds . . . he would frequently stop and point out exactly that object or effect that would strike the eye of a painter. He said he always liked to have a dog with him in his walks, if for nothing else but to furnish a living object in the *foreground of the picture* [Leslie's italics]. . . . He talked of scenery as he wrote of it—like a painter; and yet for pictures, as works of art, he had little or no taste, nor did he pretend to any. To him they were interesting merely as representing some particular scene, person or event; and very moderate merit in their execution contented him.[15]

There is unfortunately no evidence that would illuminate Turner's attitude towards Scott prior to 1831. Neither are there any indications of his having read Scott's poems or novels before this time; according to Falk's list, his library did not contain any work by Scott in an edition earlier than 1830.[16] Once engaged on the illustrations, however, it would appear that Turner warmed to his task. The character of the engravings and of the paintings connected with them, most notably *Staffa, Fingal's Cave* (coll. the Hon. Gavin Astor), affirm that this was the case.

The terms of Cadell's agreement with Turner stipulated that he would supply twenty-four designs at twenty-five guineas apiece, thus providing a frontispiece and title-page vignette for each of the twelve volumes of the edition. On being so informed, Scott replied on 13 March that he understood little of such matters,

But I will be happy supposing Mr. Turner comes here for a few days to receive him with all hospitality and conduct him to all the scenes most fit for the minstrelsy. They are numerous & very striking . . . Smaillholm tower near which was the abode of my Childhood Newark castle (somewhat hackd) Cessford castle Hermitage castle & many very fine views be sides. This is in some degree a plague for Mr. Turner though an artist of very great genius is not so pleasant as such persons usually are. But he will be

---

mankind in support of his arguments. Similarly, Alison's antithesis between compositions in which 'the expression of art' comes first and those marked by 'expression of
the subject', and his preference for the latter, would have been congenial to Scott.

[15] C. R. Leslie, *Autobiographical Recollections* (Boston, 1860), 62.

[16] Bernard Falk in *Turner the Painter: His Hidden Life* (London, 1938) lists only
the eleven-volume edition of Scott's poems (1830) which Cadell sent Turner in April
1831 in connection with the illustrations he then undertook.

[a] wellcome guest on this occasion & no one but myself perhaps can make him fix on the fit subjects.[17]

Cadell drew up a list of subjects which, he assured Scott in a letter of 14 March, would be sent to him for approval before it went to Turner, 'who asks suggestions'.[18] But in other respects Turner was less accommodating for reasons connected with the burden of previous commitments. He would not agree to complete the designs within a year as Cadell wished and he hoped to avoid the trip to Scotland, the more so as he had in his sketchbooks material for fifteen of the subjects. Cadell considered the journey vital, however, in order that all the engravings be based on first-hand observation.[19] It was at Cadell's suggestion that Scott invited Turner to Abbotsford and, with evident reluctance, he accepted in a letter of 20 April.[20]

Following Scott's stroke on 16 April, correspondence relating to the illustrations lapsed until the following 25 July when Cadell wrote to announce that Turner had reached Manchester in his northward course. His itinerary was based on Cadell's list of the previous March, as emended by Scott. But the subjects were tentative for some volumes and incomplete for others. Scott desired a meeting with Cadell to settle the matter fully; no such consultation had taken place, however, by late July. The letters exchanged just prior to Turner's arrival at Abbotsford on or around 4 August were thus concerned to fix the remaining subjects.[21] Cadell wrote on 29 July to make the following suggestions, which would be disputed in varying degrees by Scott: Bowes Tower (for *Rokeby*), the Round Table (*The Bridal of Triermain*), Caerlaverock, New Abbey, Douglas Castle and Ford Castle (*Minstrelsy*) and Flodden Field, the River Till and Twizell Castle (*Marmion*). Scott's reply of 1 August is as follows:

My dear Sir
I am a little disappointed at our not meeting with Mr Turner on the subject of the prints for it seems essential that we should lay our heads

[17] MS. Acc. 5131, f. 43.   [18] MS. 3917, f.69.
[19] Cadell's anxiety for the originality of the designs is explained by considerations indicated in the advertisement for the edition in the *Athenaeum* of 17 March 1832. Here it is stressed that Mr. Turner had made a journey to Scotland expressly for the purpose of gathering materials for the illustrations.
[20] MS. 3917, f.270.
[21] It is clear that Turner did not go to Berwick before Abbotsford as Finberg suggests (*Life*, 332). Conformably with Scott's calculations in his letter of 22/23 April (*Letters*, xi. 13) as to the time Turner would need for the subjects around Abbotsford, he spent about a week at Scott's estate, and then went to Berwick with Cadell, as the latter reported in a letter to Scott of 12 August (MS. 3919, f.39).

together on the subjects as each has his particular province in which he will have an especial claim to be consulted. Mr Turner is unquestionably [the] best judge of everything belonging to art. Your opinion will be necessary with regard to roads travelling and the arrangement for distributing Mr Turner's time with the greatest regard to convenience and trouble and the Author may be held the fittest judge of the adaptation of the scenery to the composition. I will therefore speak to my department as well as I can & follow the order of your letter.

At Rokeby the following subjects appear absolutely necessary. Mortham Castle a beautiful scene with the curious monument adjacent picturesquely situated burn [and] two tall trees. Mortham is about a mile & a half from the mansion of Mr Morritt down the river.

Bowes is a fine tower but would not so well connect with the subject and you are aware that it is from the happy adaptation of the works of [an] Artist to the poetry that the publick will judge that the illustrations have been actually designed for the publication. I can with perfect ease give Mr Turner an introduction to the Squire of Rokeby a man of taste & a particular friend of mine who will be very civil to him. A view of the castle of Carlisle which is a fine subject would be very desirable & indeed indispensible. Bruce's Castle & Lochmaben are the same thing the same place I mean. You should not I think attempt to fix Mr Turner to a certain route till you have actually fixd your subjects and there is good part of the subjects which I could convey the artist to without trouble or expense.

Perhaps we may leave out Hermitage though a noble & very appropriate Subject it lies perfectly out of the way. Johnie Armstrong's castle of Gillnockie within four miles of Langholme would do well instead and lies conveniently on the route. I do not see that Sweetheart Abbey perhaps scarce even Caerlaverock are strict[ly] speaking illustrations though they are beautiful subjects most beautiful they would seem stuffd in without propriety. It was my intention & I hardly think that it could be settled otherwise that we should have taken the copy and comparing it with the subjects should have fixd the one to the other when I am convinced the whole would be fixd handsomely.

There is nothing to see about flodden but a half cultivated braeside. I doubt even Mr Turner's talents could make nothing out of it. You have omitted [in] the eve of St. John *Smaylholm tower* which is a striking subject very appropriate & about a five miles drive from this place. The more we can get in my neighbourhood the better as when I cannot myself have the pleasure of accompanying Mr Turner I could send Mr Laidlaw who knows all the scenery in this country as well as I do myself. I foresee that unless we take pen & ink to it for a forenoon the sooner the better we will make a bungled job of it. I have always lookd to a full consultation viva voce I mean before fixing an arrangement on which much will depend. Twizell Castle as it now stands is a most detestable sample of modern Gothick with which Sir Francis Blake Delaval replaced what in my recollection was a genuine castle of moderate size. There is only one thing fit to draw at Twizell & that is the old bridge which consists of a beautiful Gothick arch ribbd beneath and I think pointed which would make an exquisite vignette but for God's sake no castle. Even the wise man who built the hulk is now blocking out from his eyes what cost him £50,000 to deform the situation with.

I wish we were well over with this undertaking & I foresee that if Mr Turner is to have his way in the illustrations the work will be void of that propriety which gives interest to an illustrated poem which I conceive to be the propriety of the union between the press and pencil which like the parties in a well chosen marriage should be well considered before hand. I hope you will look to this for which there is surely still time.

I have accordingly written over my list but having made a blunder I have to put off sending you my views till [I] come to look them over. But I have little doubt my know[ledge] of the locale will suppl[y] not only with local subjects but point out the easiest way of introducing them to Mr Turner which he is very unlike to know by himself but which I have been thinking upon occasionally since we first spoke of this undertaking.

Perhaps you meant to say Ford Castle instead of Twizell. The first is a grand ruin & indispensible, the second a mock castle with an extreme number of peaked windows.

I hope to have an opportunity of speaking to all this matter for without pretending to dictate I foresee there will be discreditable errors for which all parties will be blamed and I am very unwilling that it should be so. The sooner I see you the better

Always yours truly
Walter Scott

Abbotsford
1 August

Without meaning to be at all obstinate or dogmatical I transmit a list of engravings & vignettes which match pretty well but can be in many cases alterd. They lie in each others neighbourhood. I am most anxious about Loch Coriskin and the Isle of Skye these that are near me are easily accessible but we are losing fine weather a rare commodity at this time of the year. I wish to God we were got to work.[22]

Scott's fear that Turner was bent on having his way with the illustrations might appear to have some basis in the incongruous use of Highland costume in his vignette *Sandyknowe and Smailholm Tower* (Vassar College Art Gallery). This explanation, which I advanced in the *Warburg Journal* text of this paper, would account for Cadell's reassurance in a letter to Scott of 31 March: 'I shall pay the most marked attention to all you say as to Turner— I did intend to scare him from the Highland dress'.[23] The difficulty with this account is that there is no evidence that Turner visited Smailholm before August 1831 and it is unlikely that he used another artist's drawing as basis for his design. Most probably it was made at Abbotsford not as an illustration but as a gift

[22] MS. Acc. 5131, ff. 140–2, here reproduced in full with the exception of an irrelevant postscript and the partial list of subjects (including the Aisle at Dryburgh), which Scott thought better of and scratched through.
[23] MS. 3917, f. 160.

to Scott, in whose possession it remained while the designs for the engravings were put up for sale after their use. We are left then with the likelihood that Scott's notions of Turner's waywardness simply had no foundation apart from ideas he had formed at an earlier date.

Cadell's reply to Scott attempted to allay the misgivings expressed: he insisted that he had done nothing without Scott's sanction.[24] But he urged that Mortham be omitted because the subject figured in Turner's views for Whitaker's *History of Richmondshire*. To Scott's (attached) suggestion of the funeral aisle at Dryburgh Abbey he objected as an 'admission of the mortality of the Author of the Lay'. He maintained again that Flodden should be included for its associative interest.

Scott's final written pronouncements on these issues occur in a letter of 3 August which reads, in part, as follows:

[Mortham] is a principle beautiful & indispensible subject. If you have illustrations at all you must have them appropriate otherwise we shall be like

> Our auld gudeman wha gait down to the Merse
> With his breeks on his head & his bonnet &c &c

I cannot see how you can make Bowes Castle pass for Mortham a place totally unlike it in situation & appearance and so far separate—ten or twelve miles at least. I will not however plague you with more rigmarole as it is difficult to me to get through all these discussions and make myself comprehensible so will remit it till meeting when we shall understand each other.

I conceive you are still mistaken about Flodden of which you cannot have a view that will illustrate the text for you can from no corner see both the north & south side of the hill at once.

I do not care about the Domus Ultima for I am certainly in no hurry to take that journey all I thought of was it would make a pretty vignette. I do not think I mentioned to you the old Castle of Bemersid & an exquisite view from the Gate heugh within four or five miles of Abbotsford and one or two of each other. You should also keep in view Crichton Castle if wanted for Marmion. Fast Castle is I think totally unconnected with any poetry I ever wrote & could only have one vue if the publick have [?] esteemd [it] applicable to the Bride of Lammermore as to which there is no question. We have still to apply illustrations to the dramatic volume. I hope by your next to learn of Mr Turner's approach for like a carriage at a public place the affair stops the way & keeps me from attending to other things.

Yours truly
W. Scott[25]

---

[24] MS. 3919, f.1.
[25] MS. Acc. 5131, ff. 144–5; Scott wrote 'Norham' at the beginning of the extract, but obviously intended 'Mortham'.

Cadell accompanied Turner to Abbotsford and it seems likely that Turner meant to represent their arrival when he included in the foreground of his vignette *Abbotsford,* a chaise with two passengers attended by figures on horseback. The week of Turner's visit, ending on 11 August, was to see the disputed issues resolved at last and, in the main, Scott had the final word.[26] The inclusion of Mortham was conceded, albeit as a distant feature of *The Junction of the Greta and Tees,* while Twizell Castle and Flodden Field were dropped. In some measure Scott seems to have retreated in his objections to Bowes Tower, which was used for the vignette to *Rokeby* opposite *Greta and Tees,* but they may well have lost force when it was no longer a matter of substituting Bowes for Mortham. With the exception of Cessford Castle, all the subjects in the general vicinity of Abbotsford that Scott proposed—Newark, Dryburgh, Bemerside and Smailholm—were adopted. The Round Table, of uncertain fitness, became the subject of one of Turner's most inventive designs for the series, *Mayburgh,* but then Scott had conceived that it could perhaps be justified. Finally, Loch Coruisk, on which Scott set great store, was assured of adoption with confirmation of Turner's plan for a trip to the Hebrides.

As a series Turner's illustrations to Scott's poetry are the most personal he conceived, both with respect to their artistic qualities and in their wealth of specific allusions to the circumstances of the artist's visit to Scotland in 1831. It was probably because Cadell wished to emphasize the originality of these designs, as the advertisement for the edition would do, that Turner referred in *Abbotsford* to his arrival, that he depicted Scott, himself and Miss Haig in

---

[26] The terminal date for Turner's visit is indicated by the date of Cadell's letter of 12 August (see n. 21 above) in which he mentions having accompanied Turner to Berwick the previous day.

The order of the subjects as they appear in the edition is as follows:

Volume	Frontispiece	Vignette
1. Minstrelsy	Carlisle	Smailholm
2. Minstrelsy	Jedburgh Abbey	Johnnie Armstrong's Tower
3. Minstrelsy	Kelso	Lochmaben
4. Minstrelsy	Caerlaverock Castle	Hermitage
5. Sir Tristrem	Dryburgh Abbey	Bemerside
6. Lay of the Last Minstrel	Melrose	Newark Castle
7. Marmion	Edinburgh	Ashestiel
8. Lady of the Lake	Loch Katrine	Loch Achray
9. Rokeby	Junction of the Greta and the Tees	Bowes Tower
10. Lord of the Isles	Loch Coriskin [Coruisk]	Staffa
11. Bridal of Triermain	Skiddaw	Mayburgh
12. Dramas	Berwick-upon-Tweed	Abbotsford

the foreground of *Bemerside*, that he represented himself sketching during a picnic with Scott and others at Melrose, and so on. Not only were the social aspects of the visit portrayed, but also the more solitary stretches of Turner's journey, as where he includes himself and his guide in the foreground of *Loch Coruisk* or, in *The Junction of Greta and Tees*, is shown fishing in the equivocal light of a northern summer's night.

At the same time the series is about Scott himself in a more specific sense than that which would inevitably associate the author with the scenes in which his poems were set. At least four of the designs are mainly biographical, 'illustrations' of the poet's life more than of anything he wrote. Smailholm was identified with Scott's childhood, memories of which were recalled by his visit to the site in 1831 with Turner, J. G. Lockhart and James Skene. The Vassar College drawing of *Sandyknowe and Smailholm Tower* points to these associations in its depiction of Scott as a lame child with his nurse and in the abundance of detail meant to characterize life on his grandparents' farm. The engraved illustration is much less explicit—Sandyknowe is removed to the distance at the right —and yet, in the dramatic perspective of the cliffs and Tower, the directional and atmospheric turbulence and heightened value contrasts throughout. Turner does suggest the intensity of imaginative experience that marked Scott's early years.

Ashestiel, Scott's summer residence between 1804 and 1811, was made the subject of the vignette to *Marmion* in place of Flodden Field. Since Scott lived at Ashestiel during the composition of *Marmion* and descriptions of the surrounding scenery figure in the poem, it is not possible to draw any strict division between the literary context and that of the poet's life. Yet the prominence of the house itself places primary emphasis on Scott's personal history. Ashestiel here stands for his early recognition and success, culminating in the enthusiastic reception of *The Lady of the Lake* in 1810. Turner's vignette is based on a finely controlled balance between horizontal and vertical relations, and on a dialectic in which spatial penetration is asserted and then opposed by elements that draw the eye back towards the surface. The variety in the play of light and shadow is an analogy for the colour and movement of Scott's vision of nature, and the controlled tension of Turner's scheme epitomizes Scott's mastery of his material, asserted and acclaimed during his tenancy of Ashestiel.

Abbotsford was appropriately the subject corresponding to

Scott's mature position as it was architecturally its symbol.
Turner's vignette provides a suitable cachet in the framing device,
of a type which accompanies all the drawings for vignettes in this
series that I have been able to trace but survives in the engravings
only in this one instance.[27] It consists of a linear boundary that
contradicts in a strange manner the vignette character of the landscape it contains. In *Abbotsford*, this implied panel is superimposed,
as it were, on contour representations of interiors, with specimens
of Scott's armour on the left and, on the right, an intimate view of
his study. But transcending these *emblemata* is the moonlit Abbotsford of the landscape, a boldly asymmetrical vision in which the
depth of shadow massed towards the centre tells against the crisp-
ness of reflections in the water and marbled fitfulness of light in
the cloudy sky. It is high romance as compared with the relatively
direct freshness and austerity of *Ashestiel*.

The panoramic *Edinburgh from Blackford Hill* alludes to the
city's role in Scott's life; he is shown being helped up the rise by
Turner, though Scott did not in fact accompany Turner to Edinburgh on this occasion. Finally, the biographical aspect of the
series was augmented by the engraving of *Dryburgh Abbey*. It was
probably due to Cadell's wish to avoid any funereal suggestion in
this subject that Turner settled on a very remote view of the
Abbey from the opposite bank of the encircling Tweed.

J. G. Lockhart joined Scott on several of his excursions with
Turner and his mention of Scott's sadness upon visiting Smailholm
and, by inference, Dryburgh, where he declined to accompany
Turner into the inclosure, has coloured both Thornbury's and
Finberg's accounts.[28] Thornbury went so far as to interpret
Turner's designs in the spirit of Lockhart's retrospective melancholy; Turner, he claimed, 'caught all the mournful poetry of the
old poet's reveries. In how many of the scenes does he give us the
moonlight rising and the cows pacing homeward!' And further:
'Turner . . . shows us the scenes, not as they were, but as they are
—contrasting the feudal and the past as much as possible, and as
sadly as possible, with the present.' And yet it was at this point,

[27] The drawings for the vignettes that I have located are *Smailholm Tower* (Kurt
Pantzer coll., Indianapolis), *Johnny Armstrong's Tower* (Taft Museum, Cincinnati;
another version in Pantzer coll.), *Ashestiel* (Fitzwilliam Museum) and *Fingal's Cave*
(recently with Messrs. Agnew, London). The drawings for frontispieces that I have
located are *Jedburgh Abbey* (Taft Museum), *Loch Katrine* (British Museum), *Melrose*
and *Loch Coruisk* (National Gallery of Scotland).
[28] Walter Thornbury, *Life of J. M. W. Turner, R.A.*, rev. ed. (London, 1877) 131
and following; Finberg, *Life*, 332.

according to Lockhart, that Scott's anxieties were eased by his notion that the sale of the 'Magnum Opus' had virtually offset his debts. In any event, Thornbury's characterization of the engravings as mainly lugubrious is very far from apt; indeed, the gamut of sentiment is wider and richer in nuance than in any other Turner series of literary designs. It ranges from the lyrical incandescence of *Loch Achray* to the sublime of *Loch Coruisk*, from the deeply sombre *Caerlaverock Castle* to the Claudian serenity of *Kelso*. Most of the vignettes in which Turner was chiefly concerned to interpret Scott's sense of the energies of nature sound mixed notes with respect to mood.

Apart from Lockhart's remarks, written evidence about Turner's stay at Abbotsford is disappointingly scanty. However, a memento survives in the form of a tray (now in the Indianapolis Museum of Art) on which Turner created a pastoral idyll of Abbotsford and its surroundings enveloped in a melting, almost dream-like atmosphere. The tray had been in use during a picnic given to entertain the artist; with its painted decoration it was subsequently presented to Mrs. Lockhart as a gesture of appreciation for the hospitality of the Scott household.

From Abbotsford Turner journeyed with Cadell to Kelso and Berwick, where he got 'very charming sketches' according to a Cadell letter of 12 August. They next made their way to Edinburgh and thence, Cadell reported on 18 August, Turner left alone for Loch Katrine, 'in good glee'.[29] The final phase of his outward itinerary took him by steamer to the Hebrides, to Loch Coruisk in the Isle of Skye and, on a second excursion, to Staffa. His description of the landing at Staffa, where 'some got into Fingal's Cave, others would not', is given by Finberg; characteristically, Turner was among those who chose to venture.

Turner returned to Edinburgh and conferred with Cadell about the subjects for illustration before leaving Scotland. In a letter to Scott of 19 September, Cadell observed:

> I am sorry that Mr. Turner should have annoyed you all so much—it was most absurd to be in such a pother. Notwithstanding I passed a most profitable evening with him going over all the subjects and fixing their various positions—he is great in his praise of Coriskin & wishes to know if you prefer any one point more than another.[30]

What Turner did to annoy the Scott household is not known. He

---

[29] MS. 3919, f. 39 (12 August), f. 41 (18 August).
[30] MS. 3919, f. 155.

was back in London by 23 September, according to a letter published in part by Thornbury.

In spite of the apparent lack of personal affinity between Turner and Scott, they shared an adherence to the Romantic mystique of *place*, that is to the perception of nature and human history in a topographical dimension. For if Turner's over-riding goal was to unite landscape with ideas of universal significance, his approach to the collection of his materials was in large measure that of the topographical draughtsman, while Scott's feelings for locale and its visual evocation is one of the most vital elements of his poetry. It was this quality in Scott that made his work especially accessible to what a critic in 1844 referred to as 'real' illustration. 'Real' illustration depicted actual scenes described in literature in contradistinction to 'ideal' illustration of narrative incident, a distinction which reflects the prevailing dichotomy between landscape and figure in British Romantic art. 'Byron and Scott are alike in this, that they give ample scope both for real and ideal illustration. . . . But is it possible to read Byron without wishing to see the scenes he describes? and if that wish be strong in our minds with regard to Byron, whose interests lie abroad—in fact are foreign—how far stronger is it in the case of Scott, whose thoughts, and words, and scenes come home to ourselves . . .?'[31] Scott's descriptions had added substantially to the itinerary of picturesque travel, as evidenced by the pilgrimage of thousands of visitors to Flodden Field and Loch Katrine. From the standpoint of the genesis of Scott's ideas, the importance of locale as a tangible threshold of the historical imagination is exampled by the inspiration of *Rokeby*; the estate itself with its medieval associations served as Scott's point of departure (which explains his insistence on the inclusion of Mortham in the illustrations).

In France, Delacroix realized the 'ideal' illustration of Scott in the medium and on the scale of history painting, choosing subjects exclusively from the novels. 'Real' illustration was a relatively new and characteristically British solution for which the doctrine of the association of ideas had served as preparation. It was Turner himself who had made it a genuine creative option with his vignettes to *Italy*, demonstrating in the realm of illustration how topography might be fused with the coherent expression of ideas

[31] 'Illustrated Books', *Quarterly Review*, lxxiv (June 1844), 167–99, esp. p. 105.

or sentiments. In view of Turner's incapacity with the figure, the new mode was adapted to a major zone of common ground between painter and poet, the identified scene as symbol of past events or as manifestation of the energies of nature.

It was symptomatic of the final maturity of British Romanticism that Scott and Turner should have come together for an undertaking that enhanced the brief supremacy of landscape over traditional modes of illustration; its designation for a mass audience was, as well, a sign of changed conditions of patronage. To be sure, these circumstances were repeated in Turner's use of 'real' illustration for his designs to *Byron's Life and Works* (1832–4) and Rogers's *Poems* (1834), though in the latter the use of landscape *types*, in addition to identified scenes, is frequent. But the character of the Scott engravings—more private and venturesome, on the whole, than those to Rogers and more intense than the Byron series—mark these as a special triumph. They comprise the most original and sustained use of 'real' landscape in Turner's literary illustration, and they had moreover a significant bearing on his painting of the later 1830s and 1840s. His exploration of the vignette form, particularly in the Scott series, had a catalytic effect on the development of the vortical composition in his painting. The inventiveness of Turner's work for Scott was favoured by their propinquity of outlook and it was, I believe, as a testimonial to that kinship of feeling that Turner painted *Staffa, Fingal's Cave* (exhibited at the Royal Academy, 1832) following his return from Scotland. Like two other pictures that do homage to poets, *Thomson's Aeolian Harp* (1809) and *Childe Harold's Pilgrimage* (1832), it is both objectively a tribute to Scott and a highly personal statement about Turner's participation in the poet's vision of nature.

Scott and Delacroix, with some Assistance from Hugo and Bonington

MARTIN KEMP

THE entries in Delacroix's *Journal* during 1824, a seminal year for French painting, testify to the importance of the written word as a source of general inspiration for his imagination and specific inspiration for his paintings. Through his readings of great literature, he attempted to 'exert' his mind continually 'on great ideas'.[1] He believed that poets such as Dante, Shakespeare and Byron could act as 'an unfailing spur to your imagination'.[2] The stimulation which he received from his favourite authors was so powerful that he even became concerned in case he possessed no independent inspiration of his own: 'What! You are original, you say, and yet your flame is only kindled by reading Byron or Dante, etc. You mistake this fever for creative ability when it is no more than a desire to imitate.'[3] Perhaps it was as an act of artistic independence that he envisaged (but seems not to have succeeded in) creating his own sources of literary inspiration: 'it would be an excellent thing to compose verses on a subject, rhymed or otherwise, to help one kindle the fire for painting. . . . I must try to do so on Scio.'[4]

The numerous subjects in Delacroix's painted and graphic *œuvre* drawn from Shakespeare and Byron span the full range of his career, and his feeling of affinity for these authors seems never to have waned. The numerical tally of subjects derived from the novels of Sir Walter Scott is similarly impressive, but his 'spiritual' relationship with Scott as an artist was more variable and in some ways more revealing than his relationships with either Shakespeare

---

[1] E. Delacroix, *Journal*, ed. A. Joubin (Paris, 1932), entry for 8 March 1824.
[2] *Ibid*. 11 May 1824.   [3] *Ibid*. 14 May 1824.
[4] *Ibid*. 25 April 1824, referring to *Scenes from the Massacre at Chios* which he was painting for the Salon. For his early attempts to become a writer, see J. Marchand's 'Delacroix fut écrivain avant d'être peintre', *Les Nouvelles Littéraires*, August 1952, and his *Les Dangers de la cour* (Avignon, 1960).

or Byron. His changing attitude to Scott reflects an important aspect of his intellectual development.

Delacroix admired Scott during the 1820s—a sentiment which was far from exceptional in France and which must be seen as part of the wave of Anglo- (and we must add Scoto-) philia which was then sweeping the Parisian art world. Scott's reputation was rising strongly on the French Romantic tide by 1823, the year of the first reference to Scott in Delacroix's writings.

Guy Mannering had been the first of Scott's novels to be translated into French—in 1816—and five years later this novel was also the first to be dramatized for the French stage.[5] By 1820, nine of the novels had been translated, and the 1820s saw the increasingly rapid translation, dramatization, and wholesale imitation of Scott's new works. The publishers of Defauconpret's translations claimed (probably without undue exaggeration) sales of two million by 1840.[6] If this and the number of Scott imitations can be taken as reliable criteria of his popularity, the French vogue for Scott seems to have at least equalled that for either Shakespeare or Byron.

Scott was fashionable in France some years before he made any profound impact upon creative artists of the highest order. Only in the mid-1820s did his considerable influence move beyond a generally superficial level. Delacroix in painting and Victor Hugo in literature were amongst the first French artists to respond to Scott by creating genuinely original Scott-inspired works rather than mindless pastiches. And, as I hope to show, the responses of Delacroix and Hugo were for a time closely associated.

Delacroix's first documented painting of a Scott subject is lost—a loss which would not have been regretted overmuch by the painter if his disarming *Journal* entry for 30 December 1823 is to be believed: 'I recently sold to M. Coutan, the connoisseur of Scheffer, my execrable painting of *Ivanhoe*. . . . The poor fellow!'[7]

[5] H. White, *Sir Walter Scott's Novels on the Stage* (New Haven and Oxford, 1927), 233–45.

[6] E. Partridge, *The French Romantics' Knowledge of English Literature* (Paris, 1924), 123. Scott's impact in France is also discussed by White, *op. cit.*, 201–6; F. W. M. Draper, *The Rise and Fall of French Romantic Drama, with Special Reference to the Influence of Shakespeare, Scott and Byron* (London, 1923), 11–55; and E. P. Dargan, 'Scott and the French Romantics', *PMLA* xlix (1934), 599–629.

[7] Mrs. M. G. McGhee has kindly informed me that this painting is listed in the Coutan sale-catalogue, 9–10 March 1829, under Eugène LACROIX: 'no. 49. Sujet tiré d'Ivanhoë, roman de Walter-Scott. Ivanhoë blessé et malade se fait rendre compte par la jeune juive de l'attaque que l'on fait du château ou il est renfermé'. (MS. note, sold for 150 francs.)

At this date there is no question of Delacroix having drawn inspiration from a stage performance rather than from the novel itself; the first French dramatization of *Ivanhoe* did not occur until 1826.[8] This priority of the written word in providing him with inspiration for his paintings of Scott subjects appears to be the general rule; the first instances of his drawing upon *Quentin Durward* and *The Bride of Lammermoor* each precede the corresponding adaptation for the French theatre.

Did Delacroix read the French or English versions? Both texts appear on his lithograph of *Ravenswood and Lucy at the Mermaidens' Fountain*, and his knowledge of English had greatly improved since his first halting attempts to communicate with an English girl-friend in 1817. However, the only passage from Scott which Delacroix transcribed in his *Journal* is in French;[9] and none of the paintings, drawings, or lithographs precedes the relevant translation. For convenience, he probably read the novels more often in French.

At the Parisian soirées, which played such an important role in Delacroix's intellectual life, Scott (like Byron) was a regular topic of conversation. Delacroix himself recorded one instance of such a discussion in 1824.[10] It was in this year that he first sketched a narrative subject from *The Bride of Lammermoor* (pl. 1).[11] In selecting the tragic episode of Lucy Ashton's bridal night—she is discovered with 'her head-gear dishevelled; her night clothes torn and dabbled with blood, her eyes glazed and her features convulsed into a wild paroxysm of insanity . . . with the frantic gestures of an exulting demoniac'—Delacroix has chosen one of Scott's darkest creations, seizing upon those qualities in the novel that subsequently most embarrassed its author. Behind the hideously staring Lucy and the upturned chair lies her bridegroom's broken and near-dead body. The scene is drawn with an expressiveness reminiscent of Goya's *Disasters of War*; the jagged, clashing, scratched hatching-lines certainly reflect Delacroix's avid study of Goya's etchings.

The deeply disturbing power of this drawing shares more of the spirit of Goethe's *Faust* than the tone of Scott's normal productions. And, generally, there is some similarity of mood

---

[8] At the Odéon on 15 September (White, *op. cit.*, 237).
[9] *Journal*, 8 May 1862.   [10] *Ibid.* 20 July 1824.
[11] A. Robaut, *L'Œuvre complète d'Eugène Delacroix* (Paris, 1885), no. 104, provides a date of 1824 for a closely-related (lost?) water-colour. See also M. Sérullaz, *Mémorial de l'exposition Eugène Delacroix* (Paris, 1963), no. 58.

between Delacroix's visual translations of Scott, Dante, Tasso, Shakespeare, and Byron during the first half of the 1820s. It was not until 1826 or 1827 that he began to create major works that relate specifically to Scott rather than to the other authors in favour with the Romantic movement.

Scott's impact in France, as elsewhere, was substantially due to his ability to bring the past to life, through a vivid (and often scholarly) recreation of the sights, sounds and manners of a particular age—what Delacroix called the 'astonishing smell of reality . . . which took everyone by surprise in Walter Scott's novels'.[12] Hugo, Sainte-Beuve and Balzac all responded powerfully to Scott's historical realism at the very time when Delacroix was most closely associated with *avant-garde* movements in literature. The key point in Delacroix's Romantic antiquarianism came with his important but neglected collaboration with Hugo on the costume designs for *Amy Robsart* (pls. 2 and 3).[13] Hugo's play, based closely upon Scott's *Kenilworth*, was produced by Hugo's nephew, Paul Foucher, at the Odéon on 13 February 1828, surviving only one performance—and that barely. Hugo's writing was roundly condemned by the critics, but two of them singled out the staging for special praise. *Le Figaro* wrote on 14 February: 'the piece is mounted with an extreme care which does the greatest honour to the management. Like the costumes, there is nothing which is not beautiful or exact'. A day later, *Le Pandore* added: 'the sets by M. Gué are very agreeable; the costumes, of great exactitude and in charming taste, are designed by M. E. Delacroix'. Historical exactitude, it seems, was the order of the day.

Delacroix's scholarly interest in the post-classical past was at its keenest during the second half of the 1820s. On his visit to England in 1825, he studied medieval architecture and sculpture at Westminster, probably accompanied by Richard Bonington; and the two artists responded enthusiastically when they visited Dr. Meyrick's house to view what Delacroix called 'probably the most beautiful collection of armour in existence'.[14] The drawings made by

---

[12] *Journal*, 28 October 1853.

[13] For letters on the designing of the costumes, see *Correspondance générale d'Eugène Delacroix*, ed. A. Joubin (Paris, 1936–9), i. 221 (wrongly dated July 1828 by Joubin; the correspondence must have been written before the first performance in February), and E. Moreau-Nélaton, *Delacroix raconté par lui-même* (Paris, 1916), i. 93.

[14] *Correspondance*, iv. 287. A drawing of breast-plates in the Louvre (RF 9846) is dated 9 July, and a note on the drawing in the Library of the Wallace Collection (pl. 5) records that he visited Dr. Meyrick's house on the evening of 8 July. The visit is well discussed by Lee Johnson in the catalogues of the Delacroix exhibitions in

Bonington on this visit tend to strike a higher historical level of detailed accuracy than those of Delacroix, while exhibiting less facility in draughtsmanship (pls. 4 and 5). But whatever differences may be discerned in their styles, their drawings leave no doubt that they shared an antiquarian interest in the evocative paraphernalia of the past—an interest which strongly parallels Scott's own. It is highly probable that Scott's novels had already exercised some influence on Delacroix, since (as we have seen) he had completed a painting of *Ivanhoe* two years previously.

The small costume (or period) piece became a speciality of Bonington during 1825, 1826, and 1827. Delacroix readily acknowledged his friend's gifts in this direction—something which later critics have been unnecessarily reluctant to do—and implied that his own practice of this genre was partly inspired by the fresh sparkle of Bonington's history pieces.[15] The two artists delved into the same costume books for their research into the appearance of the past, and Bonington's charmingly silken painting of *Amy Robsart and the Earl of Leicester*, based upon his studies of sixteenth-century works in the Louvre,[16] provides a nice precedent for the antiquarian spirit in which Delacroix designed the costumes for Hugo's play (pls. 6 and 7). There can be little doubt that their mutual interest in 'costume drama' was closely related to a shared enthusiasm for Scott's historical novels; *Quentin Durward*, for example, proved to be a fertile source for pictures by both artists during the mid-1820s.[17]

Careful attention to historical decorum is usually regarded as a perogative of Neoclassicism. But those Romantic artists who fell under the spell of Scott showed themselves on occasions to be equally concerned with the recreation of a past age. What then differentiates Romantic from Neoclassical antiquarianism? It is possible, I think, to provide a broad answer to this question— always bearing in mind that the complex aspirations of creative artists (and of self-professed Romanticists in particular) cannot be

---

Toronto (1963), no. 68, and London–Edinburgh (1964), nos. 94–6. Bonington's drawings of Meyrick armour are listed in *R. P. Bonington*, the catalogue of the Nottingham exhibition (1965), nos. 154–65.

[15] *Correspondance*, iv. 286–7.

[16] Nottingham Exhibition Catalogue, nos. 133 and 296. A closely similar pair of figures was published as a lithograph by Bonington under the title 'Le silence favourable' in his *Cahiers de six sujets* (1826; Curtis 47). The present title is highly plausible, though it is unsupported by contemporary evidence.

[17] See D. Cooper, 'Bonington and *Quentin Durward*', *Burlington Magazine* lxxxviii (1946), 112–17, and Lee Johnson, *ibid.* cxviii (1966), 568–70.

expected to correspond with infallible neatness to the generalizations imposed upon their periods by historians of art.

In contrast to the Neoclassicists—devoted as they were to the supposed virtues of classical antiquity—the Romantics deliberately concentrated upon the non-classical past. This divergence of interest reflects the deep difference between their attitudes towards expression in art. Romanticists, in their recreation of the non-classical past, felt they could be free from the controlled Stoicism of expression which had become an automatic corollary to the French classical style. A piece of spiky armour was more easily associated in their minds with dark menace and passionate action than was a classical toga; the former seemed to exude a Romantic air of emotional excitement, the latter a chill air of philosophic calm. Overtones of controlled discipline even coloured the prevailing attitudes towards the more martial aspects of classical civilization. No such proscriptions of emotion were seen as operating in the medieval world. French Romantic artists could thus freely project their wide-ranging expression of open emotion into the conveniently distant realms of the 'dark ages'.

The Romantic form of expression was also regarded as more natural, as closer to the reality of nature in all her changing moods. Hugo, in his antiquarian phase, was one of the major advocates of nature and natural passion. And, for a short time, Delacroix closely approached Hugo's position. In 1824 Delacroix wrote: 'I am seized with a longing to use an entirely new style of painting that would consist, so to speak, in making a literal tracing of nature. . . . For small pictures one could draw in the subject and rather vaguely rub in the colour on the canvas and then copy the exact pose from the model.'[18] His actual paintings during this period make it clear that (like Hugo) he associated this naturalism with powerful expression of emotion.

Significantly, one of Hugo's first pleas for a natural art of this kind is to be found in an article on *Quentin Durward* in *La muse francaise*, the short-lived 1823 periodical. He selected 'the hideous and revolting portrayal of the orgy', during which the 'Wild Boar of the Ardennes' presides over the murder of the Bishop of Liege, as 'one of the finest chapters of the book'. Inspired by Scott's novel, he asked, 'Isn't life like a bizarre drama in which the good and the bad, the beautiful and the ugly, the high and the low are mingled? . . . Must he [the artist] then restrict himself to com-

[18] *Journal*, 20 February 1824.

posing, like certain Flemish painters, entirely dark pictures, or, like the Chinese, entirely light ones?'[19] This dramatic principle of natural contrast, later developed in his preface to *Cromwell*, is superbly exemplified in Delacroix's free variation upon the very theme from *Quentin Durward* which had so caught Hugo's imagination. I refer to Delacroix's painting of *The Murder of the Bishop of Liège*, originally exhibited as *Guillaume de la Marck, surnommé le Sanglier des Ardennes* (pl. 8).

Delacroix appears to have begun a painting of this subject by October 1827, when Hugo wrote: 'convey my best regards to Sardanpalus, Faliero, the Bishop of Liège and all your retinue'.[20] The earliest sketches, probably dating from this time, all dominantly embody Hugo's principle of contrast, both in emotion and in the Rembrandtesque *chiaroscuro* effects.[21] According to a contemporary, Ernest Chesnau, Delacroix planned to illuminate the finished painting only with 'a light from a lamp enhanced by a reflector'—a thoroughly theatrical effect of spotlighting which would have been consistent with its Hugo-like conception.[22]

The key to the tonal contrast is the vividly luminous expanse of white tablecloth. Its powerful glare gave Delacroix some trouble, and the desired effect was not finally achieved until 1828 (if Villot's account is to be believed).[23] The finished work was purchased by the Duc d'Orléans, first exhibited at the Musée Colbert in December 1829 and subsequently at the Salon of 1831.[24] Villot also mentioned the antiquarian spirit in which Delacroix designed the setting, though his contention that the vault was inspired by the Palais de Justice at Rouen is questionable. The plain woodwork of the Rouen vault certainly provided the basis for the architecture in one of Delacroix's paintings—his *Melmoth the Wanderer*—but that in the *William de la Marck* is in fact based very closely upon Westminster Hall, which he probably studied with Bonington in 1825 (pl. 9).[25]

Delacroix's use of Westminster Hall for the Bishop's Castle of

[19] Quoted by B. Barrère, *La fantaisie de Victor Hugo, 1820–51* (Paris, 1949), 53–4.
[20] Moreau-Nélaton, *op. cit.* 93, and R. Escholier, *Delacroix* (Paris, 1926), i. 196.
[21] The sketches are discussed and illustrated by Sérullaz, *Memorial*, nos. 137–40.
[22] Chesnau is quoted by Escholier, *op. cit.* i. 246.
[23] Sérullaz, *Mémorial*, no. 136.
[24] The early history of the painting is thoroughly discussed by M. Toupet, 'L'assassinat de l'évêque de Liège par Delacroix', *La Revue du Louvre et des Musees de France* (1963), ii. 90–1.
[25] In addition to the drawing illustrated, the National Gallery of Scotland possesses two further studies by Bonington of the architecture of Westminster Hall (all under no. 3598).

Schonwaldt is extremely similar to Scott's ingenious method of 'historical collage'. And it is closely related to the historical settings of Hugo's plays; in his *Amy Robsart*, Hugo shows a marked partiality for 'magnificent Gothic salons' and the fifth act of his *Cromwell* (1827) is set in the 'Great Hall of Westminster'. We know that Delacroix was aware of Hugo's new play, *Cromwell*, since his letter to Hugo announcing the near-completion of the costumes for *Amy Robsart* also contains a suggestion for further collaboration—on *Cromwell* 'or on some other work which will be completely your blood and the fruit of your entrails'.[26]

Hugo's *Cromwell* may have been inspired in a general sense by Scott's *Woodstock*. This same novel by Scott also provided Delacroix with inspiration for his small oil painting of *Cromwell at Windsor* (pl. 10),[27] which was exhibited with the *William de la Marck* at the Salon of 1831—by which time it was owned by the Duc de Fitz-James, a French grandson of an illegitimate son of James II and an acquaintance of Scott.[28] The same owner also acquired (probably in 1828) Delacroix's *Milton Dictating 'Paradise Lost' to his Daughters*, and it is not unlikely that the *Cromwell* was planned as a historical counterpart to the *Milton*.[29]

Exceptionally, the *Cromwell* does not precede the first French staging of Scott's novel (in 1826, the year of its publication).[30] In view of Delacroix's close association with the theatre at this time, his inspiration may have come from Scott as rendered on the stage, rather than from the written word. The event represented by the painter—the tense moment when Cromwell turns round a painting expecting to see a portrait of the escaped Prince but is instead confronted by Van Dyck's image of the dead King—featured prominently in the 1826 stage version (though not in Hugo's *Cromwell*).

The painting is a small costume piece in the Bonington manner. Delacroix has made considerable efforts to capture the 'look' of

[26] *Correspondance*, i. 221. The reference to a work which will be completely Hugo's own probably reflects his reservations concerning Foucher's large contribution to the final version of *Amy Robsart*.

[27] After its début at the Salon, the oil painting was exhibited (with *William de la Marck?*) in London at the Royal Academy (*Correspondance*, i. 266). It passed through the Cheramy collection and was exhibited at the Lefevre Gallery in December 1966, when it was owned by Dr. Peter Nathan. I am grateful to its present American owner for permission to publish it. The Witt Library also records a water-colour variant (the composition is modified and reversed) in a Paris private collection in 1929.

[28] E. Johnson, *Sir Walter Scott, the Great Unknown* (London, 1970), ii. 1087.

[29] The *Milton* and its dating in relation to the *Cromwell* are discussed by Lee Johnson, Toronto 1963, no. 1.   [30] White, *op. cit.* 245.

the period. The setting and the pose of the Royalist (Wildrake) behind Cromwell possesses distinctly Van Dyckish qualities, in keeping with the subject. The King's portrait does not appear to be based upon any known prototype, but seems to be a suggestive if sketchy reconstruction, perhaps based upon the hunting portrait in the Louvre. By contrast, the representation of Cromwell conspicuously fails to conform to the physiognomy of the Roundhead leader. Characteristically, Delacroix's period accuracy is less than complete.

Even during this most historically-minded phase of his art, his antiquarianism (keen though it is) never becomes the *raison d'être*, starting-point or chief ingredient in his paintings; it is always ultimately subordinate to the original conception in his imagination of the emotional heart of the narrative.

The final years of the 1820s saw the climax of his Scott subjects. In addition to the preparatory and final paintings of *William de la Marck*, the two versions of *Cromwell at Windsor* and a watercolour of *Quentin Durward and the Countess of Croye*,[31] he is known to have completed at least six lithographs (three from *Ivanhoe*, and one each from *The Bride of Lammermoor*, *Redgauntlet*, and *Quentin Durward*).[32] He also painted *Quentin Durward and Le Balafré*, probably for the Duchesse de Berri, and made drawings of several other Scott themes.[33]

This was the period when Romantic antiquarianism was at its

[31] The water-colour *Quentin and Countess Isabelle* ('Isabelle waiting upon Quentin and Louis XI', ch. iv), which was recorded by Robaut (no. 271 and photograph in Witt Coll.) and which appeared in the 'Vente succession de M. H. P. . . .' at the Hôtel Drouot (23 April 1901) may be that listed in an undated section of the *Journal* (iii. 371–5) as 'Quentin Durward et Louis XI à table servis par la dame, dessin terminé (Schnetz)'.

[32] Delteil, iii, nos. 84–6, from *Ivanhoe* (and possibly 87 as *The Death of Bois-Guilbert*), 83 from *The Bride*, 88 from *Redgauntlet*, and Robaut 272 from *Quentin Durward*.

[33] For *Quentin and Le Balafré* (Paris, Louvre, on deposit at the Mobilier National), see *Correspondance*, i. 283 and 195, and Lee Johnson, *Burlington Magazine* (1966), 568–70 (see also fig. 36 for the identification of a drawing in the Nationalmuseum, Stockholm, as 'Quentin Durward overhearing the plot of Hayraddin and Lanzknecht'). In addition to the works based upon Scott recorded here and elsewhere in the present study, and the preliminary drawings for Salon paintings discussed in Sérullaz, *Mémorial*, Robaut lists two further possible Scott subjects (nos. 48 and 141), the former of which he dates improbably early. In a letter to me of February 1972, Lee Johnson has kindly informed me of two new inclusions in the list of Scott 'illustrations' in Delacroix's *œuvre*: (i) 'The Fight between the Knight of the Couchant Leopard and the Saracen' from *The Talisman* (1825), ch. i (exhib. London–Edinburgh 1964, no. 99: Besançon, Musée des Beaux-Arts); (ii) 'Robert Bruce watching the Spider', probably from *Tales of a Grandfather*, ch. viii (exhib. London–Edinburgh 1964, no. 125: also at Besançon). The latter subject is listed as 'Robert Bruce dans la cabanne regardant l'araignée' on 'an unpublished sheet of notes which is datable to the early 1830s'.

height, and Delacroix was involved in a number of historical projects. With Boulanger and Roqueplan (illustrators of Scott and friends of Hugo), he designed lithographs of Duguesclin for the *Chroniques de France*,[34] and for the Duchesse de Berri he painted the fourteenth-century episode of *King John at the Battle of Poitiers*.[35] These works of 'picturesque history' run parallel to contemporary developments in French historical writing, as manifested in the lively narratives of Guizot, Thierry, and de Barante. Behind all this, Scott was openly acknowledged as the primary influence.[36]

Delacroix's friend, Bonington, was similarly occupied with historical projects and Scott subjects at this time. Before his death in September 1828, Bonington completed numerous Scott period pieces, including his most important history painting, *Quentin Durward at Liège*, which (unlike Delacroix's free variations upon Scott themes) follows the author's account almost word-for-word and blow-for-blow.[37] He had also executed lithographs from *Rob Roy* and *A Legend of Montrose*, published in *Vues Pittoresques de l'Écosse* in 1826, 'with an explanatory text drawn in large part from the works of Sir Walter Scott by Am. Pichot'.[38]

Bonington's paintings and lithographs of Scott subjects belong to a species of 'Romantic picturesque' rather than to the more violently emotional world of full-blooded Romanticism, as practised by Hugo and (for a time) by Delacroix. Even at his most energetic, Bonington never achieves the intensity of emotion and action of Delacroix's 'massacre' period.

In contrast to the limited range of expression in Bonington's works, Delacroix's lithographs of Scott subjects exploit an extraordinary range of mood; from the *Front-de-Bœuf and the Sorceress* (pl. 11), sharing the demoniac fervour of the Goethe illustrations, to the gentle world of romantic love in *Ravenswood and Lucy at the*

[34] Delteil, iii, nos. 81–2.
[35] 1830: Paris, Louvre. The Duchesse failed to take delivery of the painting and Delacroix was forced to seek a buyer elsewhere (*Correspondance*, i. 295).
[36] Cf. Partridge, *op. cit.* p. 290. A particularly good scholarly example of 'picturesque history' is Guizot's *Histoire de la Révolution d'Angleterre* (Paris, 1826), which provided inspiration for paintings of *Cromwell and the Coffin of Charles I* by Paul Delaroche (1831: Nîmes, Musée des Beaux-Arts, and Hamburg, Kunsthalle; and 1849: Leningrad, Hermitage) and an 'answering' water-colour by Delacroix (1831: Robaut no. 368).
[37] Cooper, *op. cit.* 112–17.
[38] Curtis, nos. 28, 42, and 43. Pichot had earlier published the first biographical essay on Scott in French ('Essai sur la vie et les ouvrages de Walter Scott') in *Sir Walter Scott, Romans poétiques, traduits de l'anglais (en prose) par le traducteur des œuvres de Lord Byron* (Paris, 1820).

Mermaidens' Fountain (pl. 12). Even in this latter instance, a sinister portent is present, in the form of a raven which (as the appended text records) 'dropped dead at the feet of Lucy, whose dress was stained with some spots of its blood'.[39] The raven cannot, however, be clearly discerned in the preliminary drawings or lithograph. Such a lack of literal correspondence between the lithograph and the actual text is typical of his casual attitude to narrative detail; for him, mood was ultimately more important than minutiae. It is not surprising, therefore, that his *William de la Marck* only loosely followed Scott's intricate and protracted account of the scene and personages at the assassination of the Bishop.[40]

This lack of narrative precision has not unnaturally caused difficulty in identifying the subject-matter of some of Delacroix's works. The figures of Ravenswood and Lucy, for example, so resemble those of Romeo and Juliet in the scene which he painted of the Capulets' ball that the preliminary drawings for the two works have often been confused.[41] Scott, no doubt, would have approved of this equation with Shakespeare; the parallel between the two pairs of doomed lovers was clearly in his mind when he conceived *The Bride*.

A similar instance of Scott-Shakespeare confusion has arisen with Delacroix's small, full-length self-portrait (pl. 13). Has he portrayed himself as Ravenswood or Hamlet? The name 'Raveswood' [*sic*] was once inscribed in Delacroix's hand on the stretcher of the painting, and the identification of the figure as Ravenswood probably dates back as far as its first owner.[42] The seventeenth-century costume argues against this identification, but the period is less clearly emphasised in *The Bride* than in most of Scott novels —so much so that one recent biographer has mistakenly placed Ravenswood's exploits in the seventeenth rather than eighteenth century.[43]

[39] First state 1829. The text is printed below the lithograph in French and English, but the chapter number is given as 'xxix' rather than 'xix'.

[40] Only William, the Bishop and Nikkel Blok (the butcher who actually murdered the Bishop) can be positively identified. Scott describes the Bishop's 'interrogation' and murder as taking place 'at the foot of his own episcopal throne', upon which William was sitting—not on the other side of an enormous table.

[41] For the correction of this confusion, see Sérullaz, *Mémorial*, nos. 62, 63 and 120.

[42] A fuller explanation of the arguments in favour of the Ravenswood identification is provided by Lee Johnson, London–Edinburgh 1964, no. 15 (see also no. 92, identified as *Ravenswood and Caleb*).

[43] Johnson, *op. cit.* i. 670. The actual episode in the history of the Dalrymple (Stair) family which provided the prototype for Scott's story occurred in 1669, but Scott reset the narrative (see the beginning of ch. xxiv) in the reign of Queen Anne.

The *Self-Portrait as Ravenswood* (as it probably should be called) has generally been dated 1821, which would give it considerable significance as the earliest of all Delacroix's Scott subjects. Stylistically, however, it can be more easily aligned with his works of 1824, and it probably dates from the same year as the bedroom scene from *The Bride*. Even at this later date, such a self-identification with one of Scott's most Romantic and psychologically interesting heroes would testify to the depth of his response to Scott during the 1820s.

After 1830, there is a rapid decline in the number of Scott subjects in Delacroix's *œuvre*. A lost painting of *The Knight and the Hermit of Copmanhurst* was rejected by Salon juries in 1833 and 1834,[44] and was followed by a gap of a dozen years before he exhibited his next Scott work. During this time, he continued to draw frequently upon the writings of Shakespeare, Goethe, and Byron, but Scott no longer seems to have held an important place in his creative imagination. He later expressed highly critical views of Scott, and we can infer that his attitude had begun to change during the 1830s—at the same time as his distrust of Hugo and the other self-professed Romanticists had begun to develop.

'The descriptive passages which overburden modern novels are a sign of sterility; for it is easier to describe the dress or outward appearance of an object than to trace subtly the developments of characters or the portrayal of the heart.' And, in a similar vein, 'the doublet and leather collar of a medieval serf are easier to describe than the movements of the human heart'. These closely related passages of criticism were both written with Scott's technique of historical realism in mind. The first was written by Delacroix in 1853 and the second by Stendhal as early as 1830.[45] The correspondence between their attitudes is almost certainly not coincidental. After an uneasy beginning to their relationship, the painter and author developed a powerful mutual regard, and they came increasingly to share their reservations concerning Romantics of the Hugo type. A standpoint close to Stendhal can be discerned in Delacroix criticism of Scott's (and Fenimore Cooper's)

---

[44] See Lee Johnson, 'Eugène Delacroix et les salons, documents inédits au Louvre', *Revue du Louvre* (1966), nos. 4–5. A related drawing is in the Budapest Museum of Fine Arts (exhib. London–Edinburgh 1964, no. 112).

[45] Delacroix, *Journal*, 9 April 1856; Stendhal, 'Walter Scott et la Princesse de Clèves', *Le National*, 19 February 1830 (trans. in *Scott: the Critical Heritage*, ed. J. O. Hayden, London, 1970, 318–21).

novels: 'the whole disappears, drowned in details, and result is
boredom . . . the mind wanders dully in the middle of this monotony and emptiness, where the author seems to be satisfied in
talking to himself'.[46]

Delacroix's criticisms were voiced at a time when he set less
and less store by the antiquarian realism which had characterized
his collaboration with Hugo. Historical detail had become all the
rage on the French stage during the 1820s, particularly in productions of Scott and Shakespeare. On a visit to France in 1826, Scott
himself had delighted in the staging of *Ivanhoe* at the Odéon: 'it
was superbly got up, the Norman soldiers wearing pointed helmets
and what resembled much hauberks of mail which looked very
well'.[47] Though originally sympathetic to this historical movement,
Delacroix later came to consider that such antiquarianism was unnecessary and even distracting in the performance of great drama:
'we are told that Shakespeare's plays were generally performed in
barns. . . . The constant changes of scene were shown by placards
with "A Forest", "A Prison" and so on. Within this conventional
setting, the spectator's imagination was free to follow the actions
of the various characters who were animated by passions drawn
from nature, and that was enough.'[48]

Behind his later condemnations of fiddling detail lies a gradual
transformation in his attitude towards 'imitation'. Even in his
early theorizing, he cannot be taken as an advocate of Realism in
its later sense—only following nature, warts and all—but, during
the 1820s, he was prepared to countenance a relatively straightforward doctrine of imitation, provided it was coupled with the
exercise of imagination and the portrayal of deeper emotional
values. These values were closely related to his admiration for
great literature. Later, partly as a reaction against the more
extreme statements of the new school of Realist painting, he set
his face much more firmly against straightforward imitation in the
Realist sense, and he emphasized with increasing insistence that the
artist should first and foremost strive to capture the deeper spirits
of nature and man. This slight shift in balance in his art theory (it
cannot be called a radical change of direction) is reflected in the
subtly changing role of detail in his painting, as exemplified by the
transformation between the originally naturalistic *Algerian*

[46] *Journal*, 9 September 1859.
[47] Scott, *Journal*, 31 October 1826; he did not, however, approve of the treatment
of the text.
[48] Delacroix, *Journal*, 9 April 1856.

Women (1834: Paris, Louvre) and the more generalized effects of the Montpellier version (1849).[49]

Along with the modern Realism of the Courbet–Champfleury school, Delacroix rejected Scott's particular kind of historical realism—because both forms of realism seemed to skate over the surface of life. This is not to say, however, that he entirely rejected Scott as an artist (or, for that matter, Courbet, whose abilities as a painter he generously acknowledged). In spite of the 'long-winded passages', he still considered that 'Walter Scott and Rousseau before him aimed to probe feelings of intangible impressions and melancholy which the old writers barely recognized'.[50] And, after 1846, Scott subjects begin to reappear in his *œuvre*. Thinking back on Scott after a long interval, he seems to have felt able to cut through the dense surface of detail and to grasp the essential qualities of the events in Scott's narratives. The novel which re-emerged most potently in his imagination was *Ivanhoe*.

Between 1846 and 1860, he is known to have painted at least four *Ivanhoe* subjects, including two major Salon versions of *The Abduction of Rebecca*; and his 1860 list of suitable literary subjects contains no less than twenty-four from this novel.[51] At the same time, he planned to rearrange his 'illustrations to Walter Scott and Lord Byron', but noted that 'the compositions from their works and from various subjects cannot be made into separate works like those from *Faust* and *Hamlet'*.[52] Finally, in the year before his death, he transcribed in French a long section from *Quentin Durward* concerning Quentin and the Countess of Croye, as they become aware of their mutual love.[53]

The later version of the *Abduction of Rebecca by Bois-Guilbert* (pl. 14), begun in 1856 and exhibited at his last Salon in 1859, provides a fine climax to his Scott 'translations'.[54] This painting was generally ill-received by the critics, and it cannot be denied

---

[49] G. Mras, *Eugène Delacroix's Theory of Art* (Princeton, 1966), 56–8. Mras provides a good discussion of Delacroix's attitude to imitation (pp. 46–71), though tending (p. 52) to gloss over the small but important difference between the artist's later (1850–60) opinions and his earlier outlook (e.g. *Journal*, 20 February 1824, quoted above, p. 218).

[50] *Journal*, 9 April 1856.

[51] The 1846 *Abduction of Rebecca* is in the Metropolitan Museum, New York. The later version is discussed below. A (lost?) painting of *Bois-Guilbert's Death* is mentioned in a letter (*Correspondance*, iv. 79), and a *Journal* entry for 5 September 1858 reported good progress upon a 'little *Ivanhoe and Rebecca*' (also lost?). The list of subjects is in the *Journal*, 23 and 29 December 1860.

[52] *Journal*, 31 December 1860.

[53] *Ibid.* 8 May 1862.

[54] Progress on the painting is recorded in the *Journal*, 26 May and 29 June 1856.

that the pictorial space is loosely defined, the figures slackly articulated and the architectural structure of the castle unclear— particularly when compared to the carefully-arranged tunnel of architectural space in the *William de la Marck*. Furthermore, even by his own standards of artistic licence, the narrative stands at a far remove from the details of Scott's account.[55] Such casualness of detail would not, in Delacroix's eyes, have lessened its essential affinity to Scott's conception of Rebecca's plight—plucked from the fire only to be plunged into the frying-pan of Bois-Guilbert's desires. He was concerned with conveying the total texture of the drama through paint, colour and light in movement; his painting is an imaginative recreation of the emotional heart of the narrative rather than a literal translation in the Bonington or Delaroche manner. This work shows supremely that, whatever his reservations about Scott's technique, certain episodes retained their ability to 'kindle' his creative 'fire'.

Scott's novels do indeed seem to possess some peculiar form of vividness in evoking visual sensations. *Ivanhoe* most particularly has stimulated literary critics of every generation to leaf enthusiastically through their dictionaries of visual metaphors. Balzac considered that 'the first landscape in *Ivanhoe* testifies to a talent for painting'.[56] More recently, this novel has been said to glow 'with vivid colour', a colour which 'reflects the keenness of the eye that saw and the skill of the hand that painted it'.[57] In a more general vein, Hugo's colleague, Sainte-Beuve, called Scott 'an immortal painter'.[58] Dumas drew an exact (and particularly relevant) art-historical parallel: 'Scott painted localities, characters, customs and manners; it was necessary to take the novel from his hands, as Raphael carried on from Perugino, and add a vivid treatment of the passions'.[59] In a sense, this is just what Delacroix was attempting to accomplish in his latest paintings of Scott themes.

[55] Scott's account describes Rebecca's removal from the Castle 'on horseback before one of the Templar's Saracen slaves' (more or less as in the 1846 version), not carried from the inferno in the Templar's arms in the manner of a Sabine woman abducted by a Roman.

[56] Letter to Mme Hanska, 20–22 January 1838 (trans. in *Scott: the Critical Heritage*, 373–7).

[57] Johnson, *op. cit.* i. 737.

[58] Obituary of Scott in *Le Globe*, 27 September 1832 (trans. in *Scott: the Critical Heritage*, 326–8).

[59] *Souvenirs de 1830 à 1842*, viii.

Scott as Pageant-Master—
The Royal Visit of 1822

BASIL C. SKINNER

THE portrait of Scott by Andrew Geddes in the Scottish National Portrait Gallery is not only the most sensitive and percipient painting of him in the years of his prime, but also shows him at the outset of his career as pageant-master. Geddes made this study in 1818 in preparation for a large picture completed in 1821 but lost in 1850, depicting 'The Finding of the Honours of Scotland'—the crown insignia of Scotland that had remained unlocated in Edinburgh Castle since 1707.

The finding of the regalia was Scott's first adventure into the realms of pageantry and a key preliminary to the ceremonies that he devised for the Royal Visit of 1822. The idea of instituting an official search for the regalia had been mooted by Scott to the future king on the occasion of their first face-to-face meeting in 1815. The Prince Regent (as he then was) seems to have been aware of the merits of Scott's writing, if Byron is to be believed, as early as 1812, and in 1813 there occurred the incident when the Poet Laureateship was offered on behalf of the Prince to Scott. Scott took advice from the Duke of Buccleuch who felt 'the "Poet Laureate" would stick to you and your productions like a piece of court plaster', and declined the honour, in effect causing no offence to the Prince Regent who in March 1815 entertained him to dinner at Carlton House.

Following this meeting and discussion, Scott's idea of a commission to search for the honours was eventually approved and the commissioners, besides himself, included Buccleuch, Lord President Charles Hope, Chief Commissioner William Adam, Thomas Thomson, Depute Clerk Register, William Clerk, Clerk of the Jury Court, and certain others. The Regalia was found in a locked box in a locked room on 4 February 1818, and in September Adam

Ferguson, Scott's close friend, was inducted into the newly-made office of Keeper of the Regalia.

While it is important to bear this series of events of 1818 in mind as a small history preceding the Royal Visit idea of 1822, another preliminary development occurred in Scotland in 1820. In January of that year two men, William Mackenzie of Inverness and Colonel David Stewart of Garth, were instrumental in founding the Celtic Society. Stewart is the more important of the two—a man with a distinguished military career and (in 1822) the author of *Sketches of the Characters, Manners and the Present State of the Highlanders of Scotland*. Their new Society had as its objects 'to promote the general use of the ancient Highland Dress in the Highlands of Scotland' for which purpose at the annual general meetings 'all members shall be dressed in the ancient costume of the Highlanders of Scotland, each member if of any clan, in its particular tartan'. Of this Society Sir Walter Scott was an original member and one of its first four vice-presidents. Much later he wrote 'I like this Society and willingly give myself to be excited by the sight of handsome young men with plaids and claymores and all the alertness and spirit of Highlanders in their native garb'. On this occasion, of course—in 1829—the Society had just served at Scott's instigation as escorts for that great piece of late-medieval artillery, Mons Meg, on its transportation from the sea-docks at Leith to Edinburgh Castle, following Scott's successful campaign through the Duke of Wellington for its return to Scotland. But that is another story.

The Celtic Society was in part a heritage association, in part a convivial dining-club, and in part a quasi-military body in the popular tradition of volunteer soldiering of the time. Their military bearing, such as it was, was imparted to them by Stewart and their potential role in the re-creation of Scottish ceremony was an idea which can hardly have been lost upon Scott from the moment of their inception. When he developed his plans for the romantic pageantry of 1822 by persuading the various chieftains of the Highlands to appear in Edinburgh with their 'tails' he was simply extending more widely the order of things initiated by the Celtic Society.

> But yonder come my canty Celts,
> With durk and pistols at their belts,
> Thank God, we've still some plaids and kilts—
>   Carle, now the King's come.

Lord, how the pibrochs groan and yell!
Macdonnell's ta'en the field himsell,
Macleod comes branking o'er the fell—
Carle, now the King's come.

The third preliminary to the Royal Visit was certainly the
coronation of George IV which Scott attended in London in 1821.
He had been offered and accepted his baronetcy in 1818, but his
illness of the following year had prevented his going south to
receive it from the King until March 1820. George was by then
King, though still uncrowned, and remarked 'I shall always reflect
with pleasure on Sir Walter Scott's having been the first creation
of my reign'. Scott's account of the coronation in July 1821 which
he wrote for the *Edinburgh Weekly Journal* shows how much he
absorbed of the ceremonial of the occasion and he seems particularly
to have been impressed by the tenaciously surviving custom, exercised on this occasion for the last time at a British coronation, of
the Public Challenge by the armoured King's Champion. The whole
coronation of George IV was one of the most elaborate and costly
ceremonies that England had ever seen. Its cost was a quarter of a
million pounds. The processions that it involved were largely
traditional and derived from a whole sequence of state weddings,
state funerals and coronations stretching back to the great renaissance triumphs, well documented in contemporary engravings, of
Emperor Maximilian and his peers.

When, therefore, it became apparent in Edinburgh in July 1822,
that the Royal Visit would definitely take place in August, Scott
had three sources of ideas upon which to draw—the recently
reestablished existence of the sceptre, crown, and sword of
Scotland; that recently-designed vehicle of Scottish tradition,
the Celtic Society; and the continuous tradition of state
ceremonial as commonly accepted both in England and in
Europe.

There were, of course, certain elements established in the Scottish scene that would never be ignored when ceremonial was
planned. These included, for example, the great law officers of
Scotland, enshrining the last vestiges of independent nationality,
and duly, in his processions, Scott invoked the presence of the
Lord President of the Court of Session, the Lord Clerk-Register
and the senators of the College of Justice. There was again, the
Court of the Lord Lyon King of Arms and his heralds who had
already played a part (as James Skene's water-colour records) at

the Mercat Cross in 1820 when they publicly proclaimed the accession of a new king.

More curious, however, is the accession to a new role of the Royal Company of Archers, today sub-titled the Queen's Body-guard in Scotland. Their carefully preserved rights to act as the personal escort of the monarch in Scotland stem in fact from the 1822 Royal Visit and indeed must have seemed a somewhat dis-torted re-creation of their historic past to those familiar with their history. Founded in the second half of the seventeenth century as a sporting club, the Company of Archers received a royal charter and a set of colours from Queen Anne in 1704. Their activities were in the eighteenth century generally those of a hunting or shooting fraternity with the social overtones of a dining-club of restricted membership. However, their reputation in the 1715–45 decades had been that of a Jacobite body, and in June 1715, we read 'upon Monday last the Royal Company of Archers consisting of about 200, all clad in old Scottish garb, made their parade through this town. At night they came to the playhouse and betwixt the acts desired Sir Thomas Dalzell (who is mad) to order the music-ians to play that air called "Let the King enjoy his own again". After it was over, the whole house clapped 3 times loud, and a few hissed.'

In 1822 the Company was headed by Lt.-General Sir John Hope, 4th Earl of Hopetoun, whose loyalty to the House of Hanover could never be challenged, but one is inclined to wonder whether Scott had his tongue in his cheek when he contemplated the situa-tion in which this hot-bed of Jacobitism was now re-heated to protect not Prince Charles but King George.

In agreeing to come to Scotland the King, from his own point of view, most certainly did the right thing. He badly needed to reinforce with his physical presence a personal popularity tarnished by his treatment of his Queen. He needed also politically to underline the unity of his kingdom, particularly in Ireland, by state visitation. In both these objects he probably succeeded and chroniclers indeed narrate his surprise and gratification at the warmth of his reception in the north, a reception which certainly surpassed his experience in Ireland and Hanover in the previous autumn.

At least part of the warmth shown by Edinburgh people towards their king was due to careful tuition by Sir Walter Scott. This, the populace came to realize, was the first visit by a reigning monarch

to Scotland since that of the youthful Charles II during the Crom-
wellian Civil War. This was the first visit of a royal member of
the House of Hanover, excepting Scotland's disastrous encounter
with the Duke of Cumberland in 1746, and this was, they could
feel, an act of official forgiveness for the Jacobite indiscretions of
1715 and 1745. 'The crowds', wrote Robert Mudie, describing the
events of the Royal Visit, 'seemed to consider the entrance of His
Majesty within the Palace as completing the solemn inauguration
of him as King of Scotland—as the active revival, under a modified
form, of the Scottish monarchy, and an open recognition of all
their public rights.'

It was with these emotional implications in mind that Scott
made his plans. Clearly he regarded three moments in the ceremonial as of prime importance and significance. The first of these
was to be the solemn removal of the Honours of Scotland from the
Castle of Edinburgh to the Palace of Holyroodhouse, there to
await His Majesty; the second was to be the King's actual entry
in state into the Palace of his ancestors; and the third was to be the
triumphal procession of the King and the Honours from Holyrood
up the ancient Royal Mile to the Castle.

It was soon clear that while Scott's general conception of the
events was happily in tune with general sentiment, some of the
more acute expressions of Scottishness were not without their
critics. The excessive prominence given to the Celtic Society even
to the point of matching it with official military units was particularly attacked. On 12 August, two days before the King's arrival,
the Honours of Scotland were escorted from Castle to Holyrood.
The company included Sir Walter Scott, the Duke of Hamilton
(premier Duke and Hereditary Keeper of the Palace), the Knight
Marischal of Scotland, and the Lord Provost of Edinburgh, and
the escort comprised the band of the 77th Regiment, the Mid-
lothian Yeomanry, and the Celtic Society led by Sir Ewan Mac-
Gregor of MacGregor. The proceedings were publicly attacked in
The Edinburgh Observer:

I cannot pass over that non-descript convention of anything rather than Highlanders, the Celtic Society—an incongruous assembly of all ranks that have
no one common band of union among them. They neither speak the language
nor know how to put on correctly the garb of the Gael, and yet, without
possessing the blood or the manly frame of that interesting race, or any other
ostensible cause whatever, they barefacedly masked themselves in Highland
Garb and trusting to the cloak of this assumed character . . . this novel and
non-descript body stopping at nothing that could be accomplished by a brazen

effrontery . . . unwarrantably pushed itself forward under false colours to the charge of the Regalia of Scotland.

But the writer of this protest was himself among the most touchy of Highlanders—Alastair Macdonnell of Glengarry, the subject of Raeburn's famous portrait which is almost the classic symbol of nouveau-Celticism. In reply to his letter, an anonymous member of the Celtic Society wrote in the same journal:

Mr. Macdonnell of Glengarry in tartan, the only person (on that occasion) mounted on horseback, joined the Celtic Society and placed himself at the head of the column when marching to the Mound—and after we were formed in the order of the procession, Mr. Macdonnell was riding about at the right of the whole . . . as if he wished to be taken for commander. He was forced to withdraw by Macdougall, younger of Macdougall, a captain in the Royal Navy, who commanded the second division of the Celts on that day.

The painting of this particular event by Denis Dighton, still in the MacGregor collection, shows something of the dignified cere-monial that Scott desired and which clearly was achieved, but in that day, in contrast to ours, the capital city was unprepared for the sudden flood of tartan. This facet, particularly when supported by the King himself, was one which was picked upon more than any other for satirical comment, and one which diminished more than any other the respect which was due to Sir Walter Scott for his pageant arrangements.

King George, in fact, wore the kilt once only—for the Levee held at Holyrood on 17 August, when he adopted the Royal Stewart tartan, under the sartorial guidance of Stewart of Garth. Harriet Scott of Polwarth, writing to her daughter, says: 'Papa went at one o'clock and returned at four; there was an immense number of people, but all was well arranged and there was no difficulty. His Majesty wore tartan Highland Dress, with buff-coloured trousers like flesh to imitate his royal knees, and little bits of tartan stocking like other Highlanders half up his legs, and he looked very well, only a little *huffle-buffle*.' Perhaps the best comment on the King's appearance and the unbecoming brevity of his kilt was that of Lady Hamilton: 'As he is to be here for so short a time, the more we see of him the better.'

Even the King's short excursion into Scottish costume might have been greeted with more restraint had it not been for his being joined in this experiment by Sir William Curtis, M.P., Lord Mayor of London, the King's confidant and drinking-companion from Regency days. This ludicrous and inappropriate donning of

Highland garb by Curtis 'cast', to quote Lockhart, 'an air of
ridicule and caricature over the whole of Sir Walter's Celtified
pageantry'.

Moving now to the other two climatic occasions of the visit from
the point of view of Scott's symbolism of Scotland's new-found
consciousness of nationality, their ceremonial was at once more
discreet and more popularly appreciated. The King's arrival at
Holyrood Palace was the first great moment of the Royal Visit.
He had landed at Leith Harbour from the yacht *Royal George* at a
spot still marked by a bronze plate with the words '15 August
1822 O Felicem Diem'. It was, appropriately, Scott's birthday. A
procession escorted by the Scots Greys, the Midlothian Yeomanry
and—inevitably—the Celtic Society, had formed and the King had
received the keys of Edinburgh at the city boundary at Picardy
Place.

As he alighted from his carriage at Holyrood 'a deafening shout
of triumph ascended from the multitude. . . . This we may say, that
the nation never before acquired more ample glory, nor even in
the field of danger, than it did this day, by the admirable conduct
displayed by the immense multitude present' (Mudie). In the court-
yard were grouped the great officers of state—the Duke of Montrose as Lord High Chamberlain, the Duke of Argyll as Keeper of
the Household, the Earl of Hopetoun as Captain General of the
Bodyguard in Scotland, and there were also there the Honours of
Scotland carried by their traditional and hereditary bearers—the
Crown by Sir Alexander Keith, Knight Marischal, the Sceptre by
the representative of the Countess of Sutherland, the Sword of
State by the Earl of Morton. The confrontation between the King
and his Honours was an entirely genuine, sincere, and valid cere-
monial and one which now belongs to the coronation custom of
Scotland.

The third grand and emotional event of the Royal Visit was the
procession of the King from Holyrood to the Castle, a day marred
only by the characteristic showers of rain of an Edinburgh August.
For this occasion Scott had ample precedent in the ancient Scottish
ceremony, 'The Riding of the Parliament', easily available to him
pictorially in contemporary seventeenth-century engravings, and
in written descriptions. This regular processing of the estates and
great officers of Scotland provided him with an exact framework
and order of marshalling upon which he welded the additional
trappings of neo-Scottishness. A comparison between the pub-

lished Orders of March of 1822 and, for example, those of 1703, shows an almost complete inter-relationship. The procession was such in fact that he might have wished for Charles Edward on his entry into Edward Waverley's Edinburgh of 1745, while on its return march down the Canongate it might have echoed to a small extent that which Henry Morton witnessed in 1679:

The attention of Morton was summoned to the window by a great noise in the street beneath. Trumpets, drums and kettle-drums contended in noise with the shouts of a numerous rabble, and apprised him that the cavalry were passing in the triumphal attitude which Claverhouse had mentioned. The magistrates of the city, attended by the guards of halberds, had met the victors with their welcome at the gate of the city, and now preceded them as part of the procession.

The halberds which Scott invoked to line the streets in 1822 were supplied by the Incorporation of the Edinburgh Trades. Their costumes provided a curious anticipation of the medievalism of the Eglinton Tournament. Singularly lacking in appropriateness, certain of them survive with greater propriety today in the wardrobe of Edinburgh's principal hirer of fancy dress.

The extent to which Scott related his arrangements in 1822 to historical tradition already invoked in the novels can perhaps best be illustrated with reference to the great Banquet in Parliament Hall on 24 August. On this occasion the Lord Provost and Magistrates of the City entertained the King to a magnificent feast attended by 300 guests at which no fewer than forty-seven toasts were drunk. It was after the dessert that a little ceremony took place at which William Howison Crawford performed the traditional *reddendo*, or symbolic act of feudal service for his estates at Braehead near Edinburgh. This act comprised the holding of a silver basin of water for the laving of the King's hands and— originally—also his feet. Students of Scott do not need to be reminded of the parallel between this and the homage of the Baron Bradwardine to Prince Charles after Prestonpans:

And ye are aware, I doubt not, that the holding of the Barony of Bradwardine is of a nature alike honourable and peculiar, being blanche *pro servitio detrahendi, seu exuendi, caligas regis post battaliam*—(the pulling off of the King's boots).

The other events of the Royal Visit were exciting and traditional certainly, but of lesser pageantry and significance. They have been recorded for us not only in the *Account of the Royal visit of 1882*,

written anonymously by Robert Mudie, and in such contemporary
documents as the letters of the Misses Grant of Rothiemurchus,
but also in the paintings of Wilkie, Dighton, J. M. W. Turner,
William Turner of Oxford, and others. They encompassed for
example the Drawing Room held at Holyrood for the ladies of
Edinburgh at which the King kissed each lady on the cheek as she
was presented—'which is a great bore,' wrote Harriet Scott, who
had been to Court before, 'and I think very ridiculous as if he were
a new King or we all new people'. There was the Parade on Portobello Sands of 3,000 troops from cavalry and yeomanry regiments
at which the 800 strong contingent of the Celtic Society, com-
prising the Sutherland, MacGregor, Drummond, and Campbell
clans under the 6th Duke of Argyll again come under criticism for
pushing their way into a properly military occasion. There was the
Royal Command Performance of *Rob Roy* in the Theatre Royal in
Princes Street, at which Charles Mackay played his type-role of
Bailie Nicol Jarvie, and there was the final procession of departure
on 29 August from Dalkeith Palace, where the King stayed, along
Princes Street and out west to Hopetoun. The King's last function
in Scotland was his reception at Hopetoun by the 4th Earl as
Captain General of the Royal Company of Archers, the King's
Bodyguard in Scotland, and his bestowing of knighthoods in the
Yellow Drawing Room upon Adam Ferguson, Keeper of the
Regalia, and upon Henry Raeburn, the painter.

From the King's point of view, Scott's arrangements for the
Royal Visit of 1822 achieved all that he could have wished. He
returned to London fortified with a sense of popular enthusiasm that
had indeed taken him by surprise but which owed its origin more
to Scott's teaching and organization than to the monarch's personality. For this George IV remained grateful. His later friendship
with Scott produced encouragement to Charles Scott and eventually to Anne; it produced the offer to Scott himself of a Privy
Councillorship—which was refused—and of a commission to research upon the Stuart papers at Windsor—which was accepted.

Sir Robert Peel, then Secretary for the Home Department, much
later remembered the success of 1822 in Edinburgh. Proposing
the memory of Sir Walter Scott in 1836 he said:

I suppose there are many of you here who were present on that occasion at
that memorable scene when the days of ancient chivalry were recalled, when
every man's friendship seemed to be confirmed—when men met for the first
time who had always looked at each other with distrust, and resolved in the

presence of their Sovereign to forget their hereditary feuds and animosities. In the beautiful language of Dryden:—

> 'Men met each other with erected look—
> The steps were higher than they took:
> Friends to congratulate their friends would haste
> And long inveterate foes saluted as they passed.'

For Scott the visit probably achieved all that he foresaw or imagined. It produced an outburst of national fervour throughout Scotland such as the country had never known before in modern historic times. It provided a medium for the embodiment of his ideas of traditional grandeur and for the re-enactment of such moments of historic splendour as he had occasionally described in the novels; and for Scott the Tory there was the satisfaction of seeing the semblance of temporary political unity in a general expression of popular loyalty. The visit marked the climax of Scott's relationship with his monarch and four years later he felt himself able to write of King George: 'He is in many respects the model of a British Monarch, . . . sincerely, I believe, desires the good of his subjects'. On 28 June 1830 Scott heard the minute-guns of Edinburgh distantly thundering the news of the King's death. By a curious trick of fate, he afterwards recalled, he was standing at that moment on the Battlefield of Preston, lost in thought upon the ephemeral glory of the Jacobite Prince who provided one inspiration for the programme of 1822.

To Lord Cockburn, the Whig, the Royal Visit appeared in retrospect differently:

This glimpse of Royalty did neither good nor harm, and could not. In giving the people a spectacle at which they gazed exactly as they would have done at a Chinese Emperor with his gongs, elephants and mandarins, his visit accomplished all that could be reasonably anticipated.

The last word may well be left perhaps to yet another commentator, M. T. Baillie, who wrote: 'The whole thing is rather incomprehensible'.

Scott's Foreign Contacts

E. H. HARVEY WOOD

WHEN it was first suggested to me that I should take as the subject of this paper 'Scott's Foreign Friends', I did not expect any particular difficulty. My readings of Scott's *Journal* and letters and Lockhart's *Life* had left me with a vague impression that a plethora of foreign names occurred throughout, and that the only problem likely to arise would be that of choosing from an over-abundance of material those relationships which had proved most durable or most fruitful. I should like, however, to begin by making it clear that a very brief period of study was enough to banish this comfortable theory for ever, and to replace it by the conviction that, although he had numerous foreign contacts, Scott, as far as his closest friends were concerned, bought British.

Rereading the *Journal* gave me other ideas as well, which are not irrelevant in considering Scott's attitude to his friends, whether British or foreign. He is commonly supposed to have been a sociable man, rich in friends and valuing their company as much as they clearly valued his. In fact Scott, the genial host of Abbotsford, the good companion, the jovial diner-out whose stories and jokes were 'wont to set the table in a roar' may well invite comparison with that most clubbable of men, Dr. Johnson. But there was a fundamental difference between them. To Johnson, with his tormented conscience and his fits of depression, solitude was a nightmare. To Scott, it was a rare delight. Scott would have found little in common with the man who was grateful to any man who visited him and who believed that there was in London all that life could afford, although he might have met him on the advisability of keeping friendships in good repair. Scott was never indifferent to the company of his fellow-men; his character was too healthy, too well-balanced for him to have been contented with an eremitical existence.

Few men leading a quiet life . . . have seen more variety of society than I [he wrote in his *Journal*]. Few have enjoyed it more or been *bored*, as it is called, less by the company of tiresome people. I have rarely if ever found any one out of whom I could not extract amusement or edification, and were I obliged to account for hints afforded on such occasions, I should make an ample deduction from my inventive powers. Still however from the earliest time I can remember, I preferred the pleasures of being alone to waiting for visitors, and have often taken a bannock and a bit of cheese to the wood or hill to avoid dining with company. As I grew from boyhood to manhood I saw this would not do and that to gain a place in men's esteem I must mix and bustle with them. Pride and an excitation of spirits supplied the real pleasure which others seem to feel in society, and certainly upon many occasions it was real. Still if the question was eternal company without the power of retiring within yourself or solitary confinement for life, I should say, 'Turnkey, Lock the cell!'[1]

It must, however, be borne in mind that the *Journal*, from which we know most of Scott's inmost feelings, cannot be regarded as being a fair reflection of his state of mind in the earlier part of his life. It was begun in the very month in which he first heard rumours of the expected failure of Hurst and Robinson; from then onwards, it is a record of public embarrassment and private loss, of ill-health and suffering, of courage and of his heroic attempts to make restitution for the debts of himself and of his associates. It is not possible that it can give any impression of the gay and care-free period of success which occupied most of his life. It was not unnatural that his troubles should have caused him to retire more from society than he had been used to do, and the many close friends with whom he was on terms of warmest intimacy throughout his life would have repudiated with indignation the idea that Scott was not capable of deep and disinterested friendship. But the reflection that his financial losses would make it necessary for him to lower his former standards of hospitality clearly cost him no particular pang: 'I am determined not to stand mine host to all Scotland and England as I have done',[2] he wrote in December 1825, and he might well have added all Europe and the United States as well. It was only in a particularly bleak moment that he could have written in Edinburgh in 1828, 'I shall be glad to be at Abbotsford to get rid of this town where I have not, in the proper and social sense of the word, a single friend whose company pleases me. In the country I have always Tom Purdie.'[3]

---

[1] Scott, *Journal*, 27 December 1825.
[2] *Ibid*. 15 December 1825.   [3] *Ibid*. 4 March 1828.

But it was an exaggeration of a reserve which always lay just below the surface.

In the ranks of his closest friends, however, we will not find any foreign names. Scott's attitude to foreigners was in general very much that of the typical bulldog Briton. He regarded most foreigners with a deep and instinctive suspicion. He distrusted their manners, their enthusiasms, their civilities, their dress and their politics. In short, he wrote,

I do not like [foreigners]. I hate fine waistcoats and breast-pins upon dirty shirts. I detest the impudence that pays a stranger compliments, and harangues about his works in the Author's house, which is usually ill-breeding. Moreover, they are seldom long of making it evident that they know nothing about what they are talking of, excepting having seen the Lady of the Lake at the Opera.[4]

He would not have been a Common Marketeer. Almost everything that foreigners did nourished his prejudices: Baron Meyendorff of Courland was 'a pleasant man, and deep-read in modern literature, but an enthusiast like many of the Germans'.[5] Baron Tripp had many attributes which might have been expected to appeal to Scott. 'But there was something exaggerated, as appeared from the conclusion of his life. Baron Tripp shot himself in Italy for no assignable cause.'[6] General Yermoloff was 'a man in the flower of life, about 30, handsome, bold and enthusiastic, a great admirer of poetry and all that'; but he left 'with many expressions of enthusiastic regard, as foreigners use to do'.[7] And the Duc de Lévis, who sent Scott a copy of his book, *The Carbonaro*, was censured because it was inscribed 'with hyperbolical phrases'.[8] 'The book', Scott admits, 'is better than would be expected from the exaggerated nonsense of the dedication.' It is amazing that he should have married a French wife.

In fairness, it must be admitted that Scott suffered more from the persecution of tuft-hunting foreign visitors than most of his contemporaries. Readers of Lockhart's *Life* will remember his description of the American tourists who had contrived, in Scott's absence, to gain admittance to Abbotsford, and who, Mrs. Scott complained indignantly, had gone so far as to 'pull out their note-book and beg an exact account, not only of his age—but of her own'.[9] It may have been with the recollection of this or a similar intrusion in his mind that he wrote later to Maria Edgeworth:

[4] Scott, *Journal*, 23 November 1825.   [5] Scott, *Letters*, xi. 156.
[6] *Journal*, 4 October 1827.   [7] *Ibid.* 4–5 August 1827.
[8] *Ibid.* 9 April 1829.   [9] Lockhart, *Life*, iv. 200.

I am not at all surprised at what you say of the Yankees. They are a people possessed of very considerable energy, quickened and brought into eager action by an honourable love of their country and pride in their institutions; but they are as yet rude in their ideas of social intercourse, and totally ignorant speaking generally of all the art of good-breeding, which consists chiefly in a postponement of one's own petty wishes or comforts to those of others. By rude questions, free and unfeeling observations, an absolute disrespect to other people's feelings and a ready indulgence of their own, they make one feverish in their company, though perhaps you may be ashamed to confess the reason. But this will wear off, and is [already] wearing away.[10]

His patience and his purse together were tried on another occasion by a large parcel which arrived for him at Abbotsford one morning at breakfast, and which he opened absent-mindedly while talking. This proved to be a bulky manuscript of a play called *The Cherokee Lovers*, sent to him by the authoress, a completely unknown young lady in New York, who desired him to oblige her by revising the play, furnishing it with a prologue and epilogue, and supervising its production at Drury Lane. For the privilege of receiving this, Scott found, he had been charged the not inconsiderable sum of over five pounds in postage. Three weeks later a similar parcel was delivered to him and again opened by Scott. 'Conceive my horror', he said to Lord Melville, 'when out jumped the same identical tragedy of *The Cherokee Lovers*, with a second epistle from the authoress, stating that, as the winds had been boisterous, she feared the vessel intrusted with her former communication might have foundered, and therefore judged it prudent to forward a duplicate.'[11] This is on a par with the Danish Captain who wrote to Scott that, being in distress for a sum of money by which he might transport himself to Columbia, he had dreamed that Scott generously made him a present of it. 'I can tell him his dream by contraries', was Scott's comment.[12]

There was one American, however, whose acquaintance consoled Scott for much that he had suffered from such irritations. In the spring of 1813, Scott had befriended an American tourist, Henry Brevoort, who, when he wrote to thank Scott for his services, sent him a copy of *The History of New York* by 'Diedrich Knickerbocker'. This was the work of a young American writer, Washington Irving, whom at that time Scott had not met. The book, however, delighted him.

I beg you to accept my best thanks for the uncommon degree of entertainment which I have received from the most excellently jocose history of New

---

[10] *Letters*, viii. 188–9.   [11] *Life*, iv. 196.
[12] *Journal*, 28 November 1825.

York [he wrote to Brevoort]. I am sensible that as a stranger to American parties and politics I must lose much of the concealed satire of the piece, but I must own that, looking at the simple and obvious meaning only, I have never read anything so closely resembling the stile of Dean Swift as the annals of Diedrich Knickerbocker. I have been employed these few evenings in reading them aloud to Mrs. S[cott] and two ladies who are our guests, and our sides have been absolutely tense with laughing. I think too there are passages which indicate that the author possesses powers of a different kind and has some touches which remind me much of Sterne. I beg you will have the kindness to let me know when Mr. Irvine takes pen in hand again, for assuredly I shall expect a very great treat.[13]

Brevoort, in reply to this request, sent Irving's *Salmagundi*. It was thus with feelings of unusual pleasure that Scott received at breakfast one morning in 1817 a card bearing the name of Washington Irving, together with a letter of introduction from Tom Moore. On his card, Irving had written that he was on his way to visit Melrose Abbey and hoped to be allowed to call on Scott some time during the course of the morning. Scott instantly left the table, went to meet Irving and brought him back to Abbotsford for a stay of several days. The story of that meeting has been described by Irving himself in his *Abbotsford and Newstead Abbey* and, more briefly, by Lockhart. It is unnecessary to describe it again in detail. But it is of interest to remember where it belongs in the life of Washington Irving. He had come to England to work in the family firm of P. & E. Irving; but its failure in the post-war depression had driven him back on literature for a living rather than as an amusement. It was shortly after this that he visited Abbotsford, and his meeting with Scott proved to be of some importance in his future literary development. In particular, Scott, no doubt with his own early studies in mind, suggested to him the rich mine of legend in German literature and folklore, and advised him to learn the language.

Save the meeting of Emerson and Carlyle at Craigenputtock in 1833 [one biographer of Irving has written], no literary encounter between an American and an English has been more seminal. Riveting Irving's enthusiasm for Campbell, whom he had just met in London, for Moore and Byron, Scott fixed in him also his predilection for legendary themes. Within a year, he had commenced the study of German, and completed the first draft of 'Rip van Winkle'.[14]

From then on the two men remained in constant touch. Scott found in Irving 'one of the best and pleasantest acquaintances I have

[13] *Letters*, iii. 259.
[14] Stanley T. Williams in *Dictionary of American Biography* (New York, 1932), *s. v.* Irving.

made this many a day'; and it was he who in 1819 proposed Irving as a possible editor of a new Edinburgh newspaper to be run on Tory principles, although in the event Irving felt he could not undertake this office. And on the last sad journey back from Italy to Abbotsford, one of the last books ever bought by Scott was Irving's *Legends of the Alhambra*, a work in which Scott's influence is seen at its happiest.

I have spoken of the influence of German on Scott's early studies, and it is time now to return to the first foreign contacts of which we have any knowledge in Scott's life. His boyhood was spent in surroundings which could hardly be described as cosmopolitan; but when he had left school and was at liberty to extend his education down extra-curricular paths, he found himself in touch with teachers whose background was far removed from Edinburgh and Scotland. He has told us himself that in his early youth, he was anxious to become proficient as a painter, and that in pursuit of this ambition, he took lessons in oil-painting from a teacher called Burrell; but, he lamented,

I could make no progress either in painting or drawing. Nature denied me correctness of eye and neatness of hand. Yet I was very desirous to be a draughtsman at least, and laboured harder to attain that point than at any other in my recollection to which I did not make some approaches. . . . Yet Burrell was not useless to me altogether neither. He was a Prussian and I got from him many a long story of the battles of Frederick, in whose armies his father had been a commissary or perhaps a spy—I remember his picturesque account of seeing a party of the Black Hussars bringing in some forage carts which they had taken from a body of the Cossacks whom he described as lying on the top of the carts of hay, mortally wounded, and like the Dying Gladiator eying their own blood as it ran down through the straw.[15]

He also took Italian lessons, spending on them the money he earned engrossing legal documents, and it is possible that his teacher was an Italian since we have the testimony of Henry Mackenzie that 'Italian masters are to be found in every street',[16] but on this point we have no real evidence. We do know, however, that he was taught German by a German, and how his interest in the language was aroused. In 1788 Henry Mackenzie had read a paper in the Royal Society of Edinburgh on the modern literature of Germany; and, in the words of R. P. Gillies,

it was enough for Scott to know that there were plays and poems worth reading, in order to make him a zealous member of a small club, who agreed

15 *Journal*, 1 March 1826.
16 *Anecdotes and Egotisms of Henry Mackenzie*, ed. H. W. Thompson (London, 1927), 66.

to study German under the instruction of Dr. Willich, a medical gentleman of considerable repute, who spent some time in Scotland, and published a treatise 'on Diet and Regimen', 'Elements of Kantesian Philosophy', etc. The doctor earnestly wished to make his pupils *au fait* of what he called the *geheimnissvolle tiefe* (mysterious depth) of his native language, which, as he well knew, could only be mastered by patient submission to grammatical exercises. According to his own statement, Scott's idleness made him the laughing-stock of his companions: but it may, of course, be doubted, whether he has given a just account of his own progress; for without labour and attention, he could not have acquired that power of reading German which he retained in after life.

Among his fellow students, Mr. John Macfarlane, advocate, always received high praise for his patience and assiduity, while Dr. Willich predicted that Mr. Scott would never succeed, as he determined to come at once to the superstructure without laying a stable foundation . . .[17]

This teacher, who introduced Scott to a language which was to be so significant in his literary development, was one of a small band of Germans who were at that time living in England and making a modest income by giving German lessons. His connexion with Edinburgh may have been brought about through the post which he held for some time as medical adviser to Count Brühl, the Saxon Ambassador to the Court of St. James's; for Count Brühl's daughter married in 1795 Walter Scott of Harden, a close kinsman of Scott, who was a frequent visitor in his cousin's house. Scott's friendship with his young cousin by marriage was of great importance to him, but her right to be included in a list of his foreign friends or contacts is questionable; for although her father was indubitably a German, her mother was the dowager Countess of Egremont, and Mrs. Scott was brought up in England in the company of her Wyndham relations. Indeed she so far considered herself an Englishwoman that she frequently felt qualified to correct Scottisicms in Scott's style:

He was most modest about himself, and showed his little pieces apparently without any consciousness that they could possess any claim on particular attention [she wrote many years later to Lockhart]. Nothing so easy and good humoured as the way in which he received any hints I might offer, when he seemed to be tampering with the King's English. I remember particularly how he laughed at himself, when I made him take notice that 'the little two dogs' in some of his lines, did not please an English ear accustomed to 'the two little dogs'.[18]

Whether the lady considered herself to be more an Englishwoman than a German, however, is of less importance in her friendship

[17] R. P. Gillies, *Recollections of Sir Walter Scott, Bart.* (London, 1837), 70–1.
[18] *Life*, i. 248; cf. N.L.S. MS. 1554, f. 60.

with Scott than the fact that, through her German connexions and
no doubt with the help of her father's diplomatic bag, she was able
to supply Scott with many standard German texts. These included
the works of Bürger to which she introduced him at a time when,
because of the Napoleonic wars, the difficulties of acquiring foreign
books are well attested by many scholars. It was to her that he
showed his first attempts at translation from German literature and
drama; and her kindnesses to him in the social sense were no less
important to him than her literary and linguistic help. He told
Lockhart later that

she was the first *woman of real fashion* that *took him up*; that she used the
privileges of her sex and station in the truest spirit of kindness; set him right
as to a thousand little trifles, which no one else would have ventured to
notice; and, in short did for him what no one but an elegant woman can do for
a young man, whose early days have been spent in narrow and provincial
circles.[19]

But it was for her encouragement of Scott's German studies that
both she and Willich have most title to be regarded with gratitude,
for the part played by German literature in starting him on his
literary career can hardly be overestimated. It is true that no
writer seems less dependent on foreign inspiration than Scott in his
greatest and most characteristic work; but the gateway through
which he entered his kingdom was German, and to the end of his
life traces of his early German reading were to reappear in his
work, thinly disguised if, indeed, they were disguised at all. The
White Lady of Avenel and Fenella in *Peveril of the Peak* are
avowedly German in origin, and the theme of the *Vehmgericht*
fascinated him always and made its final appearance in a work of as
late a date as *Anne of Geierstein*.

The story of this romantic tribunal was found by him first in the
work of the man whom, in his youth, he admired above all other
German writers, and with whom he continued to be linked in a
peculiar fashion until death. It was his admiration of Goethe's
writings that first stimulated his desire to learn German, and,
having acquired the rudiments of the language from Willich,
he happily resisted his teacher's desire to communicate to his
pupils his own admiration for the maudlin ecstacies of Gessner's
Death of Abel, and returned to grapple with the stronger meat
provided by Schiller and Goethe. His first publication of any
significance was his translation of Goethe's tragedy, *Goetz von*

[19] *Ibid.*

Berlichingen, and his friend, R. P. Gillies, with rare percipience, remarked that

> there is every reason to believe that the *Goetz of Berlichingen* had more influence in disposing his mind for the course which he afterwards pursued, than any other production, either foreign or domestic, which fell in his way. . . . Here, at least, was a real and well-known historical hero of the olden time—a man whose character was so far from being fabulous, that he has left his own very curious autobiography—and without the slightest departure from the realities of life, brought out in a manner, till then, unprecedented in modern art.[20]

Shortly after this, he began the natural transition from translation to creation, and from German to Scottish, and although there is evidence that he kept up his German reading, he became more involved in the ballads of his own country than in the ballad heroes of Germany. His first meeting with Lockhart was enlivened by the discovery that Lockhart had just returned from a tour of Germany, and, in particular, from a meeting with Goethe.

> He appeared particularly interested [said Lockhart] when I described Goethe as I first saw him, alighting from a carriage, crammed with wild plants and herbs which he had picked up in the course of his morning's botanizing among the hills above Jena. 'I am glad,' said he, 'that my old master has pursuits somewhat akin to my own. I am no botanist, properly speaking; and though a dweller on the banks of the Tweed, shall never be knowing about Flora's beauties; but how I should like to have a talk with him about trees!'[21]

It was to be one of the great disappointments of Scott's life that he never managed to talk to Goethe in person, about trees or literature or anything else; and the word 'contacts' in the title of this paper has been chosen especially to make it possible to include the type of relationship which existed between two men who, although so closely connected, never actually met. Goethe's interest in Scott seems to have been no less acute than Scott's in him, and was first given direct expression in a letter to Scott dated January 1827, in which he wrote:

> Can I remember that such a man in his youth made himself acquainted with my writings, and even (unless I have been misinformed) introduced them in part to the knowledge of his own nation, and yet defer any longer, at my now very advanced years, to express my sense of such an honour? It becomes me, on the contrary, not to lose the opportunity now offered of praying for a continuance of your kindly regard, and telling you how much a direct assurance of good-will from your own hand would gratify my old age.[22]

[20] Gillies, *Recollections*, 72–3.
[21] *Life*, iv. 146.   [22] *Ibid.* vii. 27–8.

Scott's characteristic entry in his *Journal* reveals how deeply he felt this gesture from the older writer.

I make it a rule seldom to read and never to answer foreign letters from literary folks. It leads to nothing but the battledore and shuttlecock intercourse of compliments, as light as cork and feathers. But Goethe is different, and a wonderful fellow, the Ariosto at once, and almost the Voltaire of Germany. Who could have told me thirty years ago I should correspond and on something like an equal footing with the author of the [Goetz]? Aye, and who could have told me fifty things else that have befallen me?[23]

He replied at once, and cordially, giving Goethe news of his family and domestic situation, joining with him in lamenting the premature death of Byron, of whom both men had been warm admirers and confirming his own early debt to Goethe,

of whom I have been admirer an ever since the year 1798 when I became a little acquainted with the German language: and soon after gave an example at once of my good taste and consummate assurance, by an attempt to translate Baron von Goethe's Goetz of Berlichingen,—entirely forgetting that it is necessary not only to be delighted with a work of genius, but to be well acquainted with the language in which it is written, before we attempt to communicate its beauty to others.[24]

He concluded his letter by telling Goethe that he had ordered a copy of his life of Napoleon to be sent to him. Goethe acknowledged this indirectly in a letter to his young protégé, Thomas Carlyle, who was not personally acquainted with Scott.

Should you see Sir Walter Scott [wrote Goethe], be so kind as return to him my most grateful thanks for his dear and cheerful letter,—a letter written in just that beautiful temper which makes one man feel himself to be worth something to another. Say, too, that I received his Life of Napoleon, and have read it this winter—in the evening and at night—with attention from beginning to end. To me, it was full of meaning to observe how the first novelist of the century took upon himself a task and business so apparently foreign to him, and passed under review with rapid stroke those important events of which it had been our fate to be eye-witnesses.[25]

He asked Carlyle to transmit to Scott some medals struck with his own head; and these were described to Scott by Carlyle in a graceful note in which he begs the privilege of handing the medals to Scott personally:

Being in this curious fashion appointed as it were Ambassador between two Kings of Poetry, I would willingly discharge my mission with the solemnity that beseems such a business; and naturally it must flatter my vanity and love

---

[23] *Journal*, 14 February 1827.   [24] *Letters*, x. 250.
[25] *Collected Letters of Thomas and Jane Welsh Carlyle*, ed. C. R. Sanders (Durham, N.C., 1970), iv. 353–4n.

of the marvellous to think that by means of a Foreigner whom I have never seen, I might now have access to my native Sovereign whom I have so often seen in public, and so often wished that I had claim to see and know in private and near at hand.[26]

Unfortunately, Scott inexplicably seems never to have acknowledged this letter, although his endorsement on it proves that he did read it. The reasons for this lapse were probably good ones, the illness of little Johnnie Lockhart, the bankruptcy of Daniel Terry and the general pressures of London life on a visiting lion. But although they may explain his silence to later students, they could hardly excuse it to Carlyle himself at the time. Six weeks later, he wrote more coldly, informing Scott that Mr. Jeffrey would deliver the medals and regretting that he had been unable to do so personally; this letter, too, remained unacknowledged, and the slight rankled with Carlyle for the rest of his life.

Scott's desire to meet Goethe remained unaltered, and when he went on his final journey to Malta and Italy in 1832, it was his dearest wish to visit him in Weimar on his return through Germany. But Goethe's death on 22 March prevented this. According to Lockhart, on hearing this news, 'his impatience redoubled: all his fine dreams of recovery seemed to vanish at once. —"Alas for Goethe!" he exclaimed, "but he at least died at home—Let us to Abbotsford."'[27] The story is probably as apocryphal as Lockhart's version of Scott's death-bed speech, but it is equally probably true that Scott was deeply affected by the news of Goethe's death. Edward Cheney's version of his reactions is probably more accurate:

I told him I had been to see Goethe the year before, and that I had found him well, and though very old, in the perfect possession of all his faculties. 'Of all his faculties!' he replied; 'it is much better to die than to survive them, and better still to die than live in the apprehension of it; but the worst of all,' he added, thoughtfully, 'would have been to have survived their partial loss, and yet to be conscious of his state.'[28]

He was uneasily and spasmodically aware that this was already his own condition. By the time he reached Germany, he was so ill that it is doubtful whether he could have seen Goethe, had he still been alive; and the last letter he wrote in his life was a shaky note of regret to another eminent German, Schopenhauer, who had hoped to come to visit him at Mainz.

---

[26] *Collected Letters of Thomas and Jane Welsh Carlyle*, iv. 345.
[27] *Life*, vii. 362.   [28] *Ibid*. vii. 377.

Of all the literary foreigners with whom Scott was in touch but whom he never met, Goethe was undoubtedly the most eminent and the most significant in Scott's own life and development, but there were others. In his youth, his ardent pursuit of ballads and their sources brought him into contact with men of letters of other countries who were similarly engaged. As early as 1806, he was applying through his friend Robert Jamieson, then a tutor in Riga, for the help of the Icelandic scholar, Grimur Thorkelin, in obtaining books which he was unable to find in Britain. 'I am sure you wish well to all Scottish antiquaries', wrote Jamieson to Thorkelin on this occasion, 'and you will see by the work I send you that Walter Scott is not the least respectable among them.'[29] In 1815, Scott sent Thorkelin a set of his *Border Minstrelsy* to replace the copy which had been lost in the burning of Thorkelin's library during the British bombardment of Copenhagen in 1807, and Thorkelin reciprocated with the gift of his edition of *Beowulf*, published in 1815, and handsomely inscribed to Scott in his own hand and his usual florid Latin. No letters appear to have passed directly between the two men, the ubiquitous Jamieson acting throughout as the channel of their communication; but when Scott, with his usual good nature, agreed to contribute to Jamieson and Weber's miscellaneous volume, *Northern Antiquities*, his contribution proved to be an abstract of Thorkelin's edition of *Eyrbyggja Saga*. At about the same date (1814), he was in touch with the Brothers Grimm at Cassel over matters of literary interest, and sent to Jakob Grimm a box of books, mostly by himself, which the war had prevented Grimm from obtaining sooner. In 1822, he exchanged gifts of books and letters with the Danish poet, Oehlenschläger, and went at some length into the possibility of arranging for an English translation of his works. The same year brought him a gift of a new edition of old Danish ballads from its editor, Knud Lyne Rahbek, and the presence in the Abbotsford Library of a Danish translation of Scott's *Halidon Hill* by Rahbek testifies to further communication between them. But the foreigner to whom he was for many years most indebted for literary assistance on such subjects was Henry Weber, a young refugee of mixed parentage from Jena who acted as Scott's amanuensis from about 1804 till 1814. He is first mentioned by name in Scott's correspondence in 1807 in a letter to Ellis in which he writes:

[29] Edinburgh University Library, MS. Laing III. 379, no. 471a.

I have fortunately discovered an enthusiastic German romancer in the person of a Mr. Weber, a young man whose mother was an Englishwoman his father a Hanoverian, he himself for the sake of still greater variety being born in Russia. He was studying at Jena when that university was broken up by the command of Bonaparte, and has fortunately come to our college to complete his own studies and assist me in mine. The first effect of the arrival of this Deus ex Machina has been a discovery which I think will interest you namely of a German Sir Tristrem.[30]

During the ten years of their association, Scott's kindness to his rather pathetic little protegé was endless. He employed him, he encouraged him in his own literary ventures and he gave him introductions to such men as Ellis or Heber who might be able to help him still further. His own references to Weber's 'superior attainments', his description of him as 'an excellent linguist and geographer', 'a remarkable antiquary' and 'an excellent and affectionate creature' are in sharp contrast to Lockhart's supercilious and disdainful dismissal of him as 'a mere drudging *German*'. The tolerance displayed by Scott towards Weber's erratic drinking habits and his humanity when Weber was finally overwhelmed by total insanity are what might have been expected of him. Weber's mind gave way in 1814, and after a scene in which Scott, at considerable personal risk, was obliged to disarm him of a pair of loaded pistols, he was sent to his mother in Yorkshire and placed in an asylum. He made brief and spasmodic recoveries, during which he would write to Scott to tell him of his extensive and ambitious plans for future work; and Scott, while answering kindly and encouragingly, would surreptitiously transmit subsidies for Weber's use, and tried unsuccessfully to pull strings to get him a pension from the Literary Fund. His death took place in 1818. 'The very last subject which animated him', his sister wrote to Scott, 'was in speaking of you.'[31]

Other young foreign students who visited Scott in Edinburgh and at Abbotsford had happier stories. Edinburgh University was a favourite resort of foreigners who were debarred from Oxford and Cambridge by the necessity for subscribing the Thirty-nine Articles, and Scott's house was a magnetic attraction to young men who were resident in Edinburgh for any length of time. One eminent scholar who looked back nostalgically in later years to his visits to Castle Street was the German historian, Johann Martin Lappenberg, who wrote in 1836 of the period when he had been a frequent visitor of the Scotts. Lappenberg concludes his account of

[30] *Letters*, xii. 292.   [31] N.L.S. MS. 866, f. 175.

his friendship with Scott by describing the voyage from Edinburgh to London which he made in Scott's company in 1815:

He had the kindness, when he heard of my intention of going thither, to suggest that I should take my passage in the same vessel, and be of his party, which consisted of his daughter, Mr. William Erskine, and a few other intimate friends. He had brought with him Dolinger's 'Alexis von Mainz', and some other German poems, with the intention of looking them over with me. But the inexhaustible attractions and liveliness of his conversation did not allow us to make any progress in reading. . . . Miss Scott gave us some delightful Scotch songs, especially some old Jacobite ones, which her father cherished beyond all others. Mr. Erskine having observed that the printing of such ballads within British territory was contrary to law, Mr. Scott directly suggested that Mr. König was then on board of our vessel with one of his newly-invented printing presses, which were afterwards employed at newspaper-offices in London. He insisted that, as the learned counsellor (so he styled Mr. Erskine) had interdicted the printing of these *memorabilia* on shore, there was now an excellent opportunity of putting some of them to press on the lawless sea, for which purpose he requested the assistance of the German artist. Thus some copies of 'Over the water and over the sea', with two or three of the same class, were actually printed *off Scarborough Head*, as expressed at the bottom of the leaf, which I still possess among my *keimelia*.[32]

Another young scholar from whose society Scott derived much pleasure was a scion of the Russian nobility, Vladimir Davydoff, later Count Orloff Davydoff, who first makes his appearance in the pages of Scott's *Journal* in 1825, when he arrived in Edinburgh at the age of sixteen to pursue his studies at the University. He came of no mean family in Russia, his father being of ancient Tartar stock and his mother, Countess Orloff, being the daughter of the youngest of the five magnificent Orloff brothers, two of whom had placed the Empress Catherine on the throne of Russia. The young man's education was supervised with particular care by his Orloff grandfather, himself a man of great wealth and highly-cultivated tastes who, considering the universities of France to be tainted by democracy, and those of Germany by the philosophies of Kant, decided to send his grandson to study in Edinburgh. Here the young man spent four happy years, attending the lectures of Sir William Hamilton on history and of John Wilson on moral philosophy, and laying the basis of an intense Anglophilism which he retained until the day of his death. He was a frequent and welcome visitor, at Abbotsford, and in after years he referred to

[32] Gillies, *Recollections*, 219–20. Frederick König (1773–1833), the inventor of the improved printing press, had settled in London in 1807.

his friendship with Scott as the highlight of his days in Edinburgh. Scott himself spoke with admiration of the qualities of his young guest:

It is quite surprizing how much sense and sound thinking this youth has at the early age of sixteen, without the least self-conceit or forwardness. On the contrary he seems kind, modest and ingenuous. Yet to questions which I asked about the state of Russia, he answered with the precision and accuracy of twice his years. He is but sixteen. I should be sorry the saying were verified in him.

'So wise and young, they say, never live long.'[33]

As time passed, and Scott saw his young friend become more and more enthusiastically attached to the customs and politics of Britain, he was to become more doubtful of the wisdom of sending a young man to study in a country so different in outlook from his own:

I am somewhat sorry for my young friend [he wrote in his *Journal* towards the end of Davydoff's stay in Edinburgh]. His friends permit him to remain too long in Britain to be happy in Russia. Yet this [is a] prejudice of those who suppose that when the institutions and habits by which they are governed come to be known to strangers, they must become exclusively attached to them. This is not so. The Hottentot returns from civilization to the wild manners of his krawl, and wherefore should not a Russian resume his despotic ideas when restored to his country?[34]

When Davydoff finally left Edinburgh to take up an appointment at the Russian Embassy in London, Scott notes his departure with similar forebodings: 'I hope well of this young nobleman and trust the result will justify my expectations. But it may be doubted if his happiness be well considered by those who sent a young person, destined to spend his life under a despotic government, to receive the ideas and opinions of such a people so popular as we are.'[35] Davydoff, however, seems to have weathered the transition from liberal Britain to despotic Russia without too much embarrassment. He continued to preserve his interest in British affairs, and to the day of his death took the *Times* daily; but the most important mark of his residence in Britain seems to have been the development of his views on the evils of serfdom. In 1833 he presented to the Czar Nicholas a scheme for the liberation of the serfs through the establishment of a bank to advance money to peasants willing to buy their freedom, but his plan was rudely rejected, and Davydoff was

---

[33] *Journal*, 24 November 1825.   [34] *Ibid*. 1 September 1827.
[35] *Ibid*. 25 March 1828.

obliged to content himself with promoting the welfare of the serfs on his own wide estates.

Scott's kindness to the young man produced another interesting contact for him. They became acquainted at the time when Scott was working on his *Life of Napoleon*; and he was delighted to find in his young friend a relative of the famous Black Captain, Denis Davydoff of the Russian Hussars, a hero of the campaign of 1812, who had played a large part in harrassing Napoleon's retreat from Moscow. He is now best known as the model for Tolstoi's 'Denisov' in *War and Peace*, where he is described as 'one of the most characteristic and attractive personalities of contemporary society', and his memoirs were largely drawn on by Tolstoi for his novel. For Scott, he had the irresistible attraction of being not only a valuable source of information on the 1812 campaign, but that most attractive of combinations, a poet and a soldier. Scott had achieved success as a poet, but he had never quite outgrown his early wistful longing for a military career, and he would have agreed wholeheartedly with Johnson that every man thinks meanly of himself for not having been a soldier. His interest in Davydoff, therefore, was unfeigned and eager, and in no way dependent on the use he hoped to make of him as a source of information. The beginning of their correspondence seems to have been prompted by Vladimir's report to his father that Scott had a portrait of the Black Captain hanging in his study at Abbotsford, and Denis Davydoff was moved by this information to write directly to Scott himself. His letter was forwarded to Scott by his nephew who wrote:

... [my uncle] is not without fear lest his feelings on this occasion may have made his letter to you utterly unintelligible. He flatters himself with the hope that you will honor him with two lines as least of your own writing. And though he has not taken the liberty of asking from you either this favor or that of sending your portrait to him, he expresses to me the ardent desire which he feels of having such monuments of you in his possession . . .[36]

'Curious that he should be interested in getting the resemblance of [a] person whose mode of attaining some distinction has been very different,' Scott mused, when sending him an engraving of Raeburn's portrait of himself. 'But I am sensible that if there be any thing good about my poetry, or prose either, it is a hurried frankness of composition which pleases soldiers, sailors and young

[36] Quoted by Gleb Struve, 'Russian Friends and Correspondents of Sir Walter Scott', *Comparative Literature* ii (1950), 307–26, at pp. 311–12.

people of bold and active disposition.'[37] Davydoff reciprocated with a present which would doubtless have pleased Scott enormously, had it reached him before his death. It consisted, according to Davydoff himself, of 'a Kurd pike and a Persian knife procured by a detachment under my command in a skirmish with Persian troops near Erivan, and a Circassian bow and arrows, which I acquired when crossing the Caucasian border'.[38] Unfortunately there is a strong possibility that these trophies, which would have been so much to Scott's taste, may never have been seen by him. Davydoff speaks of their dispatch in a letter in which he replies to Scott's request for comments on his *Napoleon*, but this letter, and the extensive critical notes which it contained, never reached Scott, and remained unknown until 1840, when it was published after the death of Davydoff himself in the preceding year.[39]

You desire, Sir, to have my remarks with regard to the war of 1812, described by you in your book on the life of Napoleon [he wrote in it]. I obey you not without apprehension, as I must confess at the very beginning that there will be a considerable number of such remarks.

His criticisms chiefly concerned questions of fact and matters of detail on which it must indeed have been difficult for Scott to get precise information so far from the scene of action. He also refutes the theory—and on this point he must have spoken with some authority—that the Russian retreat before the advance of Napoleon was a deliberate attempt to sever the French communications with their base, and maintains that it was due to nothing more than the fact that the Russian army was dispersed and was obliged to fall back in order to unite and reform. On one point, however, he was grateful to Scott. In common with other officers engaged in the campaign, he had strongly resented the implication of many French historians that Napoleon's defeat was due to the Russian winter rather than the Russian army, and indeed he later wrote an article on the subject in which he quoted Scott in his own support. For, Scott had written,

Winter was only the ally of the Russians; not, as has been contended, their sole protectress. She rendered the retreat of the grand army more calamitous, but it had already been an indispensable measure; and was in the act of being

[37] *Journal*, 16 June 1826.
[38] Quoted by Zoja Rozov, 'Denis Davydov and Walter Scott, *Slavonic Year-Book*, [*Slavonic and East European Review*] xix (1939–50), 300–2.
[39] *Ibid*. 302. Davydoff's letter was published in 1840 under the title 'Correspondence with Walter Scott' in the Russian periodical *Syn Otechestva*.

executed at the lance-point of the Cossacks, before the storms of the north
contributed to overwhelm the invaders.[40]

The third young student who became an habitué of the Scott
household was of even higher birth than Davydoff, and was no less
a person than the deposed Crown Prince of Sweden, Gustavus Vasa,
who had assumed the alias of Count Itterburg. Unlike Davydoff
and Lappenberg, he was not a student at the University, although
this had been his original intention. According to David Douglas,
however,

his real name becoming known, this was rendered impracticable by the
curiosity and attention of the public. He devoted himself mainly to the study
of military matters, and out-door exercises, roughing it in all sorts of
weather, sometimes . . . setting out on dark and stormy nights, and making
his way across country from point to point. This self-imposed training was
no doubt with the secret hope that he might some day be called upon by the
Swedes to oust Bernadotte, and mount the throne of the great Gustavus.[41]

He was introduced to Scott by letters from Melville and from
Harriet Swinton in Lausanne, and the Prince was of course
immediately invited to dinner in Castle Street, on which occasion,
according to Scott, he 'took a long look' at the portrait of King
Charles XII over the dining-room mantelpiece, and the company
'were all struck with the resemblance betwixt old Ironhead, as the
Janissaries called him and his descendant'.[42] During the following
February, Scott was able to invite the Prince to go with his family
to witness from Constable's shop the proclamation of George IV:

The weather was fine, the sun shone bright; and the antique tabards of the
heralds, the trumpet notes of *God save the King*, and the hearty cheerings of
the assembled multitude that filled the noble old street produced altogether a
scene of great splendour and solemnity. The Royal Exile surveyed it with a
flushed cheek and watery eye, and Scott observing his emotion, withdrew
with me to another window, whispering 'Poor lad! poor lad! God help him.'[43]

It is impossible that the situation of the Swedish prince should not
have most forcibly reminded Scott of Prince Charles Edward, and
while his practical common sense could not have approved the
restoration of a Stuart monarchy, he was able, in contemplating
the hopes and fears of his young guest, to sublimate all his
romantic prejudice in favour of the legitimate line. The Prince
himself seems to have been obsessed by the parallel, and recurred

[40] *Life of Napoleon*, vii (*Misc. Prose Works*, xiv), 245–6.
[41] Scott, *Journal*, ed. David Douglas (Edinburgh, 1890), i. 385n.
[42] *Letters*, vi. 39.   [43] *Life*, iv. 355–6.

to it frequently until an evening when, dining with the Skenes, he asked his host

what effect the failure of the enterprise [of 1745] had produced upon the prince's character, with whose gallant bearing and enthusiasm in the conduct of his desperate enterprise he evinced the strongest interest and sympathy. I related briefly the mortifying disappointments to which Charles Edward was afterwards exposed in France, the hopelessness of his cause, and the indifference generally shown to him by the continental courts, which so much preyed on his mind as finally to stifle every remnant of his former spirit and character, and to reduce him to listless indifference, which terminated in his becoming a sot during the latter years of his life. On turning round to the prince, who had been listening to these details, I perceived the big drops chasing each other down his cheeks, so that we changed the subject, and he never again recurred to it.[44]

'Count Itterburg' remained in Scotland until May 1820 and was a frequent guest of the Scotts. He was, according to Scott in a letter to his son, 'much affected when he took his leave'.[45] Several years later, when Scott was working on his life of Napoleon, he received a large cargo of papers from Bernadotte concerning various Napoleonic campaigns in which he had served. But Scott, who according to Irving 'had too high a veneration for pure blood to tolerate a mongrel', felt his sympathies too much engaged with the legitimate prince to allow him to make use of the help offered by the ursuper—a noble resolution which he was the more easily able to keep since, as he ingenuously confessed, he had already completed all the part of the work to which Bernadotte's papers referred.

It would be easy to go on indefinitely with a list of interesting foreigners with whom Scott came in contact at one time or another during his life. Nothing has so far been said about his various journeys to the continent in 1815, when he went to visit the battle-field of Waterloo, and was received in Paris by Wellington and met Blücher and the Czar of Russia; in 1826, when he went to collect materials for his *Napoleon*; and in 1831 and 1832 when he made his last vain journey to the Mediterranean in search of health. On these occasions he moved in distinguished circles and met a great number of foreigners, most of whom were of interest or conse-quence in some way or another. But in Scott's life they have little importance except as names occurring briefly on pages of his *Journal* or letters, and, for the most part, forgotten as soon as he

---

[44] James Skene, *Memories of Sir Walter Scott*, ed. B. Thomson (London, 1909), 83.
[45] *Letters*, vi. 195.

returned to Scotland, unless by an ill chance they happened to turn up on his doorstep at Abbotsford years later with letters of introduction. Princess Galitzin seems to have made a more permanent impression, and he heard of her death from Baron von Meyendorff in 1829 with genuine regret. His meeting with Fenimore Cooper in 1826 was of considerable interest to both of them, and for a time they were on cordial terms. When Cooper visited London in 1828, however, Scott was too busy to see much of him; and although Scott does not appear ever to have failed in courtesy towards his American colleague, Cooper (like Carlyle, though with less reason) seems to have considered himself slighted, and his later rancorous remarks about Scott were in sharp contrast to his first gratified reaction when Scott called on him in Paris. It would equally be possible to describe the many descents of foreign visitors on Abbotsford, from the visit of Prince Leopold in 1819, which is described by Scott in a letter to Lord Montagu as being very much after the style of the entertainment of Charles II at the Castle of Tillietudlem, to the arrival of ladies of the French royal family with their entourage. They were entertained by Scott at dinner in the French which he had picked up in his early reading of chronicles and romances ('Mon Dieu!' exclaimed one of them afterwards, 'comme il estropiait, entre deux vins, le francais du bon sire de Joinville!'[46]). A group of Italian visitors in 1828 do not seem to have received equal consideration. 'After all,' Scott excused himself peevishly, 'it is not my fault. They who wish to see me should be able to speak my language.'[47]

One of these casual visitors was a Mr. Alexander Turgenev, who was imperceptibly related to his later, more illustrious namesake, the novelist. Alexander Turgenev was a man of breeding and culture, who, apart from a prosperous career as a civil servant, may almost be said to have been a professional traveller. His extensive journeys seem to have been motivated only by his insatiable curiosity and his desire to meet eminent literary people. He visited Goethe in Weimar, he frequented the *salon* of Mme Récamier in Paris, he hob-nobbed with Stendhal in Italy, and it was therefore natural that, when he came to Britain in 1828, he should wish to add Scott to his list. He did actually meet him at an evening party given by Mrs. Alexander in London in May, but this was not sufficient. Abbotsford was his target. He left for Scotland in late July, armed with letters of introduction to various prominent

[46] *Life*, i. 130.   [47] *Journal*, 18 June 1828.

personalities, some of which he was given by his compatriot, Vladimir Davydoff; it perhaps casts significant light on Turgenev's character that Davydoff did not give him a recommendation to Scott as he could easily have done. Turgenev, unperturbed by this, wrote to Scott from Keswick (where he was visiting Southey), announcing his desire to call at Abbotsford and asking Scott to send a note to await him at Melrose to fix a time for his visit. When he arrived at Melrose, he found that Scott had not answered his letter; but he presented himself, nothing daunted, at Abbotsford, where he found Scott just returning from a funeral. Unfortunately there is a six-month gap in Scott's *Journal* at this point, so that we do not know what he thought of this invasion; but he seems to have put a good face on it, and probably found his uninvited visitor more interesting than he expected, for, in the event, Turgenev spent two days and nights at Abbotsford. He was a man of wide and miscellaneous knowledge, and he was able to recommend to Scott various German books on the subject of the *Vehmgericht* which we find Scott ordering through Cadell the following week for his work on *Anne of Geierstein*. On the last night of his stay at Abbotsford, he apologized to Scott for his unceremonious arrival and, according to his own account, was reassured by Scott in a few words that were 'not only flattering but almost affecttionate'.[48]

Another visitor of the same type was Baron Meyendorff of Courland, who has already been mentioned (Scott calls him 'Meyersdorff') and who arrived at Abbotsford during the following year. His enthusiasm, if one may judge by the bread-and-butter letter he wrote on his return to Riga, seems to have been divided between his host and his host's whisky, which clearly made a powerful impression on him. But what is even more interesting is the fact that he not only visited Goethe on his return to Europe, and gave him the latest news of Scott, but that he also acted as emissary between Scott and Alfred de Vigny, in whose diary we read in May 1829:

This month, M. de Meyendorff, a Russian colonel, came to visit me with my friend, Edouard Lagrange. He saw Sir Walter Scott in Edinburgh. Walter Scott begged him to see me and to say that the only French book he ever read was *Cinq-Mars*. He found in it only one blemish; this was that people were not given sufficient importance. He believes our ordinary people to be

[48] Quoted by Gleb Struve, 'A Russian Traveller in Scotland in 1828: Alexander Turgenev', *Blackwood's Magazine*, cclvii (1945), 345.

as picturesque as his own, and that our public would be as tolerant of popular dialogue; he is mistaken. His Scotland is concerned with every individual mountain, but when did France ever care about her own provinces?[49]

It would be impossible to conclude this brief survey of some of Scott's foreign contacts without making some mention of the Dumergues, the French family who were so closely associated with Lady Scott in her early youth, and who were always treated by the entire Scott family with the affectionate regard of close relations. Charles Dumergue had prospered in London as surgeon-dentist to the Royal Family, and according to Lockhart,

M. Dumergue's house was, throughout the whole period of the emigration, liberally opened to the exiles of his native country; nor did some of the noblest of these unfortunate refugees scruple to make the freest use of his purse, as well as of his hospitality. Here Scott met much highly interesting French society, and until a child of his own was established in London, he never thought of taking up his abode anywhere else, as often as he had occasion to be in town.[50]

Miss Dumergue was the godmother of Scott's elder daughter, Sophia, and Scott never allowed any of his children to forget the debt of gratitude they owed the family on their mother's account. After Sophia was settled in London, he reminded her, 'Never forget they were your poor Mother's earliest and best friends, and when a little civility can give them pleasure, it is easily afforded'.[51]

But when all is said and done, no one at all acquainted with Scott through his writings or his letters or his *Journal* can be under much illusion as to the small part which any of these foreign contacts played in his life and work. The essential man remained untouched by any foreign influence to an extent which is almost unique among the other Romantic writers of his time. Scott, who could walk with kings without losing the common touch, could equally mingle with the best and most talented society of Paris and Rome and return unshaken in his conviction that one Englishman (or Scotsman) was worth three foreigners. But deeper still in him was the instinct which built up a wall of reserve against all so-called friends of any nationality whose coming wasted his time, whose conversation failed to satisfy his most deeply-felt needs, and whose presence only served to remind him of the place and the company where he was always most at ease: '. . . in the country I have always Tom Purdie'.

[49] Translated from a passage quoted by Gleb Struve, 'Russian Friends of Scott', p. 324.
[50] *Life*, i. 372.   [51] *Letters*, xi. 399.

Waverley Ueber Alles—
Sir Walter Scott's German Reputation

PAUL M. OCHOJSKI

T HAT the novels of Sir Walter Scott were held in the highest
esteem in the English-speaking world throughout most of
the nineteenth century is well known, but that the Waverley
novels were as highly prized by appreciative foreign readers is not
generally understood. Especially in Germany did Sir Walter Scott
enjoy a reputation hardly exceeded by any other foreign writer.
Thus Goethe, Germany's foremost poet, hailed Scott as 'a great
genius who does not have an equal'. A German scholar, Luise
Sigmann, writing almost a century later, can proclaim, 'The popularity of Scott is so great that we may regard him as almost a
German writer'. Not only was Scott much appreciated in Germany,
but his effect on German literature was incalculable. Of this, the
critic, Julian Schmidt, wrote in his *History of German Literature*
(1869), 'No matter how we measure it, the influence of Walter
Scott is enormous. Yes, I do not hesitate to proclaim it, it is the
greatest which any of the authors of the nineteenth century
wielded.' As if in corroboration, Heinrich Spiero's *History of the
German Novel* (1950) lists the following novelists as having been
influenced by Sir Walter Scott: Steffens, Hauff, Rehfues, Spindler,
Van der Velde, Herloszsohn, von Tromlitz, Koenig, Alexis,
Schuecking, Dahn, Fontane, and May. In no other European
nation can a list of Scott-followers be found to equal this.

The Waverley novels at first made their way slowly in German
notices and were not too well received. The Stuttgart *Morgenblatt*,
ever alert to current British literature, comments in No. 75
(1816) on *Guy Mannering*, Scott's second novel. *Waverley*, writes
the anonymous reviewer, had brought its author so much acclaim
that he felt urged to try again too soon. 'But he showed that he
brought to market only a new broth in a dish that was basically
the same, Scottish scenes and Scottish dialect.'

The objection to Scottish dialect is found also in an article in the *Literaturblatt*, edited by Wolfgang Menzel. In No. 7 (1817), in a survey of English literature, notice is taken of the Waverley novels of which a 'Herr Forbes, a young Scotsman of rank', is thought to be the author. The critic admits that they enjoy some popularity in Britain, but he does not expect a like response in Germany. In the next number of the same journal, however, an anonymous reviewer compares *Guy Mannering* favourably with *Les Battuécas*, a historical romance by Madame de Genlis. Scott's 'natural characters' and his historical accuracy are contrasted to the perversities and inaccuracies of the other writer. By No. 15 of 1817, the *Literaturblatt* has dismissed its 'Herr Forbes' as the Waverley author and now suspects that Walter Scott, 'the epic poet, who has so well portrayed the living past', is the real author.

The Germans were not long fooled by the mystifications of 'The Great Unknown' in hiding his identity, as Luise Sigmann points out. *The Weimarisches Journal*, in May 1818, still asks plaintively why Walter Scott, 'the greatest English writer', is not better known and distributed in Germany, 'especially as he is said to be an admirer of German literature'. But this plaint is exceptional; Walter Scott was not only well-known, but also his novels, now translated, soon appeared under his own name. In 1823, a publisher in Zwickau printed translations of *Waverley* (as *Eduard*), *The Heart of Mid-Lothian*, *The Bride of Lammermoor*, and *Ivanhoe*, all 'aus dem Englischen von Walter Scott'. In 1824, *Kenilworth* followed from the same publisher, while in Reutlingen that same year, translations of both *The Fortunes of Nigel* and *Peveril of the Peak* appeared, with Walter Scott named as the author. During these same years in Great Britain the novels were still appearing anonymously and Sir Walter Scott was still coyly denying authorship, although many suspected it.

It was not until after 1820, with the publication of *Ivanhoe*, that Scott's German vogue really developed. The *Jenaische Literaturzeitung* ran a series of articles on Scott in its Nos. 173–175 of that year. The *Elegante Welt* (No. 52, 1820), not to be outdone, featured a poem addressed to 'England's Poet', written by a Herr Haug,

> Wer Scotts Gesaenge hoert,
> (Sein Nachruhm ist gegruendet)
> Und ihm nicht Kraenze windet,
> Ist nicht des eigenen wert.

> Who hears Scott's songs,
> (His fame is established)
> And wreathes him not in laurels,
> Is not worthy of his own.

A few numbers later (No. 57), it ran an advertisement for *Ivanhoe* and an article on Scott, appraising his rise to fame. 'The truly romantic writer had become scarce,' it reads in part,

No wonder that the novels of Scott among us found enthusiastic reception. His newest novel Ivanhoe surpasses his others. All the persons appearing in this novel are portrayed in a manner betraying the brush of a master, and not seldom reminding one of Shakespeare's great genius.

Menzel's *Literaturblatt*, which had in 1817 expected nothing of significance for Germany from Scott, by No. 55 (1819), is holding one of his novels up for emulation.

One thing can be highly praised in it and recommended to our writers for imitation; there is not one suggestive, sexually-exciting scene in it. . . . This is more than can be said of 99 out of 100 German novels.

The article goes on to say that the popularity of Scott's novels proves that German readers are tired of 'erotic trash'.

This praise of Scott's novels for their irreproachable morality is found in another German periodical. The Leipzig *Literarisches Conversationsblatt* (No. 199, 1821), in reviewing *Das Kloster* (*The Monastery*), lauds 'the total lack of moral filth and suggestive situations'. In a review of *The Fortunes of Nigel*, the same paper (No. 234, 1822) again praises Scott for his moral purity.

This same journal later threw some light on the manner in which the Waverley novels were so rapidly translated and spread in Germany. In No. 13 (1823), the *Conversationsblatt* describes the functioning of 'translation factories'. The publisher-printer would have the latest sections of a Waverley novel, acquired by devious means, sent from Edinburgh by fast packet, given to a translator, and immediately set up in type. When the final section had been collected and sent through the assembly-line, the book would be bound and on the bookseller's shelves before the English editions reached Germany. Needless to say, Scott received no royalties.

Even the poorer novels of Scott found an enthusiastic German audience in the early 1820s. The *Weimarisches Journal*, in June 1822, tells its readers that the latest Scott novel, *The Pirate*, 'is being devoured by the modish world of readers'. The *Wegweiser*, a Dresden paper, in No. 6 (1822), is able to give its subscribers a synopsis of *The Pirate* 'taken from a British literary journal', which it had 'acquired by rapid means'. Having whetted the appetites of its readers, the paper (in its No. 17) announces the translation of *The Pirate* into German, soon to be on sale.

Competition among publishing firms was keen, each trying to outdo the other in printing a cheaper and more complete set of Waverley novels. In 1825 the publishing house of Gebrueder Schumann in Zwickau announced the launching of a Pocket Edition of twenty Scott novels in 79 volumes to be sold at 8 Groschen each, paper-backed, and 9 Groschen each, bound. Furthermore, they were planning another edition 'on the finest vellum paper' for only 4 Groschen each. Another publisher, Gebrueder Frankh, announced in the *Intelligenzblatt* (No. 2, 1827), that of 30,000 copies of their pocket edition only a few are left, 'a delightful proof of the advance of the people in culture and of spiritual progress'.

For those Germans who still preferred to read Scott in the original, help was also forthcoming. In 1826, the firm of Gebrueder Borntraeger in Koenigsberg, East Prussia, published a *Pocket Dictionary of the Scottish Idiom*. This bilingual glossary by Robert Motherby was, according to the sub-title, 'chiefly calculated to promote the understanding of the works of Sir Walter Scott, Robert Burns, Allan Ramsay, etc.' and contained also 'an Appendix containing notes explicative of Scottish customs, manners, traditions, etc.'

Not all Scott novels fared well in German critical notices. *Peveril of the Peak* and *Redgauntlet* received but scant attention in the press. *St. Ronan's Well* was not well thought of and even the Leipzig *Conversationsblatt*, once so full of praise for Scott the moralist, sadly fears that 'his pen has become dull'. The Dresden *Wegweiser* (No. 152, 1824) even ranks the novel beneath the pseudo-Scott romance, *Walladmor*. This novel, a brazen literary hoax from the pen of Willibald Alexis, had appeared in time for the Leipzig spring fair of 1824, written apparently because no new real Scott novel was on hand. 'A new romance by the author of *Waverley*' or 'from the English of Walter Scott' set beneath the title of the veriest trash was enough to ensure sales to the enthusiastic German public. Sir Walter Scott was indignant over the attribution of *Walladmor* to him, as a letter to Lady Abercorn, dated 4 March 1824, shows.

Lockhart suspected that a pirate had spirited to Germany some advance sheets of *The Betrothed*, which Scott had begun and then laid aside, although in galleys, because Ballantyne did not like it. This is barely possible. Not only does *Walladmor* have a Welsh setting, like *The Betrothed* (the first novel Scott set in Wales), but we have seen that German printers did rely on advance sheets for their own rapid publishing. It is entirely possible that when no further sections of the novel arrived, the impatient publisher had Alexis fabricate an approximation of the genuine article, or an Ersatz-Scott. Sir Walter Scott was so annoyed by this German competition trading on his name, that, writes Lockhart, he hastened to complete and publish *The Betrothed*.

While the critics occasionally carped at the Waverley-mania, the German reading public continued to venerate Walter Scott. Some wrote fan-letters to their idol, so many that Scott made it a rule never to answer complimentary foreign letters—a rule he broke only for Goethe. Typical of these adulatory epistles is the letter from Heinrich Voss to Scott, written in March 1822. Voss, a Heidelberg professor, son of the great scholar and friend of Goethe, Johann Heinrich Voss, writes,

The name of Scott is a very dear one in our house, that you would sense if you could hear my dear mother speak. . . . Every evening when I have completed my academic lectures I read to her out of your works, and each reading we close with, not 'what a priceless composition'—but with 'what a priceless Man!'

The deification of Scott as a household god was not the only aspect of his immense vogue. He was held up to German writers as a model of excellence. When E. T. A. Hoffmann finished writing his *Prinzessin Brambilli* it was severely criticized by his friend Hitzig. Hitzig urged Hoffmann to study Scott, especially *Guy Mannering*, as a model of what the German public wanted. Hoffmann proceeded to read *Der Astrolog*, as *Guy Mannering* was titled in German translation. When finished, he wrote to Hitzig that he found it 'a very excellent, excellent book, in the greatest simplicity of vital, living Life and vigorous Truth'.

Hoffmann's greatest contemporary, the Olympian Goethe, discovered Scott comparatively late and was not at first favourably impressed. He apparently read *Kenilworth* in 1821, directed to Scott through Byron's satirical mention. On 12 October 1823, he tells Eckermann that he has read two novels by Scott and now knows what he (Scott) can do. 'He would always amuse me, but I can not learn anything from him. I have time only for the truly excellent,' he says. Also, according to Eckermann, on 25 November 1824, Goethe told Chancellor Mueller contemptuously that Walter Scott had earned £80,000 through his authorship, but had sold his true fame. He added that although the novels are not worth much, they are too good for the public.

It was only after the famous exchange of letters between Goethe and Scott in 1827 that Goethe really settled down to reading the Waverley novels. On 18 July 1827, a few days before he received Scott's answer to his letter, Goethe told Eckermann that he was going to read *Waverley* in order to compare Scott with Manzoni. On 17 August 1828, writes Eckermann, Goethe told Riemer that he was unable to finish reading *The Fair Maid of Perth*, which though interesting, he felt held little content. Yet two months later, on 3 October 1828, he is praising the novel to Eckermann, who is now reading it.

Walter Scott's *Fair Maid of Perth* is excellent, is it not? There is finish! There is a hand! What a firm foundation for the whole, and in details not a touch which does not lead to the climax.

He then goes on to discuss episodes in the novel with Eckermann and Frau Goethe, who has also read it. Goethe is full of praise for Scott's novelistic techniques. Scott has 'a remarkable sureness and thoroughness in his delineation', which, adds Goethe, 'proceeds from his comprehensive knowledge of the real world. He has not a single passage in *The Fair Maid of Perth* to make you feel that his knowledge and talent are not sufficient.'

On 9 October, Eckermann and Goethe are again discussing *The Fair Maid of Perth*, Goethe advises Eckermann to read *Waverley* next, which he says can 'be set beside the best works that have ever been written in this world'. The next day at a dinner for the Tiecks, Walter Scott is the chief topic of conversation, and Ludwig Tieck claims that it was he who had brought the first copy of *Waverley* to Germany.

Goethe's admiration for Scott increased with the years. In 1831 he read *Ivanhoe* and reported to Eckermann on 8 March, 'Walter Scott is a great genius, who does not have an equal. . . . He gives me much to think about, and I discover in him a wholly new art, which has its own laws. . . .' On the following day, 9 March, he tells of beginning *Rob Roy*, for, he says, he will read Scott's best novels in succession. 'We should only read what we admire,' he says, 'as I did in my youth, and as I now experience with Sir

Walter Scott.' Goethe waxes almost ecstatic, 'All is great—material, import, characters, execution, and then what infinite diligence in the preparatory studies!' Finally, he mourns 'the poverty of German history'.

Several days later, on 11 March, at a dinner, Goethe again speaks of *Ivanhoe*, but this time critically, finding fault with the over-detailed descriptions. But when Eckermann asks him to put his views on paper, Goethe refuses, saying that Scott's art is so great that it is difficult to make a public statement about him.

Some scholars claim that Scott influenced Goethe in some of his thinking and even in his works. Fritz Strich maintains that Goethe welcomed Scott as an ally in his battle against the sickly aberrations of Hoffmannesque romanticism, and recommended Scott's essay 'On the Supernatural in Fictitious Composition' to his readers. In this, Scott set up Hoffmann as a warning example of what he called 'the ill-regulated imagination'. Another scholar, James Boyd, feels that Scott gave Goethe some hints for *Faust*, part II. From December 1830 to January 1831, Goethe was reading Scott's *Letters on Demonology and Witchcraft*. At the same time he was completing *Faust*, and, claims Boyd, Act IV and certain characteristics of the scene, *Auf dem Vorgebirge*, point to Scott's book.

It is curious that Goethe, 'Europe's sagest head', admired Scott immensely in the very years when the first flush of his German reputation was fading. As early as 1825, Friedrich von Gentz, the Anglophile translator of Burke, had written a friend, von Pilat, that he considered the exaggerated admiration of Scott 'one of the idiocies of our time, but luckily one of the innocent ones'. One of the manifestations of this 'idiocy' (*'Narrheit'*) was the turning of Waverley novels into operas, a good example of which was Heinrich Marschner's *Templer und Juedin* (1829), based on *Ivanhoe*. But the novelty of Scott wore off and the fickle public soon pursued other literary idols. The *Conversationsblatt* (No. 297, 1831) reports on the performance of a comedy, Raupach's *Die Schleichhaendler*, which has a zany Scott-enthusiast as a character. Five years ago, the critic mourns, the dialogue brought down the house; now the allusions to Scott's novels cause the audience to ask to what they refer. A year later, the *Jenaische Literaturzeitung* (Supplement 23, 1832) finds it necessary to defend Sir Walter Scott against the wave of 'now fashionable deprecation'.

The vogue for Scott had passed like a prairie-fire over the literary landscape of Germany. The enthusiasm with which his novels were received from about 1820 to 1830 can only be understood in the light of the contemporary German novels with which his competed. Many references to Scott's novels couple praise for his works with unfavourable references to the local product. Thus Frau von Schiller, writing Knebel on 26 June 1829, deplores the 'hopeless state' of the German novel. She writes that Scott's works develop interest because the Germans find the Scottish world strange and attractive, and 'the former heroes of our novelists are for us no longer heroic'. Earlier, in 1822, the *Jenaische Literaturzeitung* (No. 93), while ridiculing the popular craze for *Ivanhoe*, admits that no *Ritterroman*, German or foreign, could equal it.

To realize fully the tremendous impact of Scott's novels on the German scene, it is necessary to examine some of these horrendous, pseudo-historical *Ritterromane*, products of the German Gothic school. These sub-literary works were historical, like their British counterparts, only in so far as they were set in a period vaguely medieval. They were almost all traceable to the impetus given this genre by Goethe's *Goetz von Berlichingen* and by Schiller's *Die Raeuber*. *Goetz* especially made a strong impression on the literary world, and imitation being the sincerest form of flattery, forty plays directly copied from it appeared soon after. Translations also abounded; Walter Scott, a *Goetz*-enthusiast himself, had published his translation in 1799.

The effect of *Goetz* on the German hack-novelists was just as great, and soon dozens of imitations in novel form were published. Rebellion, betrayal, death by poison, the secret tribunal, castles, towers, dungeons, and gypsy encampments were all incorporated directly from Goethe's drama and appeared in but slightly changed form in the novels. So flagrant was this imitation that even the dialogue form of the play was left unchanged and that announcements of time, place, and scene were made in the manner of stage-directions.

Just as the Waverley novels in Great Britain swept away their Gothic competitors, so Scott's novels, appearing in Germany after 1815, made serious inroads upon the popularity of the *Ritter-romane*. That the German hack writers, seeing this great competition, should turn to imitating their foreign rival, was a foregone conclusion. The externals of Scott's technique were not difficult to copy, and the fact that no acknowledged canon of his works existed, made duplicity easier. Some writers took advantage of this by signing their own products 'by the author of *Waverley*', or even flagrantly affixing Scott's name in direct forgery.

Goedeke in his *Grundriss zur Geschichte der deutschen Dichtung aus den Quellen* lists nineteen German imitators and forgers of Scott, of whom ten are examined in a dissertation by Frederick Bachmann. Bachmann had an excellent source for his study in the Lincke Library, a Leipzig lending library of the period 1790–1850, purchased intact by the University of Chicago. This collection, representing German popular taste of the time, contains over 400 *Ritterromane*, twenty translations of Scott, and a number of imitations.

These Scott imitations were sub-literary works aping his manner, style, and subject-matter, but without ability approaching his. The same people who had concocted the pre-Scott *Ritterromane* now wrote in the manner of 'The Great Unknown'. One was Heinrich August Mueller, a preacher in Wolmissleben, who fabricated such pseudo-Waverley novels as *Ritter Angus, Der Praetendent*, and *Lady Glamis, oder, Der Kerker von Stirling*. The first-named, which Mueller subtitles 'a Caledonian story after Walter Scott', is typical of these imitations. The usual Scott motifs appear: the Attack, Eavesdropping, the Prison, the Dream, the Duel, the Faithful Servant, the pointing out of coming events, and the use of disguises for escape. The imitator fails in the use of nature-descriptions; scenery is never mentioned, and a trip to London is merely a listing of towns on the way. Unlike Scott also is the total lack of descriptions of interiors—as, for instance, when the King is entertained by the Earl of Angus at Kerburn Castle. One need only compare Scott's magnificent description of a similar scene in *Kenilworth*.

Der Praetendent (1823), another 'Roman nach Walter Scott bearbeitet von Heinrich Mueller', is a pseudo-historical tale supposedly set in the time of Queen Anne. Unlike a Scott novel it is full of historical inaccuracies and imaginary events. James III, the Pretender of the novel, should be James VIII, and the Duke of Argyle, who fights for him, actually fought against him. All sorts of imaginary skirmishes are recounted, but actual battles such as Preston and Sheriffmuir are not even mentioned. More than this, the dialogue betrays Mueller. His characters fall into only two types: the 'good', who deliver pious orations, and the 'bad', who utter fustian. Walter Scott's people are so real and memorable because no two of them speak alike.

Writing under the pseudonym 'F. P. E. Richter' was another Scott-imitator, a woman, Wilhelmine von Gersdorf. One of her works, *Meg Merrilies, die Zigeunerin*, is in the Lincke Library. She was so flagrant a plagiarist that she not only affixed Scott's name to another of her fabrications, *Jacobine oder der Ritter des Geheimnisses*, but stole the plot itself from a novel, *Jacobine von Holland* (1791). Other Scott-imitations were Heinrich Doering's *Das Schloss von Pontefract* (1824), Heinrich Mueller's *Tremnor, der Zerstoerer des Druidenreichs* (1824), and F. W. Moser's *Redmund und Mathilde, oder der Verrath* (1823), based on *Rokeby*. The best-known imitation, and like those above 'aus dem Englischen von Walter Scott', was *Walladmor*, previously mentioned.

In the first decade after *Waverley* was introduced into Germany no work of lasting value reflected Scott's influence. Imitations and outright forgeries abounded, but none of the authors thought of applying the principles of Scott's technique to their own native material, German history. The scenes of the imitators' works were laid almost invariably either in Scotland or England. They failed to realize the true significance of Scott, that his novels were the new epics of national history, and that his ideas could be applied to the historical fiction of any nation. To them Scott was merely another fellow-Gothicist, perhaps a little more successful than the rest, but not different. Therefore they were content to mimic his tricks of style, his use of mottoes for chapter-heads, his locales, and even his motifs and characters. Never having visited Scotland or England, they either ignored descriptions entirely, or were satisfied to get their material from guide-books. Not until 1826, when Hauff's *Lichtenstein* was published, did a first-rate novel embody Scott's ideas, using German history for its subject-matter.

The flow of historical novels under the inspiration of Sir Walter Scott which poured from the pens of German writers during the remainder of the nineteenth century is not the subject of this paper, although I have written of it elsewhere. Suffice it to say that many contended for the proud title, 'the German Walter Scott'. Almost every province of Germany in almost every period of history was the subject of a historical novel. Almost always the formula was that invented by Sir Walter Scott, that of a fictitious hero moving among real historical personages. The historical novel in Germany was a strong factor in promoting national unity, and it would be no exaggeration to state that it played a large part in the psycho-logical preparation for the foundation of the German Reich in 1871.

During the nineteenth century, the novels of Scott continued to go through numerous German editions, attesting to his abiding popularity. Even as late as the period 1896–1910, when Scott had been overtaken by Dickens, Marryat, and Stevenson in popularity, there were still 51 separate editions of his novels published.

It is not difficult, in retrospect, to agree with Julian Schmidt that the influence of Sir Walter Scott in Germany was greater than that of any other foreign writer.

REFERENCES

Frederick W. Bachmann, *Some German Imitators of Walter Scott: an attempt to evaluate the influence of Scott on the Subliterary Novel of the Early Nineteenth Century in Germany* (Chicago, 1933).

James Boyd, *Goethe's Knowledge of English Literature* (London, 1932).

Paul M. Ochojski, *Sir Walter Scott and Germany: a Study in Literary Cross-Currents*, diss. Columbia 1960, University Microfilms MIC 61–255.

Luise Sigmann, 'Die englische Literatur von 1800–1850 im Urteil der zeitgenoessigen deutschen Kritik', *Anglistische Forschungen* lv (1918), 50–72.

F. Strich, *Goethe und die Weltliteratur* (Bern, 1946).

The Impact of Sir Walter Scott in Hungary

ANNA KATONA

In the 1780s the interest in things English was prompted in Hungary by the sharpening of the anti-Habsburg, anti-Austrian feeling in the nation and the growing desire for national, political, and cultural independence. The source of knowledge of English literature was Vienna, where the liberal trends under Emperor Joseph opened up new possibilities for gathering information about the outside world. In 1783 Joseph Retzer published the first English book in Vienna, an anthology of English poetry. At about the same time the first Hungarian writers with a knowledge of English came to the forefront of cultural life. József Péczeli, the editor of the periodical *Mindenes Gyüjtemény*, directed the attention of his readers to the political and cultural aspects of English life. The interest in English culture spread as far as Transylvania where it slowly replaced the predominance of French, and Gábor Döbrentei in the pages of *Erdélyi Muzárion* in 1817 urged young people to learn English, and as he put it 'to translate the works of that noble and original literature in order to show the nation that the English mind is much akin to that of the only half-awakened Hungarian nation'. Against this background of growing interest, English literature became a major shaping force in nineteenth-century Hungary, in the great Golden Age of Hungarian literature. Two figures stand out as far as the novel is concerned: Dickens who contributed largely to the development of Hungarian fiction, and Walter Scott whose impact led to the creation of the Hungarian historical novel—and the Hungarian novel for that matter, since fiction before that time was almost non-existent. Through his own collections of Scottish ballads and poems Scott strengthened the interest in popular poetry as well.

The interest in Walter Scott goes back to the 1820s and co-incided with the beginning of the Age of Reform in Hungarian political and cultural life. The struggle for national independence went hand in hand with a desperate move to get rid of the feudal past and to create a modern nation, an endeavour in which the most radical and most intellectual members of the Hungarian nobility played a leading role. In a country where political freedom was greatly limited by the Austrian government, where feudal conditions stood in the way of liberalization and modernization and where the bourgeoisie was still in an embryonic stage, 'homeland and progress' became the slogan of those radical intellectuals who in an amazingly short time succeeded in stirring up the apathetic country. As we see, two trends went hand in hand: the fight for national independence and that for a more progressive, more democratic form of government. Patriotism and democracy, a more plebeian outlook on life, were inseparable.

The influence of English literature in Hungary in the period before the 1848/49 War of Independence comes as no surprise if we consider the fact that our prominent men of letters discovered in English literature a model they were looking for, a literature that owing to historical conditions after the Norman Conquest was national and popular at a very early stage, as the periodical *Athenaeum* emphasized in an article in 1839 based on an argument in the *Edinburgh Review*. The same article also drew attention to the fact that unlike French literature, English literature always reflected a deep sympathy for the people. If we take into consideration the fact that *Athenaeum* was edited by the three leading literary figures of the early Reform Age, the three Romantics Vörösmarty, Toldy and Bajza, it is easy to conclude that the purpose of the short review on the character of English literature was quite deliberate.

It is just as easy to see why radical Hungarian writers came to be interested in Walter Scott. Their revolutionary patriotism was attracted to a writer who, as George Lukács has it, 'is a patriot . . . proud of the development of his people', one who concentrated on the great crises in the life of the people, one who skilfully showed the complex interaction among all layers of society, thus presenting the fullness of national life, never for a minute forgetting the real social and economic basis of popular life. Lukács praised Scott above all for presenting the historical process as a development in the life of the people. Besides being a patriotic writer Scott also differed from the Romantics, according to Lukács, by creating the average, prosaic hero in his novels and attributing to this type of hero a central role in the structure of his fiction.

Lukács explains in his well-known essay on the historical novel that the awakening of national feeling in the time of the Napoleonic wars prompted an interest in national history and prepared the ground for the historical novel. The patriotic awakening in the early nineteenth century in Hungary, the increasing interest in the way of life of the Hungarian people, the peasantry, well accounts for the keen interest of leading poets and writers in this country in the poetry and prose of Walter Scott. When his *Ivanhoe* was first translated into Hungarian in 1829 the translator made it clear that he undertook the job as a patriotic duty, and so did the publisher who declined all profit. A reviewer in *Figyelmező*—another periodical, also edited by the triumvirate of Vörösmarty, Toldy, and Bajza—made it plain in 1837 that if a writer wants to influence his nation he must be the embodiment of the national spirit, i.e. he must be a patriot. Scott's average, everyday hero, on the other hand, corresponded to the democratic tendencies of our own literature. Furthermore the radical section of our nobility became increasingly history-conscious because of the ever-sharpening political conflict between Hungary and Vienna. As the patriotic ideals of the nation took shape in the best minds, the hitherto popular historical themes in Romantic poetry came to be treated in a more deliberate way and with an educational purpose. Literature became highly conscious of its role as the conscience and brain of the backward nation. The writers of the important lyrical and epic works of the twenties were all committed to serve the national awakening. They showed up the drabness of the present against the background of past glory, or pointed to tragic crises in the history of the country as frightening examples. In spite of the remarkable achievements of Hungarian Romantic poetry with historical themes, historical fiction was slow to catch up owing to the general backwardness of Hungarian prose. But the whole atmosphere urgently required a development in this direction.

All these phenomena of Hungarian cultural life in the twenties of the last century made the cultural atmosphere receptive to the art of Walter Scott. As a later reviewer summed it up in *Pécsi Lapok* in 1860, the character of his writing corresponded to the general tendency of the age. One more feature may be added to the general picture. Nineteenth-century Hungarian literature was strongly moral-based and the previously mentioned article in *Figyelmező* prefers Walter Scott to Goethe for the moral tendency of his writings. Conceding that the main purpose of art is the beautiful, the reviewer strongly emphasizes that the beautiful should never contradict the true and the good. This strong emphasis on the moral issue can be understood against the serious commitment and almost messianic drive of our prominent writers to influence and awaken the backward country, to exercise a teaching, educating mission.

Walter Scott was first read in Hungary in German translations or in the original by those few eminent intellectuals who knew English. He was first introduced to a larger public when his ballad 'The Search after Happiness, or the Quest of Sultaun Solimaun' appeared in *Hasznos mulatságok* in 1822. Here we find the first comment on him. He is described as a Scottish novelist and praised for the use he makes of old chronicles. The same periodical praised him in 1825 for his collection of popular ballads. In 1824 in *Szépliteraturai Ajándék* the translator of a Scottish tale commented on his translation, expressing his desire for similar Hungarian tales to be collected and retold by talented young writers. The major endeavour of introducing Scott to a larger audience, however, was András Taisz's six-volume translation of *Ivanhoe*.

The intention of those who wanted to make Scott available was two-fold as is clearly shown in Taisz's introduction to his translation. He translated *Ivanhoe* with one eye on the slowly increasing Hungarian reading public, whose taste needed guidance and whose interest demanded entertaining reading of some value. At the same time Taisz ardently hoped that his modest work would influence writers and be followed by those of an original Hungarian Scott.

The discrepancy between the most prominent minds and the average reader was enormous. In 1835, when the poet Kölcsey, who was responsible for the slogan 'homeland and progress', possessed in his library the 1834 Frankfurt edition of *The Poetical Works of Scott*, the fashionable lady's reading habits came in for mockery by the writer József Gaál in the pages of *Rajzolatok*. Gaál referred to Kotzebue and other minor German writers as favourites, while Walter Scott, if read at all, was considered only out of utter boredom on a rainy day, and *Kenilworth* was found boring anyway. This article, besides bitterly criticizing the then fashionable reading-matter, also recommended Scott as good reading.

Scott was upheld as a model for Hungarian poets as early as 1824 by Pál Illés in the pages of *Tudományos Gyüjtemény* where he praised Scott as the poet of the people and most urgently emphasized the need in Hungary for similar poets. The previously mentioned 1839 article in *Athenaeum*, which emphasized the national and popular character of early English literature, summing up recent trends, pointed to Scott and held up his poetry as a model to be followed. 'Scott', it says, 'turned to the literature of democracy, to that of legends and ballads, there his poetry takes its roots.' To Hungarian poets of the Age of Reform, such an attitude was congenial. The collection of popular poetry was very much in vogue in the forties, and as early as 1836 *Tudományos Gyüjtemény* praised the poet Károly Kisfaludy for 'knowing that the most sophisticated stanzas must be strongly related to the sounds of popular songs'. No wonder Kisfaludy was attracted by Scottish ballads and even took over motifs from some contained in Scott's *Minstrelsy of the Scottish Border*, which he knew in German translation. But even János Arany, the greatest writer of popular ballads in Hungarian literature, could not escape the influence of both the *Minstrelsy* and of some original ballads by Scott. Two major ballads of his show an influence in more than motifs, and echo the atmosphere of the Scottish original: The *Ejféli párbaj* [Midnight Duel] can easily be linked with Scott's *The Eve of St. John* and the *Both bajnok özvegye* [The Widow of Knight Both] is a song of lament like *The Lament of the Border Widow* in the *Minstrelsy*. Arany was the greatest poet of the Age of Reform besides Petőfi. He embodied the national spirit both before and after the War of Independence and he paid a lasting tribute to Walter Scott in 1860, describing his works as representatives of a collective thought and comparing them to a wonderful symphony directed by a god-like artist. Arany had a high esteem for all those who like Scott directed themselves 'to collecting the bypassed treasures of popular literature'.

In 1833 *Muzárion* recommended Walter Scott to the attention of writers. In 1837 a volume of selected short stories from abroad appeared with Scott's 'The Tapestried Chamber' in it. The introduction clearly stated that the chosen stories were meant as models for young poets. Far more important, however, was the fact that József Bajza, considered by some the most European-minded of our poets in the early Age of Reform, recognized Walter Scott's importance. 'Blessing to such writers as Goethe and Walter Scott, as Cooper and Irving, who teach us with their immortal works what a novelist has to strive for.' His statement in 1833 in *Kritikai Lapok* is the more important since Bajza was a man who had a talent for organizing; he was the first to try to bring order, purpose, intention into the chaotic literary life of Hungary, and became something of a minor Dr. Johnson.

The prominent figures of cultural life in the thirties and the early forties were Mihály Vörösmarty, József Bajza, and Ferenc Toldy. All these men formed a literary circle. According to Toldy's reminiscences in *Budapesti Szemle* in 1875 they called themselves 'the men of Alsatia' in reference to Scott's *The Fortunes of Nigel*. As early as 1823, in a letter to Bajza, Toldy confessed: 'I am so fascinated by the novels of Walter Scott that I will not give up the desire to translate them myself. Toldy never carried out this plan, though Bajza made it plain in his reply that the translator of Scott would be entitled to the gratitude of the nation. It is important to note that Toldy read Scott in the original, indeed the desire to read Scott, Byron, and Shakespeare in the original launched him on the venture of learning English.

In 1833 Bajza published in *Kritikai Lapok* his essay *A román költészetről* [On Novel Writing]. This was the first important critical writing on fiction in Hungarian literature. Bajza intended to give some guidance to future Hungarian novelists. He based most of his arguments on Scott's fiction and most of his examples were drawn from the same source. Scott's *œuvre* served Bajza as a model. Whether he tries to define the novel as a literary form, or to distinguish it from the epic, whether he describes fictional devices or gives advice as to plot, structure and characterization, his constant reference is to Walter Scott. No wonder Bajza's own ventures into a fictional type of literature were strongly based on Scott's example as his unfinished *Kámor* proves.

Such was the prelude to the year 1836 when three novels emerged almost simultaneously on the hitherto blank fictional scene: *Az elbujdosott vagy egy tél a fővárosban* [The Emigrant, or a Winter in the Capital] by Lázár Petrichevich Horváth, *Szirmay Ilona* by József Gaál and the most important one *Abafi* by Miklós Jósika. All three were reviewed in the contemporary press by standard of Scott, and rightly so since all three were evidently products of that influence which, according to the twentieth-century poet and critic Mihály Babits, started fiction as such in Hungary.

The novel *Szirmay Ilona* about the 1716 Tatar invasion is modelled on Scott's technique of putting the story into the mouth of a humorous figure, and follows the Scottish master in mixing the lives of people belonging to different layers of society, in pointing out the relationship between historical events and the lives of ordinary people. There is a tendency, though very weak, to disclose the historical process underlying the events. Gaál's talent, however, was minor and he failed to conjure up a truly historical atmosphere. Even the first reviewer in *Figyelmező* blamed him for neglecting the background, 'though it is the step-by-step unveiling of the background which accounts for the suspense and which makes Scott's novels so exciting'. Gaál originally planned a whole series of novels under one single heading adopting in this Scott's device in such works as *Tales of my Landlord* and *Tales of the Crusaders*. But as a whole Gaál's novel remains on the adventure-story level.

The really important and decisive work of the year 1826, however, was Jósika's *Abafi*, the first readable Hungarian novel. The dream of Taisz, the unselfish translator of *Ivanhoe* was realized at last: the Hungarian Scott entered the literary scene. Jósika himself belonged to the most intellectual section of the Hungarian nobility, to those who were deeply involved in the struggle of the Age of Reform and for whom the hope of national independence deepened the interest in the national past. It is no mere chance that the Hungarian historical novel emerged in Transylvania, nor is it an accident that a Transylvanian created in Hungary fiction similar to that of the Scottish novelist. There is a close parallel between the Scotland which Scott wrote about and Transylvania in the nineteenth century. Transylvania was then as much a distinctly separate unit within Hungary as Scotland is in Great Britain, with a cultural, political and social life of its own. Like Scotland, Transylvania is a mountainous country with ancient castles and churches which bear witness to the events of a glorious past. Transylvania was similar to Scotland also in the fact that as its present was much less exciting, its people were inclined to live on the vivid memories of past glories. A living memory of the past among the people was a necessary condition for the birth of the historical novel. In Hungary proper conditions were much less favourable. There most historical monuments had been destroyed by the Turks during a century and a half of occupation. Pest had ceased to be a capital and the country was governed from Vienna. Transylvania on the other hand had been an independent prince-dom during the time of Turkish occupation and had a diplomatic history on a European level, with a princely court and all that belonged to it. It is not surprising then that the Hungarian historical novel was born in Transylvania and written by a Transylvanian. Even the early reviewer in *Figyelmező* in 1838 noticed how fortunate Jósika's choice was. 'Transplanted to Hungary the story would lose its fullness', he wrote.

All contemporary reviewers recognized the influence of Scott and hailed it with the greatest enthusiasm. In *Tudományos Gyüjtemény* in 1836, the reviewer of Hungarian literature remarked of Jósika that 'he accepted the English novel as his model since he knew it closely. This single fact recommends him to me. The English have saved the novel from that mixture of frivolity and sentimentality to which it had sunk in the hands of French and German writers.' And when Toldy tried to explain to the readers in *Figyelmező* in what way Jósika's work differed from an epic poem, his obvious reference was Walter Scott.

The reviewer of *Abafi*'s German translation listed Jósika among the followers of Scott, though he conceded that Jósika possessed more poetic power than most of the imitators. Ever since the appearance of *Abafi* in 1836 critics and writers had commented on the relationship between Scott and Jósika, and on the degree of influence that could be detected in the fiction of the Transylvanian novelist.

Before we consider the problem of outright influence one point must be made clear. Jósika's historical fiction was the clear outcome of several combined forces. The prevailing interest in past history in Hungary, and the high achievements of a Vörösmarty (who by the way read Scott eagerly in 1824) in the field of Romantic epic, dealing with the national past and all the factors that went into the creation of widespread interest in Hungary's history, prepared the ground for a receptive attitude in Jósika when his eager reading led him to Walter Scott.

The parallel or similarity between some of their novels can be questioned, and literary critics may agree or disagree on the close resemblance of some characters. Some motifs may come from Scott like the passionate lover ready to murder, the lost and refound child, the robbers, the tournament, the portrayal of the Jews. *Abafi*'s first chapters certainly contain quotations from *Ivanhoe*, and the novel has an epilogue-like last chapter. Jósika also followed the device of the author of *Waverley* when he published his novels after the War of Independence, as having been written by 'the author of *Eszter*' rather than under his own name. He also made ample use of longish chapter-titles. All these items, however, are ultimately of minor importance—for example, all passionate lovers in world literature cannot be traced back to a single origin. More important than motifs is the overall character of Jósika's *œuvre*. He was as much a prolific writer doing hasty work as Scott, and like his Scottish model delighted in complicated, exciting plots.

All this, however, would not account for Jósika's role as the creator of Hungarian fiction, nor does it establish beyond question Scott's influence on the emergence of the Hungarian historical novel. The really decisive factor was the adaptation of Scott's conception and method to Hungarian circumstances. Jósika accepted, at least in his masterpiece *Abafi*, Scott's device of introducing an average hero as the main character of the historical novel. The main hero consequently is not an historical character, and since he is a fictional figure much of the plot is fiction as well. As Jósika himself explained in his critical essay on fiction-writing (*Regény és regényítészet*) 'the story only leans on history'. In the same essay Jósika also emphasized how much serious study goes into the writing of a good novel. He certainly followed Scott's example in bringing the past alive through a very minute and detailed description of the environment. All these details, however, were entirely original to Jósika, since he reproduced specifically Hungarian or Transylvanian conditions. He accepted the method but used it in a way proper to his own Transylvanian subject-matter. Again, if (as with Scott) we can find popular legends in Jósika's fictional world, this is no mere imitation, since Jósika—like the best minds of the Hungarian literary scene of his time—was interested in the life of the people. In the developments of his plots he adopted Scott's method in bringing the story rapidly to an end once the climax had been reached. Indeed in his critical essays he brought this device to the attention of fellow-novelists, adding to his advice 'as we see it in the first and best novelist of the world, Walter Scott'.

These words alone would testify to Jósika's unlimited admiration for the Scottish novelist, and yet in his essay on the novel he refused to accept the title of 'the Hungarian Walter Scott'. Critics disagree about Jósika's motive. Some believe that he considered it much too great a praise, others think he was hurt to be called an imitator. An imitator he certainly was not. Jósika transplanted into prose Vörösmarty's historical epic, and consequently belongs to the main stream of development in Hungarian literary history. And yet he could not have achieved this important step without adapting to Hungarian circumstances the conception and methods of the Scottish master whose congenial genius released the novelist in him.

Jósika had a tremendous influence in shaping the literary taste of female readers and in creating a solid novel-reading public. In consequence, the creation of a Hungarian fiction-reading public can indirectly be attributed to Scott. Similarly, the fact that Jósika's activity made fiction-writing a respectable profession can be traced to the indirect impact of the Scottish novelist.

The fascination exercised by Dickens on Hungarian writers pushed the image of Scott into the background; the forties, fifties, and sixties of the last century were dominated by the figure of Boz. When in 1842 it was decided to start a series of foreign novels in translation, *Oliver Twist* was the first choice. In spite of this, Scott's continuous influence cannot be disregarded. Such an important figure on the Hungarian cultural scene as József Eötvös, a novelist himself, wrote on Scott's death: 'When we think of him we are not reminded of the place he left empty but of the fact that he filled a place that had been previously empty, that he created works which will keep his memory alive like that of the stones of Phidias'. The most popular Hungarian novelist in the second half of the nineteenth century, Mór Jókai, declared that the first novel he had ever read was Walter Scott's *Ivanhoe* in Hungarian translation. Jókai's techniques display evident signs of similarity to those of Scott. They are both excellent story-tellers, introduce humorous elements into the historical novel, delight in excursions into the field of folklore and popular customs. They both make ample use of descriptions and build up suspense through contrasts. The tournaments, the epilogues, the long chapter-titles in Jókai's novels can be attributed partly to English origins.

According to the more recent poet and critic Babits, even that lonely ambiguous figure of nineteenth-century Hungarian fiction Zsigmond Kemény is unimaginable without Scott—if only for the reason that Scott created the historical novel as such. Kemény has a special concept of the historical novel, and he withholds this title from works where the plot is fictional and has only loose connexions with historical events, where historical personalities play no role or unimportant ones, and where history is reduced to the evocation of a certain atmosphere. This attitude, however, does not amount to a dismissal of Walter Scott. Kemény concludes his argument on the historical novel by saying 'this is frequently

Walter Scott's way, some of his delightful novels happen in history, but they are not historical novels'. The fact that Kemény built one or the other of his stories around a motif that was predominant in Scott, should by no means be exaggerated. Kemény certainly admired Scott and fell under his impact, as did all European writers of historical novels, but none the less if Jósika and to some degree Jókai were congenial to Scott in their outlook, Kemény was not. Most of Scott's novels have a happy ending; he was the writer of the post-Napoleonic period of relief. Kemény was a pessimist, the novelist who wrote after the defeat of Hungary in the War of Independence. His works are dramatic rather than epic in character. If Kemény was impressed by Scott's accuracy in describing environmental details, this minute precision went into the psychoanalysis of his characters. One of the Hungarian critics who drew a parallel between the two novelists put it very plainly: 'Scott depicts the prison while Kemény concentrates on the soul of the prisoner'.

In 1871 the centenary of Walter Scott was marked in Hungary by long series of commemorative articles. Some of them provided a detailed analysis of Scott's works, both prose and poetry. By that time, however, interest in Walter Scott had withered away, and even the attraction of Dickens had given way among intellectuals to new interests, to the impact of the Russian and the French novel. A voice of discontent was raised in some rather popular magazines which complained about the fact that the only novel by Scott available in Hungarian in 1871 was *Ivanhoe*. The writers in popular magazines had the average public in mind. They would have enjoyed Scott's exciting stories, though the sophisticated had abandoned him for new literary trends. If we recall the patriotic enthusiasm of the translator of *Ivanhoe* and the intellectual delight in Scott of Bajza and his circle, the lack of further translations seems a paradox without explanation. The paradox should not be easily explained away, though it is true that when the novel as such became fashionable in Hungary with a wider reading public after the appearance of Jósika on the literary scene, translators looked for more recent works and turned with interest to Dickens. The intellectuals had already read their Scott either in the original or in early cheap German translations which are still in the possession of the Budapest Széchenyi Library.

The complaint of the popular magazines was repeated on a more academic level in 1915 in *Budapesti Szemle* in an article which paid tribute to the writer of *Waverley* on the centenary of that novel. Ferenczi, the writer of the article, had to concede the sore fact that *Waverley* had not been translated into Hungarian. Indeed the first Hungarian translation appeared only in 1949. In the late nineteenth century, after the 1871 anniversary, *Peveril of the Peak* and *The Bride of Lammermoor* were made available in Hungarian. In the late twenties and the thirties of this century *Kenilworth*, *Quentin Durward*, *The Talisman*, and *The Heart of Mid-Lothian* were translated, *Ivanhoe* appeared in a new and more modern guise for the second time in the century. In the late fifties and in the sixties publishers made *Ivanhoe*, *Rob Roy* and *Quentin Durward* available in translations which in their poetic quality do justice to the original.

The paradox, however, remains. Outstanding minds of the early twentieth century paid tribute to Scott, as did the poet Gyula Junász, or recognized and emphasized the importance of his influence in Hungary, as did Babits and the excellent critic Antal Szerb. Lukács attributed to him a specific role in world literature. In spite of this, the sad fact remains that literary critics in Hungary turn away with disdain from one whom they regard as an old-fashioned novelist. Critics dealing with nineteenth-century Hungarian literature attempt to minimize Scott's influence instead of trying to discover new evidence that would complete the picture of an impact that had been recognized by outstanding literary figures, writers themselves, even in the twenties and thirties of this century.

Hungarian literary criticism has proved rather ungrateful for and forgetful of the indirect contribution of Walter Scott to the creation of Hungarian fiction and the Hungarian reading public.

Scott and Italy[1]

R. D. S. JACK

THE purpose of this paper is twofold. It first seeks to analyse the nature of Scott's reading in Italian and the use made of this—as well as of his wide cultural acquaintance with Italy —in his novels. Then, by adducing more evidence of Scott's influence on the Italian novel, it explores the process operating in reverse. It is hoped that such a study may help to advance and explain the claim that his work is most profitably to be viewed in a European context.

If Scott came to the country of Italy even later than Smollett, his interest in Italian literature and language proves immeasurably superior to that of his predecessor. At college his love of Ariosto was so great that he alienated the Greek department by staunchly upholding the Italian's superiority to Homer in a class essay. Scott confesses that his first knowledge of Ariosto and Tasso came via the translations of Hoole, from whose notes he learned 'that the Italian language contained a fund of romantic lore'. This was the period when he and Irving amused themselves by composing romantic tales, and thus it is not surprising that the young Scott followed up Hoole's lead by attending Italian classes twice a week. He naturally preferred the original texts and became acquainted with 'Dante, Boiardo, Pulci, and other eminent Italian authors'.[2] Thus it is, that when reminiscing with Cheney in Rome, at the end of a long and successful career, he attributes his first interest in novel writing to *Don Quixote* and to the Italian romances of Boiardo and Ariosto, which he had earlier read once every year.

Inevitably this wide reading determined his critical thinking as well as the eventual form and content of his novels. The *Encyclopaedia Britannica* 'Essays on Chivalry, Romance and the Drama' bear witness to the influence of English and Scottish writers, but

---

[1] Most of this paper is included in my *The Italian Influence on Scottish Literature* (Edinburgh, 1972).

[2] Lockhart, *Life*, i. 46.

Scott as critic follows on naturally from the European focus of
Adam Smith. If we isolate the Italian line, it should be remembered that French, Spanish, and German references also abound.
Indeed, while praising Ariosto and Tasso, he puts forward the
interesting thesis that Italians 'received . . . the forms and institutions of chivalry' but were 'in a considerable degree strangers to
its spirit'. He places Ariosto correctly in the context of old
Romances, and shows how the form of his poetry seems controlled
when compared to their more rambling and diffuse style. One
gathers pleasure not only from his digressions, but from the
'extreme ingenuity with which he gathers up the broken ends of
his narrative, and finally weaves them all handsomely together in
the same piece.'[3] Scott's own novels, with their apparently limit-
less flexibility yet overall authorial control, and their tantalizing
mixture of realism and romance, present a variation on Ariosto's
model as here defined.

Obviously Scott is most interested in the Italian Romance, but
his reading has also taken him to the 'profligate novels' of Ban-
dello, the 'licentiousness of Aretino', and the 'politics of Machiavel'.
His study of the drama includes some material which probably was
derived at second hand from Walker's *Essay of the Revival of the
Drama in Italy*. But he has a wide knowledge of the traditions
behind the Commedia dell'arte. Bibbiena's *La Calandra* is given
credit for being the first Italian comedy and for beginning the line
of 'commedie erudite' composed by Ariosto and Trissino among
others. As with the Romance, however, he questions whether the
climate of opinion in Italy aided the development of this promising
tradition, and concludes that it died prematurely because 'it did
not take kindly root in the soil, and lacked that popularity which
alone can nurse it freely'.[4] None the less Scott's own knowledge of
Italian drama, though in part drawn from Walker and from the
Italian critic Riccoboni, is almost as extensive as his knowledge
of Italian Romance. The innovations of Goldoni in combining the
best features of the Commedia dell'arte with improved and witty
plots, are recognized. The somewhat stony path of tragedy from
Trissino to Alfieri is briefly traced, and the same conclusions of
poor audience reaction reached. He shares his century's over-
estimation of the operas of Metastasio but overall his assessment

---

[3] *Miscellaneous Prose Works*, vi ('Essays on Chivalry, Romance, and the Drama'),
195.
[4] *Ibid*. 292.

of European literature seems to me to have much more breadth
and authority than Carlyle's *Lectures on Literature*.

In the eighteenth and early nineteenth centuries men of letters,
like philosophers, strove to possess a detailed knowledge of European developments in their field. This knowledge in its turn
influenced their own original work, not usually in the form of
direct imitation or adaptation, but in determining more general
aspects of form or content. Already the link between Scott's view
of Ariosto and the shape of his own novels has been noticed. This
is no fanciful critical parallel, for Scott himself was aware of it, and
not infrequently uses his narrator to force home the point. Thus in
Chapter 16 of *The Heart of Mid-Lothian*, when Scott needs to
explain some background to the story of Robertson and Effie, he
prefaces his transition of focus with the comment:

Like the digressive poet Ariosto, I find myself under the necessity of connec-
ting the branches of my story, by taking up the adventures of another of the
characters, and bringing them down to the point at which we have left those
of Jeanie Deans. It is not, perhaps, the most artificial way of telling a story,
but it has the advantage of sparing the necessity of resuming what a knitter
(if stocking looms have left such a person in the land) might call our
'dropped stitches'; a labour in which the author generally toils much, without
getting credit for his pains.

The point here is not only that Scott consciously models himself
on Ariosto, but that the modest tone adopted by the narrator contrasts with the clearcut praise given to this technique by Scott in
the Essays. The use of digression, the changing of scene, the tying
up of loose ends had there been related to the traditions of
Romance and to the greater ingenuity of the author's controlling
vision. This may not prevent a critic's distaste for the device
carried to excess in, say, the last few chapters of *The Antiquary*,
where an eldest son, an explanation about treasure and startling
new information about the hero are all needed to bring the plot
harmoniously to a close, but it does place such a method in its
proper context and clarifies the author's own attitude to it.

This formal similarity to the Romances of Ariosto means that
Italian readers were not estranged by Scott's genre, as they had
been by Smollett's use of the Picaresque. But of course the influence of Ariosto, Boiardo and Tasso on Scott does not stop there.
It extends to content as well. Again, this does not imply the recreation of scenes already handled in *Orlando furioso* or *Gerusalemme liberata*. At the simplest level, it involves frequent retreats

to the periods immortalized in these works. The Crusades for example are the centre of the *Gerusalemme* and of the *Orlando*. They are also the centre of Scott's *The Talisman* and *Count Robert of Paris*, and play a marked part in *Ivanhoe, Anne of Geierstein* and others. Clearly Scott viewed these works as to some extent growing out of the Italian originals. For the most part this betrays itself in the form of parallels. In the *Talisman*, the hermit of Engaddi is modelled to some extent on Tasso's Peter the Hermit and is twice explicitly compared to him. In *Count Robert of Paris*, when Prince Tancred advances to participate in the parley of Chapter 32, the narrator describes him as 'remarkable for that personal beauty which Tasso has preferred to any of the Crusaders, except Rinaldo d'Este, the creature of his own poetical imagination'. It will be noted that in this latter instance the Italian parallel is used not only to boost the stature of Scott's character but also to distinguish him from the fictitious characters of Romance. This technique is often used by Scott. There is a further example in the same novel, where the countess of Paris, Brenhilda, is not only presented as a martial leader, but as one who 'gave the real instances of the Marphisas and Bradamantes whom the writers of romance delighted to paint'. Thus Italian Romance is employed sometimes to determine the form, the topic and the characters of Scott's novels, but also to point by way of contrast, the reality of his own heroes.

A variation on this is to present a character who has been brought up on Romances and then bring him face to face with actuality. Scott's knowledge of Italian literature thus becomes part of his skill in characterization. The most obvious example is, of course, Waverley, who 'had perused the numerous romantic poems, which, from the days of Pulci, have been a favourite exercise of the wits of Italy'. As a result his expectations are consistently drawn in terms of Romance. He expects Donald Bean Lean to be a 'stern, gigantic, ferocious' banditto. The effect of course lies in the contrast, when Donald eventually appears. And at length Waverley is to shed the excesses of his Romantic imagination. What is less frequently realized is the extent to which the reader is conditioned into sharing Waverley's initial romantic vision, and thus into sharing his disillusionment. The narrator plays a large part in this. He tells a story, whose form has much in common with the Italian Romance. He then compares his aims to those of Tasso: 'I may be here reminded of the necessity of rendering instruction agreeable to youth, and of Tasso's infusion of honey into the medicine prepared for a child'. At times too his outlook merges with that of his hero, as when he describes a scene which 'was not quite equal to the gardens of Alcina; yet wanted not the "due donzellette garrule" of that enchanted paradise' or compares Flora to a 'fair enchantress of Boiardo or Ariosto'. Through the form of the novel we live through those very temptations of Romance to which Waverley has succumbed, and there is little doubt that Scott's achievement at this level could not have been so successful, had he not been widely acquainted with his hero's own reading matter. Indeed even the characters who scorn Romances and play a large part in teaching Waverley the lessons of life, are not entirely ignorant of Italian writers. Fergus MacIvor, of all people, can quote these lines from the first canto of Folengo's *Orlandino*:

> Io d'Elicona niente
> Mi curo, in fé di Dio, ché 'l bere d'acque
> (Bea chi ber ne vuol) sempre me spiacque!

And the fact that he considers their author a 'crack-brained Italian romancer' cannot obliterate the initial impression. Of course this is the first of Scott's novels and more material from his Romance reading goes into it than into any other single work. The fact remains that if, from one view, the world of Romance is seen as a world of illusion, then like M. Jourdain's world of the 'mama-mouchi' it is a world in which the sane must also participate, in order to accommodate the major protagonist. The reactions vary from Fergus's scorn to Rose's admiration, via the sly irony of Flora's 'he can admire the moon and quote a stanza from Tasso'. But in the opening Waverley novel, every major character must define himself with reference to the values of Romance, thus permitting Scott to make the fullest possible use of his personal reading in Italian literature.

If the works of Ariosto and Tasso play a large part in advancing one of the principal themes in *Waverley*, they also play an important if different part in advancing the plot of *Rob Roy*. Here, the reading and translating of Italian classics become part of the story-line in a fashion which inevitably points back to *Roderick Random*. Thus it is one of Francis Osbaldistone's dearest ambitions to translate the whole of *Orlando furioso* into English. At one point in his relationship with Die Vernon, he shows her the start of this work, and

Scott actually translates the first thirteen lines by way of specimen. But Francis's interest in Ariosto, and in Italian writers generally, is used in more subtle fashions during the development of the Romance. When Die wishes to lure Francis away, she pretends to have 'encountered this morning a difficult passage in the *Divina Commedia* of Dante . . . the obscure Florentine'. So, initially, Francis's interest in Italian enables Die to manipulate him and to flatter him ('now that the passage in Dante is made so clear'), blinded as he is by his own enthusiasm. Later, when he realizes her cunning, he expresses his revised opinion of her, again in terms of his ruling interest: 'The society of half a dozen of clowns to play at whisk and swabbers would give her more pleasure than if Ariosto himself were to awake from the dead.' Smollett in *Roderick Random* has used one instance of this sort. Scott develops on his example, until Francis's copy of Ariosto seems almost to become a character in the novel.

All the novels so far discussed have been in one way or another appropriate receptacles for Scott's knowledge of Italian literature. The Crusades, the character of Waverley, the interests of Osbaldi-stone, all lend themselves to the introduction of Italian literary references. Yet the reader of Scott will find similar references appearing in much more unlikely contexts. The theme and characters of *Old Mortality* for example do not obviously suggest Italian parallels. Nor does Scott obtrude them incongruously on his readers. At the same time, he cannot fully hide his own interests, and one is not entirely surprised to find the threatened stroke of Gibbie's pike in Chapter 3 being compared to 'the celebrated thrust of Orlando, which, according to the Italian epic poet, broached as many Moors as a Frenchman spits frogs'. Or to hear the Sub-Prior in *The Monastery* back up one of his arguments by citing the following lines from Ariosto:

> O gran bontà dei cavalieri antiqui!
> Erano nemici, eran' de fede diversa.

In short, Italian literature in one form or another becomes part of the texture of Scott's novels. In some it supplies only a chance quotation or parallel, in others it may play an essential part in determining form, content, themes or characters. But in very few indeed is it non-existent.

And this is to confine ourselves to literary references! When one considers the references to Italian culture more generally, the material from the novels proves overwhelming. Naturally the various characters do not think alike, so that in *A Legend of Montrose* we learn of the high quality of Italian music, only for Osbaldistone in *Rob Roy* to counter that he prefers an old Scottish ditty to 'all the opera airs ever minted by the capricious brain of an Italian Mus. D.!' Italian paintings may decorate the homes of characters, as does Oldbuck's prized Spagnoletto, or they may be used by a lover when boasting of his lady: 'the baker's nymph of Raphael d'Urbino shall seem but a gipsy in comparison of my Molinara' (Sir Piercie Shafton in *The Monastery*). Indeed one sometimes wonders where Scott's characters would be without the various arts and crafts of Italy on which they rely. The heroes of *The Abbot* in their 'gay Milan armour' mix with other martial figures brandishing 'Andrea Ferraras' or 'poniards of Parma' in the world of Scott. Piercie Shafton blazes forth in all the glory of a 'peach-coloured doublet of Genoa velvet', then in a cuirass 'laid over with goldsmith's work . . . by Bonamico of Milan'. His skill in fencing derives from the Italian school of Vincentio Saviola who is also mentioned in *Waverley*. On the other hand, there is the salutary memory of the character in *Woodstock*, who fell to 'a trick of the sword which was not familiar in the days of old Vincent Saviolo'. These are only a few representative examples. To them could be added Oldbuck's server, 'wrought by the old mad Florentine, Benvenuto Cellini', or the various discussions on the Commedia dell'arte raised in *St. Ronan's Well*, *Redgauntlet*, *The Fortunes of Nigel*, *The Abbot* and elsewhere. But the point is surely made. Italian culture generally, as well as Italian literature, is a force in the novels of Scott. In some instances it serves to accentuate authenticity, in others it highlights one aspect of a character's personality, in others it reflects passing fashions at home or abroad, in others it merely adds a touch of mystery. Above all it strengthens the essentially international background against which Scott was often to set Scottish actions and customs. He is working on a much more ambitious scale than either Smollett or Urquhart, but his works like theirs reflect this mixture of national and international—of parochially defined viewpoint within cosmopolitan framework.

Scott then has a wider knowledge than Smollett of Italian culture on this broad level. But it is a knowledge drawn from books and from his antiquarian researches. Both writers for example refer to the type of sword known as an Andrea Ferrara, but Scott is the only one who is still actively doing research on the topic in Italy a few months before his death. Particular interests of this kind may have their drawbacks, and certainly rather many of the Waverley heroes brandish Andrea Ferraras, but generally extensive booklore serves those authors well who give their novels a European background.

If Scott surpasses Smollett in the building of up an authentic Italian cultural background in his novels, he cannot be said to be demonstrably superior in satirizing the false Italianate culture adopted by British subjects. On the other hand, he does continue this line and Dr. Lundin in *The Abbot* clearly belongs to the same family as Squire Burdock's son in *Humphry Clinker*. At once a fop and a pretender to extensive knowledge, he persists in sprinkling his language with quotations in Latin and Italian, thus rendering himself universally unintelligible. A follower of the medical school of Salerno, he is especially anxious that acquaintances should be aware of his Italian background. So, when the pageboy remarks on his many cures, he retorts:

Toys, young sir—trifles, the hit or miss practice of a poor retired gentleman, in a short cloak and doublet—Marry, Heaven sent its blessing—and this I must say, better fashioned mediciners have brought fewer patients through— *lunga roba corta scienzia*, saith the Italian—ha, fair sir, you have the language?

Yet, despite the undoubted success of Lundin or Sir Piercie Shafton as comic, humorized creations, it is still a fair generalization to say that Scott's antiquarian interests led him to prefer an outward-looking, serious depiction of Italian culture, while Smollett's satirical bent favoured an ironical analysis of the culture as it affected the more pretentious among his fellow countrymen.

In the presentation of Italian characters in his novels, Scott seems again to be following Smollett's lead, at least in part. Most obviously the character of the Paduan doctor, with his reputation for necromancy, in *Peregrine Pickle* proves the natural predecessor of one of the main figures in *My Aunt Margaret's Mirror*:

About this period there appeared in Edinburgh a man of singular appearance and pretensions. He was commonly called the Paduan Doctor, from having received his education at that famous university . . . Many persons . . . alleged that Doctor Baptista Damiotti made use of charms and unlawful arts in order to obtain success in his practice.

Like Smollett, Scott leaves the final judgement on the doctor's abilities open. He does practise necromancy, but in the matter of Sir Philip Forester he does so successfully. And if one character, the German doctor, scorns Italian learning as represented by Damiotti, Lady Bothwell is prepared to counter his assertions with the wry remark that 'What comes from Italy may be as good as what comes from Hanover, doctor'.

Yet this is still a character developing from a British generalization about a group of Italians, and so is not very far from Urquhart's Italian swordsmen and cultured courtiers. Although Scott does go further in individualizing Italian characters than Smollett, they never entirely escape from the 'type' background. In particular the idea of Machiavellianism, as popularly interpreted, aids Scott in the creation of two of his most memorable Italian characters, Montserrat in *The Talisman* and Campo Basso, who first appears in *Quentin Durward*, then plays a major role in *Anne of Geierstein*. In *Quentin Durward*, of course, the prime Machiavellian figure is Louis XI, as Scott makes clear in his Introduction. Campo Basso appears primarily as 'the unworthy favourite of Charles', who seems likely to become married to the Lady Isabelle. But he does on one occasion act as the king's counsellor, and then it is to give the Machiavellian counsel, 'that he should crush his mortal enemy, now that chance had placed his fate at his disposal'. It is this aspect of his personality which is stressed in *Anne of Geierstein*, where he emerges as a cunning politician who has wormed his way even further into the trust of Charles of Burgundy, 'chiefly . . . by accommodating himself to his master's opinions and prejudices, and placing before the Duke specious arguments to justify him for following his own way'. Yet he is also a mercenary, whose loyalties are guided by monetary considerations throughout. This image of the Italian as avaricious and unprincipled was rife in the eighteenth century particularly, due to the poverty at that time of the States. Scott includes it in many of his Italian character portraits, and certainly Campo Basso in *Anne of Geierstein* is introduced as one 'who waits but the highest price to sell his Highness like a sheep for the shambles'. In the event he does desert Charles, when his power is lessened, and so merits Arthur Philipson's epitaph, 'a more accomplished traitor never drew breath, nor one who drew his net with such success'.

This connexion of treachery with the Italian character is also a leitmotive in Scott's novels. We even find Henry Warden in a

sermon in *The Abbot* using it as a formulaic epithet of the sort
scorned by Ratchkali in *Ferdinand Count Fathom*. Warden is condemning weapons, and stresses that the exact nature of the
weapon matters not, 'whether it be a stilet, which we have
borrowed from the treacherous Italian, or a dirk, which is borne
by the savage Highlandman'. The Marquis of Montserrat in *The
Talisman* enters into a conspiracy against Richard the Lionheart
and so also is viewed primarily as a traitor. Again, like Campo
Basso, he is a Machiavellian traitor, 'proud, ambitious, unscrupulous and politic'. Like Campo Basso, his aims are largely mercenary
ones; and like Campo Basso he dies a violent death, his plans
frustrated. Thus, although the Italian characters in Scott's novels
are often well drawn, they seem to stem rather often from currently
held opinions about Italians in general—their Machiavellianism,
their avarice, their interest in the supernatural. Even Galeotti in
Quentin Durward, based though he is on a historical character, fits
into this last classification, and is presented very much as a 'type'.

These repetitions, whether they be of 'Andrea Ferraras' or
Machiavellian traitors, show that Scott's advance on the example
of Smollett is not as great as might at first appear. His wider
reading and antiquarian interest enable him to produce a wider
range of detail, a wider variety of characters, but cultural details
are drawn from a limited pool of interests and recur from novel to
novel. Characters seldom escape entirely from the 'nationality
typing' favoured by Smollett, though again this is more ingeni-
ously done. Scott is nonetheless looking at Italy from the outside
and through literature rather than experience. This is why his use
of Italian literature is generally more ambitious. At the same time,
Italian culture and characters do add much colour to his novels.
The repetitions are only noticeable when the Italian material in
all the novels is placed together, and are unlikely to spoil our
enjoyment of particular works. To a degree the same argument is
applicable to the lack of variety in characterization. The humorized
creation has the same literary validity as any other, and as such
Damiotti, Galeotti, Campo Basso, and Montserrat may be
deemed successful. Nonetheless one must also admit that Scott's
knowledge of Italy had limitations, which made such characters
the bounds of its expression and would have rendered more
individualized portrayals difficult indeed. Other arts also play their
part in this court, where the Italian Renaissance was most enthusiastically received. At Kenilworth itself, Tressilian notes the 'great

basins of Italian marble' in the gardens, and elsewhere the influence of Italy is inescapable. The casual reader may not remember these references, and in a way this is the triumph of Scott's art. He works them unobtrusively into the novel, but they do play an important role in establishing the historical authenticity of a court imbued with the vigour of the Italian Renaissance. This influence lingered on into the court of Charles II, the setting of *Peveril of the Peak*. Again, to the casual reader, this novel will not be remembered for its Italian references. There is nothing in the nature of plot or theme to demand the use of Italian material. Yet Christian and the Duke of Buckingham often speak in Italian; Earl Philip boasts of a cameo Cupid bought 'from Signor Furabosco at Rome'; the dwarf, Sir Geoffrey Hudson, has an Italian nickname, 'piccoluomini'; Buckingham refers to Boccaccio's tale of the King of Garba, is planning an Italian garden and is surrounded with 'paintings of the Venetian school', while the success of the 'Italian puppet show' at court is widely celebrated. The cult of Machiavelli is still strong, and Chiffinch is at one point rebuked for having 'turned a very Machiavel', while Julian Peveril, when wishing to underline the seriousness of a vow, urges Chiffinch to 'rely upon this, as if Machiavel had sworn it'.

It is this development of a greater variety of Italian influences which places Scott at the head of the new type of imitation, begun in the late seventeenth and eighteenth centuries. Now Italian social life can be quietly infiltrated into the overall scheme of a Scottish novel. While earlier ages had concentrated on a conscious, literary imitation, the European culture of the eighteenth century encouraged also the social, political, and geographical influences which the artist could introduce less selfconsciously. Ramsay and Thomson, Urquhart and Smollett has each in his own way been moving towards this goal, but has been restricted either by his chosen genre or by his lack of knowledge. Scott has limitations as well, all of which have been noted, but his literary and cultural researches, his skill in character-depiction and his genuine interest in the cosmopolitan philosophy of his predecessors enable him to realize more fully what the others only realized in part. If Drummond represents the acme of one line, then Scott must be the culmination of the other.

This is an angle which has not been adequately stressed when assessing Scott's success in Europe. It is true of course that Europe thrilled to the Scottish themes in the Waverley novels, to

the romantic descriptions of Scotland in *Waverley*, to the authoritative discussion of Scottish traditions in *The Antiquary* and elsewhere. Europe was intrigued to hear of the ancient Scottish
Romance writers, of Barbour, Blind Harry, and Thomas the
Rhymer, or to meet the many characters whose background
rendered them exclusively Scottish. But there are two points to
bear in mind. First, this is only the Scottish element in novels
which throughout are European in their focus. Scotland necessarily
has a prime place in Scott's novels, as he is a Scot and most inti-
mately acquainted with it. But his aim seems to be to relate Scotland and its contribution to the general pattern of European
achievement. It is important to remember that the geography of
other European countries is introduced, though Scotland's is most
minutely examined; to compare the analysis of Scottish traditions
with those advanced concerning Spain, France, and Italy; to note
that Ariosto, Tasso, and Cervantes play as important a part in
some novels as Barbour or Thomas the Rhymer in others; to set
the specifically Italianate or French characters against the Nicol
Jarvies and the Davie Deans. And secondly, Scott soon became
conscious of the popularity of his novels in Europe. He did not
need radically to alter his approach to art, which had been basically
cosmopolitan from the outset, but popularity did, I believe,
occasionally alter the emphasis. For example, Ossian enjoyed a vast
popularity abroad. Scott, with his eye as usual on the market, made
the most of this, especially perhaps in *The Pirate* or *A Legend of
Montrose*, both of which abound in Ossianic references. The two
ingredients, Scottish and European, are essential elements in
Scott's success abroad, and although the former is more obvious, to
regard him as a European novelist is a much less distorting generalization than to focus on the passages of Scots dialect and label him
parochial. Properly, he is the literary equivalent of Hume and the
eighteenth-century philosophers, making his (necessarily Scottish)
contribution to European art.

It is a corollary of this new type of 'imitation', that it too can be
imitated. Italian translations of the major novels began to appear,
headed by the 1823 Pisa edition of *Waverley; o sia la Scozia
sessant'anni addietro*. Sometimes the titles of these works are
identical to Scott's own, as with the Milan translations, *Ivanhoe*
and *Kenilworth*. Sometimes a slight adjustment appears, as in
Quentino Durward. But there are other occasions when the Italian
title is more fanciful. *Carlo Il Temerario* is the title of the 1882

Milan translation of *Anne of Geierstein*, while *The Heart of Mid-Lothian*, *A Legend of Montrose* and *The Bride of Lammermoor* become respectively, *La prigione di Edimburgo*, *L'officiale di Fortuna* and *La promessa sposa ovvero Lucia di Lammermoor*.

There would have been no point in rendering Drummond's imitations or Stewart's *Roland Furious* back into Italian, but the freer use of foreign influences preferred in the eighteenth an nineteenth centuries encourages such an approach. And with Scott, there comes the first occasion, when a Scottish vernacular writer is accepted as being a major contributor to European literature. In this too he marks a culmination of the movement earlier begun by Thomson and Ossian. Nor is his influence confined to translations such as those listed above. For many European writers of historical romance he became a model on which to pattern their own novels. Thus literature advanced by a process of accretion. Scott benefits from past European writers like Cervantes or Ariosto, then works their example into the creation of his own literary world. His world in its turn serves as an example for later Spanish and Italian authors, and so the process continues.

Manzoni's *I promessi sposi* is the example usually favoured when critics wish to exemplify Scott's influence in Italy.[5] Manzoni had after all confessed his own debt, when he wrote, 'già, se non ci fosse stato Walter Scott a me non sarebbe venuto in mente di scrivere un romanzo'. This path has however been so thoroughly trodden by others that I may be forgiven for turning the reader's attention to an even more faithful, though less fashionable figure, that of Tommasso Grossi (1790–1853). Grossi, like Manzoni, acknowledged his debt to Scott openly and wrote his fifteen-canto epic poem, *I Lombardi alla prima crociata* under the joint influence of Scott and Tasso. His novel, *Marco Visconti*, composed between 1831 and 1834, is even more heavily indebted to the Scottish writer, yet undoubtedly worthy of study in its own right.[6]

Set in one of Scott's favourite periods, the Crusades, it concerns the love of Bice for a young knight, Ottorino. Their passion is threatened from the outset by various forces, including the intervention of the powerful Marco Visconti, who had earlier loved Bice's mother. The tone of the novel, throughout bleak, anticipates

---

[5] See M. F. M. Meiklejohn, 'Sir Walter Scott and Alessandro Manzoni', *Italian Studies* xi (1956), 91–8 and bibliography at end of article; Francis R. Hart, 'The Fair Maid, Manzoni's *Betrothed*, and the Grounds of Waverley Criticism', *Nineteenth-Century Fiction* xviii (1963), 103–18.

[6] Quotations from Grossi follow the third edition of *Marco Visconti* (Firenze, 1835).

the eventual tragic outcome, when Bice dies. Visconti discovers that due to the treacherous behaviour of his servant Pelagrua, he is indirectly responsible for her fate. He makes Ottorino his heir in a bid to alleviate his guilt, but is murdered shortly afterwards through the treachery of Pelagrua's ally, Visconti's own kinsman, Lodrisio. Such a bare outline does not do justice to the novel, whose debts to Scott are throughout striking. Apart from the setting, the form is just such as Scott favoured. Thus the 'dropped stitches' policy referred to in *The Heart of Mid-Lothian* is followed, and Grossi turns from one centre of interest to another with the same versatility, as in Chapter 11:

Non incresca ora ai lettori di tornare un passo indietro per andare fino a Limonta, dove abbiamo lasciato alcuni nostri amici, addosso ai quali stava per versarsi la piena . . .

(Let it not displease the reader, if we now turn back, and journey as far as Limonta, where we have left our rural friends, exposed to the danger of a coming storm . . .)

But this is just one of many general similarities. Grossi also shares Scott's antiquarian interest in authenticity when describing armour, buildings and customs in the middle ages. His description of a tournament is held up for a long analysis of the principles on which a quintain works or to explain why some knights bear shields with no heraldic device. Like Scott he relies heavily on the character of his minstrel Tremacoldo, many of whose songs and ballads are reproduced in the text. Dreams and prophecies too play an important role in *Marco Visconti*, as in many Scott novels. Thus, as early as Chapter 22, Bice is made to foresee her own dismal fate, and does so in the heightened poetic language favoured by Scott in similar situations:

Ricordatevi di me! Brevi sono i giorni che Iddio mi ha numerati; e quando vi giugnerà la novella che il mio corso è finito, date una lagrima alla memoria della povera Bice, che nata e cresciuta fra voi, sperava di posare il suo capo, stanco dai travagli della vita, nella dolce sua terra, fra le lagrime e il compianto de' suoi cari.

(Remember me! Few are my appointed years on earth; but when you shall hear that my course is run, give a tear to the memory of one who was born and grew amongst you, and who once trusted to breathe her last sigh, when wearied with the sorrow of life, in her own dear land, surrounded by the fond regrets of those most dear to her.)

This interest in the supernatural is effectively worked into the structure of the novel, with prophecies and dreams foreshadowing obliquely some truth that is to be revealed. When, for example, the loyal servant Lupo is unsuspectingly setting off to deliver a crucial message to Marco, for whom he has a soldier's unquestioning admiration, he is warned in a dream that all is not as it seems. Marco's eyes in the dream seem glazed and he will not accept the note. Lupo does not understand his vision, but it puts him on his guard against the treachery that awaits him on the road.

It is clear that Grossi's confessed indebtedness to Scott is not a matter of convention. He has learned much from the author of *Waverley*. A copy of Dante even plays a part in the drama, as had the copies of Dante and Ariosto in *Rob Roy*, while his conclusion, rounding up the main themes and tracing the lives of his major characters briefly forward in time, must again derive from the practice of his master.

There are two Scott novels in particular which help to mould the final form of *Marco Visconti*. They are *Ivanhoe*, hailed by Italians as 'il capolavoro dello Scott' from time immemorial, and, more surprisingly, *The Antiquary*. There were no Italian translations of these works prior to Grossi's novel, but he could have read them, either in the original or, in the case of *Ivanhoe*, in a French translation. Certainly the lengthy description of the tournaments in *Marco Visconti* are closely modelled on the similar descriptions in *Ivanhoe*. There is even an unknown knight on a black horse, who appears to offer a challenge by striking the displayed shields. The parallel with the actions of the Disinherited Knight in Chapter 9 of *Ivanhoe* could scarcely be closer:

Allora l'ignoto, cui ne veniva data la balìa, attraversò esso pure a lento passo tutto lo steccato, fino alla tenda dei tenitori, e fermatosi dinanzi allo scudo di Ottorino, invece di toccarlo colla lancia, come usavasi, lo strappò dal luogo in cui era posto, gettandolo per terra; poi ve lo tornò ad appiccare, ma col capo in giù; il che era il più grande oltraggio che potesse farsi a cavaliere, e importava una disfida *a tutto transito*, o, come noi diremmo, all'ultimo sangue. [Chap. 18.]

(The unknown being now duly authorized, slowly crossed the palisade, until he reached the tent of the holders of the just, when, stopping short before Ottorino's shield, instead of touching it with his lance, as was customary, he pulled it rudely from the place where it hung, and threw it on the ground. He then lifted it up again, and put it with the head downwards; this being considered the greatest insult which could be offered to a knight, and signifying that he was defied to death.)

The influence of *Ivanhoe* pervades the novel, but three major features at least derive from *The Antiquary*. First and most

obviously, the storm described in Chapter 5 derives much of its
inspiration from the storm which maroons Sir Arthur and Miss
Wardour. The atmospheric openings are similar. Ottorino and his
companions are also marooned, and the rescue is in each case
effected by a daring piece of rock-climbing, performed by Lovel in
The Antiquary and by Lupo in *Marco Visconti*. There are diver-
gences as well, but the interrelationship of the two passages will
surely be admitted by all who read them. In addition, Grossi takes
over from *The Antiquary* the idea of contrasting his noble families
with the lives of a loyal, unpretentious family of boatmen. Thus
the Mucklebackits live again in the characters of Martha and
Michael, who bravely continue to face life after the tragic death of
their son, Arrigozzo. There is even (in Chapter 11) a detailed
description of their cottage, paralleling Scott's description of the
Mucklebackits' home in Chapter 26 of *The Antiquary*:

La capanna del barcaiuolo, padre dell'annegato, era posta, come abbiam
detto, di là del paese, tirando a tramontana. Quel che si vedeva di essa
guardando dal lago, non era che un po'di tettuccio di paglia con una croce di
legno piantata in vetta; tutto il resto veniva nascosto da due vecchi castagni,
i quali parevano chinarsi per abbracciarla. Al di dentro era una cameraccia
non ammattonata, col palco ingraticolato e le muraglie tutte nere dal fumo.
Si vedeva in un canto un letticciuolo coperto di una grossa e ruvida coltre, di
quelle che si chiamavano *catalane*, dalla Catalogna d'onde venivano; nome
che conservano ancora in alcuni paesi del lago di Como; era quello il giacitoio
del povero Arrigozzo e in quel momento vi dormiva sopra un barboncino, il
suo cane fedele. A piè del letto, alla distanza di non più di due passi, stava un
cassone massiccio, ripieno di terra, dentro il quale, secondo l'uso comune a
quel tempo per tutta Europa (perocchè era ancor fresca l'invenzione dei
cammini) si faceva il fuoco, e v'era posto un laveggio a bollire sopra un
trepiede; più innanzi, e proprio nel mezzo della camera, sorgeva un desco di
faggio: quattro seggiolette impagliate, una mezza dozzina di remi, una
rastrellieretta a piuoli appiccata al muro, sulla quale erano, messi in parata
alcuni piattelli, tre scodelle di terra e tre cucchiai d'ottone luccicanti come
un oro; una cassa, una fiocina e un bertovello compievano il mobile di tutta
la casa.

(The cottage of the boatman, the father of the drowned Arrigozzo, was
situated, as we have before said, a little to the north of the village. From the
lake, nothing could be seen of it, but the lowly straw-covered roof with the
wooden cross planted at the top; all the rest was hidden by two old chestnut
trees, which seemed to bow themselves down to embrace it: its interior consisted of a shabby unpaved room, with a low cross-beamed roof, and walls
blackened with smoke. In one corner stood a small bed, with one of these
coarse thick coverlets, which were called *catalans*, (a name still preserved in
many of the villages on the Lake of Como,) from Catalonia, whence they
first came. This had been the nightly resting place of poor Arrigozzo, and it

was still tenanted by his faithful spaniel, who, at the moment we are describing, was sleeping upon it. At the foot of the bed, at the distance of a few paces only, stood a strong chest, full of earth, in which, according to custom then common throughout Europe, (the invention of chimneys being of recent date,) the fire was made; a kettle was placed on a trivet before it; in the middle of the room stood a table of beechwood, four little straw chairs, half-a-dozen oars, a small rack, fastened against the wall with pegs, and on which were ranged a few dishes, three earthen porringers, and as many brass spoons, shining like gold; a box, a spear, and a net, completed the inventory of the household furniture.)

It is hoped that this lengthy quotation will not only prove the initial point raised, but suggest that Grossi's detailed vision and parenthetically erudite style is also to some degree modelled on Scott. Certainly the latter has no more faithful Italian follower known to me, and the influence of *The Antiquary* extends even to the character of the Count del Balzo, with his obsession for etymological explanations: 'Sapete quel che vuol dir giostra? ve lo diro io; giostra vien da *juxa*, da presso, perche è un combattimento che si fa da vicino a corpo a corpo.' ('Do you happen to know the meaning of the word just? I will tell you; it comes from *justa*, signifying near, because it is a combat which takes place between two persons close to each other'.) He clearly owes something to the immortal figure of Jonathan Oldbuck. Indeed, a reader coming to the tale of *Marco Visconti* in translation might be forgiven for believing it to be one of Scott's own minor works. But this would be a superficial reaction, and despite its heavy indebtedness this Italian novel does make its own particular contribution to the development of the Historical Romance in Europe.

This study of Scott from an Italian viewpoint serves to underline the important part played in the novels by his knowledge of foreign cultures. As these borrowings enrich the texture of his work, and as he in turn becomes a model for the Italian successors of his own beloved Ariosto, we see again that 'universal coltura' of eighteenth and early nineteenth-century Europe referred to by Algarotti. Scott's 'Scottishness' must not be allowed to obscure his equal loyalty to 'la gran famiglia' of Europe.

Scott and Old Norse Literature

JOHN M. SIMPSON

A great creative writer, or a great critic, can have insights that are denied to the mere scholar who is qualified to trip up the great ones on a host of technical inaccuracies. This is why it's worth commemorating Scott's interest in Old Norse literature. Scott was, like almost everyone in Britain at that time, largely a prisoner of the very one-sided view of Old Norse literature that seems now to have been almost a historical necessity for the writers of the Romantic revival. But Scott was equipped, if anyone was, to gain glimpses of the larger reality of Old Norse literature, and in one single but crucial instance, he took the opportunity to introduce readers of English to an important new aspect of the literature and life of medieval Iceland.

My hero Georg Lukács is another case in point. He can easily be faulted in his knowledge of the historical background to the Waverley Novels, but he has still taught us some key lessons about them.[1] My text in this paper, if you like, is the familiar one from Lukács, that Scott was a *realist*. As Lukács says: 'It is precisely because of his character that Scott did not become a Romantic, a glorifier of elegist of past ages. . . . Objectively, in a large historical and artistic sense: he saw at one and the same time [the] outstanding qualities [of past social formations] and the historical necessity of their decline. This objectivity, however, only enhances the true poetry of the past.'

In Scott's youth, English poetic imitations of Old Norse literature were of course very fashionable. Norse mythology and history had become part of the staple diet of romantic imaginations since the publication of Thomas Gray's *Fatal Sisters* and *Descent of Odin* in 1768. If we take the fashion for things Norse that Gray set on the one hand, and the vogue for things Celtic created by Mac-

---

[1] Georg Lukács, *The Historical Novel*, trans. H. and S. Mitchell (London, 1962), 30–63; my quotation is from pp. 54–5.

pherson's supposed translations of Ossian on the other, we can see that the two fashions were in an obvious sense complementary. The Celtic past seemed to offer endless vistas of misty melancholy, whereas the Norse past seemed to afford an ample supply of horror, violence, and total and reckless courage. It's unnecessary now to belabour the point that the stereotypes of the wistful twilit Celt and of the bloodthirsty rapacious Viking were unbalanced and therefore unhistorical and misleading caricatures of the spirit of Celtic and Norse literature. As far as the Old Norse literature goes, the writers of Gray's generation and of Scott's were reliant on secondary books rather than on the original texts, and on secondary book that gave one very definite slant. In addition, they were able to find out much more about Skaldic and Eddic poetry than about the Sagas. It's the Sagas of Icelanders, in particular, that have led us to our more rounded modern picture of Old Norse literature: in the Sagas of Icelanders there are plenty of heroes, certainly, but heroes whose exploits occur in and stem naturally from the settled farming communities of Iceland. As well as the blood and thunder, we can appreciate the side of Old Norse literature epitomized by the saying: 'With law shall the land be built up and with lawlessness wasted away'. Now Scott, as a realist in his historical interests, was interested in medieval Scandinavia for its own sake. His medievalism wasn't a mere reaction against modern trends, an exalting of the age of faith above the age of reason. He was concerned to place the writings of the heathen and the christianizing periods in the broad development of history. In the poem *Harold the Dauntless*, for instance, we shall find plenty of the stage trappings of the bloodthirsty Viking, but I think we shall find something else too. Even here, when Scott was certainly not at his best, I don't accept that he was merely doing what David Craig describes as skimming 'off manners—idiom, costume, furniture, raw history'.[2] And when Scott published his *Abstract of the Eyrbiggia Saga* in 1814, his was for English readers the pioneering step into that branch of Old Norse literature, the Sagas of Icelanders, that modern audiences value most for its own sake.

From Lockhart, and from Scott's notebooks, we know quite a lot about Scott's youthful enthusiasm for Old Norse literature in the

[2] David Craig, *Scottish Literature and the Scottish People*, 1680–1830 (London, 1961), 152.

1790s.[3] Lockhart says that Scott was drawing on Anglo-Saxon and Norse material as early as 1789 or 1790 in discussions at the Literary Society in Edinburgh. And the third address that he gave to the Speculative Society on 11 December 1792 was on 'The Origin of the Scandinavian Mythology'. One prefers to believe that it was the Edinburgh winter rather than Scott or the Scandinavian Mythology that was to blame for the attendance being 'uncommonly thin' on that occasion. Scott's notebooks at that time contain among other things a lengthy item about the *Vegtams Kviða*, the Eddic poem from which Gray had taken his *Descent of Odin*. He also transliterated two lines of the Gray into runic characters, a procedure that puzzled scholars for a bit. Another notebook has notes on Scandinavian beliefs and customs drawn from several secondary sources, as well as a table of the runic alphabet, and the Roman, Anglo-Saxon and Gothic alphabets in parallel columns.

This, then, was the foundation of Scott's interest in Old Norse literature. It was of course only one of his many scholarly enthusiasms and certain things should be said, in order to place it in context.

Firstly, what we have so far was the reading of a young man, even if of an intellectually voracious one. To utilize it in his own creative work was a large further step. Scott himself made this point when he described the youthful reading of Edward Waverley; there's clearly an element of self-portrait here. Waverley, he says, 'had read, and stored in a memory of uncommon tenacity, much curious, though ill-arranged and miscellaneous information'. At the end of the list of Waverley's reading there is the following item: 'the earlier literature of the northern nations did not escape the study of one who read rather to awaken the imagination than to benefit the understanding'. Scott, with his great intellectual balance, is here criticizing himself more sternly than anyone else would be entitled to do. For after all, Scott continued to read about Norse literature throughout his life, and, quite apart from making it the central inspiration of a few of his works, he constantly supplies, throughout his poems and novels, information drawn from Norse history and mythology.

Secondly, Scott was as a young man, and continued to be, partly

---

[3] See Arthur Melville Clark, *Sir Walter Scott, the Formative Years* (Edinburgh, 1969), esp. 220–1, 236–7; P. R. Lieder, 'Scott and Scandinavian Literature', *Smith College Studies in Modern Languages* ii. 1 (1920), 8–57, and review of same by F. W. J. Heuser, *Modern Language Notes* xxxvii (1922), 303–7.

the prisoner of the secondary authorities from whom he derived much of his knowledge of Scandinavia. This essential limitation, which he shared with all his contemporaries, can be illustrated briefly. Perhaps the single most influential book on the Norsemen for Scott was one that he mentioned in a letter of September 1792: 'I am poring over Bartholine in the long evenings, solitary enough'. Thomas Bartholin was a Danish doctor who in 1689 published his *Antiquitatum Danicarum de Causis Contemptae a Danis adhuc gentilibus mortis*. This Latin work gave a whole series of passages of Old Norse, in original and Latin translation, in the course of a discussion of why the Vikings had displayed indifference, or rather defiance, in the face of death. Bartholin must take responsibility for the fact that, for the Romantic poets, the archetypal Viking came to be Ragnar Loðbrók, who, in the poem *Krákumál*, dies laughing at the thought of the welcome awaiting him from Odin, even though he is being stung to death by serpents. On top of this extravagance, a seventeenth-century mistranslation of *Krákumál* supplied the English and French Romantic poets with one of their favourite bloodthirsty images, the Vikings in Odin's hall drinking beer from the skulls of their enemies. In fact the Old Norse, literally 'the curved branches of skulls' is a kenning for drinking horns. I don't know if this piece of pseudo-Norse lore was in Kitchener's mind when, as it's said, he wanted to make the Mahdi's skull into a drinking cup to present to Queen Victoria. But it certainly appears, among other places, in Scott's *Harold the Dauntless*:

> In wild Valhalla has thou quaff'd
> From foeman's skull metheglin draught . . .

Scott, of course, merely inherited the mistranslation: the essential point is that the secondary authorities on which he and his contemporaries drew were not conducive to, as it were, a sober look at Old Norse literature.

I must however say, that Scott added primary sources to his library wherever he could, and he built up a collection of the Danish editions of the Sagas that were produced by the Anna-Magnaean Commission in Copenhagen from the 1770s on. These editions gave the Old Norse text and a Latin translation, and at last made the Old Norse Sagas texts available to the scholarly world. One of the editors of these texts was the Icelander Grimur Thorkelin, a man with many Scots connexions, and it is from his 1787 edition of *Eyrbyggja Saga* that Scott prepared his abstract.

Scott, then, collected the primary source material when he could, but the final and most basic limitation on his knowledge of Old Norse literature was the linguistic equipment he could bring to bear on the texts. There is no reason to quarrel with Dr. Melville Clark's assessment that, when Scott in the 1790s studied his secondary sources with their Old Norse quotations, he 'is pretty certain to have picked up a limited knowledge at least of the language of the originals'. But it seems that it was the same sort of knowledge that Scott himself said that he and his friends sought of German, given that they were 'averse to the necessary toil of grammar, and the rules'. Scott's knowledge of Old Norse vocabulary was, in other words, ahead of his grasp of morphology and syntax. It can easily be shown, and I don't propose to do so today, that if Scott had an Old Norse text with a Latin or English translation, then he followed the translation for good or ill, and that he was capable of linguisitic howlers. If he had read Old Norse fluently, than he would have been exceptional for his day among scholars of a type with whom he never claimed to class himself in any case. If I mention one instance, which I take from Edith Batho, it is to illustrate, as she intended, not Scott's necessary limitations as a scholar of his time, but the fact that Scott's intellectual enthusiasm, and his sheer spirit, knew virtually no limits, even *in extremis*[4].

In late 1830 Scott's *Letters on Demonology and Witchcraft* were published. By this time in his life financial cares and ill-health would have curbed the intellectual curiosity of almost anyone else. But one curious mistake that Scott makes in the *Letters*, when he refers to the tale of Gunnar Helming, suggests that he was still reading Old Norse. Gunnar Helming's story occurs in the *Saga of King Olaf Tryggvason*. Gunnar travelled round Sweden with the shrine containing the image of the god Freyr, and the priestess who was known as Freyr's wife. Gunnar got into a fight with Freyr (who materialized in person), and vanquished him. Thereafter he pretended to be Freyr, and was accepted. When Freyr's wife was found to be pregnant, then his reputation was really made. Scott muffles the story in retailing it, by making the priestess simply the attendant of the female god Freya and not the wife of a male god. Now, if Scott had gone back to Bartholin, or even

---

[4] Edith C. Batho, 'Sir Walter Scott and the Sagas: Some Notes', *Modern Language Review* xxiv (1929), 409–15; her article 'Scott as a Mediaevalist' in *Sir Walter Scott Today*, ed. H. J. C. Grierson (London, 1932), 133–57, incorporates the same arguments.

remembered him correctly, he would have got it right. Edith Batho suggests, very plausibly, that Scott had refreshed his memory of the story by looking at *Olaf Tryggvason's Saga* in volume III of the *Fornmanna sögur*, where he could get a general sense of the Old Norse, but be misled by the word used for the priestess—'kona'—which can be either a wife or simply a woman. Now we know that Scott subscribed to the *Fornmanna sögur*, which were published in Copenhagen from 1825 onwards. That he should still be keeping up his Old Norse reading in the late 1820s is noteworthy. If Miss Batho is right, then as she says, 'his treatment of Gunnar Helming shows, besides his glorious carelessness, a persistent intellectual curiosity which, in the circumstances, is not much less than heroic'.

I want to turn to those works where Scott used Old Norse material in a more than illustrative way, and I'll take them out of chronological order, so as to leave *Eyrbyggja Saga* to the last. *Harold the Dauntless* is never taken, so far as I know, to be one of the best of Scott's longer poems. Even at the time Scott had an experience similar to the story told of Bing Crosby, that he once entered a talent contest anonymously only to come second to a man doing a Bing Crosby imitation. *Blackwood's* said that it 'admits not of dispute' that Harold was 'generally inferior to the works of Mr. Scott, in vigour and interest'. The *Scots Magazine* invoked Scott and suggested that 'as that great master seems, for the present, to have left his lyre unstrung, a substitute, even of inferior value, may be welcomed by the public'. The *Critical Review* was even more emphatic: '*Harold the Dauntless*, like *The Bridal of Triermain*, is a tolerably successful imitation of some parts of the style of Mr. Walter Scott; but, like all imitations, it is clearly distinguishable from the prototype; it wants the life and seasoning of originality'.[5] One must admit that the poem has the excesses of the Romantic view of the Viking. Here is Harold, the *berserkar* hero, giving his father a brief autobiography:

> For me, I am yet what thy lessons have made,
> I was rock'd in a buckler and fed from a blade;
> An infant, was taught to clasp hands and shout,
> From the roofs of the tower when the flame had broke out;
> In the blood of slain foeman my finger to dip,
> And tinge with its purple my cheek and my lip.

[5] *Blackwood's Magazine* i (1817), 76–8; *Scots Magazine* lxxix (1817), 131–4; *Critical Review* 5th ser. v (1817), 379–84.

But if the plot is melodramatic and the characterization unsubtle, there is surely in Harold the coiled spring within the verse that marks all Scott's narrative poetry. If a poem can be described after a hundred and fifty years as not great art, it's something at least if one can say it still makes pleasant reading. And here and there, I hope it's not too fanciful to suggest, Scott the realist peeps out. He's dealing with the assimilation of the Norse element into pre-Conquest England, and shows as always that he's aware of social processes. The conversion to Christianity of the old reprobate warrior Harold's father lets Scott make a couple of telling if not too solemn points. We can share the apprehension of the priests at the party after the baptism, when

> The mead flow'd around, and the ale was drain'd dry,
> Wild was the laughter, the song, and the cry;
> With Kyrie Eleison, came clamorously in
> The war-songs of Danesmen, Norweyan, and Finn.

Before that, there is a neat counterpoint as the Bishop of Durham labours to convert the old Viking:

> 'Fiends hast thou worshipp'd, with fiendish rite,
> Leave now the darkness, and wend into light.
> O! while life and space are given,
> Turn thee yet, and think of Heaven!'
> That stern old heathen his head be raised,
> And on the good prelate he steadfastly gazed;
> 'Give me broad lands on the Wear and the Tyne,
> My faith I will leave, and I'll cleave unto thine.'

The medievalist of today, preoccupied as he often is with the major cultural change of the conversion of the Dark Age invaders, would be hard put to it to deny that that little verse sums up a good deal of the conversion process.

Scott lived too early to have been able to write a poem on a Norse theme of the quality of William Morris's *Sigurd the Volsung*; Morris was writing at a time when the Sagas were making a much greater impact on English readers. But *Harold the Dauntless* does show Scott's historical curiosity at work; he is interested in the Viking world for its own sake. Lockhart's judgement of the poem, that 'the confusion and harsh transitions of the fable' lessened public interest in it may be just; but the other fault he finds, that of 'the dim rudeness of character and manners' is surely wide of the mark. 'The dim rudeness of character and manners' indeed!

—the tone could hardly diverge more from Scott's own attitude to his theme.

Two of Scott's *Encyclopaedia Britannica* essays, that on 'Chivalry' published in 1818, and that on 'Romance' published in 1824, make interesting use of the sagas. In the latter essay we find the following:

Scandinavia, as was to be expected, may be safely considered as the richest country in Europe in ancient tales corresponding with the character of Romance. . . . There are . . . very many of the sagas, indeed by far the greater number of those now known to exist, which must be considered as falling rather under the class of fictitious than of real narratives; and which, therefore, belong to our present subject of enquiry. The *Omeyinga* [recte *Orkneyinga*] *Saga*, the *Heimskringla*, the *Saga of Olaf Triggwason*, the *Eyrbiggia Saga*, and several others, may be considered as historical; whilst the numerous narratives referring to the history of the Nibilungen and Volsungen are as imaginary as the Romances which treat of King Arthur and of Charlemagne. These singular compositions, short, abrupt, and concise in expression, full of bold and even extravagant metaphor, exhibiting many passages of forceful and rapid description, hold a character of their own; and while they remind us of the indomitable courage and patient endurance of the hardy Scandinavians, at once the honour and the terror of Europe, rise far above the tedious and creeping style which characterised the minstrel efforts of their successors, whether in France or England. In the pine forests, also, and the frozen mountains of the North, there were nursed, amid the relics of expiring Paganism, many traditions of a character more wild and terrible than the fables of classical superstition; and these the gloomy imagination of the Skalds failed not to transfer to their romantic tales.

Scott then properly goes on to pay tribute to the way that German scholarship was already opening up this field of medieval literature. He continues

It must, however, be remarked, that although the north possesses champions and Romances of its own, unknown to southern song, yet in a later age, the inhabitants of these countries borrowed from the French minstrels some of their most popular subjects; and hence we find sagas on the subject of Sir Tristrem, Sir Percival, Sir Ywain, and others, the well-known themes of French and English Romance. These, however, must necessarily be considered later in date, as well as far inferior in interest, to the sagas of genuine northern birth.

And he concludes this passage by showing that it is a scholarly error to use the later romantic sagas, as had been done, to impugn the authenticity of the home-grown Old Norse sagas.

Now this is a very striking passage in various ways. Firstly, Scott seeks to place the sagas in the process of literary and historical evolution, from paganism to Christianity, from epic (though he doesn't use the term) to romance, and finally from a period of Scandinavian cultural self-sufficiency to one of heavy influence from the south. This presages the theme of much subsequent scholarship. Again, Scott suggests a classification of sagas in terms of their historicity or lack of it; Sagas of Icelanders and Kings' Sagas on the one hand, Mythical-Heroic Sagas on the other. This too is a main concern of modern saga-scholarship. (Incidentally, Scott's library contained Peter Erasmus Müller's *Sagabibliothek*, published in 1817–20 in Copenhagen, which may be classed as the first modern attempt at scholarly classification of the sagas. Müller knew about Scott's *Abstract of Eyrbiggia Saga*, but from what Scott says about his own poor command of Danish, in a letter of 1824 to Adam Oehlensläger, I doubt whether Scott can have gained a lot from Müller). Finally, in the essay on 'Romance', we should note the decided preference Scott expresses for the sagas as against other medieval literary genres—'these singular compositions, short, abrupt, and concise in expression', reminding 'us of the indomitable courage and patient endurances of the hardy Scandinavians, at once the honour and the terror of Europe' and rising 'far above the tedious and creeping style which characterized the minstrel efforts of their successors'. National characteristics are dangerous beasts to handle, but perhaps I may suggest that there is a Northern hardness about the Scots that gives us a particular relish for the sagas. Among more modern Scots sagamen one has only to instance W. P. Ker and Sir William Craigie.

Now for the *Abstract of Eyrbiggia Saga*. I should stress at this point something that is well enough known, that Scott was one of a circle of scholarly men in Edinburgh, who were well read in foreign medieval literatures as well as their own. They were keen to create a public awareness of the connexions between Scottish and foreign material, as well as to explore the foreign material for its own sake. This is a respectable occupation nowadays: there are even university chairs in comparative literature. But Scott's friend Robert Jamieson, for instance, who has been hailed as a pioneer in among other things the study of Latvian folklore, even though he couldn't read it in the original,[6] was very dependent on the support and patronage of the influential Sir Walter. The *Illustrations of Northern Antiquities*, published in 1814, in which Scott's *Abstract of*

---

[6] See Haralds Biezais, 'The Studies of the Scottish folklorist Robert Jamieson into Latvian mythology and folklore', *Arv* xiv (1958), 62–82.

Eyrbiggia Saga appeared, resulted firstly from the work of Jamieson and of Scott's tragic protégé, the German refugee Henry Weber, and secondly from the patronage of Scott. Weber was, of course, Scott's amanuensis, and Scott encouraged him in scholarly editing.[7] Weber's unstable temperament, made worse by heavy drinking, led to his mental collapse in the year when the *Illustrations of Northern Antiquities* was published. There was the tragic episode where he offered to fight a duel with Scott, and Weber died in 1818 in an asylum at York, where he had lived at Scott's expense. Lockhart believes that Scott supplied Weber with poetic translations from the German for the *Northern Antiquities*, as well as backing its publication. Lockhart clearly can't see why Scott bothered himself with 'a mere drudging *German*': but I think we may safely prefer Edgar Johnson's description of Weber as 'a scholar who pursued knowledge for its own sake'. For this alone he was to Scott a friend for whom no amount of support and encouragement was too great.

The main contents of the *Northern Antiquities* were an abstract of the *Nibelungenlied* and material on such German texts as the *Heldenbuch*, supplied by Weber, and Jamieson's work on Danish and other popular ballads which, as Scott said, bore a curious relation to the popular ballads of England and Scotland. Even without Scott's own contribution this would have been a notable volume and one worthy of Scott's cosmopolitan view of literature.

I want to emphasize Scott's role as entrepreneur here. His promotion of medieval literature shows as exceptional an enthusiasm as does his writing about it. We know what Constable thought of Scott's support for scholarly publishing: 'I like well Scott's *ain bairns*, but heaven preserve me from those of his fathering'. Scott not only encouraged the Ballantynes to publish the *Northern Antiquities*, but as early as 1810, when it was clearly being planned on more ambitious lines than finally proved possible, he was soliciting a contribution from the Rev. Richard Polwhele. Polwhele was a West of England clergyman and had published in 1792 two volumes of poetry by himself and others. Several of the poems were odes in the Scandinavian style, and Scott in one of his 1792 notebooks had transcribed Polwhele's *Death-Song of Ragnar Lothbrog*. In 1810 Scott promised Polwhele a review copy of the

[7] For Weber, see Lockhart, *Life of Scott*, ii. 16, 138, 168, 215, 331; iii. 58, 109, 112, 114; vi. 259; Edgar Johnson, *Sir Walter Scott, The Great Unknown* (London, 1970), esp. 434–5.

first volume of *Northern Antiquities* (this of course turned out to be the only volume). The conclusion of this letter shows Scott's scholarly generosity well: 'I have little share in [the *Northern Antiquities*], excepting my wish to promote the interest of the prime conductors, whose knowledge is rather more extensive than their financial resources.'

This, of course, is too modest of Scott, and even if his *Abstract of Eyrbiggia Saga* does represent his only major contribution to the volume, it is notable in itself. For the first time English readers were told what one of the Sagas of Icelanders was about, and why it was interesting and worthwhile. Scott tells the story with gusto, and his remarks on it are usually very much to the point. In the first few lines he shows his limitations on questions of factual detail, and more importantly his shrewd grasp of the spirit of the saga. He says that it was probably composed before 1264, 'when Iceland was still subject to the dominion of Norway'. It was of course in the 1260s that Iceland *became* subject to Norway. He then proceeds, rightly I am convinced, to seize the essentials of the saga without regard for a supposed problem that has worried students of *Eyrbyggja Saga* too much.[8] It has often been described as a troublesome saga, lacking in what is thought to be proper unity. The central figure is Snorri goði, the local bigwig, but he's not a heroic figure, as Scott says later on. The narrative line lacks any obvious cohesion, but this doesn't matter, because the theme is that of the overall development of a society. The man who was to write such fine novels of what I shall call a social realist type took *Eyrbyggja Saga* in his stride. Scott says of it:

[These annals] contain the history of a particular territory of the Island of Iceland, lying around the promontory called Snæfells, from its first settlement by emigrants from Norway: and the chronicle details, at great length, the feuds which took place among the families by whom the land was occupied, the advances which they made towards a more regular state of society, their habits, their superstitions, and their domestic laws and customs.

Now naturally Scott revelled in the supernatural elements in the story, particularly the hauntings at Froða that began with the appearance of a sudden cloud from the north during the hay harvest.

[8] For a fuller discussion of this point, see my 'Eyrbyggja Saga and Nineteenth-Century Scholarship' in the forthcoming proceedings of the First International Saga Conference, to be published by the Viking Society. The most accessible text of Scott's *Abstract* is in the *Miscellaneous Prose Works*.

The cloud approached with great celerity, and sunk so heavily around the farm, that it was scarce possible to see beyond the limits of the field. A heavy shower next descended, and so soon as the clouds broke away, and the sun shone forth, it was observed that it had rained blood. That . . . which fell upon the ricks of the other labourers soon dried up, but what Thorgunna had wrought upon remained wet with gore. The unfortunate Hebridean, appalled at the omen, betook herself to her bed, and was seized with a mortal illness.

But when the ghosts begin to appear thick and fast at Froða, and they are ejected by due process of law, by a court constituted at the door of the house, Scott the social historian takes up the discussion:

All the solemn rites of judicial procedure were observed on this singular occasion; evidence was adduced, charges given, and the cause formally decided . . . it is the only instance in which the ordinary administration of justice has been supposed to extend over the inhabitants of another world, and in which the business of exorcising spirits is transferred from the priest to the judge. Joined to the various instances of the Eyrbiggia-Saga of a certain regard to the forms of jurisprudence, even amid the wildest of their feuds, it seems to argue the extraordinary influence ascribed to municipal law by this singular people, even in the very earliest state of society.

Scott's concluding remarks on the saga once more demonstrates his sure grasp of what constitutes its essence. He shows how the character of Snorri goði unobtrusively unifies the action. Now Snorri is neither a tragic doomed hero, nor does he carry all before him; he bobs up to the surface of the story every now and then, suffering reverses from time to time, but on the whole maintaining his ascendancy in the district. A modern critic, Professor Turville-Petre, has described Snorri thus: 'he is calculating, cold, and cynical, gifted with cunning rather than bravery, but at the same time wise, prudent, and sometimes generous'.[9] Scott shows exactly how this sort of figure acts as focus for what is less an epic, though it has epic qualities, than an ancestor of the social novel:

That such a character, partaking more of the jurisconsult or statesman than of the warrior, should have risen so high in such an early period, argues the preference which the Icelanders already assigned to mental superiority over the rude attributes of strength and courage, and furnishes another proof of the early civilisation of this extraordinary commonwealth. In other respects the character of Snorro [sic] was altogether unamiable, and blended with strong traits of the savage. Cunning and subtlety supplied the place of wisdom, and an earnest and uniform attention to his own interests often, as in the dispute between Arnkill and his father, superseded the ties of blood and friendship. Still, however, his selfish conduct seems to have been of more service to the settlement in which he swayed, than would have been that of a generous and high-spirited warrior who acted from the impulse of momentary passion.

[9] E. O. G. Turville-Petre, *Origins of Icelandic Literature* (Oxford, 1953), 242.

I come now to the second brilliant scholarly aperçu in this paper. Just like the first one, it belongs not to me but to Edith Batho. She points out that Scott's novel *Waverley* was begun and abandoned in 1805: Scott looked at it again in 1810, and again set it aside because of the criticisms of his friends. He finished his *Abstract of Eyrbiggia Saga* in October 1813, and it was in three weeks of the following summer that *Waverley* was completed. Admitting that Scott did not consciously react to the stimulus of the saga, Dr. Batho suggests that the stimulus may nevertheless have been there. Adapting Saintsbury's expression that Scott was the father of the later novel, and Jane Austen its mother, she wonders if the author of *Eyrbyggja Saga* may be described as a grandparent. She herself would not resist the application of the good Scots verdict of 'not proven' to this hypothesis, but it's an attractive one surely. And in general terms, of course, more than one modern saga scholar would see the sagas as ancestors of the modern social novel.

Just as Scott relished the sagas, so have modern Scandinavian readers and writers taken to Scott. In Iceland, I believe, an interest in his works (indicated by translations, for example) continues to the present day. And nineteenth-century poets and novelists in Scandinavia witnessed to Scott's influence on them. Against the cheeky aphorism of George Brandes that Scott is 'a writer whom everybody has read, but nobody reads', we may set the remark of Strindberg in connexion with one of his own works: 'to get myself into the proper mood and into the presence of the past I did the same thing, as I usually do, when I am writing historical plays, I read Walter Scott'.[10] But this could have been the theme of another paper.

One of the truly tragic vignettes of Scottish history is Lockhart's account of the argument between Scott and Francis Jeffrey on the subject of legal reform: Scott exclaimed 'No, no, 'tis no laughing matter: little by little, whatever your wishes may be, you will destroy and undermine, until nothing of what makes Scotland Scotland shall remain', and Jeffrey saw that Scott was weeping. In general terms all too many of Scott's forebodings have proved correct, and our outlook has become steadily less cosmopolitan, more and more drearily provincial. We would do well, as a corrective, to seek to emulate Scott's zest for the literature of

[10] Quoted in S. Blöndal, 'Scott in Swedish Literature', *Sir Walter Scott Quarterly* i (1928), 169–75.

other lands. And so, if Sir Walter noted the events of 1971, he was perhaps pleased that his conference was followed immediately in Edinburgh by the First International Saga Conference. It may be a small sign that all is not yet lost.

Periodicals in the Age of Scott

DONALD A. LOW

T HE founding of the *Edinburgh Review* by Francis Jeffrey and others in 1802 came as a shock to authors and readers accustomed to the undemanding standards of late eighteenth-century periodicals. Journals with established reputations suddenly looked old-fashioned. Before long, the example of the *Edinburgh* reviewers was being followed generally, though seldom matched. A new impetus had been given to the analysis of society and its institutions. Conventions of political commentary and literary reviewing both changed. In 1817 Coleridge summed up the feelings of an admiring but still bemused public when he described Jeffrey's initiative as marking 'an epoch in periodical criticism'.

Of the first *Edinburgh* reviewers, Sydney Smith was an Englishman educated at Winchester and Oxford; but Jeffrey, Brougham, and Horner all drew directly on the intellectual traditions of the Scottish Enlightenment. They cared passionately about the nature of the social contract, about law, and about economics. Their style was that of advocates trained to debate general questions in such clubs as the Speculative Society in Edinburgh University, and since hardened for battle by strenuous competition for each legal case. They did not give or crave quarter, but instead argued for one view of a subject in the manner of men whose livelihood depended upon victory in the argument. The characteristic method of the *Edinburgh Review* is to relate an issue to first principles, and then to argue a case to score points and win. Only those English-born authors who combined the pursuit of truth with a combative style were likely to be welcome as contributors. Smith was the first; and later, Hazlitt wrote with a pugnacious authority which led some to confuse his work with that of Jeffrey himself. As a literary form, the polemical essay flourished in the *Edinburgh Review* as never before.

Jeffrey told Scott, who was for a time one of his contributors, that the 'right leg' of the *Edinburgh* was politics. His confidence and success in arguing the Whig case came to rankle in Scott's mind. When to this general complaint there was added resentment at a patronizing review of one of his own poems by Jeffrey, Scott took action. It was largely owing to his enterprise that the *Quarterly Review* came into being in 1809 as a Tory rival to the *Edinburgh*. He was determined that a seriously argued pro-Government view of current affairs should be placed before people who might otherwise be won over to opposition and even anti-war policies. The same political motive prompted him to establish an annual publication summarizing recent events from what he judged to be an enlightened conservative viewpoint. The *Edinburgh Annual Register* was started with this object.

As an essayist on contemporary history in the *Edinburgh Annual Register* and elsewhere, Scott sought to be objective and accurate; but these principles of selection were inevitably at variance with his Tory propagandist aim. His essays in periodicals on political and social history thus illuminate one of the principal tensions in his work, between the demands of politics on the one hand and of general truths about human nature on the other. This is an aspect of a more complex problem. When he wrote *The Antiquary*, a novel set in the Scotland of his own (and Jeffrey's) youth in the politically divisive 1790s, he had great difficulty in reconciling the sometimes contradictory impulses of political conviction, historical narration, and fictional art. The conflict recurred in a modified but still intense form towards the end of his life when he wrote a large-scale biography of Napoleon. In his journalism, the strains are less marked because he could avoid treating his subjects in depth, but the evidence of conflict is plain. The letters of 'Malachi Malagrowther', for example, which first appeared in the *Edinburgh Weekly Journal* in 1826, reveal that he did not always find it easy to combine his support of the government with his pride in Scotland. The tone of the letters is that of affronted nationalism and political frustration. Yet these powerful feelings are indulged over a subject of limited significance—disagreement as to whether Scottish banks should be allowed to issue their own bank-notes. Aggressive emotion is diverted from political actuality to an almost irrelevant area of play. The manœuvre, which is only in part a conscious one, is highly characteristic of Scott's mature political philosophy. A parallel instance is the encouragement he gave to football matches between the men of Selkirk and Ettrick. Old rivalries must have an honourable outlet. No tradition in the Scottish Borders is more clearly in accord with his outlook than one which he did not live to see: the development of intense competition among the rugby teams of neighbouring towns, a competition which extends to supplying players to national teams dedicated above all to victory over the English.

The great quarterly reviews transformed discussion of politics and of literature. In 1824 the *Westminster Review* was started, in John Stuart Mill's words, as 'a Radical organ to make head against the Edinburgh and Quarterly'. The *Westminster* was the mouthpiece of the English Utilitarians and was strongly affected by the thought of Bentham. James Mill's association with the new journal nevertheless ensured that it resembled the other quarterlies in possessing something of the distinctively broad range of interests of the Scottish Enlightenment.

Rational debate concerning a wide variety of subjects distinguishes the reviews. They remain very impressive publications, beside which much twentieth-century journalism looks deficient in ideas. But there is a sense in which they are too impressive to be interesting as periodicals. They aspire to the condition of books. Many of their leading contributors had a gentlemanly contempt for the rest of the periodical press, and especially for newspaper journalism. One result of this attitude is that while the reviews have a great deal to tell us about the history of ideas, including the theory of romanticism, they appear remote from ordinary life. They lack the immediate appeal of direct reporting of news. For a sense of direct involvement in the times—perhaps the most valuable thing old periodicals offer—a modern reader has to turn to newspapers and magazines.

George Steiner has commented recently on the revolutionary nature of the historical period in which Scott passed from youth to early middle age:

No string of quotations, no statistics, can recapture for us what must have been the inner excitement, the passionate adventure of spirit and emotion, unleashed by the events of 1789 and sustained, at a fantastic tempo, until 1815. Far more than political revolution and war, on an unprecedented scale of geographical and social compass, is involved. The French Revolution and the Napoleonic Wars—*la grande épopée*—literally quickened the pace of felt time. We lack histories of the internal time-sense, of the changing beat in men's experience of the rhythms of perception. But we do have reliable evidence that those who lived through the 1790s and the first decade and a half of the 19th century, and who could recall the tenor of life under the old dispensation, felt that time itself and the whole enterprise of consciousness had formidably accelerated. [*The Listener*, 18 March 1971.]

Periodicals are probably the best of all guides to rapidly altering local and national life—when they are read in temporal sequence, as periodicals. Time is the dimension which they are especially equipped to measure. They make possible the partial recovery of the actual experience of change in the past, and, with their inbuilt time-sense, subtly indicate how rhythms of perception were transformed.

Journalists were responsive to ongoing life from within its flux, not from the detached vantage-point of posterity. Not only their accurate comment, but their admission of bewilderment is vitally important as evidence of what it felt like to be confronted by change on a radically new scale. If one reads the file of, say, a Regency weekly newspaper over only a year of its existence, and then its summary of the year's events, the nature of the journalist's achievement—and of his predicament—is made plain. Here is part of the summary of the year 1813 which appeared in *The Champion*, a London Sunday paper, on 9 January 1814:

Those who have quitted the old world for that on the other side of the Atlantic, find that creation has been there conducted on a scale of magnitude which reduces what they have left behind to mere miniature landscape. The lakes are seas; the rivers rolling gulphs; the mountains 'make Ossa like a wart'. The occurrences of the present period have a similar superiority in extent and importance over those of past times. We do not now take up a daily newspaper but with the expectation of seeing an event recorded, which once would have formed a distinction for an age, or at least a reign, The year 1813 has included within its extremes, an entire change in the condition,—not of a nation, but of Europe. In its course the war has rolled from Russia to France on one side, and from Portugal into France on another. . . . Twelve months have totally altered the basis of political reasonings; they have opened totally new prospects; they have struck down within their own space a system which was thought preternaturally rapid in its growth, inasmuch as it arrived at maturity within twenty years; they have dispersed the settled gloom that enveloped the minds of men, and set them upon all sorts of cheerful speculations;—in short, they have reversed Europe in every respect, converting friends to enemies, and enemies to friends,—slaves to conquerors, invincibility to weakness, and vassalage to independence.

These comments on the speed and extent of developments in 1813 concerned life in Britain as well as a new turn of events in the war against Napoleon. Throughout the year the newspaper had included home news and leading articles about social questions, politics, and the arts. Its editor, John Scott, noted significant changes in every department of life. Hope for the future, and a sense of shock, dominated his response. Both attitudes were present in the minds of many of his readers. Because it was a time of very rapid change, feelings swung quickly from visionary optimism to nostalgic attachment to the past. Most people reacted with complicated feelings to what was new and unfamiliar.

Magazines responded to change less directly than newspapers, but from the point of view of the modern literary student in a no less meaningful way. Unlike the reviews, early nineteenth-century magazines published personal essays, poetry, and fiction. To read the best magazines of the period is to see a major part of British romantic literature in its original cultural context.

Periodicals attracted imaginative writers at this time not merely because the most successful paid very well, but because of the periodical form itself. Edward Young's definition of original genius can be borrowed to describe a periodical: it is not made, it *grows*. The possibility of spontaneous, unpredictable growth drew variously gifted writers together in a common allegiance. Much of the interest of a series such as 'Noctes Ambrosianae' in *Blackwood's Magazine* lies in its unpredictability—and it was one variant of the concept of creative imagination which helped to unite John Wilson, James Hogg, and others in a new kind of team-writing. At its best, a magazine like *Blackwood's* enacted the process of 'dynamic organicism'. We can watch the Scottish regional novel growing to maturity within a few years in *Blackwood's*. But the best work of Galt and Hogg was quickly followed by inferior serialized tales exploiting at a sentimental level the interest in Scotland which Scott had aroused. Predictability then became the distinguishing feature of Scottish fiction in *Blackwood's*, which had, from the beginning, achieved its literary distinction by ignoring settled conventions.

Organic growth, then, was one possibility which made some periodicals exciting in the eyes of their contributors. The spirit of comradeship among the early writers in Baldwin's *London Magazine* was as marked as that of Blackwood and his associates; and the work of some of these men—notably of Hazlitt, Lamb, and De Quincey—defines a new and important phase in the evolution of the periodical essay.

This suggests another main effect of the periodical form upon writers contemporary with Scott. The theme of mutability, which runs through so much romantic writing, took on peculiar urgency against the background conditions governing the periodical press. Magazines, their very existence defined by time, and disappearing at once to likely oblivion, acted as a catalyst for the expression of that theme. 'Time's handiworks by Time are haunted.'

The Scottish regional novelists who wrote in *Blackwood's* had a semi-documentary purpose. They sought to describe life in the Scotland of their youth, which was receding at an increasing rate from the view of a new generation. In this sense, they were, like Scott, memorialists of society, although none of them had his capacity to write with elegiac power about the Scottish past, and all were more nearly contemporary in their subject-matter. The atmosphere of early fiction in *Blackwood's* is partly satirical, and partly nostalgic.

There is a clear parallel to be drawn between the nostalgia for an older Scotland of the *Blackwood's* group of novelists, and the recoil from the present to the past which is observable in the imaginative prose contributed by English essayists to the *London Magazine*. Lamb's nostalgia in the 'Essays of Elia' is freely indulged, and it is complemented by the less obvious but recurrent inclination to live in the past which Hazlitt shows in 'Table Talk'. The detailed recreation of childhood experience in 'Confessions of an English Opium-Eater' shows another variation on the same pattern.

The contents of magazines were varied in such a way that an up-to-date summary of political affairs or an article on recent developments in science might be placed next to a personal essay. Certainly, all three kinds of contribution were likely to be included in the average monthly magazine. In indulging his memories, or in tracing the swift disappearance of today's customs into those of yesterday, the essayist could claim that he was performing an essential function of the periodical: charting the movement of past, as distinct from present and future time. The *London Magazine* aimed to 'catch the manners living as they rise', and also to recreate those of the recent past in its evocative essays.

The Romantics, after all, saw change everywhere. Mutability is one of their most insistent major themes, just as it is with the Elizabethans. It is a common preoccupation of Spenser and Keats, and forms a connexion between Shakespeare's sonnets and the most popular poem of the Regency, *Childe Harold's Pilgrimage*. For the Elizabethan actor-writer, the 'two hours' traffic of our stage' was the medium which seemed best adapted for its expression. One underlying reason for this preoccupation common to the two periods was the occurrence of rapid social and cultural change,

accompanied by visions of a new social order which were not fulfilled. Old manners and customs were swept away, but were not
replaced by ideal practices. Ancient abuses remained. In Scott's
age, therefore, whether you were a Tory or a Whig, you were
shocked into recognition of the tyranny of Time. *Marmion* shares
this recognition with Canto 4 of *Childe Harold's Pilgrimage*.

It is no accident that one of the central ideas in Wordsworth's
Prelude is a strategy for withstanding time's conquest, the 'spots
of time' motif, which is clearly stated in Book 12. We can compare
with this Byron's claim,

> But I have lived, and have not lived in vain:
> My mind may lose its force, my blood its fire,
> And my frame perish even in conquering pain;
> But there is that within me which shall tire
> Torture and Time, and breathe when I expire.

In Byron's poetry, as in Wordsworth's, time is a more formidable
agent than any of the invented characters.

But Byron's approach is radically different from Wordsworth's
—and this will lead us back to periodicals. Wordsworth, recollecting emotion in tranquillity, offers in *The Prelude* an artificially
arranged past, which is surveyed from a stable position in the
present. Byron does not provide this reassuring dimension of calm
recollection. Instead, he offers as the basis of his poetry the flux
of a continuous present which is charged with uncertainty and
bewilderment. In *Childe Harold's Pilgrimage* the reader shares
with its author his existential predicament. He is involved in the
moment's chaos of conflicted moods and disappearing choices.
There are also flashbacks, and reflective passages which take a
longer view of events. These suggest another angle on the problems posed by time, and a Byronic version of philosophical resignation. Byron characteristically returns to the multiple contradictions confronting him now. His refusal to subordinate experience
to the ideal forms of memory helps to account for a very modern
note in his poetry.

Periodicals resemble *Childe Harold's Pilgrimage* rather than *The
Prelude* in that they offer the illusion of a continuous present, and
not an artificially arranged past. Inevitably, a twentieth-century
reader brings his own time-scale to the reading of periodicals of
Scott's age. But it is still possible to make the approach with the
kind of curiosity and suspension of prejudice which are appro-

priate in foreign travel. Instead of dismissing old newspapers and magazines as ephemeral, the willing reader recognizes that they have a special role in the imaginative reconstruction of social and literary history. They can do no less than take him into the age in which Scott wrote, and accustom him to its tempo and values.

Susan Ferrier

WENDY CRAIK

SUSAN FERRIER suffers through no deficiency of her own.
Like Mark Antony's before Caesar's, her genius is rebuked.
Heresy though it is to say it in this context, it would have
been much to Miss Ferrier's advantage if Sir Walter Scott had
stuck to poetry and never turned his mind to novel-writing. It
would also be to her advantage if no critic of her had ever heard of
Jane Austen. Being Scots—and an Edinburgh Scot at that—she is
inevitably compared with the former; and being a woman who
writes novels of manners, she is unavoidably likened to the latter.
She is not really like either of them. She is not, let me admit from
the start, playing in their league. Though not among the great
novelists of the world, she *is* among the good ones, and among
those of the good ones who offer lasting and undating enjoyment.
Her general claims, not only to fame, but to being read a century
and a half after she wrote, rest upon the very little historical sense
needed to relish her, because she writes best about characters—
and eccentric ones at that—and because she is at her best in the
comic sides of a novelist's business. Although, unlike Cleopatra,
she has far from infinite variety, her merits are of the kind that age
cannot stale nor custom wither. What is more, they are very much
her own merits, unlike those of other novelists before or after.
Her Scottish characters—that is, all her best characters—are
different from Sir Walter's, Galt's or Smollett's, not only in kind,
but in the uses to which she puts them and the means by which she
presents them. They are also, of course, unlike Jane Austen's. But
the temptation to look at her as if she were a Scottish Jane Austen
is equally a disservice, because her intentions and her means are
unlike Miss Austen's, and the quality of the entertainment she
provides is even more dissimilar.

To be just, one must admit Miss Ferrier's deficiencies, but I
should like to concentrate, in the short space before me, upon her
virtues and delights, which can all be collected under one general

head—humour. Susan Ferrier's greatest power is that of pro-
voking the kind of amusement that vents itself in mirth, and she
has that rare power of prodding even the silent solitary student
into outright laughter. She has no rigid or limited formula for
comedy, but, rather, a wide variety of methods. Before coming on
to them, though, in the interests of fairness, I must point out her
limitations, at the risk of going over perhaps familiar, and probably
uninspiring, ground.

Miss Ferrier has the deficiencies as well as the virtues of the
minor and the amateur writer. She wrote three novels: *Marriage*
in 1816, *The Inheritance*, in 1824, and *Destiny* in 1831. She was
wise to do so. Reading them, one doesn't regret her small output.
Plainly she had only material enough for three, if that. *Marriage*
has by far the most gusto; and if *The Inheritance* has more polish,
it has also more *longueurs*; by the time she writes *Destiny* the
sands of inspiration are running out. Illness and domestic circumstances may account partly for the tiredness of the writing, the
lifeless morality and trite sentiment, but there is no doubt that she
suffered from restricted subject matter. She admitted to drawing
from life, from using real acquaintances as starting-points, if not
models; and even in Regency Edinburgh, and in the castles and
estates of the West Coast and Highlands, the supply of memorable
and outrageous eccentrics of a kind she could use was not inexhaustible. The kind she could use is drawn from the gentry—if
so English a term can have currency—the landed and professional
range, from the clergy to the titled—never the poor nor the very
rich (indeed, there is a striking lack of ready cash throughout her
novels). Her range of characters is limited also by her talents. She
never tackles the coarse or the brutal, or gets her fun from cruelty,
as Smollett could; nor is she in any real sense a satirist. The ridiculous arouses her delight; folly, providing it is ludicrous, her
mirth. She exposes and exploits them. She does not make them
serve any moral end. The reader is heartily thankful that she does
not. By nature she is seriously and conventionally moral and high-
principled, in the Evangelical way. She feels herself obliged to be a
moral writer, not only by personal conviction, but also by the
conventions of the novel of manners. But her didacticism flour-
ishes quite apart from her humour; it exercises itself upon her
young heroines, and upon her serious portraits—which are undeni-
ably and regrettably dull. Fortunately it doesn't seem to occur to
her that caricature may be personally cruel, that these kinds of

foibles, and grotesqueries of behaviour, or the ridiculous manifestations of stupidity, may yet exist alongside honest good
nature. She is not, in fact, an intelligent or a self-conscious writer.
Her thinking is hardly worth the name, her standards are sound
eighteenth-century ones, but naïve. One instance of many will
suffice, when Mary, the heroine of *Marriage*, struggles for several
pages to justify herself for going to church when her irresponsible
and pleasure-loving mother has forbidden it. Duty to God and
duty to the silliest of parents tie her in knots. When her cousin
invites her to go to a ball, also forbidden by her mother, she gets
into further knots trying to explain why, in this case, the duty to
obey her parent carries the day.

Just as the spirit of the age and the models before her thus
oblige her to write at times what does not suit her, they oblige her
also to have a story; and so, after *Marriage*, she chooses incidents
and hangs them on to plots that could have been, and were, done
by any lady novelist from Fanny Burney and Maria Edgeworth
onwards: clichés as plots, they can be summarized in clichés:
separated twins, long-lost relatives, heiresses who, through being
changed over at birth, are not heiresses at all; charming but unprincipled wastrel suitors, long-lost kinsfolk and heirs, the honest
country girl caught up in the heartless and frivolous society of
profligate London, villainous blackmail and mysterious secrets.
She has to write novels of the customary length, and so digresses
and discourses like Fielding on an off day; she pads with quotations
from the standard poets, from *Elegant Extracts*, and from pious
tracts like a conscientious schoolgirl; and she introduces passages
of instructive and stilted sentimental dialogue like the worst parts
of *Sir Charles Grandison*. When she tries, as in *Destiny*, to write a
more serious work, her evangelical principles, honest though they
are, drag her down. When she attempts, as in *The Inheritance*, to
write a coherently-plotted one, any reader can see from a third of
the way through, that the charming suitor is no good, and that the
virtuous one will win in the end, that the heiress is not who
she thinks she is, and that the villainous American, though he may
be able to deprive her of her title, will never succeed in establishing
himself as her parent. Though the reader may not know whose
daughter she is, he knows whose *grand-daughter*, and he knows that,
in the atmosphere of this novel, nobody of refinement is a bastard,
and that no young man of impeccable virtue who marries a heroine
is ever doomed to have a drunken, swearing father-in-law. If one

cannot actually guess the outcome of the plot—as Oliver Elton thinks[1]—one can guess more than one is really interested to know. Even in character-drawing she can sometimes flag. There are times when, realizing that she is temporarily stale, she abruptly and deliberately thrusts a fresh character before the reader to refresh him, herself, and her story. An instance in *The Inheritance* is Miss Becky Duguid, the poor spinster whom all her relations impose on and exploit. When she appears, not only does the story halt, but the technique falters. The account of Miss Duguid is static, like the analyses of personages found in Goldsmith's history and (ultimately) in Clarendon; the letters sent to her by those who make a convenience of the poor willing spinster are both improbably grotesque, and far too long.

But enough of the drawbacks. Homer can nod, and Susan Ferrier can yawn, but neither happens often. One might perhaps call her a 'primitive', because she invents new means, and embarks on new material, without seeming to realize her originality. She began *Marriage* some time before Scott produced *Waverley*, although it was published five years after. Although she may have read Smollett and the other Scots writers, she makes no sign in her manner of writing of being aware of others who *are* near her in her good things, Smollett and John Galt immediately, and Fanny Burney further off, none of whom she much resembles in effect, although like Smollett and Galt she draws on Scottish types and dialect speakers. Her great powers are to invent and handle all kinds of comic social situations, and to render farcical and grotesque ones credible; to invent and to delineate from life all kinds of comic characters, from the eccentric to the outright grotesque, both men and women, and to handle these characters both individually and in groups; and to present her incidents and characters with a remarkably wide range of techniques: all the usual ones of description and idiosyncratic speech, and many much less predictable ones of racy idiom, reported thought, literary allusion and quotation, unexpected interaction, wit, deflation, anti-climax, prolific and marvellously chosen detail, and even manipulation in the reader of some of the emotions most difficult to handle, like embarrassment.

The intentions she presents to herself before embarking on her first novel are just right for her, and indicate exactly how much

[1] Oliver Elton, *A Survey of English Literature*, 1780–1830 (London, 1912), i. 366–9.

part design should play in her kind of work, and what strengths she should exploit. She writes to Charlotte Clavering, the friend who was to be her collaborator—although the collaboration came to very little in the end—as follows:

I don't think, like all penny-book manufacturers, that 'tis absolutely necessary that the good boys and girls should be rewarded and the naughty ones punished. Yet I think, where there is much tribulation, 'tis fitter it should be the *consequence* rather than the *cause* of misconduct or frailty.

This is not a moral stance that can produce a Jane Austen, but it is one that gives much freedom. So also is her idea of the material:

I do not recollect ever to have seen the sudden transition of a high-bred English beauty, who thinks she can sacrifice all for love, to an uncomfortable solitary Highland dwelling, among tall red-haired sisters and grim-faced aunts.

The joint correspondence thereafter on the book is mostly concerned with *characters*—and very entertaining it is—showing what Miss Ferrier felt her novel to be about and what interested her most.[2] Authors' explicit intentions are, of course, not necessarily criteria for assessing their achievement, but such spontaneous ones as Susan Ferrier's are a good guide, on the simple principle that what she likes best she is likely to do best. And by character she does not mean, plainly, mere description of personality. Her characters are people in action, so that, although her books have little *plot*, they have plenty of events; in *The Inheritance*, though one may hardly recall who the young heiress Gertrude St. Clair (otherwise Lady Rossville) ultimately marries, one cannot forget the scenes in which she takes part with the Scottish characters who surround her: her uncle Mr. Ramsay, for instance, old, miserly, crotchety, and rich, when she returns £500 she has borrowed from him, reproves her for not giving him the interest, and, says the author, 'Taking up an old blackened stump of a pen, began to cast up his account on the back of the bill; then showing it to Lady Rossville, "There's what I was inteetled to frae you; but I tell you I dinna want it—I only want to mak' you sensible o' what you're aboot".'[3] The point made and the principle established, he

   [2] *Memoir and Correspondence of Susan Ferrier*, ed. John A. Doyle (London, 1898), ch. 2, esp. pp. 75–6.

   [3] *The Inheritance* ii. 25. References to *The Inheritance* are to volume and chapter of the first edition (Edinburgh, 1824). The two-volume 'Edinburgh' edition (London, 1882) prints i. 1–34 and ii. 1–17 of the first edition (renumbered 1–51) in its first volume, and ii. 18–37, iii. 1–35 (renumbered 1–55) in its second. The limited edition (London, 1929) introduced by Lady Margaret Sackville gives all 106 chapters in one sequence.

immediately asks her whether she has got her feet wet in the snow.

While the plot plods its weary way, with Gertrude spending her fortune, suffering at the hands of her feckless, selfish betrothed and of her mother's mysterious blackmailer, a rich succession of continuous comic situations absorbs and entertains us, alongside and inter-related. Mr. Ramsay provides much of the fun, along with the chatterbox and busy-body Miss Pratt. Her garrulity is a delight, and Miss Ferrier's inspiration magnificently employs Miss Pratt's talents: for mis-hearing and getting things wrong, for loving to be right and know what others don't, and for money. So she and Mr. Ramsay have a bet on the identity of whom Gertrude really admires, and their respective suspenses, about this and the respective five guineas that they have staked, gives true comic coherence to the action. Mr. Ramsay provides another kind of coherence. He is held captive at Gertrude's house, not by her pleas, or by social decorum, but by a copy of *Guy Mannering*. The stresses of serious existence at the house are registered, on a comic level, by the strength of Mr. Ramsay's fascination with his reading, opposed to his wish to get home away from it all.

Over the shorter interval, too, Susan Ferrier has a wholly original method of rendering drama by farce. A superb, rightly well-known instance is the death of Gertrude's uncle, Lord Rossville. Since he must die to leave Gertrude as heiress, his death must be dealt with. Since he is himself another of Miss Ferrier's fine range of comic bores, he plainly cannot die tragically or even melodramatically. Miss Pratt's personality gives Susan Ferrier means for introducing the perfect machinery. In a blinding snow-storm in the middle of winter the splendid sequence of incidents begins: when Miss Pratt, to Lord Rossville's utter horror, consternation and outrage, arrives in a hearse, with all the trappings. Miss Ferrier's invention, once on the wing, soars higher and higher. When Miss Pratt has made her entry,

'There's eight horses and four men,' said Lady Betty, who had been pleasing her fancy by counting them. 'Whose burial is it?'

'It's Mr M'Vitae's, the great distiller. I'm sure I'm much obliged to him— for if it hadn't been for him, poor man! I might have been stiff and stark by this time.'[4]

The outrage perpetrated on the Earl's sense of his own dignity by the arrival of a hearse at his front door, is worsened by its being a

4 *Inheritance*, ii. 21.

distiller's hearse, and receives a worse blow when, the snow being impassable, he has to give lodging to horses and men for the night:

There was something in having a hearse, and the hearse of Mr. M'Vitae, the radical distiller, thus forced within his walls, he could not away with. Death, even in its most dignified attitude, with all its proudest trophies, would still have been an appalling spectacle to Lord Rossville; but in its present vulgar and burlesque form, it was altogether insupportable. Death is indeed an awful thing, whatever aspect it assumes. The King of Terrors gives to other attributes the power of terrifying: the thunder's roar—the lightning's flash—the billow's roar—the earthquake's shock—all derive their dread sublimity from Death. All are but instruments of his resistless sway.

From these, and even from his more ordinary emissaries, Lord Rossville felt secure; but still a lurking fear had taken possession of his mind, and he could not divest himself of the train of ideas, which had been excited by beholding, in horrid array, Death's cavalcade approach his dwelling. He passed a restless night—he thought of what the county would say, and what he would say to the county—he thought of whether he would not be justified in banishing Miss Pratt for ever from his presence. When the first faint grey streak of light appeared, he rang his bell to enquire whether the funeral procession had departed—but a fresh fall of snow during the night had placed the castle and hearse in a complete state of blockade. He rose and opened the window to ascertain the fact, but nothing was to be seen but a fast-falling, blinding snow—he next went to the door, but there the snow lay six feet deep—he returned to bed, but not to sleep—and when his servant entered in the morning he found his master a lifeless corse.[5]

The regulation of tone is superb. The mixture of idioms—the tritely rhetorical and the homely—serves to make us acknowledge the serious aspects of death, and prepare us for it as an actual event, while the very rhetoric, in its emptiness, preserves the comic spirit. The arrival of the hearse is such a fine grotesque event in itself, and Miss Pratt's emergence from it so hilarious an anticlimax, that the idea of death, thus introduced, enters the reader's mind almost without his noticing it, with all the atmosphere of comedy that Miss Ferrier requires to subdue the Earl's death, when it happens, to her comic design, and to make it, though not at all callous, superbly funny.

It is this kind of narrative art that constitutes Susan Ferrier's claim to be a novelist, and not, as so many accounts of her would suggest, merely a creator of a gallery of superb characters. Her most famous characters are of course well known and much praised: Lady Maclaughlan in *Marriage*, Mr. Ramsay and Miss Pratt (already mentioned) in *The Inheritance*, the Rev. Duncan McDow

[5] *Inheritance*, ii. 22.

in *Destiny*. But she has a nice and original skill (which later novelists such as Dickens were to use, though perhaps never to better
effect): the group portrait. Take the bunch of nieces in *Marriage*:
Bella, Becky, Betty, Baby and Beeny, 'five awkward purple girls'
indistinguishable in name and virtually so in personality.

> They had . . . exchanged their thick morning dresses for their muslin gowns,
> made, by a mantua-maker of the neighbourhood, in the extreme of a two-
> year-old fashion, when waists *were not*.
> But as dame nature had been particularly lavish in the length of theirs, and
> the stay-maker had, according to their aunt's direction, given them *full
> measure* of their new dark stays, there existed a visible breach between the
> waists of their gowns and the bands of their petticoats, which they had vainly
> sought to adjust by a meeting. Their hair had been curled, but not combed,
> and dark gloves had been hastily drawn on to hide red arms.[6]

Independent life they never have after this introduction, but as a
corporate unit they never fail. Their effect is such that, after a few
chapters, one of their three aunts, or the author herself, has only to
refer to one of them to produce the effect of the whole quintet.

At the other extreme I must mention one of Miss Ferrier's most
memorable of all creations: Miss Pratt's nephew, Anthony Whyte,
who achieves immortality by never appearing at all. Earlier by
nearly forty years than Mrs. Gamp's Mrs. Harris, he is perhaps
even finer than her because there is, indubitably, 'sich a person',
though such as what remains a hilarious mystery: it is inconceiv-
able that he should be as Miss Pratt represents him, because she
never interprets aright anyone whom we do meet. He is even
more of a literary mystery than the nature of Hamlet.

There is plainly more to Miss Ferrier's humour than merely
describing characters, or even endowing them with personal
idioms like Miss Bell Black's reiterated appeal to 'the eyes of the
world' or 'a woman in her position': she contrives never to pay
visits anywhere, you remember, in her position as successively
betrothed, bride, wife, and mother. These excellences are obvious
to any responsive reader, as is her sure hand with bores, whom, in
Marriage and *Inheritance* at least, she represents by a fine short-
hand of their own boring qualities, or even better, by having bores
mutually cut each other out by all sorts of ingenious interruption.
Miss Ferrier has learned the great truth that no one is as soon
wearied of a bore as another different kind of bore.

She herself, as narrator, provides much of her own comedy, and
is almost another character from what she is in her serious,

[6] *Marriage*, i. 10.

reflective, or sentimental moods. Both her relations with her reader and her idiom are engaging and disarming. After one of her most successful comic letters from a comic character she remarks:

The perusal of this letter was a severe tax on Gertrude's patience, as it has doubtless been upon all who have read it.[7]

and later, she describes the scene which her unhappy heroine is listlessly watching, which contains an 'old gentlewoman knitting a large thick-shaped white lamb's-wool stocking':

Much might be said upon this subject [of her dexterity]; but, doubtless, my readers love a well knit story as much as a well knit stocking; and it would be like letting down a stitch to enter upon a long digression at present.[8]

The digression she has already supplied has in fact been a most useful one, since it re-creates for the reader the sense of nothing happening, of time standing still or only drearily proceeding, which has afflicted the heroine. The mood of a homely Scottish Mariana in a moated Grange has been beautifully caught.

Others of her talents associated with creating mood cannot be so easily instanced, because they depend on the length with which they are told. A nice instance occurs, in chapter iv of *The Inheritance*, of real comedy springing from manipulated embarrassment when Gertrude tries to offer help to an invalid cottar and his loquacious wife. The cottar is, if not bed-ridden, chair-ridden, and hag-ridden. His wife never lets him speak, and rejects for him Gertrude's proffered soup, milk, coat, carpet and chair, and asks instead for money to buy grave-clothes.

If Miss Ferrier is not a literary writer, she has the amateur's power to put her reading to effective and very unselfconscious use. Shakespeare is clearly in her blood and breath. Quotations, mis-quotations, echoes, and paraphrases abound, used with wonderful freedom and ingenuity. How brilliantly Lord Rossville exposes his own self-complacent rhetoric in this ghastly paraphrase:

'It was a maxim of Julius Caesar's, unquestionably the greatest conqueror that ever lived, that his wife must not only be spotless in herself, but that she must not even be suspected by others.'[9]

His own quality as a bore is thus put quite *beyond* suspicion. And how brilliantly the Colonel Delmour reveals both another bore, Miss Pratt, and also his own intolerance when he declares: 'to endure her company for a nine mile *tête-à-tête* was more than my

---

[7] *Inheritance*, ii. 2.   [8] *Ibid.* ii. 7.   [9] *Ibid.* i. 5.

philosophy dreamt of '.[10] How Miss Pratt herself delights us with 'we're too soon for breakfast yet, so we may just scent the morning air, as what do you call the man's ghost says in the play'.[11]

We are here not so much in the Smollett world of Tabitha Bramble saying 'Spout a little of the ghost of Gimlet', as in the P. G. Wodehouse world of the following:

'I say, Jeeves, who was the fellow who threw the jolly old pearl down the jolly old drain?'
'I suspect, sir, that you have in mind the base Indian.'
'Threw a pearl away, what?'
'Yes, sir. Richer than all his tribe, sir.'

Finally I should like to offer a word of praise, not the less genuine and fervent for being both negative and positive, and to remark, not only how little she uses phonetic transcript of Scottish speech, but how well she suggests it, and how pointedly she contrasts it with her formal, if rather lifeless, English. Her ear for the Scottish tongue—her own tongue—is so sensitive that she uses idiom to suggest accent, and only for her broader speakers resorts to unorthodox spelling. I must however quote one of these. Bell Waddell and her Major, having just produced their first-born, a girl, suggest names to the crusty Mr. Ramsay:

'I think Andromache is such a beautiful name, and so off the common——'
'Andrew Mackaye's a very gude name for her, to be sure,' said Uncle Adam, gravely.[12]

I have not hoped at this late date to rescue Susan Ferrier in any very grandiose sense from oblivion. She is of course above ground still in the operating theatre of academic research, which will disinter and anatomize almost any dead writer who reached the printed page. But a look at the more 'popular' historians of literature shows that many do not even mention her. Neither Walter Allen nor Ian Watt has even a passing reference, nor has Richard Church, though his theme *The Growth of the Novel* would seem to call for notice of one who wrote about Scottish moors and *mores* before either Scott or Galt. She rates a paragraph and a quotation from Walter Allen, and from Ian Jack. To go to an older generation, Oliver Elton speaks sense of her, and Saintsbury, whose priorities are as right as his judgements generally are, gives her space equal with Galt. But what I should really desire for Susan Ferrier, is not so much that she should be studied and discussed as relished and read.

[10] *Ibid*. i. 7.   [11] *Ibid*. i. 16.   [12] *Ibid*. iii. 118.

John Galt and the Analysis
of Social History

JOHN MACQUEEN

SCOTT was never much of a traveller. He belonged to the more conservative East of Scotland; his natural haunts were the monuments and antiquities of Edinburgh and Tweeddale from which normally he felt little inclination to remove himself. Byron's comment in a letter to Moore is not without an occasional relevance:

'. . . half of these Scotch and Lake troubadours are spoilt by living in little circles and petty societies. . . . Lord, Lord, if these home-keeping minstrels had crossed your Atlantic or my Mediterranean, and tasted a little open boating in a white squall—or a gale in "the Gut"—or the Bay of Biscay, with no gale at all—how it would enliven and introduce them to a few of the sensations!'

The remark is smug and unfair; at best it is an exaggeration. A gale in the Minch or the Pentland Firth is a sensation which obviously had been denied to Byron. But, given Scott's background, it is not surprising that in his novels the present with its sensations tends to be kept at a distance, to be seen through and in terms of the past.

To turn from Scott to his younger contemporary, John Galt, is to become aware of a change. Galt's roots were in the commercial and radical West, which formed the scene of much of his fiction. At the same time, as *Letters from the Levant* and his American and Canadian novels show, he was a traveller whose journeys, east and west, made those of Childe Harold seem parochial. His concern was with new worlds—the New World beyond the Atlantic as well as the New World of the Industrial and Agricultural revolutions which was to culminate in the triumphs of Victorian prosperity. His outlook however was philosophic and theoretical; he was not only a business man, but also a student of *The Wealth of Nations* and Adam Ferguson's *Essay on the History of Civil Society*

(1767). In other words, he was by no means unconscious of the past, but his tendency was to see it partly as the organically necessary prelude to the present, partly as the obstacle which, sometimes tragically, had delayed or impaired the delivery of freer and more enterprising times.

Annals of the Parish is the most obvious example. In it he treats the period from 1760 to 1810, the period which saw both the personal reign of George III and the personal ministry of his narrator, the Rev. Micah Balwhidder in the Ayrshire parish of Dalmailing. The period covered overlaps that which Scott attempted in his first three novels—'the age of our fathers . . . that of our own youth, and . . . the last ten years of the eighteenth century'. Galt was younger than Scott by almost a decade, so, relative to the author, the chronology is almost precisely the same. Although the novel, or 'theoretical history', as Galt preferred to call it, was not published until 1821, the first draft antedated the publication of *Waverley* in 1814.

In narrative technique the two novelists differ strikingly. When Scott began his career as novelist, he had not yet developed the distancing framework utilized in *Tales of My Landlord*; the omniscient, detached and therefore relatively unemphasized narrator sets out the sequence of events. The opening of *The Antiquary* will illustrate:

It was early on a fine summer's day, near the end of the eighteenth century, when a young man of genteel appearance, journeying towards the north-east of Scotland, provided himself with a ticket in one of those public carriages which travel between Edinburgh and the Queensferry, at which place, as the name implies, and as is well known to all my northern readers, there is a passage-boat for crossing the Firth of Forth. The coach was calculated to carry six regular passengers, besides such interlopers as the coachmen could pick up by the way and intrude upon those who were legally in possession.

Even when he developed the more advanced technique found in *Tales of My Landlord*, Scott's narrators themselves remained uninvolved. The regression of *personae* distances and reduces to perspective the people and events presented. Much of Galt's best work has the directness of fictitious autobiography:

In the same year, and on the same day of the same month, that his Sacred Majesty King George, the third of the name, came to his crown and kingdom, I was placed and settled as the minister of Dalmailing. When about a week thereafter this was known in the parish, it was thought a wonderful thing, and everybody spoke of me and the new king as united in our trusts and temporalities, marvelling how the same should come to pass, and thinking the hand of Providence was in it, and that surely we were pre-ordained to fade and flourish in fellowship together; which has really been the case, for in the same season that his Most Excellent Majesty, as he was very properly styled in the proclamations for the general fasts and thanksgivings, was set by as a precious vessel which had received a crack or a flaw, and could only be serviceable in the way of an ornament, I was obliged, by reason of age and the growing infirmities of my recollection, to consent to the earnest entreaties of the Session, and to accept of Mr Amos to be my helper.

(*Annals of the Parish*, Introduction)

The narrator is at once placed; he is an elderly man writing for younger contemporaries; a retired, egalitarian, Presbyterian, and unconsciously self-important ('me and the new king') clergyman, who can remember a time when news took a week to travel from London to rural Ayrshire. His language with its biblical overtones, marked alliteration, and Scots legal and colloquial idiom ('in the same year, and on the same day of the same month', 'the third of the name', 'placed and settled', 'trusts and temporalities', 'thinking the hand of Providence was in it'), clearly stems from education in a Scottish university at a period before the Enlightenment and the rise of polite letters. The word 'pre-ordained' emphasizes Mr. Balwhidder's moderate but entirely orthodox Calvinism. At the same time, the passage emphasizes that the narrator's powers, like those of George III, have begun to decline, and so in a sense warns the reader that his own reading of the *Annals* must make allowance for human frailty, that a more enlightened intelligence must analyse and fill the gaps in the recollections of an old man somewhat bewildered and left behind by the tempestuous later eighteenth and early nineteenth century. Mr. Balwhidder is an anachronism, a survival from earlier days, who nevertheless has observed the events of the modern world. The very inadequacy of his responses defines the shape of events more penetratingly than investigations apparently more subtle.

Mr. Balwhidder belongs, however tenuously, to the present of the novel; he draws on his store of memory and observation, to bear witness to 'the work of a beneficent Providence, even in the narrow sphere of my parish'. Even for Mr. Balwhidder, that is to say, his parish is no more than part of the general Calvinistic Providential scheme: the reader may not share his Calvinism, but Galt assumes that at worst he will be prepared to substitute the idea of progress, or at least of a predestined progressive movement in history, the reality of which may be seen on the small scale in Dalmailing, on the larger scale in the American and French

revolutions, the growth of industry, the fall of the old local aristocracy and the rise of an educated working class, all of which help to
form the general background shaping the course of events in the
parish. To the end of his life Galt remained a modified Calvinist.
His poems include extended philosophical pieces entitled *The
Demon of Destiny* and *The Star of Destiny*. 'I . . . profess myself
openly a predestinarian', he observed in the *Literary Life* (1834),
and continued: 'In the order of things and the succession of events,
the providence of God is constantly seen; and such is the harmony
of the universe, that the smallest occurrence affects its whole frame
and system.' In *Annals of the Parish* and indeed in his work generally Galt is concerned with the smallest occurrences, but in a way
which shows how they affect, and still more how they are affected
by the whole frame. That is why the novels of so widely travelled
a man, who spent much of his life outside Scotland, concern themselves so markedly with Scottish local affairs, and the local affairs
of Scotsmen overseas. Galt recognizes the significance of small
events. Mr. Balwhidder, on the other hand, recognizes only very
imperfectly the interconnectedness of the events which he described;
his narrow perspective leads him to treat secondary and even
tertiary causes as if they were prime movers. Some critics mistakenly hold that this is the limit of Galt's achievement. Mr. Craig,
for instance, observes, 'Because the minister is as conservative and
credulous as many of his parishioners, and because everything is
felt through his mentality, all other possible life is diminished to his
kind of understanding'. In a way, such a remark is a tribute to the
art which conceals art, and to Galt's complete realization of the
minister's character, but even a brief analysis of the opening
sentences has shown, I believe, the inadequacy of Mr. Craig's
response. Galt's choice of language inevitably directs the reader
to a more extended and philosophical perspective than Mr. Balwhidder or Mr. Craig seems able to command.

Galt is writing a theoretical history and his treatment of the
commercial and industrial developments which followed the opening of the Ayrshire coalfield will demonstrate his methods. For
Mr. Balwhidder everything apparently springs from chance and
from personal contingencies—a dearth of fuel in the winter of
1765 and an accident to Lord Eglesham in March 1767. Admittedly
under 1762 the coal trade between Irville and Ireland is already
mentioned and Mr. Balwhidder suggests rather than states that
fuel shortage caused the new pits to be opened. It would perhaps

be more accurate to say that he regarded the opening of the pits as the providential remedy for the hardships of the preceding winter. Notably too he makes Providence an ally of commercial prosperity in a way to delight the heart of the author of *Religion and the Rise of Capitalism*:

In the winter there was a dearth of fuel, such as has not been since; for when the spring loosened the bonds of the ice, three new coal-heughs were shanked in the Douray moor, and ever since there has been a great plenty of that necessary article. Truly, it is very wonderful to see how things come round; when the talk was about the shanking of thir heughs, and a paper to get folk to take shares in them was carried through the circumjacent parishes, it was thought a gowk's errand; but no sooner were the coal reached, but up sprung such a traffic, that it was a God-send to the parish, and the opening of a trade and commerce, that has, to use an old bye-word, brought gold in gowpins among us. (Year 1765.)

For Mr. Balwhidder the paper which he mentions seems almost to lead an independent existence: at least he gives no sign of realizing that the proposals which it contained were produced as the result of human forethought and commercial ingenuity operating, one presumes, outwith the immediate neighbourhood of the parish. For him the parish is the source of all human activity: beyond it lies the field of providential operation, which sometimes acts through intermediaries, kings, governments and speculators, almost as remote as Providence itself. But this view is confined to Mr. Balwhidder; the reader is compelled to realize its inadequacy when he accepts the full implications of the reference to the paper.

Coal when it has been mined must be distributed, and the distribution depends on a satisfactory system of transport. The inevitable sequel to the opening of the local pits was the construction of a turnpike road to bypass the perils of the vennel of Dalmailing.

The king's highway, as I have related in the foregoing, ran through the Vennel, which was a narrow and a crooked street, with many big stones here and there, and every now and then, both in the spring and the fall, a gathering of middens for the fields, insomuch that the coal carts from the Dowray-moor were often reested in the middle of the causeway, and on more than one occasion some of them laired altogether in the middens, and others of them broke down. (Year 1767.)

At no point in his memoir does the minister comment on the most startling feature of this entry, the casual way in which he accepts middens on the king's highway as a natural hazard. One may deduce from Chapter XXVII of Galt's *The Provost*, the secular companion piece to *Annals of the Parish*, that by 1810 such middens elsewhere would probably have been a thing of the past:

But new occasions call for new laws; the side pavement, concentrating the people, required to be kept cleaner, and in better order, than when the whole width of the street was in use; so that the magistrates were constrained to make regulations concerning the same, and to enact fines and penalties against those who neglected to scrape and wash the plain-stones forenent the houses, and to denounce, in the strictest terms, the emptying of improper utensils on the same, and this, until the people had grown into the habitude of attending to the rules, gave rise to many pleas, and contentious appeals and bickerings, before the magistrates.

The apparent date of the new laws is 1805. Gudetown, however, was a royal burgh; Dalmailing a mere clachan, which might well be laggard in matters of public hygiene. Whatever the true assessment, Mr. Balwhidder, unlike Provost Pawkie, belongs to the past by writing of his casual acceptance of the middens. The middens however become vitally connected with transport improvements when, as the result of an encounter with the coal-carts, Lord Eglesham's carriage is accidentally overturned into one of them. For Mr. Balwhidder this is both the proximate and ultimate cause by which a turnpike was instituted.

His Lordship was a man of genteel spirit, and very fond of his horses, which were the most beautiful creatures of their kind that had been seen in all the country-side. Coming, as I was noting, to see his new lands, he was obliged to pass through the clachan one day, when all the middens were gathered out reeking and sappy in the middle of the causeway. Just as his Lordship was driving in with his prancing steeds like a Jehu at the one end of the Vennel, a long string of loaded coal carts came in at the other, and there was hardly room for my lord to pass them. What was to be done? His lordship could not turn back, and the coal carts were in no less perplexity. Every body was out of doors to see and to help, when, in trying to get his lordship's carriage over the top of a midden, the horses gave a sudden loup, and couped the coach, and threw my lord, head foremost, into the very scent-bottle of the whole commodity, which made him go perfect mad, and he swore like a trooper, that he would get an act of parliament to put down the nuisance—the which now ripened in the course of this year into the undertaking of the trust road. . . .

But to return to the making of the trust-road, which, as I have said, turned the town inside out. It was agreed among the heritors, that it should run along the back-side of the south houses; and that there should be steadings fewed off on each side, according to a plan that was laid down, and this being gone into, the town gradually, in the course of years, grew up into that orderlyness which makes it now a pattern to the countryside—all which was mainly owing to the accident that befel the Lord Eglesham, which is a clear proof how improvements came about, as it were, by the immediate instigation of Providence, which should make the heart of man humble, and change his eyes of price and haughtiness into a lowly demeanour.   (Year 1767.)

Galt's irony is unmistakable, but Mr. Balwhidder certainly has a point—Lord Eglesham's accident hastened the institution of the turnpike. His narrative nonetheless shows that road improvements had been meditated for some little time, and even without the accident would certainly have been instituted. Under the year 1765, for instance, the year in which the new pits on the Douray moor were opened, we find, probably as a direct consequence, that the king's road through the Vennel had been mended. In 1767, the year of the accident, the minister notes that 'there had been, for many a day, a talk and sound of an alteration and amendment'. Talk and action are not the same thing, but it is fairly clear once more that Mr. Balwhidder has mistakenly attributed to accident a change which, as the reader realizes, in fact resulted from general economic forces.

In isolation, this treatment of mining and transportation is remarkable enough. In the context of the book generally, it is still more remarkable. Galt continues to indicate universals by way of apparent contingencies. A rise in the price of barley in 1765, for instance, suggests as an explanation that a house for brewing whisky had been established in a neighbouring parish—another industrial innovation. The Agricultural Revolution is insinuated by way of Mr. Balwhidder's marriage to Miss Lizy Kibbock, daughter of Mr. Kibbock of the Gorbyholm, a pioneer of new farming methods. Under the year 1761 a phrase, 'the very bairns on the loan', sufficiently indicates that the playground of the old fashioned farm was the patch of ground near the steading on which during summer cows were milked in the open air; equally the reference under 1765 to Mr. Kibbock's Delap-cheese which 'spread far and wide over the civilized world' by its very hyperbole demonstrates the establishment of new dairy methods with a new magnitude of commercial operation. Nor were Mr. Kibbock's innovations confined to dairying; he improved his arable also by plantations, and enclosure, to do away with the old system of in- and out-field.

Mr. Kibbock, her father, was a man beyond the common, and had an insight of things, by which he was enabled to draw profit and advantage, where others could only see risk and detriment. He planted mounts of fir-trees on the bleak and barren tops of the hills of his farm, the which every body, and I among the rest, considered as a thrashing of the water, and raising of bells. But as his tack ran his trees grew, and the plantations supplied him with stabs to make *stake and rice* between his fields, which soon gave them a trig and orderly appearance, such as had never before been seen in the west country.
(Year 1765.)

By way of his second wife and her inherited talents, Mr. Balwhidder himself comes to share in the profits of new enterprise,
indeed to become rich, without himself ever seeming to realize
what exactly had happened. Only to a very limited extent does he
grasp the purpose of plantation and enclosure, which he seems to
regard as intended primarily to enable the countryside to vie
scenically with Italy and Switzerland. That he has some awareness,
at least of the wider geographical context, is suggested by the
reference in the annal for 1766 to Mr. Coulter, who had gained his
skill in farming in the Lothians, where the process of improvement
had by then advanced further than in Ayrshire. As his name indicates, Mr. Coulter was a specialist in ploughing methods, who
replaced the old Scottish plough with a more up-to-date and
efficient implement; and who practised crop-rotation, which in
turn implies enclosure. Mr. Balwhidder appreciates the increase
of prosperity caused by Mr. Coulter's new methods, but again
what he emphasises is the increase of visible beauty—the effect on
his own eyes. 'Nothing could surpass the regularity of his rigs and
furrows.—Well do I remember the admiration that I had, when,
in a fine sunny morning of the first spring after he took the Breadland, I saw his braird on what had been the cow's grass, as even
and pretty as if it had been worked and stripped in the loom with a
shuttle.'

Mr. Balwhidder is not entirely confined to local affairs. An
industrial event of national importance, the digging of the Forth
and Clyde Canal (1768–90) achieves mention, for instance in the
annal for 1767, but only as the source of 'a great sough of old
prophecies, foretelling mutations and adversities . . . it being
thought an impossible thing to be done'. The reference under
1766 to 'a troop of wild Irish, seeking for work' may have some
relevance here. Much of the labour on canals and other new
industrial sites was performed by Irish navigators or navvies. Of
this Mr. Balwhidder drops no hint.

Whatever their social and intellectual implications, all these are
matters in the first place of economic history. Social and intellectual
history, however, are not neglected, and to make his effects, Galt
utilizes the same indirect methods as elsewhere. In purely social
history the major event, described under the year 1766, is the
destruction by fire of the local great house, the Breadlands. Galt
here exemplifies the end of the old social order, the *ancien régime*,
for the house is never rebuilt, and the policy is let out as a farm to

the improver Mr. Coulter. The fire is the climax, but no more than the climax, of an earlier process of change. Already after the death of the Laird of Breadland in 1761, his widow and family had removed to Edinburgh letting the house to Major Gilchrist, a returned Indian nabob, and his sister Miss Girzie, Lady Skimmilk. The Gilchrists represent an early stratum of the *nouveau riche*; their social origin is obscure, and during the Major's period of service in India, Miss Girzie 'had been in a very penurious way as a seamstress, in the Gorbals of Glasgow'. Even before the fire, in other words, the Breadlands had already to some degree ceased to be the centre of settled activity in the parish. The old Laird too had been Mr. Balwhidder's patron, but after his death, the powers of patronage shifted to the more distant and anglified figure of Lord Eglesham, and after Lord Eglesham's murder in 1781, seem altogether to disappear. From 1785, the local grandee is the returned American loyalist, Mr. Cayenne, who becomes an industrialist, the founder of Cayenneville, with its mills and radical weavers. He had little more interest in Mr. Balwhidder's orthodox Calvinism than have his imported work-people, whether Utilitarians, Non-conformists or Irish Catholics. The long-term results are clear. In 1780 it is still possible for the parish to be convulsed by reports of the troubles which in London led to the anti-Catholic Gordon riots. In 1804 however an Irish priest reintroduced the Mass to the parish without disturbance; in 1806 a dissenting meeting house was opened. The externals at least of Presbyterianism suffered a corresponding dimunition. Under 1764 the story of Nichol Snipe's humiliation in church reveals the disciplinary powers of the old Kirk. By 1779 Mr. Balwhidder's sermon at the General Assembly in Edinburgh is clearly thought old-fashioned, and in 1789, although the elderly people of the parish feel that the sermon delivered by young William Malcolm is too 'Englified', 'the younger part of the congregation were loud in his praise, saying, there had not been heard before such a style of language in our side of the country'. In 1804, the Session agreed that church censures should be commuted with fines.

Lady Macadam's jointure house, first mentioned in 1763, is the nearest approach in the parish to a second great house, and a less spectacular way it suffers a change as great as that of the Breadlands. On the death of Lady Macadam, shortly after the murder of Lord Eglesham in 1781, the house stood empty until 1785, when it was temporarily rented by Mr. Cayenne. In 1787, Mr. Cayenne moved to a new house. By that time, as a consequence of developments along the turnpike road, the jointure house had come to be in the middle of town. Since 1764, the village had boasted of a change-house (ale-house), but by 1787 the increase of prosperity and the growing number of travellers on the road, made the establishment of an inn a practical possibility. For this purpose, a large unoccupied building in the centre of the town had obvious attractions, and as a result the jointure house became the Cross Keys Inn. The social implications are manifold.

Galt does not confine his social investigations to the upper levels of parish society. By 1760, for instance, the belief in witchcraft which had led to the spectacular trials and executions of the later sixteenth and seventeenth centuries, and which is present although not greatly emphasized in *Ringan Gilhaize*, had virtually disappeared, save at the level of popular superstititon. At this level, as Burns's *Tam o' Shanter* illustrates, it retained a latent vigour, which might even on occasions lead to the threat of public action. *Annals of the Parish* is a history of the Enlightenment as it affected a small country parish, and Galt twice indicates the survival of pre-Enlightenment superstitions. In the annal for 1762 Mr. Balwhidder mentions the death of Mizy Spaewell at the pagan seasonal festival of Samain (Hallowe'en). She is obviously regarded as a white witch:

Mizy had a wonderful faith in freats, and was just an oracle of sagacity at expounding dreams, and bodes of every sort and description—besides, she was reckoned one of the best howdies in her day; but by this time she was grown frail and feckless, and she died the same year on Hallowe'en, which made every body wonder, that it should have so fallen out for her to die on Hallowe'en.

Equally obviously, Nanse Birrel, whose death is mentioned in the annal for 1766, is a black witch, finally driven to suicide by her diabolic master:

An aged woman, one Nanse Birrel, a distillator of herbs, and well skilled in the healing of sores, who had a great repute among the quarriers and colliers, —she having gone to the physic well in the sandy hills, to draw water, was found with her feet uppermost in the well, by some of the bairns of Mr. Loremore's school; and there was a great debate whether Nanse had fallen in by accident head foremost, or, in a temptation, thrown herself in that position, with her feet sticking up to the evil one; for Nanse was a curious discontented blear-eyed woman, and it was only with great ado that I could get the people keepit from calling her a witchwife.

'Calling her a witchwife' is probably a euphemism for 'treating her as a witchwife' and ducking her. The 'people' are probably the ordinary villagers and farmworkers, as opposed to the more uncanny quarriers and colliers, who worked in the depths of the earth. The magic physic well in the sandy hills is itself a probable survival from pre-Christian times. After 1766, although the *Annals* still record dreams, prodigies and superstitions, there is no further hint of actual witchcraft.

To summarize—from one point of view *Annals of the Parish* indeed belongs to the parish. Few aspects of life there are ignored, and they are consistently presented from a point of view which itself belongs to the parish. The location of the parish, however, makes internal events typify what is happening in the wider world, if not from China to Peru, at least from India to the United States— the wider world too, which, under the influence of the Enlightenment, was beginning the change from an agrarian to an industrial economy. The book thus achieves something like universality. It is the immediacy of the intensely local combined with the universal which gives *Annals of the Parish*, like all Galt's best work, a vividness and intellectual range, which can sometimes seem more valuable than all but the very best of Scott.

Other Papers read at the Conference

J. H. ALEXANDER, *University of Aberdeen*
Medievalism in Scott's Poetry

J. C. BECKETT, *Queen's University, Belfast*
Scott's Novels as Historical Interpretation

W. J. CAMERON, *University of Western Ontario*
Scott as Biographer

IAN CAMPBELL, *University of Edinburgh*
The Growth of the Kailyard

ALICE CHANDLER, *City University of New York*
Chivalry and Romance: Scott's Medieval Novels

JOHN CLUBBE, *Duke University*
Scott and Byron

THOMAS CRAWFORD, *University of Aberdeen*
Scott as a Poet

D. D. DEVLIN, *Queen's University, Belfast*
Political Crisis in Scott's Novels

DOUGLAS GIFFORD, *University of Strathclyde*
The Effect of Critical Disapproval on the Development of
Hogg's Fiction

G. GOODIN, *Southern Illinois University*
Scott and the Political Novel

CATHERINE GORDON, *University of London*
The Illustration of Sir Walter Scott: Nineteenth-Century
Enthusiasm and Adaptation

IAN A. GORDON, *Victoria University, Wellington*
Galt and Blackwood

HAMISH HENDERSON, *University of Edinburgh*
Scott and Folk Song

D. S. HEWITT, *University of Aberdeen*
What should we do about Scott's Letters?

ANDREW HOOK, *University of Edinburgh*
  Jane Porter, the Historical Novel, and *Waverley*

DOUGLAS MACK, *University of Stirling*
  The Development of Hogg's Poetry

JAMES MICHIE, *University of Hull*
  The Chronicles of the Canongate

JEROME MITCHELL, *University of Georgia*
  Operatic Versions of *The Bride of Lammermoor*

JOAN PITTOCK, *University of Aberdeen*
  Scott and the Novel of Manners: the case of *St. Ronan's Well*

JOHN PYM, *Dublin*
  Scott and Ireland

WILLIAM RUDDICK, *Manchester University*
  The Fiction of John Gibson Lockhart

ALEXANDER SCOTT, *University of Glasgow*
  The Structure of *The Lay of the Last Minstrel*
  Hogg and Supernatural Comedy in Verse

DOUGLAS YOUNG, *University of North Carolina*
  The Scottish Cultural Background to Scott